A BIBLIOGRAPHY OF
THE MUSICAL WORKS
PUBLISHED BY
JOHN WALSH

1721–1766

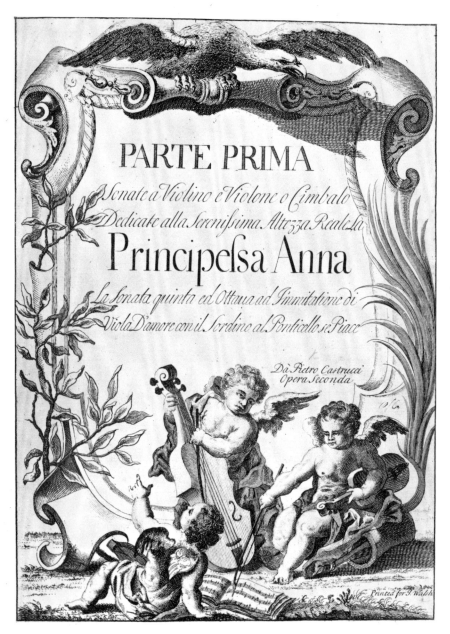

PARTE PRIMA

Sonate a Violino e Violone o Cimbalo
Dedicate alla Serenissima Altezza Reale La

Principessa Anna

La Sonata quinta ed Ottaua ad Immitatione di
Viola D'amore con il Sordino al Ponticello se Piace

Dà Pietro Castrucci
Opera Seconda

Printed for J. Walsh

Titlepage of no. 335 (reduced)

A BIBLIOGRAPHY OF THE MUSICAL WORKS PUBLISHED BY THE FIRM OF JOHN WALSH

during the years

1721-1766

BY

WILLIAM C. SMITH

AND

CHARLES HUMPHRIES

LONDON

THE BIBLIOGRAPHICAL SOCIETY

1968

BIBLIOGRAPHICAL SOCIETY PUBLICATION
FOR THE YEAR 1966
PUBLISHED 1968

CONTENTS

INTRODUCTION

I

In 'A Bibliography of the Musical Works published by John Walsh during the years 1695–1720', by William C. Smith (Bibliographical Society, London, 1948), every recorded or advertised work of that period was listed and a comprehensive Introduction dealt with the history of the firm and its successors, its association with the Hares and other publishers, its method of working and the conditions of music publishing at the time. This information has since 1948 been to some extent augmented by several articles (listed on page xx). Dr. James S. Hall has also made exhaustive investigations into the personal histories of the Walshes, father and son, and into the activities of the firm. This material has not yet been published but we are privileged to extract from it as necessary, and subsequent references will be made to it. It is not intended to incorporate in this Introduction material facts about the Walshes recorded in earlier publications, other than those necessary for a brief review of the subject, and those which are new and of importance.

The present work sets out to do for the years 1721 to 1766 what has already been done for the earlier period: 1766 was chosen as the terminal date as on the death of John Walsh junior in that year the firm became Randall and Abell. The great number of original works by Handel published by the Walshes has compelled their omission from the present volume. They are, however, listed in 'Handel. A Descriptive Catalogue of the Early Editions', by William C. Smith assisted by Charles Humphries (Cassell & Co., London, 1960). Miscellaneous works containing Handel items and extracts are included in this Bibliography (see pp. 167, 168).

The main facts of the firm's history, given in the earlier Bibliography, are that it was founded by John Walsh in about 1695, and was carried on by John Walsh alone or more frequently in association with John Hare and sometimes others until December 1721. From then until September 1725 Walsh was associated with John and Joseph Hare, and after the death of the former in September 1725, with Joseph Hare until about November 1730. From 1730 to 1766 the firm published and advertised as 'John Walsh', this form covering John Walsh the elder who died on 13 March 1736, and the younger who succeeded his father and carried on the business until his death on 15 January 1766. It seems fairly clear that John Walsh junior, when he was about 20 or 21 (he was born on 23 December 1709, according to Dr. Hall), that is in about 1730 or 1731, took an increasing share in the work of the business, and that to him may be attributed some of the changes that took place from then onwards, such as the provision of serial numbers for the works, and the adoption of different styles of title-page. Randall and Abell, the successors of John Walsh junior, continued until July 1768. After this Randall carried on alone until January 1776 when his widow Elizabeth Randall continued the business until she was succeeded by Wright and Wilkinson in or before April 1783.

The usual address of John Walsh and his successors was at first the Golden Harp and Hoboy (or Hautboy) in Catherine (Katharine, Katherine, &c.) Street in the Strand. Subsequent variations are Catharine Street, the Golden Harp and Hautboy in Katherine Street near Somerset House in the Strand, and the Harp and Hoboy in Catherine Street. Walsh was associated in the imprints with P. Randall and John and Joseph Hare and others as indicated in the Introduction to the earlier Bibliography.

The common form, with little variation of the imprint or in the advertisements from 1730 onwards, was 'Printed for and sold by John Walsh Musick Printer and Instrument maker to his Majesty at the Harp and Hoboy in Catherine-street in the Strand'. This was later generally shortened to 'Printed for and sold by John Walsh at the Harp and Hoboy in Catherine Street in the Strand' and by the time John Walsh junior was thoroughly established, the usual form was 'Printed for J. Walsh in Catherine Street (or Katherine Street) in the Strand'.

The transcriptions of the title-pages and advertisements given in this present volume include all the names mentioned in the imprints but omit unessential or repeated parts. It has been assumed hitherto that the Walshes, father and son, occupied the same premises in Catherine Street (afterwards known in Elizabeth Randall's or H. Wright's time as No. 13) but from the researches of Dr. Hall it appears that the firm moved more than once.

The earliest mention of John Walsh (not as a publisher) is his appointment on 24 June 1692 as Musical Instrument Maker in Ordinary to William III in place of John Shaw surrendered. Presumably Walsh must have been in business before that. His first child was baptized at St. Mary Strand als Savoy [the Savoy Chapel] on 26 January 1693. He must therefore have been living in the vicinity.

Introduction

At Easter 1693 Walsh took a house almost certainly on the south side of the Strand in the Dutchy Liberty[1] between the Savoy and Somerset House. He remained there until Easter 1695 when he moved into a house on the east side of Catherine Street. From the rate books it appears that this house may have been No. 18, and was formerly occupied by a Peter Veraine. From there Walsh published at least three works (*Bibliography, 1695–1720*, nos. 1, 2, 3). From October 1696 he paid a half-year's rates for a house in Dutchy Lane[2] (south side of the Strand) near his first residence, and at Easter 1697 he took a house (almost certainly No. 14 or No. 15) further up Catherine Street on the east side. This was the home of the firm until 1757 and where, presumably, John the elder died in 1736.

In June 1713 Walsh bought a messuage or tenement and three plots of land over against the north-west corner of the New Exchange [Exeter Exchange] abutting in front on the Strand, of which we know nothing further except that in 1714 and later the rates were paid by a tenant, Collett Mawhood.

At Easter 1740 Walsh junior rented additional premises in Helmet Court, probably No. 5, backing on to his Catherine Street house. These he occupied until Easter 1757 when he left the premises at No. 14 or 15 Catherine Street and took over two houses, Nos. 12 and 13 (which were previously empty) and gave up the Helmet Court address. It has been established that John Walsh junior left his business to be carried on by his cousin William Randall and his worthy servant John Abell under very definite terms. He also laid down that they should live together, one taking the first floor, the other the second, and that they should purchase the freehold of the shop and let the freehold house annexed to it which Walsh had lately rebuilt. If they could not purchase the freehold of the business premises, four years before the lease expired they were to move into his new house which was to be fitted up with shelves, &c., from the old premises (*The Library*, ser. 5, vol. 3, 1949, p. 293). There is good reason for thinking that Randall and Abell gave up the lease of the old premises in 1767–8 (perhaps after Abell's death in July 1768) and moved the business to the freehold house next door which may have been the one afterwards known as No. 13.

[1] The Dutchy Liberty was the Liberty of the Dutchy of Lancaster, stretching on the south side from Without Temple Bar to the east side of Cecil Street (Stow, *Survey*, 1720, Vol. ii, Book IV, pp. 104, &c.)

[2] He was still publishing from the Golden Harp and Hoboy or the Harp and Hautboy during the whole of 1697 (*Bibliography, 1695–1720*, pp. 8–13). There is no later reference to the Dutchy Lane house.

Introduction

William Randall died in about January 1776 and his widow Elizabeth carried on at the same premises until about April 1783. Advertisements in 1781 and after give the address as No. 13 Catherine Street. Wright and Wilkinson succeeded Elizabeth Randall in or before April 1783. In June the form was Wright & Co. and from February 1785 or thereabouts H. Wright, No. 13 Catherine Street. Lowndes's London Directory 1784, however, gives Wright and Wilkinson No. 12 Catherine Street and one imprint (Gawler's *Harmonia Sacra*, 1781) Randall's Music Shop, No. 10 Catherine Street. These may be misprints for No. 13, as there is no other evidence for them. The Randalls, Wright, and their successors all issued works from Walsh plates (with alterations) and from time to time sold copies with the old Walsh imprints.

To return to Dr. Hall's researches on the Walshes. He has listed in great detail many personal and family matters—Walsh the elder's marriage, his large family of nine daughters and six sons, most of whom died in infancy, his appointment as churchwarden at St. Mary Strand als Savoy, and his burial place in the new churchyard of St. Mary-le-Strand. Until the new church, St. Mary-le-Strand, was consecrated in 1723, the parishioners of the old church of St. Mary the Virgin, which stood on the south side of the Strand and was pulled down for the building of the Palace of the Lord Protector Somerset, were compelled to worship elsewhere, and thus some of them, including Walsh, used the Savoy Chapel. Dr. Hall also provides many entries from the Lord Chamberlain's records of payments to Walsh as musical instrument maker, repairer, and dealer to the Crown.

John Walsh junior continued the business, obviously quite efficiently, after his father's death. He retained the appointment as His Majesty's Instrument Maker, many references to him as such being recorded by Dr. Hall. His publications were generally in a bolder style than his father's and he extended the practice of partly stamping the plates from which the works were printed. He never married. The details of his and his father's wills are recorded in 'John Walsh and his Successors' by William C. Smith (*The Library*, ser. 5, vol. 3, 1949). Walsh senior is said to have left £20,000 and his son £40,000, considerable sums for those days. The latter was buried in a new vault in St. Mary-le-Strand churchyard, and the remains of his father and mother were removed from their burial place in the churchyard to the vault where the son was interred.

Introduction

II

The various catalogues which Walsh and his successors issued from time to time are invaluable sources of information and provide in many cases the only details available of some works and editions. The *Bibliography, 1695–1720* listed a number of catalogues, but others have been discovered since, and all these have been referred to and used for the present work.

Some of the catalogues are separate sheet publications issued with various works. They frequently occur in two or three states and have varying numbers of entries. Others are the fairly long lists of works in newspaper notices. Many of Walsh's publications include lists of other works. It is not essential to mention here the less important of these lists, but the following summary includes the catalogues mentioned in the *Bibliography, 1695–1720* (with necessary corrections) and many others. They are referred to in the text as 'Walsh Cat.' followed by the serial number in this list. Those already listed in the earlier Bibliography are only briefly described here, and are followed by the reference numbers given to them in that work (Smith 1, 2, &c.).

CATALOGUES

1. The Overture's and Ayrs in four Parts, &c. [1701.]
    BM. c. 105. a. 1. (5.) 26 items. Smith 1.

2. The Setts of Aires in 4 parts, &c. [1702.]
    Hirsch II. 749. RCM. Daniel Purcell, 'The Iudgment of Paris.' 20 items. Smith 2.

3a. The Overture's and Ayrs in four Parts, &c. [1703.]
    Bod. Don. C. 66. (1.) Same plate as No. 1, with additions. Smith 3a.

3b. A Catalogue of English and Itallian Musick, &c. [1703.]
    Bod. Don. C. 66. (1.) 48 items. Smith 3b.

4–8. Lists of works in various issues of 'The Monthly Mask of Vocal Music.' [1706–10.] 20–40 items in each:
    4. 1706. Mitchell Library. Kidson Collection 8449.
    5. 1707. BM. K. 7. e. 4.
    6. 1708. Richard Newton, Henley in Arden.
    7. 1709. BM. K. 7. e. 4.
    8. 1710. BM. K. 7. e. 4.

9*a*.   A Catalogue of English & Italian Musick, Vocal & Instrumental, &c. [*c.* 1721.]
BM. 7897. y. 12. (1.) Hirsch II. 90. RCM. XXXII. B. 11. (2.) 152 items. Smith 4*a*.

9*b*.   A Catalogue of English & Italian Musick for Flutes, &c. [*c.* 1721.]
BM. 7897. y. 12. (1.) Hirsch II. 90. RCM. XXXII. B. 11. (2.) 88 items. Smith 4*b*.

10.   A Catalogue of choice Musick for the German Flute, &c. [*c.* 1725.]
Dayton C. Miller Collection. Library of Congress, Washington. 23 items. Not examined.

11*a*–11*d*.   Choice Musick by the most Celebrated Authors in Europe, &c. [*c.* 1727–31.]
Four issues containing 75–84 numbered groups with additions not numbered. 11*a*. No copy traced. 11*b*. Smith Collection. 'Apollo's Feast.' Book III. 11*c*. Kenneth Mummery copy, present location unknown. 11*d*. Hirsch IV. 1111. (17.) Smith 5.

12.   Divine Musick Printed for I: Walsh. [*c.* 1730.]
BM. A. 1231. p. J. Bishop, 'A Sett of Psalm Tunes . . . The Third Edition.' 11 items. Later issues Smith 8, 11.

13.   A Cattalogue of Choice Musick for the Harpsicord. [*c.* 1731.]
Advertised on 'Thirty New and Choice Country Dances.' BM. e. 5. r. (2.) No copy traced.

14.   A Cattalogue of Solos for a Violin & a Bass, &c. [*c.* 1732.]
NLS. BH. 194. 37 items.

15*a*.   A Catalogue of English & Italian Musick Vocal & Instrumental, &c. [1733 or earlier.]
Coke 'Apollo's Feast.' Book III. 291 items. Smith 6*a*.
—Second issue. [*c.* 1733.] Hirsch IV. 1113. (13.) 298 items. Smith 6*b*.

15*b*.   A Catalogue of English & Italian Musick for Flutes, &c. [*c.* 1733.] Coke. 'Apollo's Feast.' Book III. 138 items. Smith 6*b*.
—Second issue. [*c.* 1733.] Hirsch IV. 1113. (13.) 148 items. Smith 6*b*.

16*a*.   New Musick and Editions of Musick Lately printed for Iohn Walsh. [*c.* 1733.]
BM. g. 237. Pietro Castrucci, 'Sonate . . . Opera Seconda.' 93 items and general reference.

16*b*.   —Second issue. [*c.* 1734.] Kenneth Mummery copy, present location unknown. 97 items.

16c. —Third issue. [*c.* 1737.] Hirsch IV. 1111. (18.) 114 items.

17a. Vocal Musick Just Publish'd by I. Walsh, &c. [*c.* 1737.]
  BM. C. 382. 'British Musical Miscellany.' Vol. VI. 58 items.

17b. —Second issue. [*c.* 1738.] RM. 8. b. 14. 'The Chaplet.' 60 items.

18. A Cattalogue of Musick, &c. (The 'Great Catalogue' &c.) [*c.* 1736–44.]
  Three or four issues were made of which only one has survived
  (BM. C. 120. b. 6.). Referred to under Smith 7 and 9. *See infra* for
  fuller description.

19. New Musick, and Editions of Musick, Just publish'd by J. Walsh.
  Daily Advertiser, 23 September, 1742. About 50 items, single and
  grouped.

20a. Divine Musick, Just Publish'd by I Walsh, &c. [*c.* 1743.]
  BM. 7897. y. 12. (2.) 21 items. *See supra* No. 12. Smith 8.

20b. —Another issue. Divine Musick, &c. [*c.* 1763.]
  RM. 14. d. 19. Maurice Greene, 'Forty Select Anthems.' 35 items.
  Smith 11.

21a. Musick Printed for Iohn Walsh, &c. [*c.* 1743.]
  With probably 122 items. No copy available. Smith 7.

21b. —Another issue. [*c.* 1744.] Hirsch III. 208. 128 items. Smith 7.

22. New Musick, and Editions of Musick, Just publish'd by J. Walsh.
  General Evening Post, February 21–23, 1745. 30 items, single and
  grouped.

23. New Musick, and Editions of Musick, Just publish'd by J. Walsh.
  General Evening Post, October 12–15, 1745. 31 items, single and
  grouped. Different from No. 22.

24a. A Catalogue of Vocal and Instrumental Musick. (A Catalogue of Instru-
  mental and Vocal Musick.) [*c.* 1747.]
  Hirsch IV. 1111. (16.) 380 items. Smith 9. Wrongly identified as the
  'Great Catalogue.'

24b. —Another issue. [*c.* 1748.] Handel, 'Joshua.' Smith Collection. 386
  items. Smith 9.

24c. —Another issue. [*c.* 1748.] BM. 7897. y. 12. (4.) 391 items. Smith 9.

25. A Catalogue of New Musick, and new Editions of Musick, &c. [*c.* 1755.]
  BM. 7897. y. 12. (3.) 353 items. Smith 10.

26. A Compleat Catalogue of Vocal and Instrumental Music. Price 6*d.*
  Public Advertiser, November 17, &c. 1760; July 14, &c. 1761; September 23, 1763; January 20, &c. 1764. Not identified. Smith 12.

27.   A Catalogue of Vocal and Instrumental Musick, &c. [*c.* 1765.]
        BM. g. 273. (5.) C. A. Campioni, 'Six Sonatas for two Violins . . .
        Opera VI.' 128 items and long list of Handel works.

28.   A Catalogue of Vocal and Instrumental Music, For the Year 1776.
        Printed for . . . William Randall, &c.
        BM. G. 159. 'Le Delizie dell' Opere.' Vol. I–X. Hirsch IV. 1113. (12.)
        Smith Collection. 721 items. Smith 13.

29.   A Catalogue of Vocal and Instrumental Music, Printed for . . . Elizabeth
        Randall, &c. [*c.* 1783.]
        BM. 1879. cc. 13. (22.) RM. 7. f. 1. 'Chandos Anthems.' Hirsch IV.
        1113. (11.) Smith Collection. 769 items. Smith 14.

Of the Walsh catalogues listed above, No. 18 is of the greatest importance. The only known copy, that in the British Museum (C. 120. b. 6), was purchased in 1954. It was unknown when the *Bibliography, 1695–1720* was published. The title of this catalogue is:

A Cattalogue of Musick: Containing all the Vocal, and Instrumental Musick Printed in England, For Iohn Walsh. Where may be had, variety of English, and Italian Songs, also Musical Instruments of all Sorts, and variety of Curious Pieces of Musick Printed abroad London. Sold by I: Walsh, Musick Printer and Instrument maker to his Majesty, at yᵉ Harp & Hoboy, in Catherine Street, in the Strand. Price 6*d.*
    It is an octavo, pp. 2–28.

This catalogue contains nearly 600 items. The works of the principal composers, headed by Handel, are grouped together under their respective names. Other works, about half the catalogue, are grouped under classes: 'Musick for a single Violin', 'Divine Music', 'Sonatas for 2 Violins and a Bass', &c.

As was pointed out in the *Bibliography, 1695–1720* the firm adopted a system of numbering their publications by which engraved or manuscript serial numbers usually appeared at the foot of the title-pages. As copies have come to notice, a list, albeit very incomplete, has been compiled. Catalogue 18 has provided important information on this subject and on the extent to which the practice was adopted, as most of the items in the catalogue have the Walsh serial number and the price.

From a careful examination it is clear that the catalogue was issued in an earlier form or forms with very many fewer entries, and that additions were made to it from time to time. The highest number given is No. 600, 'Locatelli's Concertos. Op. 1', published in December 1736, but many numbers are omitted, and there are over 120 entries of works bearing no number, covering publications up to about the end of 1744. When the numerical system was started, copies of many works already published were in the possession of the firm and were then given a number, which in some cases was added to the title-pages in manuscript or engraved on the plates from which subsequent impressions were made. It is clear from an examination of the entries that the practice began about 1730.

Walsh, like others, stocked works not published by him, but which he sold. This was sometimes by arrangement with existing firms, but it seems quite clear that he bought up or acquired in some way copies of works issued by publishers (English and foreign) who had ceased to market them, most probably because the firms had gone out of business. Examples of these are scattered throughout the present work. Significant examples, although not included here, are the copies of Handel operas and other works, originally issued by John Cluer and his successors, which were sold by Walsh. In most of the cases where Walsh was marketing the productions of other firms the works appear in the catalogue without any number. The Walshes did not stop numeration at 600, the highest number in the Catalogue, but carried on to 683, with many gaps in between. From about 1740 new works were no longer given serial numbers and some earlier works, when reissued, were published without them.

III

All that we know about the Walshes' methods of working has been published in the earlier Bibliography and elsewhere. It is therefore only necessary to summarize it here briefly. The metal plates employed were at first of copper but later a softer metal, pewter, was used. The whole was at first engraved, but subsequently the plates were stamped in part, as far as this was possible. These plates were of varying sizes, such as 7×10, 7×12, $7\frac{1}{2} \times 10$, $7\frac{1}{2} \times 10\frac{1}{2}$, &c., inches. The paper was not folded as in books printed from type, but was usually cut into single sheets which were sewn together. Occasionally, however, folded paper, stitched through the folds, was used. As most existing copies have been bound and trimmed it is difficult to measure the paper accurately. But as a rule the ordinary folio volume measures between 12×9 inches and 13×10 inches approximately. While a few works were issued bound, most were issued in blue-grey paper covers. If bound, the works had boards covered with mottled or patterned paper. The ordinary bibliographical descriptions cannot be applied to such publications as there are no gatherings or signatures, and sizes therefore are arbitrarily decided according to whether the shape or size of the book approximates to folio, quarto, octavo, oblong folio, &c. These terms, therefore, as used in the present bibliography are relative. Most of the works are described as folio and a few as large folio, which in some cases only means from ordinary-sized plates on larger paper. We have no printers' proofs of works published by Walsh, no details of his staff or to what extent the work was done by journeymen engravers and printers. Whether the father and son were craftsmen or skilled musicians able to supervise and correct the work we do not know, but at any rate they were capable enough to found and maintain in succession for seventy-one years one of the greatest music publishing businesses then known here or on the Continent, and one which continued in one form or another for eighty years or so afterwards.

It now remains to indicate the plan and methods under which this Bibliography has been prepared. As far as possible all copies of works in the British Museum, the Royal Music Library, the Hirsch Music Library, the National Library of Scotland, the Royal College of Music, the Royal Academy of Music, the Rowe Library, the Cambridge University Library, and the Gresham Music Library, Guildhall, London, have been examined. A number of others listed in other collections have been included although in some cases they have not been examined. The locations of some of the other copies recorded in *The British Union-Catalogue of Early Music* (BUC) have been given, most of them having been checked, but this has not been possible in every case. Some BUC identifications are incorrect.

Wherever possible the title of the work has been included, with all the names given in imprints, but with addresses shortened as necessary, and without the transcription of advertisements on title-pages unless they are of consequence or aid the identification of particular editions. When the Hares ceased to collaborate with Walsh, their names were generally erased from the imprints on the plates. In some cases the erasure was incomplete and copies were therefore issued with the Hares' names still in the imprints. This has led to confusion over the date of issue, but all such copies have been given the correct dates as far as possible.

Titles are followed by details of the first advertisement of the work, or an approximate date given in brackets, e.g. [*c.* 1730]. If no copy of the work is known, the title is given as in the advertisement. Comparison of surviving works with their advertisements suggests that the latter represented the titles with sufficient accuracy to preclude wrong identification; but where there is any ambiguity owing to an abbreviated or different form in the description

xvi

the necessary particulars have been given. Some entries have been taken entirely from Walsh catalogues, from music dealers' or sale catalogues, or from private lists of one kind or another. In all cases the available evidence or reasons for inclusion have been given.

The special circumstances governing entries from Catalogue 18 (referred to above) need explanation. Many of the items listed in that catalogue seem to be reissues or new editions of items included in the *Bibliography, 1695–1720*. Where such works appear in Catalogue 18 with a number it is assumed that copies existed with that number added to them, as we know was generally the case. Entries have therefore been made for such issues with serial numbers although actual copies have not been traced. In such entries, the title and particulars are given from earlier issues if available or from the advertisements or other form of entry in the *Bibliography, 1695–1720*. Where a former title or advertisement has either or both of the Hares (John and Joseph) in the imprint, it is assumed that these were omitted in issues after the Hares ceased to collaborate with Walsh (*c.* 1730) by deletion from the plate. It will be noticed that for this reason in many of such reissued items, seen or unseen, the statement 'Walsh only in the imprint' occurs. In cases where the particulars are given from the earlier Bibliography and are assumed to apply to a later Walsh issue, it is uncertain whether some of such works were printed on one or both sides of the paper and therefore the particulars of pagination (pp.) or foliation (ff.) given are open to correction. Size and pagination or foliation are given whenever possible. Blank pages are not as a rule indicated, but breaks in the pagination are usually noted. Instrumental works issued in parts are so described, though the number of parts is not always stated.

In the transcription of titles, capitals are given only to the first letter of a word as they appear, even if the whole word is in capitals. The spelling and punctuation have been followed, even in such details as Mᴿ Mʳ Mr., except that each title is followed by a full stop, whether one occurs on the work or not. Librettists or writers of words are not always given. If no location is recorded it can be assumed that no copy has been traced.

The order of entries is generally alphabetical under composers' names, or under the title of the work ('Apollo's Feast', 'Beggar's Opera', 'British Miscellany', &c.). In cases like 'The Favourite Songs in the Opera Call'd Antigona' (a pasticcio with no composer's name on the title-page), the work is entered under the title ('Antigona'). Some works are placed under generic headings ('Airs', 'Minuets', 'English Songs', 'Songs', &c.) even if preceded by a qualifying adjective ('Familiar', 'Select', 'New', &c.). It has sometimes been found desirable to use compound forms ('Country Dances', 'Drinking Songs', 'Song Tunes', &c.).

Some items may be entered twice under different headings where it has been difficult to be certain of identification. Cross references are given only in special cases: under the title of a work published anonymously to the composer or composers if known; and conversely in some cases from the composer's name to the title; and in cases of alternative spelling. Cross references under composers' names are also given to works (pasticcios, collections, &c.) to which the composer in question made any contribution. Quotations from the Walsh catalogues or from the works giving a Walsh number, are transcribed in the exact forms 'N°' or 'No.'. Material inserted by the authors is given in square brackets [ ]; dates supplied for works are always given in brackets and are in the form [c.   ] unless an actual date of publication can be supplied. The Randall and Elizabeth Randall catalogues are quoted only in some cases where it has been considered essential or helpful. Many other works appear in these catalogues which had been formerly published by the Walshes and were sold or reissued by the Randalls, some of them with the original Walsh imprints.

The Walsh practice of printing and reprinting music must not be considered in the same way as one would books printed from type. The same plates were generally used in the different issues, with minor or major alterations. A new plate was used here or there, with singers' names changed (especially in Handel's works), or with variations in the imprints by erasure or addition. Sometimes an entirely new title-page was given to the contents of an earlier issue. It is obviously impossible to make fine distinctions between an edition, a reissue with variants, a reprint, a much later impression, and so on; but everything has been done in the entries in this catalogue to enable the reader to distinguish between two editions or issues and as far as possible to be able to identify with certainty a particular copy.

The Walshes advertised 'New editions' but in many cases we do not know whether they were rightly described as such or were simply reprints. Some works were reprinted over many years from exactly the same plates.

References to the *Bibliography, 1695–1720* are given as 'Smith' followed by the entry number. 'Smith' without a number signifies that the work is in the private collection of William C. Smith.

The following abbreviations have been used in the locations and elsewhere:

BM   British Museum
RM   The Royal Music Library, British Museum

Hirsch	Hirsch Music Library, British Museum
Bod.	Bodleian Library, Oxford
BUL	Birmingham University Library
Cardiff	Cardiff Public Library
Coke	Gerald Coke Collection
CUL	Cambridge University Library
DAM	Irish Academy of Music, Dublin
Dublin	National Library of Ireland, Dublin
Dundee	Dundee Public Library
Durham	Durham Cathedral Library
Edinburgh	Edinburgh Public Library
Euing	Euing Musical Library, Glasgow University
Fitz.	Fitzwilliam Museum, Cambridge
GUL	Glasgow University Library
Gresham	Gresham Library, Guildhall, London
Hereford	Hereford Cathedral Library
Leeds	Leeds Central Library
Liverpool	Liverpool Public Library
Manchester	Manchester Public Library (Henry Watson Library)
Mitchell	Mitchell Library, Glasgow
NLS	National Library of Scotland
OUF	University Faculty of Music Library, Oxford
Pendlebury	Pendlebury Library, Cambridge
RAM	Royal Academy of Music, London
RCM	Royal College of Music, London
RCO	Royal College of Organists, London
Reading	Reading University Library
Reid	Reid Library, Edinburgh University
Rowe	Rowe Music Library, King's College, Cambridge
Tenbury	St. Michael's College, Tenbury

Thanks are due to the directors and librarians of these institutions who have all been most helpful in giving access to the collections, supplying details of works, or answering queries. Some of them and others have already been referred to in the Introduction to the *Bibliography, 1695–1720* and in *Handel. A Descriptive Catalogue of the Early Editions*, and it is not therefore necessary to list them again here.

The British Union-Catalogue of Early Music has been invaluable as a foundation work for checking the entries and locations in this Bibliography and the authors are deeply grateful for the information in the Catalogue which they have been able to collate and compare with their own material and to use as necessary.

With the publication of this work and the *Bibliography 1695–1720* the history of the firm of the Walshes has been covered from the beginning in 1695 to 1766. Few works which they published can have escaped notice although in many cases no copies have been traced. Perhaps some of these will be brought to light.

Other works on the subject are:

Desmond Flower, 'Handel's Publishers'. (*English Review*, vol. 62, 1936, pp. 66–75.)

Frank Kidson, 'British Music Publishers, Printers and Engravers'. (W. E. Hill & Sons, London, 1900.)

Frank Kidson, 'Handel's Publisher, John Walsh, his Successors and Contemporaries'. (*Musical Quarterly*, vol. 6, 1920, pp. 430–50.)

William C. Smith, 'John Walsh, Music Publisher. The first twenty-five years'. (*Library*, ser. 5, vol. 1, 1946, pp. 1–5.)

William C. Smith, 'John Walsh and his Successors'. (*Library*, ser. 5, vol. 3, 1949, pp. 291–5.)

William C. Smith, 'The Meaning of the Imprint'. (*Library*, ser. 5, vol. 7, 1952, pp. 161–3.)

William C. Smith, 'New Evidence concerning John Walsh and the Duties on Paper, 1726'. (*Harvard Library Bulletin*, vol. 6, 1952, pp. 252–5.)

A Catalogue of Music published by John Walsh and his Successors, with a preface by William C. Smith. (The First Edition Bookshop Limited, London, 1953.)

Frank Kidson concluded his article 'Handel's Publisher, John Walsh, his Successors and Contemporaries' with the following words:

And thus ends my story of Handel's publishers. Could a bibliography of the publications of the two Walshs be compiled, it would reveal a wealth of music of which the present day has little conception.

The task would be a great one but its compilation would be not an unpleasant one to those bibliographers who delight in such work, and its use to the musical historian would be of the utmost value. Whether any bold spirit or spirits will essay the task is a matter that time alone will show.

With the publication of the *Bibliography, 1695–1720; Handel. A Descriptive Catalogue of the Early Editions*, and the present work, the task referred to by Kidson can be considered to have been carried out, however incompletely, by the present authors. They have been inspired and helped by the great contributions made to the subject by Frank Kidson himself—a pioneer worker in this field of musical research.

A BIBLIOGRAPHY OF THE MUSICAL
WORKS PUBLISHED BY JOHN WALSH
DURING THE YEARS 1721–1766

ABBOS

See Abos (Girolamo)

ABEL (CARL FRIEDRICH)

1. Six Sonatas for the Harpsicord, with Accompanyments for a Violin, or German Flute, and Violoncello. Composed by Charles Frederic Abel.
Sold at the Author's Lodgings, the Dove and Acorn in Greek-street, Soho; J. Walsh . . . J. Johnson . . . and Tho. Smith.

Public Advertiser, July 30, 1760.

This work is presumably the same as 'Opera II'. Printed for the Author. Engraved by Pasquali. (BM. h. 3055. (4.); RM. 17. e. 1. (6.) Fol. Parts.)

See also Nos. 1155–7. Overtures. Abel Arne and Smith's Six Favourite Overtures, &c.; Nos. 1419, 1420. The Summer's Tale . . . Music by Abel, &c.; Nos. 1422, 1423. Summer's Tale. The Overture in the Summer's Tale . . . Compos'd by C. F. Abel.

ABOS (GIROLAMO)

See No. 522. Creso; No. 969. Love in a Village . . . Music by . . . Abel, &c.; No. 1129. Nerone; No. 1450. Tito Manlio.

AGRELL (JOHANN JOACHIM)

2. Six Sonatas or Duets for two German Flutes or Violins Compos'd in a pleasing fine Taste by Giovanni Aggrell Frederico Aurelli Leonardi Vinci Opera Seconda.
London. Printed for I. Walsh, &c.

General Advertiser, April 25, 1751.

Fol. pp. 2–25.
BM. g. 280. (1.) Cardiff.
Randall Cat.: 'Vinci and Agrell's Duets. 3s. 6d.'

3. Six Sonatas for two German Flutes or Violins with a Thorough Bass for the Harpsicord or Violoncello Compos'd by Sig.ʳ Giovanni Agrell &c. Opera Terza.
London. Printed for I. Walsh, &c.

London Evening-Post, Dec. 15–17, 1757.

> Fol. 3 parts.
> BM. g. 222. b. (1.) GUL.
> Walsh Cat. 27: 'Agrell and Vinci's Sonatas.'

4. Sei Sonate per il Cembalo Solo accompagnate da alcune Ariette Polonesi e Menuetti. Composte da Giovanni Agrell.
London. Printed for I. Walsh, &c.

Public Advertiser, Jan. 17, 1758. (Six Sonatas for the Harpsichord . . . A Collection of Easy Lessons, &c.)

> Obl. fol. pp. 36.
> BM. e. 4. Cardiff. Rowe.
> Presumably Book I. A second book with the title 'A Collection of Easy Genteel Lessons for the Harpsichord Composed by Giovanni Agrell Book II. To which is added Vivaldi's Celebrated 5th Concerto, Set for the Harpsicord', was issued by Randall and Abell. (*Public Advertiser*, Dec. 12, 1767.) (BM. e. 4. a. Obl. fol. pp. 2–29.)
> Walsh Cat. 27: 'Agrell's Lessons. 6s. od.'

> *See also* No. 727. Graun (Johann Gottlieb) and Agrell (Johann Joachim) Six Concertos for the Harpsicord . . .Opera 2da; Nos. 879–881. Jozzi (Giuseppe) A Collection of Lessons for the Harpsicord compos'd by . . . Agrell . . . Book I (Book II, Book III).

AGUS (Giuseppe)

> *See* No. 793. Hasse (Johann Adolph) The Comic Tunes . . . Compos'd by Sig^r Agus, &c.; No. 969. Love in a Village . . . Music by . . . Agus, &c.; No. 1154. Overtures. Six Favourite Overtures . . . Publish'd by Mr Agus.

AIRS (or AIRES) (arranged chronologically)

5. Aires & Symphonys for ye Bass Viol being a choice Collection of ye most favourite Song tunes, Aires & Symphonys out of the late Operas, Curiously contriv'd & fitted to the Bass Viol by the best Masters, also some excellent Lessons made purpose for y^t Instrument, as Almands, Corants, Sarabands & Jiggs the whole fairly Engraven and carefully Corrected.
London. Printed for J. Walsh . . . N°. 201.

[*c.* 1730.]

> Obl. fol. pp. 14.
> Walsh Cat. 18: 'Songs and Aires for the Viol. 2s. 6d. N°. 201.'
> Smith 378 (BM. c. 63.) with Walsh only in the imprint and 'N° 201' added to the title-page.

6. Aires by a Person of Quality (for 2 Flutes). 2s. 0d. N? 74.

[*c.* 1730.]

Walsh Cat. 18.
Not identified. The composer may have been William Byron, Fourth Baron Byron.
Smith 601 with 'N? 74' added to the title-page.

7. Aires by 8 Masters (for 2 Flutes). 2s. 0d. N? 75.

[*c.* 1730.]

Walsh Cat. 18.
   Smith 142 'A Collection of Aires, &c.', probably 'Aires for two Flutes by Mr. Weldon,
Sen.ʳ Gasperini & several Masters', with Walsh only in the imprint and 'N? 75' added to the
title-page.

7a. A Book of Familiar Aires, or Song Tunes for a Violin.

[*c.* 1730.]

See No. 1468. Tunes. Familiar Tunes for the Violin. 1s. 6d. N? 148.

8. Familiar Aires for the Flute. 1s. 0d. N? 11.

[*c.* 1730.]

Walsh Cat. 18.
Smith 608 with Walsh only in the imprint and 'N? 11' added to the title-page.

9. Select Airs for the Violin, as Preludes, Almands, Corants, Sarabands and Jigs.
Price 1s. 6d.

[*c.* 1730.]

Walsh Cat. 18: 'Select Lessons 1st Book. (Violin.) 1s. 6d. N? 164.'
Presumably Smith 93 with Walsh only in the imprint and 'N? 164' added to the title-
page.
For the 2ᵈ Book *see* N? 935 Lessons. Select Lessons. 2d. Book . . . N? 152.

10. A Choice Collection of Aires and Duets for two German Flutes Collected from
the Works of the most Eminent Authors viz. Mr. Handel Arcan? Corelli Sig.ʳ
Brivio Mr. Hayden Mr. Grano Mr. Kempton To which is added a favourite
Trumpet Tune of M.ʳ Dubourg's. The whole fairly Engraven and carefully cor-
rected. Price 2s.
   London. Printed for and sold by I: Walsh . . . N? 386.

Country Journal: or, The Craftsman, Sept. 26, 1730.

Obl. 8°. ff. 24 (top corner foliation; double folios, the left-hand folios 'German Flute
Primo', the right hand 'German Flute Secondo'). Printed on one side only.
   RM. 15. g. 4. Schœlcher.
   Joseph Hare's name deleted from the plate after 'Strand' and 'N? 386' probably added.
This may have been done before the work was issued (Sept. 1730) or after Hare left Walsh,

3

Nov. 1730. Copies may have been issued before the alteration was made, but no copy is known. With a top centre foliation on each part in this order: 1, 4, 3, 2, 5, 8, 7, 6, 9, 12, 11, 10, 13, 16, 15, 14, 17, 20, 19, 18, 21, 24, 22, 23. Apparently each folio plate contained two pages of music, the paper being cut in half after the impression had been made, and the top centre pagination 1, 4, 3, 2, &c. refers to a numeration on the plates which does not agree with the order of the pieces.

Walsh Cat. 18: 'Aires and Duets by Mr. Handel . . . No 386.'

This and the three following items also in Walsh Cat. 18: 'Select Aires & Duets (for 2 German Flutes) 4 Books. Each 2s. od.'

11. Select Aires or Duets for two German Flutes or two Violins By the following Eminent Authors Handel Geminiani Sᵗ Martini Weideman Quantz Pescetti 2d Book. N.B. There is just Publish'd Twelve Solos by Mʳ Weideman, &c.

London. Printed for & Sold by I. Walsh . . . No 620.

Country Journal: or, The Craftsman, July 9, 1737.

Obl. 8º. ff. 2–23. Printed on one side only.

RM. 15. g. 4.

The music is in double stave and two pages of music were engraved on each plate, the folio paper being subsequently cut in half.

12. Select Aires or Duets for two German Flutes, and a German Flute & Bass Compos'd by Mʳ Handel, and other Eminent Authors. 3ᵈ Book. N.B. There is just Publish'd Twelve Solos by Mʳ Weideman, &c.

London. Printed for & Sold by I. Walsh . . . No 642.

London Daily Post, July 19, 1738.

Obl. 8º. ff. 2–24. Printed on one side only.

RM. 15. g. 4.

'Mr. Stanley' is the only composer's name given in the body of the work: 'Minuet by Mr. Stanley' on p. 14. The music is in double stave and two pages of music were engraved on each plate, the folio paper being subsequently cut in half.

13. A Fourth Book of Select Aires or Duets, For German Flutes or Violins Being a Collection of Favourite Aires Perform'd with Universal applause at Vaux-Hall, and in all Publick Entertainments, By the following Eminent Authors Handel Geminiani Hasse Arne.

London. Printed for I. Walsh . . . Price 2ˢ of whom may be had, &c.

London Daily Post, Oct. 21, 1741.

Obl. 8º. ff. 2–27. Printed on one side only.

RM. 15. g. 4.

Two pages of music were engraved on each plate as in Nos. 10, 11, and 12.

14. Select Aires For the Guitar Collected from Operas. and the most Favourite Songs, Minuets, &c Perform'd at the Theatres. By the best Masters. N. B. These Airs may be play'd on yᵉ French Horn.

London. Printed for I. Walsh, &c.

[*c.* 1765.]

8°. pp. 2–64.
Rowe.

— Vol: II. (in MS.)

[*c.* 1765.]

8°. pp. 96.
NLS. BH. 232.
Walsh Cat. 27: 'Select Airs for the Guitar Collected from Operas, Oratorios and the Songs Sung at the Publick Gardens. 12 Books, each 1s. 6d.'

ALBERTI (DOMENICO)

15. VIII Sonate Per Cembalo Opera Prima da Dominico Alberti.
London. Printed for I. Walsh, &c.

General Advertiser, Nov. 9, 1748. (Of whom may be had, just publish'd Eight Sets of Lessons for the Harpsichord or Organ.)

Obl. fol. pp. 2–18, blank, 20–27.
BM. e. 5. (1.); e. 5. b. (1.) RAM. RCM. Fitz. Liverpool. Manchester. Reid. Rowe. Tenbury.
Walsh Cat. 25: 'Alberti's Lessons. 5s. od.'

See also Nos. 879–81. Jozzi (Giuseppe) A Collection of Lessons for the Harpsicord compos'd by . . . Alberti . . . Book I (Book II, Book III).

ALBERTI (GIUSEPPE MATTEO)

16. Alberti's Concerto's for three Violins an Alto Viola and a Thorough Bass for the Harpsicord or Bass Violin Compos'd by Giuseppe Matteo Alberti Opera Prima.
London Printed for I: Walsh . . . N.° 344.

[*c.* 1730.]

Hirsch III. 2. RAM.
Walsh Cat. 18: '10 Celebrated Concertos for Violins in Six Parts . . . N.° 344.'
Smith 546 (BM. g. 900) with Walsh only in the imprint and 'N.° 344' added to the title-page.

17. — Another edition.

General Evening Post, Jan. 17–19, 1745. (New editions. Alberti's twenty-two Concertos for Violins, in six Parts. i.e. Op. 1 and 2.)

18. — Another edition.

General Advertiser, Oct. 25, 1749. (New Editions.)

19. XII Sinfonie a Quatro Due Violini Alto Organo e Violoncello Autore Giuseppe
Matheo Alberti. Opera Seconda. Libro Primo (Secondo).
> Printed for and sold by I: Walsh . . . and Ioseph Hare, &c.

> *London Journal*, Oct. 14, 1727. (Twelve Concertos in five Parts.)
>> Fol. Parts.
>> BM. g. 900. d. RAM. Manchester.

20. — With Walsh only in the imprint and 'N⁰ 345' added to the title-page.
> [*c.* 1732.]
>> RAM.
>> Walsh Cat. 18: '12 Concertos for Violins. Opera Seconda. 10s. 6d. N⁰ 345.'

21. — Another edition.
> *General Evening Post*, Jan. 17–19, 1745. (New editions. Alberti's twenty-two
Concertos for Violins, in six Parts. i.e. Op. 1 and 2.)

22. XII Solos for a Violin with a Thorough Bass for the Harpsicord or Bass
Violin Compos'd by Giuseppe Matheo Alberti Opera Terza Note. All the Works
of this Author may be had where these are sold.
> London. Printed for and sold by I: Walsh . . . and Ioseph Hare, &c.

> *Country Journal: or, The Craftsman*, Dec. 20, 1729.
>> Large fol. pp. 47.
>> CUL. (with 'A Cattalogue of Solos for a Violin & a Bass. Printed for Iohn Walsh.') BUL.

23. — With Walsh only in the imprint and 'N⁰ 347' added to the title-page.
> [*c.* 1732.]
>> Fol.
>> BM. g. 900. a. CUL.

> *See also* Nos. 755, 756. Harmonia Mundi. The 2ᵈ Collection . . . Alberti, &c.

ALBINONI (Tommaso)

24. Albinoni's Aires in 3 Parts for Two Violins and a Through Bass Containing
Almand's Saraband's Corrant's Gavots and Jiggs &c Collected out of the Choisest
of his works with the Apro = /bation of our Best Masters the whole Carefully
Corrected and fairly Engraven.
> London Printed for I. Walsh . . . N⁰ 466.

> [*c.* 1730.]
>> Obl. fol. Parts.
>> Walsh Cat. 18: 'Albinoni's Aires Collected. 3s. od. N⁰ 466.'
>> Smith 128 (BM. d. 20. (4.)) with Walsh only in the imprint and 'N⁰ 466' added to the
title-page.

25. Albinoni's Balletti's in 3 Parts for two Violins and a Thorow Bass Consisting of Preludes, Alemands, Sarabands, Corants, Gavots and Jiggs. Compos'd by Thomaso Albinoni Opera Terza.
    London Printed for I: Walsh, &c.

   [*c.* 1726.]
       Fol. Parts.
       BM. h. 24. (1.) Tenbury.
       Smith 540 with Walsh only in the imprint.

26. — With 'N.º 340' on the title-page.

   [*c.* 1730.]
       Walsh Cat. 18: 'Twelve Aires or Ballettis . . . 6s. od. N.º 340.'

27. Albinonis Concertos in Seven Parts for three Violins Tenors and Bass Violin with a Through Bass for the Harpsicord Compos'd by Tomaso Albinoni Opera Secunda.
    London Printed for J. Walsh . . . N.º 339.

   [*c.* 1732.]
       Fol. Parts.
       Walsh Cat. 18: 'Six Concertos for Violins . . . Opera Seconda. 6s. od. N.º 339.'
       Smith 328 (BM. g. 671. a.) with Walsh only in the imprint and 'N.º 339' added to the title-page.

28. Sonate da Chiesa a Violino Solo e Violoncello o Basso Conti: da Tomasso Albinoni, &c.
    London Printed for J. Walsh . . . N.º 341.

   [*c.* 1730.]
       Obl. fol. pp. 25.
       Walsh Cat. 18: 'Albinoni's 6 Solos for a Violin and a Bass. Opera 4.º 4s. od. N.º 341.'
       Smith 366 (RCM.) with Walsh only in the imprint and 'N.º 341' added to the title-page.

29. Trattenimenti Armonici Per Camera Divisi in Dodici Sonata [altered in MS. to Sonatæ] A Violino Violine E Cembalo Da Thomaso Albinoni Opera Sexto [altered in MS. to Sexta]. An Entertainment of Harmony Containing Twelve Solos or Sonatas for a Violin with a Through Bass for the Harpsicord or Bass Violin Compos'd by Thomaso Albinoni Opera Sexta Note. there are of this Authors Several Curious Pieces lately Printed as Concertos, Ballettis and Solos, which may be had where these are Sold.
    London: Printed for I: Walsh . . .N.º 342.

   [*c.* 1732.]
       Fol. pp. 2–67.
       Walsh Cat. 18: '12 Grand Solos for a Violin and a Bass. Op.: 6ta. 6s. od. N.º 342.'

Smith 541 (BM. h. 24. (2.) with Walsh only in the imprint and 'N<u>o</u> 342' added to the title-page.

See also Nos. 753–6. Harmonia Mundi . . . Sign<u>r</u> Albinoni . . . the first (the 2<u>d</u>) Collection, &c.; Nos. 1360, 1361. Select Harmony, 2d Collection . . . from the latest opera of Albinoni, &c.; No. 1443. Thomyris.

ALCOCK (JOHN)

30. A Choice Collection of those Excellent Psalm Tunes which are used in the Parish Churches in London, &c. Set to Four Voices, by John Alcock, B.M.

Printed for the Author, and sold by him and Mr. Walsh and Mr. Johnson, Music-sellers.

Evening Advertiser, Feb. 15–17, 1757.

Not in Walsh or Randall catalogues.

31. Six Concertos In seven Parts, for Four Violins, a Tenor, a Violoncello: & a Thorough Bass for the Harpsicord. Compos'd by John Alcock, Late Organist of Reading Berks; and now Organist, Vicar, & Master of the Children of the Cathedral at Lichfield, &c.

London Printed for, & sold by the Author, and at all the Musick-shops, Price 10<u>s</u> & 6<u>d</u> MDCCL.

General Advertiser, Jan. 10, 1751. (Printed for the Author, and sold by **Mr.** Walsh, &c.)

Fol. 7 parts.
BM. g. 101. Liverpool. Rowe. Tenbury.
Not in Walsh or Randall catalogues.

ALDRICH (BEDFORD)

See No. 749. Harmonia Anglicana . . . Book I.

ALESSANDRO IN PERSIA

32. The Favourite Songs in the Opera Call'd Alexander in Persia. Just Publish'd Le Delizie dell' Opere, &c.

London. Printed for I. Walsh, &c.

— 2<u>d</u> Coll<u>n</u> (in MS.)

London Daily Post and General Advertiser, Dec. 1, 1741; *Daily Advertiser*, Nov. 17, 1742. (Two collections.)

Fol. Passe-partout title-pages. Both pp. 2–19.
BM. G. 190. (4.); H. 348. e. (9.) (Bk. I.) RAM.
Pasticcio. Music by Leo, Hasse, Arena, Pescetti, Lampugnani, and D. Scarlatti.
Republished in 'Le Delizie dell' Opere', Vol. III, pp. 181–98 and Vol. IV, pp. 181–93.
Gresham.

ALESSANDRO NELLE INDIE

33. N? I. The Favourite Songs in the Opera Call'd Alessandro nelle Indie. Price 2.ˢ London. Printed for I. Walsh, &c.

Public Advertiser, Dec. 3, 1761; Dec. 19, 1761. (2 Books.)

Fol. Passe-partout title-page. pp. 14.
BM. H. 230. e. (1.) RM. 13. c. 19. (10.)
Pasticcio, chiefly composed and performed under the direction of Gioacchino Cocchi.
Randall Cat.: 'Alessandro nel India. Cocchi.'
The reference in the advertisement to 2 Books may include Lampugnani's earlier work on the same subject (No. 914).
Republished with an additional song (pp. 15–18) in 'Le Delizie dell' Opere', Vol. XI, pp. 62–79.

ALEXANDER IN PERSIA

See Alessandro in Persia

ALMAHIDE

34. Songs In The New Opera, Call'd Almahide, &c.
Sold by I: Walsh . . . N? 242.

[*c.* 1730.]

Fol. pp. or ff. 4, 64 and Parts.
Walsh Cat. 18: 'The Opera of Almahide. 9s. od. N? 242. (With Symphonys for 2 Viol.ˢ & Bass.)'
Smith Nos. 344 (BM. H. 314) and 346 (Rowe) together, with Walsh only in the imprint and 'N? 242' added to the title-page.

35. The Airs in the Opera of Almahide for a single Flute.
Engraven and printed for J. Walsh, &c.

[*c.* 1730.]

Obl. 4°.
Walsh Cat. 18: 'Almahide for the Flute. 1s. 6d. N? 22.'
Smith 351 (title uncertain) with Walsh only in the imprint and 'N? 22' added to the title-page.

36. The Most Celebrated Aires and Duets In the Opera of Almahide. Curiously fitted and Contriv'd for two Flutes and a Bass, &c.
London Printed for I: Walsh . . .N? 97.

[*c.* 1730.]

Fol. Parts.
Walsh Cat. 18: 'Aires in Almahide (for 2 Flutes and a Bass). 3s. od. N? 97.'
Smith 367 with Walsh only in the imprint and 'N? 97' added to the title-page.

ALMERIGHI (Giuseppe)
See No. 318. Carcani (Giuseppe) Six Sonatas in Three Parts, &c.

AMADEI (Filippo)
See No. 376. Ciro; No. 1125. Muzio Scevola

AMBROGIO (Carlo)
See No. 1392. Solos. Six Solos by several Authors.

AMORE E MAESTÀ
Amore e Maestà. By G. M. Orlandini.
See No. 376. Ciro

ANNIBALE IN CAPUA
37. The Favourite Songs in the Opera Call'd Anibale in Capua.
London. Printed for I. Walsh, &c.

General Advertiser, Dec. 4, 1746.

> Fol. Passe-partout title-page. pp. 20.
> BM. G. 194. (2.)
> Pasticcio. Composers named are Hasse, Lampugnani, Cavalier Malegiac, Terradeglias (i.e. Terradellas), and Paradies. Words by Francesco Vanneschi.
> Walsh Cat. 24a: 'Anibale by Hasse'.
> Randall Cat.: 'Anibale in Capua, Hasse.'
> Republished in 'Le Delizie dell' Opere', Vol. VII, pp. 184–203.

ANTHEMS
Anthems by several Authors.
See No. 1545 Weldon (John) Divine Harmony The 2ᵈ Collection, &c.

ANTIGONA
38. The Favourite Songs in the Opera Call'd Antigona.
London. Printed for I. Walsh, &c.

Public Advertiser, May 17, 1760.

> Fol. Passe-partout title-page. pp. 2–19.
> Pasticcio. Composers named are Galuppi, Dupuis, Conforto, and Cocchi.

39. — Another edition.
[1764.]

> Fol. Passe-partout title-page. pp. 2–19.
> BM. G. 206. g. (2.)
> With additional top centre pagination 96–113.
> Republished in 'Le Delizie dell' Opere', Vol. XI, pp. 99–116.

ANTIOCHUS (ANTIOCO)

Songs in the Opera of Antiochus.
  See No. 688. Gasparini (Francesco)

APOLLO'S BANQUET

40. Apollo's Banquet. A Collection of Favourite Song Tunes Comic Dances
&c. Perform'd at the Theatres. Collected for the Improvement of Young Practitioners on the German Flute, Violin, or Harpsicord. By the best Masters. Vol. I.
(Vol. II.)
  London. Printed for I. Walsh, &c.

  London Evening-Post, Oct. 24–26, 1754. (In four Books, each 1s. 6d.)

    8°. pp. 84.
    BM. e. 24, Vol. I. Leeds, Vol. I. W. N. H. Harding, Chicago, Vol. I, pp. 84, Vol. II,
    pp. 64, 24. Dundee, Vol. I, pp. 20, Vol. II, pp. 48, 24, 20.

APOLLO'S FEAST

41. 2ᵈ Book Apollo's Feast or The Harmony of the Opera Stage being a well-
chosen Collection of the Favourite & most Celebrated Songs out of the latest
Operas Compos'd by Bononcini, Attilio & other Authors done in a plain & Intelli-
gible Character with their Symphonys for Voices and Instruments The whole
fairly Engraven & carefully Corrected Book the Second.
  London. Printed for and sold by I: Walsh . . . and Ioseph Hare at the Viol &
Flute in Cornhill near the Royall Exchange.

  Daily Post, Nov. 11, 1726.

    Fol. Frontispiece (Berchet–H. Hulsbergh), with 'Her' altered to 'His' Maᵗⁱᵉ in MS. 'A
    Table of the Favourite Songs', &c., pp. 226.
    RM. 13. d. 24. NLS. BH. 203. ('Her' not altered on frontispiece.)
    Made up from plates previously used for editions of the operas or collections of favourite
    songs from the operas, with the original pagination in most cases at the top corners in addi-
    tion to the Apollo's Feast top centre pagination. Walsh afterwards substituted a Second
    Book consisting entirely of Handel items, the series of 'Apollo's Feast' being completed in
    five books all of Handel's songs, &c., and the volume of 'Handel's Overtures in Score'
    which was sometimes advertised as the sixth volume of the series.
    Listed by Walsh, *c.* 1730, under Bononcini's works, as 'Le Delizie dell' Opere, Vol. I', with
    Walsh only in the imprint and 'N° 337' added to the title-page. (Walsh Cat. 18.)
    For details of the Handel volumes *see* Smith, 'Handel. A Descriptive Catalogue of the
    Early Editions.'

AQUILIO

42. The favourite Songs in the Opera call'd Aquilio. Publish'd for September.
Price 2ˢ 6ᵈ.
  Printed for & sold by I: Walsh . . . & Inᵒ & Ioseph Hare, &c.

  [*c.* 1724.]

Fol. ff. 17. Printed on one side only.
BM. G. 195. (1). Gresham. Cardiff. Rowe.
Published anonymously, but attributed to Attilio Ariosti.

43. — With Walsh only in the imprint and 'N.° 270' added to the title-page.

[*c.* 1730.]

Walsh Cat. 18: 'Attilio's Works . . . Aquilio. 2s. 6d. N.° 270.'
Republished in 'Le Delizie dell' Opere', Vol. I, pp. 23–24, 89–90, 146–9, 185–9, 194–7.

ARAJA (FRANCESCO)
See No. 1145. Orfeo

ARBACES

44. The Favourite Songs in the Opera Call'd Arbaces 499   Note. where these are Sold may be had all M.ͬ Handel's Operas and Instrumental Musick.
London. Printed for & Sold by I: Walsh . . . N.° 285.

Daily Journal, Feb. 5, 1734.

Fol. Passe-partout title-page used previously for 'The Favourite Songs in . . . Orlando.' (BM.H.300.) pp. 2–19.
BM. G. 206. j. (1.) RCM. Coke. Smith.
Pasticcio. Music attributed to Hasse, Porpora, and Vinci, with recitatives by Handel which are not included. Words adapted partly from Pietro Metastasio's 'Artaserse'.
Walsh Cat. 25: 'Favourite Songs. Arbaces. Vinci.'
A selection was included in 'Le Delizie dell' Opere', Vol. II, pp. 209–13.

ARENA (STEFANO CANDELORO)
See No. 32. Alessandro in Persia

ARIANNA E TESEO

45. The Favourite Songs in the Opera Call'd Arianna e Teseo.
London. Printed for I. Walsh, &c.

Public Advertiser, Jan. 15, 1761.

Fol. Passe-partout title-page. pp. 2–19.
BM. G. 760. g. (2.) RM. 13. c. 19. (4.) RCM. London University. Trinity College, London.
Pasticcio. Composers named are Galuppi, Cocchi, Jomelli, and Scarlatti.
Republished in 'Le Delizie dell' Opere', Vol. XI, pp. 142–59.

46. The Favourite Songs in the Opera Call'd Arianna.
London. Printed for I. Walsh, &c.

[*c.* 1761.]

Fol. Passe-partout title-page. pp. 2–19.
Mitchell. Rowe.
Another issue of No. 45.

ARIOSTI (ATTILIO)

47. The Favourite Songs in the Opera of Artaxerxes. 2s. od. N⁰ 256.

[*c*. 1730.]

> Fol.
> Walsh Cat. 18.
> Reissue by Walsh of 'The Favourite Songs in the Opera call'd Artaxerxes . . . Printed and Sold at the Musick Shops', [1724] with 'N⁰ 256' on the title-page. (BM. G. 206. c. (1.) Fol. ff. 16. Printed on one side only.)
> Music by Attilio Ariosti. Words by Apostolo Zeno.
> Republished in 'Le Delizie dell' Opere', Vol. I, pp. 47–48, 100–2, 109–10, 182–4, 192, 207–9.

48. Opera of Coriolanus.

Printed for and Sold by John Walsh . . . and John and Joseph Hare, &c.

Daily Courant, March 23, 1724. (Where may be likewise had, &c.)

> Fol. pp. 79.
> Walsh Cat. 18: 'Coriolanus. £1. 1s. od.'
> Presumably the edition of Richard Meares May 30, 1723, 'Il Coriolano' (BM. H. 319) which Walsh was selling.
> Music by Attilio Ariosti. Words by Nicola Francesco Haym. Loewenberg says Pietro Pariati, with alterations.
> A selection was included in 'Le Delizie dell' Opere', Vol. I, pp. 77–81, 133–7, 150–1, 193, 222–3.

49. Coriolanus for a Flute Containing the Favourite Songs and Symphonys Curiously Transpos'd and fitted to the Flute in a Compleat manner The whole fairly Engraven and carefully Corrected.

London Printed for and sold by I: Walsh . . . and In⁰ and Ioseph Hare, &c.

[*c*. 1724.]

> Obl. 4⁰. 'A Table of the Song Tunes', &c. ff. 20. Printed on one side only.
> BM. a. 209. a. (2.)

50. The Favourite Songs in the Opera of Darius. 2s. 6d. N⁰ 248.

[*c*. 1730.]

> Walsh Cat. 18.
> Issued anonymously in 1725, with imprint 'London Printed and Sold at the Musick Shops'. (BM. H. 319. a. Fol. Passe-partout title-page. 'A Table of the Favourite Songs', &c. ff. 20. Printed on one side only.) Reissued by Walsh (imprint uncertain) with 'N⁰ 248' on the title-page.
> Music by Attilio Ariosti.
> Republished in 'Le Delizie dell' Opere', Vol. I, pp. 30–32, 39–40, 45–46, 67–68, 123–6, 142–3, 173, 216–17.

51. The Favourite Songs in the Opera call'd Lucius Verus.
   Printed for and sold by I: Walsh . . . and Ioseph Hare, &c.

   [1727.]

   > Fol. Passe-partout title-page. ff. 2–18. Printed on one side only.
   > BM. G. 206. c. (3.) Rowe.
   > Music by Attilio Ariosti, words by Apostolo Zeno.

52. — With Walsh only in the imprint and 'N⁰ 261' added to the title-page.

   [*c.* 1730.]

   > Walsh Cat. 18: 'Attilio's Works. The Favourite Songs in . . . Lucius Verus. 2s. od. N⁰ 261.'
   > One number included in 'Le Delizie dell' Opere', Vol. II, p. 230.

53. Vespasian an Opera as it was Perform'd at the Kings Theatre for the Royal
   Accademy Compos'd by Sig^re Attilio Ariosti Publish'd by the Author.
   London Printed and sold by I: Walsh . . . and In⁰ & Ioseph Hare, &c.

   Daily Courant, March 23, 1724.

   > Fol. 'A Table of Songs', &c. pp. 79.
   > BM. I. 350. a. RCM. Rowe.
   > Words by Apostolo Zeno.

54. — With Walsh only in the imprint and 'N⁰ 232' added to the title-page.

   [*c.* 1730.]

   > Walsh Cat. 18: 'Opera of Vespasian. 12s. od. N⁰ 232.'
   > A selection was included in 'Le Delizie dell' Opere', Vol. I, pp. 6, 33–36, 60–64, 71–72,
   > 82–84, 86, 113–14, 127–8, 218–19.

55. Vespasian for a Flute Containing the Favourite Songs and Symphonys
   Curiously Transpos'd and fitted to the Flute in a Compleat manner. The whole
   fairly Engraven and carefully Corrected.
   London Printed for and sold by I: Walsh . . . and In⁰ and Ioseph Hare, &c.

   [*c.* 1724.]

   > Obl. 4⁰. 'A Table of the Song Tunes', &c. ff. 18. Printed on one side only.
   > BM. a. 209. a. (3.) Rowe.

56. — With Walsh only in the imprint and 'N⁰ 29' added to the title-page.

   [*c.* 1730.]

   > Walsh Cat. 18: 'The Opera of Vespasian for the Flute. 1s. 6d. N⁰ 29.'

   See also No. 41. Apollo's Feast. 2^d Book Apollo's Feast . . . Songs . . . by . . .
   Attilio, &c.; No. 42. Aquilio; No. 376. Ciro.

ARMINIO

57. Songs in the Opera of Arminius as they are Perform'd at the Queens Theatre. London Printed for J: Walsh . . . N⁰ 236.

[*c.* 1730.]

> Fol. ff. or pp. 56.
> Walsh Cat. 18: 'The Opera of Arminius. 9s. od. N⁰ 236.'
> Smith 447 (BM. H. 322.) with Walsh only in the imprint and 'N⁰ 236' added to the title-page.
> Composer unknown, one number attributed to A. Scarlatti, and another ('Per dicesti') frequently given as by A. Lotti.

58. The Aires and Song Tunes for two Flutes in the Opera Call'd Arminius. London. Printed for I. Walsh . . . N⁰ 64.

[*c.* 1730.]

> Obl. 4⁰. 2 parts.
> Walsh Cat. 18: 'Opera of Arminius (for 2 Flutes). 2s. od. N⁰ 64.'
> Smith 456 (Rowe) with Walsh only in the imprint and 'N⁰ 64' added to the title-page

59. Opera of Arminius for the Flute. 1s. 6d. N⁰ 21.

[*c.* 1730.]

> Obl. 4⁰.
> Walsh Cat. 18.
> Smith 457 (title uncertain) with Walsh only in the imprint and 'N⁰ 21' added to the title-page.
> May have been the First Flute part of the previous entry.

60. The Favourite Songs in the Opera Call'd Arminio. London. Printed for I. Walsh, &c.

Public Advertiser, April 7, 1760.

> Fol. Passe-partout title-page. pp. 2–17.
> BM. G. 206. a. (1.) RCM. DAM. Rowe.
> Pasticcio, by D. Perez, &c. A different work from No. 57.
> Randall Cat. as anonymous.
> Republished in 'Le Delizie dell' Opere', Vol. XI, pp. 192–207.

ARNE (Michael)

61. A favourite Collection of English Songs Sung by Mʳ Beard & Miss Young &c. at the Publick Gardens and both Theatres. Compos'd by Mʳ Michael Arne. Book III. London. Printed for I. Walsh, &c.

London Evening-Post, Sept. 13–15, 1757. (A Collection of Songs sung at Ranelagh Gardens.)

> Fol. pp. 2–20.
> BM. G. 234. a. BUL. Rowe.
> Randall Cat.: 'Michael Arne's Songs. 3d Book 3s. od.'

62. The Flow'ret. A New Collection of English Songs Sung at the Public Gardens. Compos'd by Master Arne.
    London. Printed for I. Walsh, &c.

    General Advertiser, May 29, 1750.

    > Fol. pp. 2–11.
    > BM. G. 234. RCM. RCO. Rowe.
    > Randall Cat.: 'Michael Arne's Songs. 1st Book. 1s. 6d.'

63. The Violet A Collection of XII English Ballads Compos'd by M͏ͬ Arne Jun͏ͬ Book II.
    London. Printed for I. Walsh, &c.

    London Evening-Post, Jan. 27–29, 1756. (A Collection of Twelve English Songs.)

    > Obl. fol. pp. 17.
    > BM. D. 267. (4.) Cecil Sharp Library.
    > Randall Cat.: 'Michael Arne's Songs. 2d Book. 2s. od.'

ARNE (THOMAS AUGUSTINE)

The Agreeable Musical Choice. Numb. V–VIII.

> *See* Nos. 95–98. Arne (Thomas Augustine) [Vocal Melody. Books V–VIII.]

64. Songs in the Masque of Alfred Compos'd by M͏ͬ Arne.
    London. Printed for I. Walsh, &c.

    Whitehall Evening-Post, May 20–22, 1756. (Songs in the Mask of Alfred. Several of which are now sung by Miss Young at Ranelagh Gardens.)

    > Fol. pp. 1–9, blank, 1–23 (bottom centre).
    > BM. G. 226. f. RCM. Others in BUC not examined.
    > With additional bottom left corner pagination 24–32 on pp. 1–9.

65. A Second Set of Song's in the Masque of Alfred Compos'd by M Arne.
    London. Printed for I. Walsh, &c.

    Public Advertiser, Jan. 27, 1757. (A Second Book of Songs in Alfred, with the Overture in Score, which compleats the Masque.)

    > Fol. 'A Table of the Songs in the Masque of Alfred. Overture 1 . . . See Liberty, Virtue, and Honour appearing 80'. pp. 1–9 (Overture), 42–83 (top corner).
    > Reid.
    > 'A Second Set of Song's in' is in MS.

66. The Masque of Alfred Compos'd by M͏ͬ Arne.
    London. Printed for I. Walsh, &c.

    [1757.]

    > Fol. 'A Table of the Songs in the Masque of Alfred. Overture 1 . . . See Liberty, Virtue, and Honour appearing 80'. pp. 1–9 (Overture, top corner), blank, 1–23 (bottom centre),

blank, 1–9 (bottom centre, with additional left corner pagination 24–32), 42–86 (top corner, with additional top centre pagination 62–64 on pp. 84–86).

RCM.

This copy is made up of the two collections of 'The Songs in . . . Alfred' (Nos. 64 and 65), but in a different order, with the addition of pp. 84–86 which are not listed in the 'Table' (*see* No. 67). Pp. 84–86, 'The Score of the celebrated Ode, in Honour of Great Britain call'd Rule Britannia' are from the same plates as pp. 62–64 of T. A. Arne's 'The Music in the Judgment of Paris . . . To which . . . are added the celebrated Ode, in Honour of Great-Britain call'd Rule Britannia', &c. London. Printed for Henry Waylett.' [*c.* 1745.] (BM. G. 230. (1.)) The first edition of the Masque of Alfred was issued by J. Oswald, advertised in *The General Advertiser*, May 8, 1751.

67. The Masque of Alfred Compos'd by Mr Arne.
London. Printed for I. Walsh, &c.

[*c.* 1757.]

Fol. 'A Table of the Songs in the Masque of Alfred. Overture 1 . . . When Britain first at Heav'n's Command 84'. pp. 1–9 (Overture), blank, 10–32, blank, 33–86 (top corner).

BM. G. 226. e.; G. 229. (1.) (Wanting title-page). RCM. (Wanting pp. 84–86).

With additional bottom centre pagination 1–23 on pp. 10–32, bottom centre pagination 1–9 and bottom left corner pagination 24–32 on pp. 33–41, from 'Songs in . . . Alfred' (No. 64) and top centre pagination 62–64 on pp. 84–86 as in No. 66.

Randall Cat. 1776: 'Dr. Arne's Masque of Alfred: 10s. 6d.'

68. The Songs in As you like it. Compos'd by Dr Arne Price 3s: 6d
London   Printed for & Sould by I: Walsh, &c.

[*c.* 1765.]

Fol. Passe-partout title-page (Collins frame). pp. 25.

Manchester.

The title is in MS.

A reissue of 'The Songs in As you like it, with the Duet in the Rival Queens. To which are added, The Songs in Twelfth Night, with a Song in the Fall of Phæton, and the Tender Husband, As sung by Mr. Lowe and Mrs. Clive, at the Theatre-Royal, in Dury-Lane. Compos'd by Thomas Augustine Arne', published by William Smith, 1741 and reissued by John Cox *c.* 1755. Walsh probably purchased the work at the sale of the stock-in-trade of John Cox, at Simpson's Music Shop, in 1764.

69. Britannia A Masque as it is Perform'd at the Theatre-Royal in Drury-Lane.
Compos'd by Mr Arne.
Printed for I. Walsh, &c.

Public Advertiser, June 14, 1755.

Fol. pp. 23.

BM. G. 229. (2.) RM. 11. a. 3. Gresham. RAM. RCM. BUL. CUL. Euing.

According to an advertisement on 'The Agreeable Choice', No. 7, &c. by Arne, this work was issued as No. X of the series of song collections beginning with 'Vocal Melody'.

Words by D. Mallet.

British Melody. No. XI.

See No. 100. Arne (Thomas Augustine) [Vocal Melody. Book XI.]

70. Two English Cantatas for a Voice and Instruments. Compos'd by M.ʳ Arne.
N.B.A 2.ᵈ N.⁰ of M.ʳ Arne's Cantatas will be Publish'd in a few Days.
   London. Printed for I. Walsh, &c.

   Public Advertiser, April 30, 1755.

>   Fol. pp. 20.
>   RAM. Bod.
>   Consists of 'The School of Anacreon. Cantata I' and 'Lydia, from Sappho, Cantata II.'
>   Subsequently issued as part of 'Six Cantatas', &c.

71. — Another issue. Two English Cantatas for a Voice and Instruments. Compos'd
by M.ʳ Arne.
   London. Printed for I. Walsh, &c.

   [*c.* 1756.]

>   Fol. pp. 20. N.B. &c. erased from the title-page and 'Britannia' added to list of works
>   advertised.
>   BM. H. 1648. c. (1)

72. — Another issue. A Book of Two English Cantatas for a Voice and Instruments Compos'd by M.ʳ Arne.
   London. Printed for I. Walsh, &c.

   [*c.* 1760.]

>   Fol. pp. 20.
>   Gresham. CUL.

73. A 2.ᵈ Book of Two English Cantatas for a Voice and Instruments. Compos'd
by M.ʳ Arne. N.B. A 3.ᵈ N.⁰ of M.ʳ Arne's Cantatas will be Publish'd in a short time
which compleats this Work.
   London. Printed for I. Walsh, &c.

   London Evening-Post, June 26–28, 1755; *Public Advertiser*, June 27, 1755.

>   Fol. pp. 21–45.
>   RCM.
>   Consists of 'Cantata III. The words by the late Lord Landsdown' (Begins: 'Frolick and
>   free') and 'Bacchus and Ariadne. Cantata IV.'
>   Subsequently issued as part of 'Six Cantatas', &c.

74. — Another issue. A 2.ᵈ Set of Two English Cantatas for a Voice and Instruments. Compos'd by M.ʳ Arne.
   London. Printed for I. Walsh, &c.

   [*c.* 1756.]

>   Fol. pp. 21–45.
>   Gresham.

75. Six Cantatas, For a Voice and Instruments Set to Musick by Thomas Augustine Arne.

London Printed for and Sold by John Walsh, &c.

Public Advertiser, Sept. 4, 1755. (A Third Book of Arne's Cantatas, which compleats the Set, for the Harpsichord, Voice, or German Flute.)

> Fol. pp. 1–45, blank, 47–70. (63–70 is the Flute part.)
> CUL. Rowe. Dundee (imperfect). BM. G. 323. (1.) (With the original title-pages of the first and second books of two cantatas also, wanting pp. 63–70.) BM. G. 321. (1.) (Wanting pp. 63–70.) Others listed in BUC, which have not been examined.
> Originally issued in three books each consisting of two cantatas. Book III consists of 'The Morning. Cantata V.' and 'Delia. Cantata VI.'

76. — A reissue. Six cantatas, &c.

London Evening-Post, April 1–3, 1760.

> Fol. pp. 1–45, blank, 47–70.
> Gresham.

A Choice Collection of Songs sung at Vaux-Hall Gardens by Miss Brent and M.r Lowe . . . Book XII.

See No. 101. Arne (Thomas Augustine) [Vocal Melody, Book XII.]

A Collection Consisting of Favourite Songs and Cantatas Performed by M.r Tenducci, M.r Lowe, &c.

See No. 102. Arne (Thomas Augustine) [Vocal Melody. Book XIII.]

A Collection of Songs (No. IX) . . . in which are The New Songs Sung by Miss Brent in the Jovial Crew, &c.

See No. 99. Arne (Thomas Augustine) [Vocal Melody, Book IX.]

77. The Musick in the Masque of Comus. Written by Milton. As it is perform'd at the Theatre Royal in Drury-Lane. Composed by M.r Arne. Opera prima.

London. Printed for I. Walsh . . . Of whom may be had, compos'd by the same Author, The Songs in As You Like It, &c.

[*c.* 1765.]

> Fol. pp. 2–47.
> BM. G. 321. a. RCM. CUL. OUF.
> Printed from the plates of the edition issued by J. Simpson *c.* 1748 (BM. G. 227. (2.)) with the imprint altered to Walsh. Probably purchased by Walsh at the sale of the stock-in-trade of John Cox at Simpson's Music Shop in 1764.
> BUC gives Reid and Rowe copies of different Walsh issues, not examined.

78. Songs in the New English Opera call'd Eliza. as it is Perform'd at the Theatre Royal in Drury Lane. Compos'd by M.r Arne.

London. Printed for I. Walsh, &c.

Public Advertiser, Feb. 19, 1757. (Songs in . . . Eliza.) *Public Advertiser*, March 8, 1757. (A Second Set of Songs.) *London Evening-Post*, March 24–26, 1757. (A Third Set of Songs . . . which compleats the Opera.)

Fol. pp. 2–105.
CUL. (pp. 2–9, 48–83, consisting of the overture and probably the second set of songs.)
Words by Richard Rolt.

79. Eliza; an English Opera, As perform'd at the Theatre Royal in Drury-Lane. Compos'd by Mʳ Arne.
London. Printed for I. Walsh, &c.

[*c.* 1758.]

Fol. 'A Table of the Songs', &c. pp. 2–105.
BM. G. 228.(1.) RAM. RCM. Fitz. Reading. Rowe.
The three collections of Songs with a new title-page.

A Favourite Collection of Songs with the Dialogue in the Arcadian Nuptials, &c. *See* No. 103. Arne (Thomas Augustine) [Vocal Melody. Book XIV.]

80. Judith an Oratorio as it is Perform'd at the Theatre-Royal in Drury Lane Compos'd by Dʳ Arne.
London. Printed for I. Walsh, &c.

Public Advertiser, March 31, 1761. (Songs in . . . Judith.); May 14, 1761. (Second Set of Songs in Judith, with the Overture which Compleats the Oratorio.)

Fol. 'A Table of the Songs', &c. pp. 97.
BM. G. 231. (1.) RAM. RCM. Bod. CUL. Fitz.
Words by Isaac Bickerstaff.

81. The Second Volume of Lyric Harmony Consisting of Eighteen entire new Songs and Ballads The Words collected from the best Poets, ancient and modern With Damon and Cloe in Score as Perform'd at Vaux-Hall Gardens By Mʳˢ Arne, Mʳ Lowe & Mʳ Reinhold Compos'd by Thomas Augustine Arne Opera quinta Price 4ˢ 0ᵈ.
London Printed for and sold by I. Simpson, &c.

[1764.]

Fol. Privilege verso of title-page. pp. 26.
BM. G. 322. (6.)
This copy bears the manuscript note 'Printed for I Walsh—64' after the imprint. The work was issued by John Simpson and advertised in *The General Advertiser*, Oct. 4, 1748, and was probably purchased by Walsh at the sale of the stock-in-trade of John Cox at Simpson's Music Shop in 1764.

82. The Songs in the Merchant of Venice &c Composed by Dʳ Arne Price ˢ4/.
London Printed for & Sould by I: Walsh, &c.

[c. 1765.]

> Fol. Passe-partout title-page (Collins frame). pp. 28.
> Manchester.
> The title is in MS.
> A reissue of 'The Songs and Duetto, in the Blind Beggar of Bethnal-Green; As perform'd by Mr. Lowe, and Mrs. Clive, at Theatre-Royal, in Drury-Lane. With the Favourite Songs, Sung by Mr. Lowe, in The Merchant of Venice, At the said Theatre. To which are added, A Collection of Songs, The Words carefully Selected from the best Poets. Compos'd by Thomas Augustine Arne,' published by William Smith 1742, and reissued by John Cox, c. 1755. Walsh probably purchased the work at the sale of the stock-in-trade of John Cox, at Simpson's Music Shop, in 1764.

83. Medley Overture in 4 parts. 6d.
   Printed for and sold by John Walsh, &c.

Country Journal: or, The Craftsman, Dec. 25, 1736. (Medley Overtures by Arne, Lampe, Charke and Prelure, in Four Parts—Just publish'd.)

> Fol. Parts.
> Walsh Cat. 18: under 2 Violins and a Bass.
> Subsequently issued in a collection, 'Six Medley or Comic Overtures', No. 1160. (BM. g. 100. c. 1763.) *See* No. 1160. Overtures.)

84. Eight Overtures in 8 Parts, Four for Violins, Hoboys, or German Flutes and Four for Violins, French Horns, &c. with a Bass for the Violoncello & Harpsicord. Compos'd by Thomas Augustine Arne.
   London. Printed for I. Walsh, &c.

London Evening-Post, Jan. 8–10, 1751.

> Fol. 8 parts.
> BM. g. 100. RM. 17. d. 4. (8.) RM. 26. b. 2. (16.) RAM. RCM. BUL. Manchester. Rowe.

85. VIII Sonatas or Lessons for the Harpsichord Compos'd by Thomas Augustine Arne.
   London. Printed for I. Walsh, &c.

London Evening-Post, Nov. 16–18, 1756.

> Obl. fol. pp. 2–32.
> BM. D. 263. (1.) London University. RCM. Leeds (Brotherton Collection). Reid. Rowe.
> Randall Cat.: 'Dr. Arne's Lessons. 6s. od.'

86. VII Sonatas for Two Violins with a Thorough Bass for the Harpsicord or Violoncello Compos'd by Thomas Augustine Arne. Opera Terza.
   London. Printed for I. Walsh, &c.

Public Advertiser, April 6, 1757.

> Fol. 3 parts.
> BM. g. 100. a. RAM. CUL. Manchester.

87. A Loyal Song call'd The Subscription, sung by Mr. Low at the Theatre Royal in Drury-Lane, set by Mr. Arne.

    Printed for J. Walsh, &c.

    General Evening Post (London), Nov. 26–28, 1745. (Just published.)

      Fol.

88. Thomas and Sally or The Sailor's Return, A Dramatic Pastoral. With the overture in Score, Songs, Dialogues Duettos and Dance-tunes, as perform'd at the Theatre Royal in Covent Garden By M.ʳ Beard and Miss Brent, M.ʳ Mattocks, M.ʳˢ Vernon and Chorus: The Music Compos'd by Doct.ʳ Arne.

    London. Printed for I. Walsh, &c.

    Public Advertiser, Oct. 15, 1765.

      Fol. pp. 2–51.
      BM. G. 230. (3.) Hirsch M. 1363. Gresham. RCM. Leeds (Brotherton Collection). Manchester. Rowe.
      Words by Isaac Bickerstaff.
      A reissue of the edition issued with the imprint 'Printed for and sold by the Author' in 1761. (BM. H. 130. (2.))

89. Thomas and Sally. A Dramatic Pastoral As Perform'd at the Theatre Royal in Covent Garden by M.ʳ Beard M.ʳ Mattocks Miss Brent and Miss Poitier. Compos'd by D.ʳ Arne. For the Harpsicord, Voice, German Flute, or Violin. Price 1ˢ 6.ᵈ

    London. Printed for I. Walsh, &c.

    Public Advertiser, Oct. 15, 1765.

      Obl. fol. pp. 2–17.
      BM. D. 262. (5.) Manchester. Mitchell. Rowe.

90. Thomas and Sally A musical Entertainment Set for a German Flute, Violin, or Guitar Compos'd by D.ʳ Arne   Price 1ˢ 6.ᵈ

    London. Printed for I. Walsh, &c.

    [*c.* 1765.]

      8°. pp. 2–16.
      BM. e. 340. h. (5.) Dundee.

91. Vocal Melody. An Entire New Collection of English Songs and a Cantata Compos'd by M.ʳ Arne. Sung by M.ʳ Beard, M.ʳ Lowe, and M.ʳ Baker, at Vaux-Hall, Ranelagh, and Marybon-Gardens.

    London. Printed for I. Walsh, &c.

    General Advertiser, August 31, 1749.

      Fol. Privilege (dated 29 January 1740–1) verso of title-page. pp. 20.
      BM. 321. (2.) RM. 9. i. 18. (1.) RCM. Gresham.

92. Vocal Melody Book II. An Entire New Collection of English Songs and a Cantata Compos'd by Mr Arne. Sung by Mr Beard, Mr Lowe, and Miss Falkner at Vaux-Hall, Ranelagh, and Marybon-Gardens.
London. Printed for I. Walsh, &c.

London Evening-Post, Oct. 16–18, 1750.

> Fol. Privilege (dated 29 January 1740–1) verso of title-page. pp. 21–42.
> BM. G. 321. (2.) RM. 19. i. 18. (1.)

93. Vocal Melody Book III. A Favourite Collection of Songs and Dialogues Sung at Marybon-Gardens by Master Arne and Miss Falkner. and at Vaux-Hall-Gardens by Miss Stevenson and Mr Lowe. Compos'd by Mr Arne.
London. Printed for I. Walsh. &c.

London Evening-Post, August 13–15, 1751.

> Fol. Privilege (dated 29 January 1740–1). pp. 2–21.
> BM. G. 321. (2.) RM. 19. i. 18. (1) RCM.

94. Vocal Melody Book IV. A Favourite Collection of English Songs Sung at the Publick Gardens. with the Songs in Harlequin Sorcerer, and the Oracle Sung by Mrs Cibber. Compos'd by Mr Arne.
London. Printed for I. Walsh, &c.

London Evening-Post, June 4–6, 1752.

> Fol. Privilege (dated 29 January 1740–1). pp. 22–40.
> BM. G. 321. (2.) RM. 9. i. 18. (1.)
> Walsh Cat. 25: 'Arne's Songs call'd Vocal Melody. 4 B. each 3s. od.'

95. [Vocal Melody. Book V.] Numb. V. The Agreeable Musical Choice An Entire New Collection of English Songs, with the Duet in Harlequin Sorcerer Sung by Mr Lowe and Mrs Lampe. Never before Printed. Compos'd by Mr Arne.
NB. There are 4 Collections of Songs Publish'd by the same Author, call'd Vocal Melody.
London. Printed for I. Walsh, &c.

Public Advertiser, May 7, 1753.

> Fol. Privilege (dated 29 January 1740–1). pp. 2–22.
> BM. G. 321. (3.) RM. 9. i. 18. (2.)
> Nos. I–IV were published as 'Vocal Melody', Books I–IV.

96. [Vocal Melody. Book VI.] Numb. VI. The Agreeable Musical Choice. A Favourite Collection of English Songs Never before Printed. Compos'd by Mr Arne.
London. Printed for I. Walsh, &c.

London Evening-Post, May 30–June 1, 1754.

Fol. pp. 2–22.
BM. G. 321. (3.) RM. 9. i. 18. (2.) RCM.

97. [Vocal Melody. Book VII.] Numb: VII. The Agreeable Musical Choice. A Pastoral Collection of Songs Sung at the Publick Gardens. Compos'd by Mͬ Arne. London. Printed for I. Walsh, &c.

Whitehall Evening-Post. June 26–29, 1756.

Fol. pp. 2–22.
BM. G. 321. (3.) RM. 9. i. 18. (2.) RCM.

98. [Vocal Melody. Book VIII.] Numb: VIII. The Agreeable Musical Choice. A Favourite Collection of English Songs Sung at the Publick Gardens. Compos'd by Mͬ Arne.
London. Printed for I. Walsh, &c.

Whitehall Evening-Post, July 4–6, 1758.

Fol. pp. 24–43.
BM. G. 321. (3.) RM. 9. i. 18. (2.) RCM.
Walsh Cat. 27: 'Dͬ Arnes Musical Choice. 4 Books, each 3s. od.'

99. [Vocal Melody. Book IX.] Nͦ IX. A Collection of Songs compos'd by Dͬ Arne. in which are The New Songs Sung by Miss Brent in the Jovial Crew &c. London. Printed for I. Walsh, &c.

Public Advertiser, April 24, 1760.

Fol. pp. 2–22.
BM. G. 323. (7.); G. 321. (4.) RM. 9. i. 18. (3.) RAM. Birmingham. Rowe.
Nos. I–VIII were published as 'Vocal Melody' and 'The Agreeable Musical Choice'.
Randall Cat. gives Nͦ IX as a separate entry: 'Dr. Arne's New Songs in the Jovial Crew. 3s. od.'

[Vocal Melody. Book X.]
See No. 69. Arne (Thomas Augustine) Britannia.

100. [Vocal Melody. Book XI.] Nͦ XI British Melody. A Favourite Collection of English Songs and a Cantata Compos'd by Dͬ Arne. Sung by Miss Brent & Mͬ Lowe at Vaux-hall Gardens.
London. Printed for I. Walsh, &c.

London Evening-Post, August 26–28, 1760.

Fol. pp. 19.
BM. G. 323. (4.) RM. 9. i. 18. (4.) RCM. Bod. Fitz. Rowe.
'XI' altered from 'X' in MS.

101. [Vocal Melody. Book XII.] A Choice Collection of Songs sung at Vaux-Hall Gardens by Miss Brent and M.ʳ Lowe Set to Musick by D.ʳ Arne. Book XII. Price 1.ˢ 6.ᵈ

London. Printed for I. Walsh, &c.

Public Advertiser, Sept. 1, 1761.

> Fol. pp. 13.
> BM. G. 323. (5.) RCM. Manchester. Rowe.

102. [Vocal Melody. Book XIII.] A Collection Consisting of Favourite Songs and Cantatas Performed by M.ʳ Tenducci M.ʳ Lowe, M.ʳ Mattocks M.ʳˢ Lampe, Miss Stevenson and Miss Brent, At the Theatre Royal in Covent Garden Vaux-hall and Ranelagh. The whole composed by Thos. Arne Mus: Doc: Price 5s.

London Printed for I. Walsh, &c.

[*c.* 1765.]

> Fol. pp. 2–40.
> Gresham. Fitz. (Wanting pp. 63–70.)

103. [Vocal Melody. Book XIV.] A Favourite Collection of Songs with the Dialogue in the Arcadian Nuptials Sung by M.ʳ Beard & Miss Hallam. Compos'd by D.ʳ Arne. Book XIV.

London. Printed for I. Walsh, &c.

Public Advertiser, Feb. 4, 1764.

> Fol. pp. 14.
> BM. G. 323. (3.) RAM. RCM. Dundee. Fitz. Manchester. Rowe.
> Randall Cat. gives this as a separate item: 'Dr. Arne's Arcadian Nuptials. 2s. od.'

[Vocal Melody.]
> *See also* No. 1404. Songs. Miss Brents Songs sung at Vauxhall.

104. Winter's Amusements, a favourite Collection of English Songs and Cantatas by Mr. Arne, sung at the Theatres, Vauxhall and Ranelagh.

Printed for J. Walsh, &c.

Public Advertiser, Jan. 29, 1762.

> Probably a reissue of the edition 'Printed for the Author'. (BM. G. 320. (4.) Fol. pp. 2–40.)

See also No. 13. A Fourth Book of Select Aires or Duets, For Two German Flutes ... By ... Arne; No. 267. British Orpheus. No. III; No. 315. Canzoniere; No. 546. Defesch (Willem) M.ʳ Defesch's Songs, &c.; No. 549. Delightful Musical Companion. A second set of celebrated Duets for two German Flutes . . . by Arne &c.; Nos. 602–4. English Songs; No. 747. Harlequin Restored; No. 748. Harlequin Sorcerer; No. 749. Harmonia Anglicana . . .

by . . . Dr Arne, &c.; No. 768. Hartley (James) Six Sonatas . . . Revised . . .by
Thomas Augustine Arne; No. 840. Hornpipes. A fourth Book of Hornpipe's
In which is that Celebrated Hornpipe . . .Compos'd by Dr Arne; No. 969.
Love in a Village . . . Music by . . . Arne, &c.; Nos. 1155–7. Overtures. Abel
Arne and Smith's Six Favourite Overtures, &c.; No. 1160. Overtures. Six
Medley or Comic Overtures . . . Compos'd by Dr Arne, &c.; Nos. 1419,
1420. The Summer's Tale . . . Music by . . . Arne, &c.

ARNOLD (Samuel)

Comic Tunes in Dr Faustus.
  See No. 748. Harlequin Sorcerer; Nos. 1419. 1420. The Summer's Tale . . .
  Music by . . . Arnold, &c.

ARSACE

The Favourite Songs in the Operas of Cyrus and Arsaces.
  See No. 376. Ciro

ARSINOE

Songs in the Opera Call'd Arsinoe Queen of Cyprus.
  See No. 379. Clayton (Thomas)

ARTASERSE

The Favourite Songs in the Opera of Artaxerxes.
  See No. 47. Ariosti (Attilio)

ASTARTO

  See No. 193. Bononcini (Giovanni) The Overture, Symphonies, or Instru-
  mental Musick in . . . Astartus, &c.; No. 195. Bononcini (Giovanni) The
  Song Tunes with their Symphonys for the Flute in . . . Astartus, &c.; No. 196.
  Bononcini (Giovanni) Astartus for the Flute.

ASTIANASSE

The Favourite Songs in the Opera call'd Astyanax.
  See No. 197. Bononcini (Giovanni)

ATTALO

105. The Favourite Songs in the Opera Call'd Attalo.
  London: Printed for I. Walsh, &c.
  Public Advertiser, Dec. 5, 1758.

Fol. Passe-partout title-page. pp. 24.
BM. G. 206. g. (3.) RM. 13. c. 19. (7.) RCM. DAM.
Pasticcio. Composers named are Auresichio, Coffarello, Perez, Potenza, and Cocchi.
Republished in 'Le Delizie dell' Opere', Vol. IX, pp. 93–116.

ATTILIO

See Ariosti (Attilio)

AULETTA (PIETRO)

See No. 833. Hasse (Johann Adolph) N.º III. Venetian Ballads, &c.

AURELLI (FEDERICO)

See No. 2 Agrell (Johann Joachim). Six Sonatas or Duets for two German Flutes
or Violins Compos'd . . . by Giovanni Aggrell Frederico Aurelli, &c.

AURESICHIO (ANTONIO)

See No. 105. Attalo

AVISON (CHARLES)

106. Eight Concertos for the Organ or Harpsicord Compos'd by M.ʳ Charles
Avison Organist in Newcastle upon Tyne.
   N.B. The 1ˢᵗ & 2ᵈ Ripienos, Tenor, & Basso Ripieno of His Violin Concertos,
[Op. 2] are the Instrumental Parts to yᵉ above.
   London. Printed for I. Walsh, &c.

General Advertiser, April 21, 1747.

Fol. pp. 2–8, blank, 10–31.
BM. g. 256. d. Tenbury.
The Instrumental parts referred to were the 'Six Concertos in Seven Parts . . . Opera
Secunda', published by Joseph Barber, Newcastle, 1740. (BM. g. 256. c.)

AYRTON (EDMUND)

See No. 1233. Psalms.

BABELL (WILLIAM)

107. Chamber Music. XII Solos, For a Violin or Hautboy: with a Bass, figur'd for
the Harpsicord. With proper Graces adapted to each Adagio, by the Author.
Compos'd by M.ʳ W.ᵐ Babell, Late Organist of Allhallows Bread street, and
One of his Majesties Private Musick. Part the First of his Posthumous Works.
   London Printed for and sold by I : Walsh . . . and I.ⁿ and Joseph Hare, &c.

[*c.* 1725.]

Fol. Illustrated title-page. Preface. pp. 59.
BM. g. 1090. (5.) Rowe.

108. — Another issue, with 'N.° 357' added to the title-page and without the preface.

> [*c.* 1730.]
>> Fol. Illustrated title-page. pp. 59.
>> BM. g. 908.
>> Walsh Cat. 18: '12 Solos for a Violin or Hoboy. Opera Prima. 7s. od. N.° 357.'

109. Babell's Concertos, in 7 Parts: The first four for Violins and one small Flute and the two last for Violins and two Flutes. The proper Flute being named to each Concerto. Compos'd by the Late Mr Will.ᵐ Babell. Perform'd at the Theatre with great applause Opera Terza. Note: All the Works of this Author may be had where these are sold.

> London, Printed for and sold by I. Walsh . . . and Ioseph Hare, &c.

> [*c.* 1726.]
>> Fol. Parts.
>> York Minster Library.
>> Walsh Cat. 11c. 'Babel's Concertos for Flutes.'

110. — With Walsh only in the imprint and 'N.° 359' added to the title-page.

> *Country Journal: or, The Craftsman,* May 8, 1731.
>> Walsh Cat. 18: '6 Concertos for small Flutes and Violins. Opera Terza. 8s. od. N.° 359.'

111. The 3.ᵈ Book of the Ladys Entertainment or Banquet of Musick being A Choice Collection of the most Celebrated Aires & Duets Curiously Set and Fitted to the Harpsicord or Spinnet: With their Symphonys introduc'd in a Compleat man.ʳ by M.ʳ W.ᵐ Babel.

> London, Printed for J. Walsh . . . N.° 169.

> [*c.* 1730.]
>> Fol. pp. 22.
>> BM. f. 39. a. (1.)
>> Smith 484 with modified title-page, blank space after 'Duets', with Walsh only in the imprint and 'N.° 169' added to the title-page.
>> Walsh Cat. 18: '2 Books call'd the Ladys Entertainm.ᵗ . . . 7s. od. N.° 170.'
>> The 1st and 2nd Books were published anonymously. (*See* Nos. 896 and 897. Lady's Entertainment.)
>> Walsh Cat. 25 gives: 'Ladies Entertainment. 4 Books of Aires from Operas Set by Babell. Each 3s. od.'

112. The 4.ᵗʰ Book of the Ladys Entertainment or Banquet of Musick Being a Choice Collection of yᵉ most Celebrated Aires & Duets in the Operas of Hydaspes & Almahide Curiously Set and fitted to the Harpsicord or Spinnet With their Symphonys introduc'd in a Compleat manner by M.ʳ W.ᵐ Babell.

> London   Printed for I: Walsh . . . N.° 170.

[*c.* 1730.]

Fol. pp. 31.

BM. f. 39. a. (2.)

Smith 501 with Walsh only in the imprint and 'N<u>o</u> 170' added to the title-page, the Table omitted and the order of the plates slightly different.

Walsh Cat. 18: '2 Books call'd the Ladys Entertainment . . . 7s. od. N<u>o</u> 170.'

XII Solos For a Violin or Hautboy: with a Bass . . . Part the First of his Post-humous Works.

See No. 107. Babell (William) Chamber Music.

113. XII Solos for a Violin Hoboy or German Flute with a Bass figur'd for the Harpsicord With proper Graces adapted to each Adagio by y<u>e</u> Author Compos'd by M<u>r</u> W<u>m</u> Babell Late Organist of Allhallows Bread-street, and One of his Majestys Private Musick. Part the Second of his Posthumous Works.

London Printed for and sold by I: Walsh . . . and In<u>o</u> Ioseph Hare, &c.

[*c.* 1725.]

Fol. pp. 51.

BM. g. 1090. (4.)

114. — Reissued with Walsh only in the imprint and 'N<u>o</u> 358' added to the title-page.

[*c.* 1730.]

Walsh Cat. 18: '12 Solos for a German Flute or Hoboy. Op: 2da 6s. od. N<u>o</u> 358.'

115. Suits of the most Celebrated Lessons Collected and Fitted to the Harpsicord or Spinnet by M<u>r</u> W<u>m</u> Babell with Variety of Passages by the Author. Note there are two precedent books for y<u>e</u> Harpsicord by y<u>e</u> same hand.

London Printed for I: Walsh, . . . N<u>o</u> 174.

[*c.* 1730.]

Fol. 'A Table of the Lessons', &c., pp. 2–77.

BM. g. 908. a. RCM. Edinburgh. Fitz. Liverpool. Smith.

Smith 505 with Walsh only in the imprint and 'N<u>o</u> 174' added to the title-page.

Walsh Cat. 18: 'Babell's Works. His Celebrated Book of Lessons for y<u>e</u> Harpsi<u>d</u> 5s. od.'

BACH (CARL PHILIPP EMANUEL)

116. Sig<u>r</u> Bach (of Berlin) Concertos for the Harpsichord, or Organ. with Accompanyments for Violins &c. Op. 3<u>za</u>

London. Printed for I. Walsh, &c.

Public Advertiser, Nov. 26, 1765.

29

Fol. 5 parts.
RM. 16. b. 19. (Harpsichord and Violino Primo parts only.) Euing. (5 parts.) Rowe (imperfect).
Randall Cat.: 'Bach of Berlin's Concertos. 7s. 6d.'

117. Sei Sonate per Cembalo Composte dal Sig.ͬ Carl Philipp Emanuel Bach. [1st Set.]
London. Printed for I. Walsh, &c.

Public Advertiser, April 25, 1763.

Obl. fol. pp. 2–35.
BM. f. 46. j. RM. 16. a. 15. (3.) OUF. Rowe.
Walsh Cat. 27: 'Bach's Lessons. 2 Sets. each 6s. od.'

118. A 2.ᵈ Set Sei Sonate per Cembalo Composte dal Sig.ͬ Carl Philipp Bach. Opera Seconda.
London. Printed for I. Walsh, &c.

Public Advertiser, Oct. 15, 1763.

Obl. fol. pp. 33.
BM. f. 46. k. OUF. Rowe.
Walsh Cat. 27: 'Bach's Lessons. 2 Sets. each 6s. od.'

BACH (Johann Christian)

119. N.º I The Favourite Songs in the Opera Call'd Orione, o sia Diana Vendicata. Bach.
London. Printed for I. Walsh, &c.

Public Advertiser, March 5, 1763; April 4, 1763. (A Second Set.)

Fol. Passe-partout title-page. pp. 1–15, blank, 17–30. (Two sets in one.)
BM. H. 348. c. (2.) (With 'Bach' in MS. on title-page.) RM. 11. a. 18. (1.) (Two sets. 'N.º 1' not on title-page.) RM. 13. c. 22. (1.) (N.º 1 only.) Gresham. RCM. Manchester.
Republished in 'Le Delizie dell' Opere', Vol. XI, pp. 33–61.

120. Number I. A Favourite Overture: Compos'd by Sig. Bach, in the Opera Orione, for Violins, French Horns, Clarinets, &c. Printed for J. Walsh, &c.

Public Advertiser, July 14, 1763.

Fol. Parts.
Included in 'Six Favourite Overtures in 8 Parts', &c. (*See* No. 126.)

121. No. II. A Favourite Overture in 8 Parts for Violins, Hoboys, French Horns, with a Bass for the Harpsicord and Violoncello. Compos'd by Sig.ͬ Bach.
London Printed for I. Walsh, &c.

Public Advertiser, August 2, 1763.

Fol. Parts.
Hirsch IV. 1586. (Two copies of the Bass part.)
'II' has been altered from 'I' in MS.
The overture is 'La Calamita', subsequently included in 'Six Favourite Overtures in 8 Parts', &c. (*See* No. 126.)

122. A Third favourite Opera Overture for Violins and French Horns, in 8 Parts, composed by Sig. Bach, Price 2s.
Printed for J. Walsh, &c.

Public Advertiser, Sept. 1, 1763.

Fol. Parts
Presumably the overture to 'Artaserse', subsequently included in 'Six Favourite Overtures in 8 Parts', &c. (*See* No. 126.)

123. A Fourth favourite Opera Overture, in eight Parts, for Violins and French Horns; by Sig. Bach. Price 2s.
Printed for J. Walsh, &c.

Public Advertiser, Oct. 1, 1763.

Fol. Parts.
Presumably the overture to 'Il Tutore e la Pupilla', a pasticcio, subsequently included in 'Six Favourite Overtures in 8 Parts', &c. (*See* No. 126.)

124. A Fifth favourite Opera Overture, for Violins, French Horns, &c. in eight Parts, by Sig. Bach.
Printed for J. Walsh, &c.

Public Advertiser, Nov. 2, 1763.

Fol. Parts.
Presumably the overture to 'Cascina', a pasticcio, based on the opera of Giuseppe Scolari, subsequently included in 'Six Favourite Overtures in 8 Parts', &c. (*See* No. 126.)

125. A Sixth favourite Opera Overture, for Violins, French Horns, in 8 Parts. Compos'd by Sig. Bach. Price 2s.
Printed for J. Walsh, &c.

Public Advertiser, Dec. 1, 1763.

Fol. Parts.
Presumably the overture to 'Astarto', a pasticcio, subsequently included in 'Six Favourite Overtures in 8 Parts', &c. (*See* No. 126.)

126. Six Favourite Overtures in 8 Parts For Violins, Hoboys, French Horns, with a Bass for the Harpsicord and Violoncello. Compos'd by Sig.^r Bach.
London. Printed for I. Walsh, &c.

Public Advertiser, Dec. 10, 1763.

Fol. Parts.

RAM. RCM. Bod. Rowe.

Contains overtures to 'Orione', 'La Calamita', 'Artaserse', 'Il Tutore e la Pupilla', 'La Cascina' and 'Astarto'.

Listed as 'Fourth Set' on the title-page of 'Six Overtures in 8 parts . . . Compos'd by Sig.ʳ Bach Jomelli Galuppi Perez Sixth Collection'. (BM. g. 212. a. 1764. *See* No. 1158.)

Walsh Cat. 27: 'Bach's 6 Overtures. 5.ᵗʰ Coll.ⁿ 12s. od.'

127. Six Favourite Opera Overtures Set for the Harpsichord or Organ Compos'd by Sig.ʳ Bach, &c.

London. Printed for I. Walsh, &c.

Public Advertiser, Dec. 13, 1763. (Also set for the Harpsichord.)

Obl. fol. pp. 2–31.

BM. e. 12. (2.) RM. 16. a. 15. (2.) Manchester. Rowe.

No. 1 is overture to 'Orione', No. 2 to 'Zanaida', No. 3 to 'Artaserse', No. 4 to 'La Cascina' and No. 5 to 'Astarto'. No. 6 is by 'Sig. Galuppi'. Nos. 4 and 5 were pasticcios.

Number VII. Price 2s. A Favourite Overture for Violins, French Horns &c. in 8 Parts. Compos'd by Sig. Galuppi.

See No. 675 Galuppi (Baldassare)

128. An Eighth favourite Opera Overture for Violins French Horns, &c. in 8 Parts. By Sig. Bach. Price 2s.

Printed for J. Walsh, &c.

Public Advertiser, Feb. 2, 1764.

Fol. Parts.

The overture is to 'Zanaida', subsequently included as No. 2 of 'Six Overtures in 8 Parts . . . Compos'd by Sig.ʳ Bach Jomelli Galuppi Perez Sixth Collection.' (BM. g. 212. a. 1764. *See* No. 1158.)

Nos. 9–12 of this series are under B. Galuppi, L. V. Ciampi, D. Perez and N. Jomelli.

Public Advertiser, June 5, 1764. (Eleven favourite Opera Overtures for Violins, &c.)

129. The Favourite Songs in the Opera Call'd Zanaida By Sig.ʳ Bach. Price 4.ˢ

London. Printed for I. Walsh, &c.

Public Advertiser, May 23, 1763.

Fol. Passe-partout title-page. pp. 31.

BM. G. 136. b. RM. 11. a. 18. (2). Gresham. Manchester. Rowe.

Republished in 'Le Delizie dell' Opere', Vol. XI, pp. 1–31.

See also No. 276. Calamita de Cuori; Nos. 566, 567. Delizie dell' Opere. Vols. X, XI; No. 1158. Overtures. Six Overtures . . . Compos'd by Sig.ʳ Bach, &c.; Nos. 1419, 1420. The Summer's Tale . . . Music by . . . Bach, &c.

BAILDON (Joseph)

130. The Laurel. A New Collection of English Songs Sung by M.ʳ Lowe and Miss Falkner at Marybon-Gardens. Compos'd by M.ʳ Joseph Baildon.

London Printed for I. Walsh, &c.

General Advertiser, Aug 17, 1750.

> Fol. pp. 11.
> BM. H. 1650. a. (1.) RCM.
> Randall Cat.: 'Baildon's Songs, Book 1st. 1s. 6d.'

131. The Laurel. Book II. A New Collection of English Songs and Cantatas Sung by Mʳ Lowe and Miss Falkner at Vaux-Hall and Marybon-Gardens. Compos'd by Mʳ Joseph Baildon.
London. Printed for I. Walsh, &c.

London Evening-Post, Sept. 21–23, 1752.

> Fol. pp. 2–19.
> BM. H. 1650. a. (1.) RCM.
> Randall Cat.: 'Baildon's Songs, Book 2d. 3s. od.

132. A Collection of Songs sung at Vauxhall Gardens by Mr. Lowe and Miss Stevenson. Set by Mr. Baildon. No. 2. Price 1s. 6d.
Printed for J. Walsh, &c.

London Evening-Post, Sept. 13–15, 1757.

> Probably, Randall Cat.: 'Baildon's Songs, Book 3d. 1s. 6d.'

See also No. 969. Love in a Village . . . Music by . . . Baildon, &c.; No. 1233. Psalms; No. 1419. Summer's Tale

BALLAD OPERAS

133. A Collection of all the Ballad Operas Bound.

> [*c.* 1736.]

> Walsh Cat. in Caledonian Country Dances . . . 3ᵈ Edition. (*London Daily Post, and General Advertiser*, Nov. 3, 1736.) Mitchell.
> A collected edition of works previously issued separately, contents not known, but presumably listed separately in this bibliography.

BANISTER (JOHN)

134. Banisters . . . Opera Airs . . . His Collection for two Violins.
Printed for J. Walsh, &c.

> [*c.* 1727.]

> Walsh Cat. 11*b*.
> Presumably Smith 527. 'A Collection of Choice Airs and Symphonys for two Violins, out of the most celebrated Operas . . . by the best Masters.'

135. — With Walsh only in the imprint and 'Nº 430' added to the title-page.

> [*c.* 1730.]

> Walsh Cat. 18: 'Opera Aires (for 2 Violins). 2s. od. Nº 430.'

136. A Collection of the most Celebrated Song Tunes with their Symphonys taken out of the Choicest Operas and Fitted to the Violin for the Improvement of Practicioners on that Instrument by Mr. Ino. Banister. Price 1s. 6d. (in MS.)

London. Printed for I. Walsh ⋮ . . . N⁰ 165.

[*c.* 1730.]

> Obl. 8⁰. 'Table of the Song Tunes.' ff. 20. Printed on one side only.
> Smith 503 (Fitz.) with Walsh only in the imprint and 'N⁰ 165' added to the title-page.
> Walsh Cat. 18: 'Banister's choice Opera Aires (for a single Violin). 1s. 6d.'

137. A 2nd Collection of the most Celebrated Song Tunes with their Symphonys out of the Choicest Operas and Fitted to the Violin for the Improvement of Practicioners on that Instrument by Mr. Ino. Banister.

London Printed for I. Walsh . . . N⁰ 154.

[*c.* 1730.]

> Obl. 8⁰. Table. ff. 20. Printed on one side only.
> Smith 526 (Fitz.) with Walsh only in the imprint and 'N⁰ 154' added to the title-page.
> Walsh Cat. 18: 'Banister's 2d Collection (for a single violin). 1s. 6d.'

BARBANDT (Carl)

138. Six Sonatas for Two Violins, two German Flutes or two Hautboys with a Bass for the Violoncello & Harpsicord Compos'd by Charles Barbandt Musician to His Majesty at Hanover. Opera 1ᵐᵃ.

[London.]

Daily Advertiser, Feb. 15, 1752. (Printed for the Author; and sold by J. Walsh, &c.)

> Fol. 3 parts. 'To Her Royal Highness the Princess of Wales.' 'A List of Subscribers names.'
> 2 pp.
> BM. f. 14.

BARSANTI (Francesco)

139. A Collection of old Scots Tunes, with the Bass for the Violoncello or Harpsichord By Francesco Barsanti. Price 5s.

Printed for the Author; and sold by J. Walsh in Katherine-Street in the Strand.

Daily Advertiser, Jan. 27, 1743.

> Presumably the advertisement refers to the work published in 1742 with the imprint 'Edinburgh, Printed by Alexander Baillie, & sold by Messrs Hamilton & Kincaid.' (BM. f. 74. Fol. pp. 15.)

140. Ten Great Concertos for Violins, Hautboys, French Horns, Trumpets and Kettle-Drums, with a thorough Bass for the Harpsichord. Compos'd by Francesco Barsanti. Opera 3.

Printed for the Author; and sold by J. Walsh in Katherine-Street in the Strand.

Daily Advertiser, Jan. 27, 1743.

Presumably the advertisement refers to 'Concerti Grossi . . . Opera Terza. Sold by the Author, at Edinburgh', &c. published *c.* 1743. (BM. g. 261. Fol. Parts.)

141. Solos for a German Flute a Hoboy or Violin with a Thorough Bass for the Harpsicord or Bass Violin Compos'd by Francesco Barsanti Opera Terza. N.B. The rest of the Works of this Author may be had where these are sold Also great variety of new Musick for the German Flute.

London. Printed for and sold by I: Walsh . . . and Ioseph Hare, &c.

Country Journal: or, The Craftsman, July 6, 1728.

Fol. pp. 31.

142. — With Walsh only in the imprint and 'N°. 355' added to the title-page.

[*c.* 1732.]

BM. g. 270. l. (1.)

143. Sonatas or Solos for a Flute with a Thorough Bass for the Harpsicord or Bass Violin. Compos'd by Francesco Barsanti.

London. Printed for & sold by I: Walsh . . . and Ioseph Hare, &c.

London Journal, Sept. 16, 1727.

BM. g. 70. c. (1.)
Walsh Cat. 11*a*: 'Barsanti's Solos for a Flute and a Bass. Opera Prima.'

144. — With Walsh only in the imprint and 'N°. 106' added to the title-page.

[*c.* 1730.]

Walsh Cat. 18: 'Six Solos . . . 3s. od. N°. 106.'
The same, or a similar, work was printed for the Author and sold by Mr. Bressan, London. (*Daily Post*, April 30, 1724.)

Six Sonatas for 2 Violins and a Bass. Opera Seconda made from Geminiani's Solos.

See Nos. 710, 711. Geminiani (Francesco) Sonatas of three Parts, &c.

See also No. 1304. San Martini (Giovanni Battista) Concerti Grossi . . . Opera Sesta . . . Questi Concerti sono composti da diversi Notturni del Sr Martini da Francesco Barsanti.

BASEVI *detto* CERVETTO (GIACOB)

See Cervetto (Giacobbe) *the Elder*

BASSANI (GIOVANNI BATTISTA)

See No. 753. Harmonica Mundi . . . Bassani . . . the first Collection, &c.; No. 1527. Voluntaries. Voluntarys & Fugues . . . by . . . Bassani, &c.

BASTON (JOHN)

145. Six Concertos in Six Parts for Violins and Flutes viz. a Fifth, Sixth and Consort Flute. The proper Flute being nam'd to each Concerto Compos'd by M.ʳ Iohn Baston.

London. Printed for and sold by I: Walsh . . . and Ioseph Hare, &c.

Daily Post, April 2, 1729.

> Fol. Parts.
> BM. i. 53.

146. — With Walsh only in the imprint and 'N.º 363' added to the title-page.

[*c.* 1730.]

> Walsh Cat. 18: 'Baston's Concertos for Violins & small Flutes. 6s. od. N.º 363.'

See also No. 936. Lessons. Select Lessons, or a choice Collection of easy Aires by . . . Baston, &c.

BEDFORD (ARTHUR)

147. The Temple Musick: or, an Essay Concerning the Method of Singing the Psalms of David, in the Temple, Before the Babylonish Captivity. Wherein, The Musick of our Cathedrals is Vindicated . . . By Arthur Bedford, &c.

[*c.* 1730.]

> 8º.
> Walsh Cat. 18: 'The Temple Musick . . . 2s. od.'
> An earlier edition with Walsh's name in the imprint was published by H. Mortlock in 1706 (Smith 208) and an edition, 'Printed for the Author, 1712'. There is no evidence that Walsh issued an edition with his own imprint, but probably acquired and sold copies of the 1712 edition.

BEGGAR'S OPERA.

148. The Songs and Dialogues, Duets and Trios, in the Beggar's Opera as they are perform'd at the Theatre in Lincolns Inn Fields. The Songs Transpos'd for the Flute. Those that are not in yᵉ compass of yᵉ Flute are at the end of the Book. also the Original Songs may be had where these are sold.

Printed for I: Walsh and I: Hare and sold at the Musick-shops. Price 1.ˢ 6.ᵈ

[*c.* 1729.]

> 8º. pp. 60 and 4 unnumbered pages.
> BM. A. 869. b.
> With an earlier imprint erased and the above substituted.
> Ballad opera, words by John Gay.

149. — With 'N.º 303' added to the title-page.

[*c.* 1730.]

> BM. A. 869. a. (6.)
> Walsh Cat. 18: 'Beggar's Opera. 1s. 6d. N.º 303.'

150. Original Songs.
  Printed for I: Walsh and I: Hare, &c.

[*c.* 1730.]

> On title-page of No. 148. This may refer to editions of the complete text with the music, published by John Watts, 1728, &c.

The Beggars Opera Songs for Voices, or two German Flutes and a Bass.

  See No. 1184. Pepusch (Johann Christoph) The Excellent Choice, &c.

BEGGAR'S WEDDING

151. Songs in the Opera call'd the Beggar's Wedding as it is Perform'd at the Theatres. The Tunes proper for the German Flute, Violin or Common Flute. Price 1.ˢ
  London. Printed for I: Walsh I: Hare and I: Young, &c.

Daily Post, June 28, 1729.

> 12°. pp. 32.
> BM. K. 5. a. 11.
> Ballad opera, words by Charles Coffey.

152. — Songs in the Opera call'd the Beggar's Wedding . . . the 2.ᵈ Edition Price 1.ˢ
  London. Printed for I: Walsh I: Hare and I: Young, &c.

> *Daily Post,* Sept. 6, 1729.
> 12°. 'A Table of the Songs', &c. pp. 55.
> BM. K. 1. d. 22.

153. — With Walsh only in the imprint and 'N.º 304' added to the title-page.

[*c.* 1730.]

> Walsh Cat. 18: 'Beggar's Wedding. 1s. od. N.º 304.'

BENEGGER (ANTONIO)

Forest Harmony. Book IV. Being a Collection of Airs, Minuets and Marches, made on purpose for two French Horns, compos'd by Antonio Bennegger.
  See No. 640. Forest Harmony.

BENNETT (JOHN)

  See No. 1233. Psalms

BERETTI (PIETRO)

154. Six Sonatas for two Violins with a Thorough Bass for the Harpsicord or Violoncello Compos'd by Sig.ʳ Pietro Beretti.
London. Printed for I. Walsh, &c.

London Evening-Post, Sept. 25–27, 1755.

Fol. 3 parts.
BM. g. 274. (2.) Rowe (imperfect).

BERG (GEORGE)

See No. 1233. Psalms

BERKENSTOCK (JOHANN ADAM)

See Birckenstock

BERNASCONI (ANDREA)

See No. 358. Ciampi (L.V.) Arie 6, &c.

BERTONI (FERDINANDO GIUSEPPE)

See No. 522. Creso; No. 1201. Pescatrici; No. 1388. Solimano; No. 1419. Summer's Tale.

BESOZZI (ALESSANDRO)

155. Six Solos for a German Flute or Violin with a Thorough Bass for the Harpsicord or Violoncello. Compos'd by Sig.ʳ Alexandro Bezozzi. Opera Seconda.
London. Printed for I. Walsh, &c.

General Advertiser, March 3, 1750.

Fol. pp. 27.
BM. g. 422. b. (4.)

156. VI Sonatas in Three Parts for a German Flute, a Violin with a Thorough Bass for the Harpsicord or Violoncello Compos'd by Sig.ʳ Alexandro Bezozzi Musician in Ordinary to the King of Sardinia.
London. Printed for I. Walsh, &c.

General Advertiser, Sept. 30, 1747.

Fol. 3 parts.
BM. g. 241. (2.) RM. 17. d. 2. (5.)
Walsh Cat. 24c: 'Bezozzi's Sonatas (for 2 Gerⁿ Flutes or 2 Violins and a Bass). 5s. od.'
Randall Cat.: 'Bezozzi's Sonatas. Op. 1.'

157. VIII Sonatas for Two German Flutes or Two Violins with a Bass for the

Violoncello or Harpsicord Compos'd by Sig.ʳ Alexandro Bezozzi Musician in Ordinary to the King of Sardinia. Opera Terza.
London. Printed for I. Walsh, &c.

London Evening-Post, May 17–19, 1750.

Fol. 3 parts.
BM. g. 241. (1.) RM. 17. d. 2. (6.) RAM. GUL. Rowe.

158. Six Sonatas, For Two Violins and a Thorough Bass for the Harpsicord Compos.ᵈ By, Signior Alexandro Bezzozi, Musician in ordinary to the King of Sardinia. Opera 4.ᵗᵃ Price 5.ˢ
London Printed for I. Walsh, &c.

[*c.* 1760.]

Fol. 3 parts.
BM. g. 241. a. (1.) RM. 17. c. 6. (1.) Rowe.

159. Six Sonatos for two Violins and a Bass. By Sig. Bezozzi. Op. 5th.
Printed for J. Walsh, &c.

Public Advertiser, August 3, 1764.

Originally published by John Cox with the title of 'Six Sonatas for Two Violins or two German Flutes with a Thorough Bass compos'd by Sig.ʳ Alexandro Bezozzi Musician in ordinary to the King of Sardinia Opera V.ᵃ London Printed for I. Cox', &c. The title-page of the BM. copy (g. 241. a. (2.)) bears a manuscript note 'Printed for I. Walsh–64'. This work was probably purchased by Walsh when the stock-in-trade of Cox was sold at Simpson's Music Shop in 1764.

See also No. 1396. Solos. Six Solos for a German Flute . . . Compos'd by Several Eminent Authors, &c.

BETTY (Martino)

See Bitti.

BIRCKENSTOCK (Johann Adam)

160. XII Solos for a Violin with a Thorough Bass for the Harpsicord or Bass Violin Composed by Gio: Adamo Birckenstok. Opera Prima.
London. Printed for and sold by John Walsh . . . and Joseph Hare, &c.

Mist's Weekly Journal, Dec. 2, 1727.

Fol. pp. 71.

161. — Reissued by John Walsh and Joseph Hare.

Daily Journal, Jan. 29, 1730. (New Musick, and Editions of Musick, Just Published.)

162. — With Walsh only in the imprint and 'N⁰ 353' added to the title-page.
   [*c.* 1730.]
   BM. i. 5.
   Walsh Cat. 18: 'Birckenstocks Solos. 7s. od. N⁰ 353.'

163. — Another issue.
   General Advertiser, June 10, 1746. (Printed for J. Walsh . . . Of whom may be had . . . Twelve Solos for a Violin and Bass by Sig. Berkenstock.)

BIRD FANCIER'S DELIGHT

164. The Bird Fancyer's Delight, Or Choice Observations, And Directions Concerning the Teaching of all sorts of Singing Birds, after the Flagelet and Flute when rightly made as to Size and tone, with Lessons properly Compos'd within the Compass and faculty of each Bird, viz for the Canary-Bird, Linnet, Bull-Finch, Wood-Lark, Black-Bird, Throustill, Nightingale and Starling. The whole fairly Engraven and Carefully Corrected, price 1ˢ [Drawing of Flagelet.]
   London Printed for I: Walsh . . . and I: Hare . . . N⁰ 4.

   [*c.* 1730.]
   Obl. 8⁰. 5 ff. text (with foliations 2, 5, 6), ff. 6–20 music. Printed on one side only.
   BM. K. 4. a. 1. (Imperfections supplied in photostat, but it may not have had 'N⁰ 4' on title-page.) Cardiff. Rowe.
   Smith 513 with 'N⁰ 4' added to the title-page, but not included in Walsh Cat. 18.

165. The Bird Fancyer's Delight . . . price 6ᵈ 2ᵈ Book.
   London, Printed for I. Walsh . . . and I. Hare . . . N⁰ 4.

   [*c.* 1730.]
   Obl. 8⁰. 6 ff. text (with foliations 1, 2, 5, 6), ff. 6–20 music. Printed on one side only.
   Euing.
   Another edition of No. 164, with slight variations including different spelling in 'To the Reader' ('value' not 'Vallue', 'Having' not 'haveing', 'airs' not 'aires', &c.) and a tune for the starling on f. 10 not found in No. 164.

BIRKHEAD (   ) AND EGERTON (   )

166. Twenty four new Country Dances for the Year 1722. Compos'd by Mr. Birkhead and Mr. Egerton. Price 6d.
   Printed for, and sold by J. Walsh . . . and John and Joseph Hare, &c.
   Post-Boy, Feb. 20–22, 1721 [1722].

BIRON, *Lord*

See Byron (William) *Lord Byron*.

BISHOP (JOHN)

167. A Sett of New Psalm Tunes, in Four Parts: Containing Proper Tunes to all the different Measures of the Psalms which are to be found in the Old, or any of the New Versions, or Supplement: With variety of Tunes for the most common Measures; contrived within a moderate Compass for the Ease of the Voice, and may be sung in 1, 2, 3, or 4 Parts, with a Figured Bass for the Organ, and a Table shewing what Psalms are proper to each Tune. With Variety of Anthems, in four Parts, for the Delight and Improvement of all who are truly Lovers of Divine Music. Taught by *Tho. Batten.* Cantus. By *John Bishop*, Organist of the College at *Winton. The Second Edition, with Additions.*

London: Printed by *W. Pearson* for the Author, and Sold by *J. Walsh* at the *Harp* and *Haut-boy* in St. *Katherine's-street, J. Hare* near the *Royal Exchange*, and at *Winchester.* [Price 2s.]

Weekly Journal: or Saturday's Post, Dec. 8, 1722. (Sold by John Walsh . . . and John and Joseph Hare . . . and by the Author, at Winton.)

8°. 4 parts. Cantus, Medius, Tenor, Bassus. Medius, Tenor and Bassus parts bear the title of 'A Set of New Psalm Tunes in Four Parts.'

BM. C. 523; A. 1230. e. NLS.

The first edition ('The New Psalm Book') was advertised in *The Post Man*, Nov. 16–18, 1710. (Smith 372.)

168. A Sett of Psalm Tunes, in Four Parts: Containing Proper Tunes to all the Different Measures of the Psalms which are to be found in the Old, or any of the New Versions, or Supplement: With variety of Tunes for the most common Measures; contrived within a moderate Compass for the Ease of the Voice, and may be sung in 1, 2, 3, or 4 Parts, with a Figured Bass for the Organ, and a Table shewing what Psalms are proper to each Tune. With Variety of Anthems, in four Parts, for the Delight and Improvement of all who are truly Lovers of Divine Music. Cantus. By *Iohn Bishop*, Organist of the College at *Winton. The Third Edition, with Additions.*

London. Printed for and sold by I: Walsh . . . and may be had at I: Hare's . . . and I: Young's in S.̲ Paul's Church-yard. [Price 2s. 6d.]

Country Journal: or, The Craftsman, Aug. 8, 1730.

8°. 4 parts. Cantus. Medius. Tenor. Bassus. Medius, Tenor and Bassus parts bear the title of 'A Set of New Psalm Tunes in Four Parts.'

BM. A. 1231. p; A. 1230. f. (Bassus only.)

169. — Reissued with the Supplement to the New Psalm-Book (*see* No. 170), with Walsh only in the imprint and 'N.̲ 205' added to the title-page.

[*c.* 1730.]

Royal School of Church Music, Addington Palace, Croydon. (Cantus part only.)

Walsh Cat. 18: 'Mr. Bishops 2 Books of Psalms. 4s. 0d. N.̲ 205.'

170. A Supplement To the New Psalm-Book. Consisting of Six New Anthems, and Six New Psalm-Tunes, after a different Manner. By John Bishop, Organist of the College at *Winchester*.

London: Printed by *William Pearson* . . . and Sold by *John* and *Joseph Hare* and *John Walsh*, at the *Harp* and *Haut-Boy*, in St. *Catherine's -Street*, near the *Strand*. And by the *Author* at *Winchester*. MDCCXXV. Price 1s. 6d.

> 8°. Title-page, verso advertisement. pp. 3–56, [9,] 01. Sigs. A2, B, B2, C, C2, D, E, E2, F, F2, G, G2, 2 leaves after each without sigs.
> BM. B. 616.

171. — Presumably reissued with the Psalm Tunes, with Walsh only in the imprint and 'N⁰ 205' added to the title-page.

[*c.* 1730.]

> Walsh Cat. 18: 'Mr. Bishops 2 Books of Psalms. 4s. od. N⁰ 205.'

BITTE ( )

See Bitti (Martino.)

BITTI (MARTINO)

172. Solo's for a Flute, with a through Bass for the Harpsichord or Bass Violin. Compos'd by Martino Bitti, &c.

London, Printed for J. Walsh . . . N⁰ 129.

[*c.* 1730.]

> Obl. fol. pp. 32.
> Smith 401 (BM. e. 201. b. (3.)) with Walsh only in the imprint and 'N⁰ 129' added to the title-page. This is the same work as No. 173.
> Walsh Cat. 18: 'Martino Bitty's Solos (for a Flute and a Bass) 4s. od. N⁰ 129.'

173. Sonate a due Violino e Basso Per Suonarsi con Flauto, o' vero Violino del Signor Martino Bitti, &c.

London, Printed for J. Walsh . . .N⁰ 418.

[*c.* 1730.]

> Obl. fol. pp. 32.
> Smith 396 (BM. d. 161. a. (4.)) with Walsh only in the imprint and 'N⁰ 418' added to the title-page.
> Walsh Cat. 18: 'Martino Bitty's Solos (for a Violin and a Bass) 4s. od. N⁰ 418.'
> Walsh Cat. 11a: Solos for a Violin and a Bass. Opera Prima. Also issued as 'Solo's for a Flute', &c. (*See* No. 172.)

See also No. 764. Harpsicord Master. XIII⁰ᵗʰ Book; No. 893. The Lady's Banquet Fifth Book; No. 1392, Six Solos by several Authors; No. 1458. Torelli (Giuseppe) and Vivaldi (Antonio) Torelli and Vivaldi's Concertos.

BLAVET (MICHEL)

174. Six Solos for a German Flute, Violin or Harpsichord, composed by Mr. Blavet, one of the greatest Performers on the German Flute in Europe.
Printed for J. Walsh, &c.

General Advertiser, Nov. 29, 1749.

Walsh Cat. 25: 'Blavet's Solos. 5s. od.'

175. Six Sonatas or Duets, for two German Flutes. By Mr. Blavet, Sig. Groneman, &c. Price 3s.
Printed for J. Walsh, &c.

General Advertiser, Oct. 21, 1752.

Walsh Cat. 25: 'Blavet, &c. Sonatas or Duets. 3s. od.'

176. Sonatas or Duets for two German Flutes or Violins Compos'd by M.r Blavet, Sig.r Groneman &c. Book 2.d.
London. Printed for I. Walsh, &c.

[*c.* 1755.]

Fol. pp. 26.
BM. g. 280. (3.)

BLOW (JOHN)

177. A Choice Collection of Lessons for the Harpsicord, Spinnet, &c. Containing four Setts, As Grounds, Almands, Corants, Sarabands, Minuets, & Jiggs, by D.r Iohn Blow.
London. Printed for I. Walsh . . . N.o 173.

[*c.* 1730.]

Obl. 4.o ff. 21.
Smith 162 (RCM. I. F. 50. (2.)) with Walsh only in the imprint and 'N.o 173' added to the title-page.
Walsh Cat. 18: 'Dr Blow's Lessons (for the Harpsicord Spinnet or Organ). 1s. 6d. N.o 173.'

178. The Psalms by D.r Blow Set full for the Organ or Harpsicord as they are Play'd in Churches or Chapels.

[*c.* 1730.]

Obl. fol. Without title-page or imprint, but with title and 'N.o 184' on p. 1. pp. 10.
BM. c. 93. RCM. Rowe (imperfect).
Walsh Cat. 18: 'Dr Blow's Psalms (for the Harpsicord Spinnet or Organ). 1s. 6d. N.o 184.'

See Smith Nos. 130, 176, and 537.

179. Dr Blow's Songs. 15s. od. N° 327.

[*c.* 1730.]

> Fol.
> Walsh Cat. 18.
> Not identified. Presumably a reissue of Smith 602, or may refer to stock copies of 'Amphion Anglicus' (Pearson 1700. BM. G. 106.) or to another Walsh work first published 1720 or earlier. Walsh catalogues 17*a* and 17*b* give: Just Publish'd by I. Walsh 'Dr. Blow's Songs.' The work does not appear in later Walsh catalogues.

See also Nos. 339–42. The Catch Club or Merry Companions . . . Catches . . . Compos'd by . . . Dr. Blow, &c.; Nos. 749–54. Harmonia Anglicana . . . by . . . Dr Blow, &c.; No. 757. Harmonia Sacra.

BOMPORTI (Francesco Antonio)

See Bonporti

BONI (Giovanni)

180. Solos for a German Flute, a Hoboy or Violin, with a Thorough Bass for the Harpsicord or Bass Violin Compos'd by Sig^r Giovanni Boni. Note The following Pieces, &c.

London. Printed for and sold by I: Walsh . . . and Ioseph Hare, &c.

[*c.* 1728.]

> Fol. pp. 1–15, 17–19.
> BM. g. 1090. (2.)

181. — With Walsh only in the imprint and 'N° 356' added to the title-page.

Country Journal: or, The Craftsman, Feb. 13, 1731.

> Walsh Cat. 18: 'Boni's Solos. 3s. od. N° 356.'

BONONCINI (Antonio Maria) [Wrongly known as Marc' Antonio Bononcini.]

Astyanax. Opera.
> *See* No. 197. Bononcini (Giovanni)

182. The Opera of Camilla as it is perform'd at the Theatre in Lincoln's-Inn Fields, composed by Bononcini.

Printed for and Sold by John Walsh . . . and Joseph Hare, &c.

Daily Post, Dec. 8, 1726.

> Libretto by Silvio Stampiglia.
> Reissue of Smith 221, 298, and 560 'Songs In The New Opera, Call'd Camilla' for the revival 1 December 1726.

183. — With Walsh only in the imprint and 'N⁰ 221' added to the title-page.

[*c.* 1730.]

> Walsh Cat. 18: 'The Opera of Camilla with Addi! Songs. 10s. 6d. N⁰ 221.' (*See also* No. 184.)

184. The Additional Songs in the Opera call'd Camilla as it was perform'd at the Theatre in Lincolns Inn Fields.
London Printed for & sold by I: Walsh . . . and Ioseph Hare, &c.

[1726.]

> Fol. Passe-partout title-page. ff. 7. Printed on one side only.
> RM. 11. b. 20. (2.)
> Presumably a new edition of Smith 402 for the revival 1 December 1726.
> Walsh Cat. 18: 'The Opera of Camilla with Addi! Songs. 10s. 6d. N⁰ 221.'

> *See also* No. 183 and No. 1174 Pepusch (Johann Christoph) The Additional Songs in the Opera's of Thomyris & Camilla.

185. A Collection of the Song Tunes and Ariets in the Opera of Camilla Contriv'd and Fitted to the Harpsicord or Spinnett by M⁰ Ramondon . . . price 3ˢ
London   Printed for I. Walsh . . . and I. Hare, &c.

[*c.* 1730.]

> Fol. 'A Table of the Lessons . . . N⁰ 176.' 2 unnumbered folios, ff. 1–3, 1–24. Printed on one side only.
> Rowe.
> Smith 211 with 'N⁰ 176' added to the Table.
> Walsh Cat. 18: 'Camilla Set for the Harpsicord. 3s. od. N⁰ 176.'

186. A Collection of the Song-Tunes, Duets and Ariets in the Opera of Camilla, contriv'd and fitted for two Flutes and a Bass, by Mr. Ramondon.
Printed for J. Walsh . . . N⁰ 81.

[*c.* 1730.]

> Walsh Cat. 18: 'Camilla for 2 Flutes and a Bass. 3s. od. N⁰ 81.'
> Smith 216 with Walsh only in the imprint and 'N⁰ 81' added to the title-page.

Camilla. Overture.

> *See* No. 220. Bononcini (Giovanni) and (Antonio Maria) and others. Bononcini's Six Overtures for Violins . . . in the Operas of Camilla, &c.

187. Overture in Camilla (for 2 Flutes). 2s. od. N⁰ 73.

[*c.* 1730.]

> Walsh Cat. 18.
> Not identified unless Smith 262: 'A Choice Collection of Airs or Ariett's for two Flutes with the Overture of Camilla & Arsinoe. . . London   Printed for I. Walsh, &c. (BM. b. 171. a. (2.) obl. 4⁰.)

188. Camilla made into Concertos for Violins, &c. 6s. od. N⁰ 351.

[*c.* 1730.]

> Walsh Cat. 18.
> Reissue of Smith 521 (Camilla Concertos, for 2 Violins and a Bass) with Walsh only in the imprint and 'N⁰ 351' added to the title-page.

BONONCINI (GIOVANNI) [Wrongly known as Giovanni Battista Bononcini.]

189. The Anthem which was Performed In King Henry the Seventh's Chapel at the Funeral of The most Noble & Victorious Prince Iohn, Duke of Marlborough. The Words taken out of Holy Scripture And Set to Musick by Mʳ Bononcini.
    London. Printed for & Sold by I. Walsh .. N⁰ 631.

[*c.* 1738.] *London Daily Post, and General Advertiser,* Feb. 17, 1739. (Where may be had.)

> Fol. pp. 2–19.
> BM. G. 499. Gresham. RCM. Bod. CUL. Fitz. Rowe.
> First published by Richard Meares, 1722.
> Walsh Cat. 18: 'A Funeral Anthem for the Duke of Marlbʰ 2s. od.'

190. — Another copy or reissue.

Public Advertiser, Dec. 24, 1761. (Divine Music. This day is published.)

191. Astartus an Opera as it was Perform'd at the Kings Theatre for the Royal Accademy. Compos'd by Bononcinj.
    London. Printed for and Sold by I: Walsh ... and I: Hare, &c.

Daily Courant, April 1, 1721.

> Fol. 'A Table of the Songs', &c. pp. 81.
> BM. I. 296. RM. 11. b. 18. Hirsch II. 90. RAM. RCM. XVIII. E. 11. Bod. Fitz. Rowe.
> Words by Apostolo Zeno and Pietro Pariati.

192. — With Walsh only in the imprint and 'N⁰ 220' added to the title-page.

[*c.* 1730.] *Daily Journal,* Feb. 26, 1734. (Where may be had, &c.)

> Fol.
> Walsh Cat. 18: 'The Opera of Astartus. 12s. od. N⁰ 220.'
> A selection was included in 'Le Delizie dell' Opere', Vol. I, pp. 9–10, 25–29, 85, 91–92, 95–96, 112, 152–3.

193. The Overture, Symphonies, or Instrumental Musick, in that most celebrated opera, call'd Astartus, as they were performed at the King's Theatre, for the Royal Academy.

Printed for and sold by J. Walsh, &c.

Post-Boy, May 16–18, 1721.

> Fol.

194. — With Walsh only in the imprint and 'N<u>o</u> 352' added to the title-page.
   [*c.* 1730.]

> Fol.
> Walsh Cat. 18: 'Astartus Symphonies made into Concertos for Violins, &c. 6s. od.
> N<u>o</u> 352.'

195. The Song Tunes with their Symphonys for the Flute in that Celebrated Opera call'd Astartus fairly Engraven & carefully Corrected. Price 1<u>s</u> 6<u>d</u> note: Several Operas are done for the Flute in this manner & may be had where these are sold.
   London: Printed for and sold by I: Walsh . . . & I: Hare, &c.

Post-Boy, Sept. 12–14, 1721.

> Obl. 4º. 'A Table of the Song Tunes', &c. ff. 22. Printed on one side only.
> BM. a. 209. a. (4.)

196. — With Walsh only in the imprint and 'N<u>o</u> 27' added to the title-page.
   [*c.* 1730.]

> Obl. 4º.
> Walsh Cat. 18: 'Astartus for the Flute. N<u>o</u> 27.'

Astartus. [Two numbers from Astartus.]
   See No. 890. Lady's Banquet. Second Book.

Astartus. Overture.
   See No. 220 Bononcini (Giovanni) and (Antonio Maria) and others. Bononcini's Six Overtures for Violins . . . in the Operas of Astartus, &c.

197. The Favourite Songs in the Opera call'd Astyanax. [Astianatte. By Giovanni Bononcini.] London. Printed for and sold by I: Walsh . . . and Ioseph Hare, &c.

London Journal, June 17, 1727.

> Fol. Passe-partout title-page. ff. 2–15. Printed on one side only.
> BM. H. 317. Manchester. Rowe.
> Words by Antonio Salvi.

198. — With Walsh only in the imprint and 'N<u>o</u> 262' added to the title-page.
   [*c.* 1730.]

Fol.

Walsh Cat. 18: 'The Favourite Songs in . . . Astyanax. 1s. 6d. N⁰ 262.' One number included in 'Le Delizie dell' Opere', Vol. II, pp. 219–21.

Antonio Maria Bononcini also wrote an opera 'Astianatte'. (Loewenberg. Grove. Fifth edition. I, p. 809.)

199. The Favourite Songs in the Opera call'd Calphurnia. [By Giovanni Bononcini.]

London Printed for and sold by I: Walsh . . . and In⁰ & Ioseph Hare, &c.

[1724.]

Fol. ff. 20. Printed on one side only.

BM. H. 230. f. (1.) Gresham. RAM. RCM. Cardiff. Reid. Rowe.

Words altered by Nicola Francesco Haym from Grazio Braccioli. Some of the Songs were issued in 'The Monthly Mask of Vocal Music', July 1724.

200. — With Walsh only in the imprint and 'N⁰ 258' added to the title-page.

[c. 1730.]

Fol.

Walsh Cat. 18: 'The Favourite Songs in . . . Calphurnia. 2s. 6d. N⁰ 258.'

Republished in 'Le Delizie dell' Opere', Vol. I, pp. 93–94, 107–8, 111, 144–5, 172, 174–181, 214–15.

201. Bononcini's 3 Cantatas. 3s. 0d.

[c. 1747 or earlier.]

Walsh Cat. 24a: 'Vocal Musick, Italian'.

Not identified, assumed to be by Giovanni Bononcini.

202. Bononcini's Cantatas. £2. 2s. 0d.

[c. 1752.]

Walsh Cat. 25: 'Vocal Musick, Italian.'

This presumably refers to copies of 'Cantate e Duetti dedicati alla Sacra Maestà di Giorgio Rè della Gran Bretagna &c. Da Giovanni Bononcini. Londra MDCCXXI.' (BM. D. 360. Obl. fol. pp. 99.)

203. The favourite Songs in the Opera call'd Crispus. [By Giovanni Bononcini.]

London Printed for & sold by I: Walsh . . . and In⁰ & Ioseph Hare, &c.

Post-Boy, Aug. 23–25, 1722.

Fol. Passe-partout title-page. ff. 20. Printed on one side only.

BM. H. 230. f. (2.) (Wanting the title-page.) RAM. RCM. Pendlebury. Rowe. Tenbury.

Words by Gaetano Lemer, altered by Paolo Antonio Rolli.

204. — With Walsh only in the imprint and 'N⁰ 254' added to the title-page.

[c. 1730.]

Walsh Cat. 18: 'The Favourite Songs in . . . Crispus. 2s. 6d. N° 254.'
Republished in 'Le Delizie dell' Opere', Vol. I, pp. 37–38, 43–44, 73–74, 87–88, 158–61, 202–3, 210–11.

205. The favourite Songs in the Opera call'd Cyrus.
London Printed for & sold by I: Walsh . . . & In° & Ioseph Hare, &c.

[1721.]

Fol. ff. 14. Printed on one side only.
BM. H. 230. f. (3.) (Wanting the title-page.) RCM. Rowe.
Attributed to Giovanni Bononcini.

See also No. 376. Ciro

206. The Favourite Songs in the Operas of Cyrus & Arsaces. 3s. od. N° 253.

[*c.* 1730.]

Walsh Cat. 18: under 'Bononcini's Works'.
Arsaces was a pasticcio produced 1721 (Burney) although listed by Walsh as by Bononcini.
Loewenberg says it was an altered version of Orlandini's 'Amore e Maestà' with additional music by F. Amadei.

See also No. 376. Ciro

Le Delizie dell' Opere. Vol. 1, containing the Favourite Songs out of all his [Bononcini's] Operas. £1. 1s. od. N° 337.
See No. 554. Delizie dell' Opere. Vol. I.

207. The Favourite Songs in the Opera Call'd Erminia. [By Giovanni Bononcini.]
London Printed for and sold by I: Walsh . . . & In° & Ioseph Hare, &c.

[*c.* 1723.]

Fol. pp. 10.
Rowe.
Words by Gaetano Lemer, altered by Paolo Antonio Rolli.

208. — With Walsh only in the imprint and 'N° 263' added to the title-page.

[*c.* 1730.]

Walsh Cat. 18: 'The Favourite Songs in . . . Erminia. 1s. 6d. N° 263.'
Republished in 'Le Delizie dell' Opere', Vol. I, pp. 54–56, 121–2, 157, 212–13.

209. [Farnace.] The favourite Songs in the Opera call'd Pharnaces Publish'd for March price 2ˢ 6ᵈ [By Giovanni Bononcini.]
London Printed for & sold by I: Walsh . . . In° & Ioseph Hare, &c.

[1723.]

Fol. Passe-partout title-page. ff. 20 Printed on one side only.
BM. H. 318. H. 230. f. (4.) (Wanting title-page.) RAM. Euing. Rowe.
Words altered from Lorenzo Morani.

210. — With Walsh only in the imprint and 'N̷ 260' added to the title-page.
[*c.* 1730.]
> Fol.
> Walsh Cat. 18: 'The Favourite Songs in . . . Pharnaces. 2s. 6d. N̷ 260.'
> Republished in 'Le Delizie dell' Opere', Vol. I, pp. 11–12, 19–20, 69–70, 75–76, 103–6, 168–71.

211. Griselda an Opera as it was Perform'd at the Kings Theatre for the Royal Accademy Compos'd by M̷ Bononcini. Publish'd by the Author.
London Printed and sold by I: Walsh . . . and In̷ and Ioseph Hare, &c.

Post-Boy, May 19–22, 1722.
> Fol. 'A Table of Songs', &c. pp. 76.
> BM. H. 321. b. Hirsch II. 91. RCM. (Wanting last leaf.) BUL. Bod. Rowe.
> Words by Paolo Antonio Rolli, altered from Apostolo Zeno.

212. — With Walsh only in the imprint and 'N̷ 231' added to the title-page.
[*c.* 1730.]
> Fol.
> Walsh Cat. 18: 'The Opera of Griselda. 12s. od. N̷ 231.'
> *Daily Journal*, May 25, 1733. (Readvertised for revival, May 1733.)
> A selection was included in 'Le Delizie dell' Opere', Vol. I, pp. 1–5, 51–53, 65–66, 97–99, 115–18, 138–141, 154–6, 190–1, 204–6.
> Antonio Maria Bononcini also wrote an opera, 'Griselda'. (Loewenberg. Grove. I, p. 809.)

213. Griselda for a Flute The Overture Symphonys and Ariets for a single Flute and the Duets for two Flutes of that Celebrated Opera Compos'd by M̷ Bononcini. Price 2ˢ
London Printed and sold by I: Walsh . . . and In̷ & Ioseph Hare, &c.

Post-Boy, May 29–31, 1722. (Done for the Flute.); June 14–16, 1722. (Just published.)
> Obl. 4°. 'A Table of the Song Tunes', &c. ff. 32. Printed on one side only.
> BM. a. 209. a. (1.)

214. — With Walsh only in the imprint and 'N̷ 26' added to the title-page.
[*c.* 1730.]
> Obl. 4°.
> Walsh Cat. 18: 'The Opera of Griselda for the Flute. 2s. od. N̷ 26.'

Bononcini's Six Overtures in all their Parts, &c.

See No. 220. Bononcini (Giovanni) and (Antonio Maria) and others.

215. Six Solos for two Violoncellos compos'd by Sig.ʳ Bononcini and other eminent Authors.
London Printed for J. Simpson, &c.

[1764.]

> Fol. pp. 2–24.
> BM. g. 500. (5.)
> This copy bears the manuscript note 'Printed for I. Walsh—64.' after the imprint. The work was issued by Simpson in 1748 and was probably purchased by Walsh at the sale of the stock-in-trade of John Cox, at Simpson's Music Shop, in 1764.
> Walsh Cat. 27: 'Bononcini's Solos. (For 2 Violoncellos.) 4s. 0d.'

216. Sonatas, or Chamber Aircs, for a German Flute, Violin or Common Flute: with a Thorough Bass for the Harpsicord or Bass Violin. Being all choice Pieces Compos'd by Sig.ʳ Giovanni Bononcini. Opera Settima.
London. Printed for and sold by I: Walsh . . . N.º 494.

Daily Post, Nov. 14, 1733.

> Obl. fol. ff. A, B, pp. 30.
> Leeds.
> Walsh Cat. 18: 'Bononcini's Chamber Aires Op: 7ᵐᵃ 3s. 0d. N.º 494.'

217. — Another edition.

Country Journal: or, The Craftsman, Oct. 26, 1734. (Where may be had, a new edition on fine Dutch paper.)

218. 12 Sonatas for 2 Violins and a Bass. £1. 1s. 0d.

[*c.* 1732.]

> Fol. Parts.
> Walsh Cat. 18.
> This presumably refers to 'XII Sonatas For the Chamber For two Violins and a Bass doubled Dedicated To her Grace the Dutchess Dowager of Marlborough By John Bononcini. Printed at London Anno 1732 Price One Guinea.' (BM. g. 46.)

219. Suites de Pieces Pour le Clavecin. Composées par Giovanni Bononcini.
London Printed, & sold by John Walsh . . . N.º 490.

[*c.* 1735.]

> Obl. fol. Passe-partout title-page used previously for 'Suites de Pieces Pour le Clavecin. Composées par G. F. Handel . . .N.º 490.' pp. 40.
> BM. e. 403.
> Walsh Cat. 18: 'Lessons for the Harpsicord. 3s. 0d.', without any number.

See also No. 41. Apollo's Feast. 2.ᵈ Book Apollo's Feast . . . Songs . . . by Bononcini, &c.; Nos. 221–4. Bononcini (Giovanni Maria); Nos. 554–7, 559, 565. Delizie dell' Opere. Vols. I, II, IV, X, XI; No. 936. Lessons. Select Lessons . . .

by ... Bononcini ... for the Flute; Nos. 1028, 1029, 1039. Minuets; No. 1125. Muzio Scævola; No. 1443. Thomyris.

BONONCINI (GIOVANNI) and (ANTONIO MARIA) and others.

220. Bononcini's Six Overtures for Violins in all their Parts as they were perform'd at the Kings Theatre in the Operas of Astartus, Crœsus, Camilla, Hydaspes, Thomyris, Elpidia. NB: There may be had where these are sold, all the Operas in Italian and English that have been printed in England.
   London, Printed and sold by I: Walsh ... N⁰ 410.

> [*c.* 1730.]
>> Fol. Parts.
>> RM. 17. d. 4. (12.) RCM.
>> This work was probably previously issued by Walsh and Hare, 1725 or after, without 'N⁰ 410'.
>> For an earlier edition by John Walsh, John and Joseph Hare, *c.* 1724, with Handel's 'Rinaldo' in place of 'Elpidia' and without 'N⁰ 410', *see* Smith. Handel. A descriptive Catalogue. p. 289. No. 2.
>>   'Astartus' was by Giovanni Bononcini, 'Camilla' by Antonio Maria Bononcini, 'Hydaspes' by Francesco Mancini, 'Elpidia' by Leonardo Vinci, 'Crœsus' and 'Thomyris' were pasticcios.

BONONCINI (GIOVANNI BATTISTA)

See Bononcini (Giovanni)

BONONCINI (GIOVANNI MARIA)

221. Bononcini's Ayres in 3 Parts, as Almands Corrants Preludes Gavotts Sarabands and Jiggs. With a Through Bass for the Harpsicord. [All in capitals.]
   London Printed and Sold by I: Walsh and I: Hare ... N⁰ 348.

> [*c.* 1730.]
>> Obl. fol. Parts. Printed on one side only.
>> BM. d. 26. a. (Wanting title-pages of Violino Secondo and Bassus parts.)
>> Walsh Cat. 18: 'Six Sonatas for 2 Violins and a Bass. 3s. od. N⁰ 348.'
>> Probably by Giovanni Maria Bononcini, but sometimes attributed to his son Giovanni.
>> Smith 63 (BM. d. 150. (2.)) with 'N⁰ 348' added to the title-page.

222. Six Solos for a Violin or Flute with a Bass. 5d. od. N⁰ 349.

> [*c.* 1730.]
>> Walsh Cat. 18.
>> Not identified. Walsh lists this under 'Bononcini's Works', with 'Camilla' (by Antonio Maria Bononcini) and 'Astartus' (by Giovanni Bononcini), &c.
>> Walsh Cat. 16*a*: 'Bononcini's Solos. 5s. od.'

Six Sonatas for 2 Violins and a Bass.

  See No. 221. Bononcini (Giovanni Maria) Bononcini's Ayres in 3 Parts.

223. 6 Sonatas or Aires for 2 Flutes and a Bass. 3s. od. № 92.

[*c.* 1730.]

> Obl. fol. Parts.
> Walsh Cat. 18.
> Presumably a reissue of Smith 178 (BM. d. 150. (1.) 'Bononcini's Aires for two Flutes and a Bass', &c.), with Walsh in the imprint and № 92 added to the title-page. The work was probably by Giovanni Maria Bononcini, but generally attributed to his son Giovanni. Walsh lists this under 'Bononcini's Works', with 'Camilla' (by Antonio Maria Bononcini) and 'Astartus' (by Giovanni Bononcini), &c.
> Walsh Cat. 24a: 'Bononcini's Airs (for 2 Flutes and a Bass). 3s. od.'

224. Six Sonatas or Aires for 2 Violins. 3s. od. № 350.

[*c.* 1730.]

> Walsh Cat. 18.
> Not identified. May refer to an edition of G. M. Bononcini's 'Sonate a due Violini con, il BC. Op. 6.' (Eitner. Quellen-Lexicon; Grove.) Walsh lists this under 'Bononcini's Works, with "Camilla" (by Antonio Maria Bononcini) and "Astartus" (by Giovanni Bononcini), &c.'
> Walsh Cat. 24a: 'Bononcini's Airs (Sonatas for 2 Violins) 3s. od.'

BONONCINI (MARC' ANTONIO)

See Bononcini (Antonio Maria)

BONPORTI (FRANCESCO ANTONIO)

225. 10 Solos for a Violin and a Bass. Opera Settima. 4s. od. № 362.

[*c.* 1730.]

> Walsh Cat. 18.
> Presumably a reissue of Smith 277d and 603 with Walsh only in the imprint and '№ 362' added to the title-page.

226. Bomporti's Sonata's or Chamber Aires in three Parts for two Violins and a Thorough Bass Compos'd by Francisco Antonio Bomporti Opera Seconda.
London Printed for I. Walsh . . . № 360.

[*c.* 1730.]

> Fol. Parts.
> Smith 482 (BM. g. 407. a.) with Walsh only in the imprint and '№ 360' added to the title-page.
> Walsh Cat. 18: '10 Sonatas for 2 Violins and a Bass. Op: 2da. 4s. od. № 360.'

227. Bomporti's Sonata's or Chamber Aires in three Parts for two Violins and a Through Bass Compos'd by Francisco Antonio Bomporti Opera Quarto.
London. Printed for I. Walsh . . . № 361.

[*c.* 1730.]

Smith 267 (BM. g. 407.) with Walsh only in the imprint and 'N⁰ 361' added to the title-page.

Walsh Cat. 18: '10 Sonatas for 2 Violins and a Bass. Op: 4ta. 4s. od. N⁰ 361.'

BOOK

A Book of Familiar Aires, or Song Tunes for a Violin.

See No. 1468. Tunes. Familiar Tunes, &c.

228. A new Book for Learners on the Violin containing the finest Opera-Aires and Tunes.

Printed for and sold by J. Walsh . . . and J. Hare, &c.

Post-Boy, May 16–18, 1721.

See also No. 1472. Tutor. The 6ᵗʰ Book of the Compleat Tutor to the Violin, &c.

229. A new Book of Instructions for the Flute, with easy Lessons for Learners. Price 1s. 6d.

Printed for John Walsh, &c.

Country Journal: or, The Craftsman, July 1, 1732.

BOOKS

230. Books for Learners on the Flagelet, Gamut-way. 1s. od. N⁰ 5.

(*c.* 1730.)

Walsh Cat. 18.
Smith 618 with Walsh only in the imprint and 'N⁰ 5' added to the title-page.

231. Books for Learners (Single Flute). 1s. 6d. N⁰ 1.

[*c.* 1730.]

Walsh Cat. 18.
Smith 619 with Walsh only in the imprint and 'N⁰ 1' added to the title-page.

232. Books for Learners (Harpsicord, Spinnet or Organ). 2s. od. N⁰ 186.

[*c.* 1730.]

Walsh Cat. 18.
Smith 622 with Walsh only in the imprint and 'N⁰ 186' added to the title-page.

233. Books for Learners on the Hoboy. 1s. 6d. N⁰ 140.

[*c.* 1730.]

Walsh Cat. 18.
Smith 620 with Walsh only in the imprint and 'N⁰ 140' added to the title-page.

234. Books for Learners (Single Violin). 1s. 6d. N⁰ 131.

[*c*. 1730.]

Walsh Cat. 18.
Smith 621 with Walsh only in the imprint and 'N⁰ 131' added to the title-page.

See also Nos. 1472, 1473 Tutor. The 6th (13th) Book of the Compleat Tutor to the Violin, &c.

BOYCE (WILLIAM)

235. D⁰ Boyce Anthem and Serenade, performed at Cambridge.
Printed for J. Walsh, &c.

Public Advertiser, Dec. 24, 1761. (Divine Music.)

This presumably refers to copies of 'An Ode; perform'd in the Senate House at Cambridge on the first of July, 1749 . . . To which is added, An Anthem, perform'd at St. Mary's Church', &c. Without imprint. [1752.] (BM. K. 7. i. 5. Fol. pp. 2–67, 2–70.)

236. The Chaplet. A Musical Entertainment. As it is Perform'd at the Theatre-Royal in Drury-Lane. Compos'd by Dr. Boyce.
London. Printed for I. Walsh, &c.

London Evening Post, Jan. 23–25, 1750.

Fol. Privilege (dated 10 April 1745). pp. 2–46.
BM. G. 225. (2.) RM. 11. b. 21. RCM.
Words by Moses Mendez.

237. — Another issue, with privilege in different type.

[*c*. 1755.]

Hirsch II. 93.

238. M⁰ Boyce's 2d Tune to Jessy.
Printed for I. Walsh, &c.

[*c*. 1750.]

S.sh. fol.
BM. G. 305. (171.)
The earlier setting of the song was published in Book II of Boyce's 'Lyra Britannica'.
The words 'How blest has my Time been' by E. Moore.

239. Lyra Britannica: Book I. Being a Collection of Songs, Duets, and Cantatas, on Various Subjects. Compos'd by M⁰ Boyce.
London. Printed for and Sold by I. Walsh, &c.

General Advertiser, March 30, 1747.

Fol. pp. 21.
BM. G. 330. RCM.

240. — Book II.

General Advertiser, July 11, 1747.

>Fol. Privilege (dated 10 April 1745). pp. 22–33.
>BM. G. 330. Gresham. RCM.
>Same title-page as Book I.

241. Lyra Britannica Book 3ᵈ. A Cantata and English Songs Set to Musick by Dʳ Boyce in which is inserted the Songs of Iohnny Ienny. To make the kind, you Say you love &c. Sung at Vauxhall, and Ranelagh Gardens.
London. Printed for and Sold by Iohn Walsh, &c.

General Advertiser, Sept. 9, 1748.

>Fol. pp. 35–47.
>BM. G. 330. RCM.

242. Numb: IV. Lyra Britannica. A Collection of English Songs Compos'd by Dʳ Boyce. In which are inserted some Songs in Lethe.
London. Printed for I. Walsh, &c.

Whitehall Evening-Post, March 19–21, 1754.

>Fol. Privilege (dated 10 April 1745). pp. 49–68.
>BM. G. 330. RCM.

243. Numb: V. Lyra Britannica. A Collection of English Songs and Cantatas Compos'd by Dʳ Boyce.
London. Printed for I. Walsh, &c.

London Evening-Post, Feb. 5–7, 1756.

>Fol. Privilege (dated 10 April 1745), verso of title-page. pp. 70–87.
>BM. G. 330. RCM.

244. Numb: VI. Lyra Britannica, &c.

Whitehall Evening-Post, July 19–21, 1759.

>Fol. pp. 89–108.
>BM. G. 330.
>Same title-page as No. 5, with 'VI' altered from 'V' in manuscript.

245. The Non-pariel. Set by Mʳ Boyce.
Printed with the Consent of the Author by I. Walsh with His Majesty's Royal Licence.

>[*c*. 1745.]
>S.sh. fol.
>BM. G. 312. (66.)
>Song, begins: 'Tho' Chloe's out of Fashion.' Different from 'The Non-Pareille', in Book VI of 'Lyra Britannica'.

246. The Shepherd's Lottery. A Musical Entertainment. As it is Perform'd at the Theatre-Royal in Drury Lane. Compos'd by Dr Boyce.
London. Printed for I. Walsh, &c.

General Evening Post: Whitehall Evening-Post, Dec. 19–21, 1751.

Fol. Privilege verso of title-page (dated 10 June 1745), pp. 52.
BM. G. 225. (1.) RAM. RCM. Manchester. Rowe. Tenbury.
Words by Moses Mendez.

247. Solomon. A Serenata, In Score, Taken from the Canticles. Set to Musick By William Boyce, Composer to His Majesty.
London: Printed and Sold for the Author, by J. Walsh . . . M.DCC.XLIII.

Daily Advertiser, May 19, 1743.

Fol. 'A List of the Subscribers' [4 pp. unpaginated.], pp. 2–101.
BM. H. 1081. RAM. RCM. Rowe. Others in BUC, not examined.
Libretto by E. Moore.

248. Solomon. A Serenata, In Score, Taken from the Canticles. Set to Musick By Mr. William Boyce, Composer to His Majesty, and Master of His Majesty's Band of Musick.
London. Printed for I. Walsh, &c.

Public Advertiser, Feb. 2, 1760.

Fol. pp. 2–101.
RCM. Birmingham. Fitz. Oriel College, Oxford. OUF. Rowe.

249. Twelve Sonatas For Two Violins; with a Bass for the Violoncello or Harpsichord. By William Boyce, Composer to His Majesty.
London, Printed for the Author. & sold by I. Walsh . . . MDCCXLVII.

London Evening-Post, Jan. 27–29, 1747.

Fol. 3 parts.
BM. g. 263. b. RCM.

250. — Second Edition.

General Advertiser, March 14, 1747.

251. — A New Edition of twelve Sonatas, &c.

General Advertiser, Jan. 16, 1751. (Of whom may be had.)

Fol. 3 parts.
BM. g. 263. a. RCM. Fitz. Rowe.

252. Eight Symphonies in Eight Parts. Six for Violins, Hoboys, or German Flutes.

and Two for Violins, French Horns and Trumpets. with a Bass for the Violoncello and Harpsicord. Compos'd by Dr Wm Boyce. Opera Seconda.
London. Printed for I. Walsh, &c.

Public Advertiser, Jan. 5, 1760.

Fol. 10 parts.
BM. g. 263. RM. 17. d. 4. (6.) RM. 26. b. 2. (15.) RAM. RCM. Fitz.

See also Nos. 266, 268. British Orpheus. Books II, IV; No. 749. Harmonia Anglicana . . . by . . . Dr Boyce, &c.; No. 907. Lampe (Johann Friedrich) and Howard (Samuel). The Vocal Musical Mask, &c.; No. 969. Love in a Village . . . Music by . . . Boyce, &c.; No. 1223. Psalms; Nos. 1419, 1420. The Summer's Tale . . . Music by . . . Boyce, &c.

BREMNER (Robert)

See No. 1348. Scotch Songs

BREUNICH (Johann Michael)

See No. 318. Carcani (Giuseppe) Six Sonatas in Three Parts, &c.

BRIOSCHI (Antonio)

See No. 1313. San Martini (Giovanni Battista) Six Sonatas For Two Violins . . . Compos'd by . . . Sigr Brioschi, &c.

BRITISH MISCELLANY

253. No I. The British Miscellany. A Selected Collection of the most Favourite Songs Perform'd at the Theatres. &c. For the Harpsicord, Voice or German Flute. Price 2s
London. Printed for I. Walsh, &c.

Public Advertiser, Nov. 11, 1762. (The British Miscellany; a Collection of English Songs; in which are inserted the favourite Songs in the Pastoral called The Spring; The Music by Mr. Handel, and the most eminent Masters, &c.)

Obl. fol. pp. 12.
BM. E. 151. a. RCM.

254. — Another issue, with additional advertisement on title-page.

[*c.* 1762.]

BM. E. 151.

255. No II. The British Miscellany, &c.

Public Advertiser, June 25, 1763.

Obl. fol. pp. 13–25.
BM. E. 151.
'II' altered from 'I' in MS.

256. Number III. The British Miscellany, &c.

Public Advertiser, August 5, 1763. (Number III. The British Miscellany The Music by Mr. Handel and the most eminent English and Italian Masters.)

Obl. fol. pp. 27–38.

257. No IV. The British Miscellany, &c.

Public Advertiser, Feb. 4, 1764.

Obl. fol. pp. 39–49.
BM. E. 151. E. 151. a.
'IV' altered from 'I' in MS.

258. No V. The British Miscellany, &c.

Public Advertiser, August 18, 1764. (Number V. The British Miscellany . . . The Music by Mr. Handel.)

Obl. fol. pp. 51–62.
BM. E. 151.
'V' altered from 'I' in MS.
Walsh Cat. 27: 'Spring, Fairies, &c. 5 Books, each 2s. od.'
Randall Cat.: 'The Spring, a Pastoral called the British Miscellany, in 5 Books, each 2s. od.'

BRITISH MUSICAL MISCELLANY

259. The British Musical Miscellany, or, the Delightful Grove: Being a Collection of Celebrated English, and Scotch Songs, By the best Masters. Set for the Violin, German Flute, the Common Flute, and Harpsicord. Vol. I. Engraven in a fair Character, and Carefully Corrected.

London. Printed for & Sold by I. Walsh . . . 514.

[1734.]

8°. Frontispiece. 'A Table of the Songs' I–IV. pp. 145.
BM. C. 382. Coke. Dundee. Mitchell. NLS.
Issued in parts. No. I. (For November. To be continued monthly.) *Grub-street Journal*, Dec. 6, 1733. No. II. *Country Journal: or, The Craftsman*, Dec. 29, 1733. No. III. *Grub-street Journal*, Jan. 24, 1734. No. IV. *Country Journal: or, The Craftsman*, Feb. 9, 1734. No. V. *Country Journal: or, The Craftsman*, March 23, 1734. No. VI. (With frontispiece which compleats First Volume.) *London Evening-Post*, April 4–6, 1734.

260. The British Musical Miscellany or, the Delightful Grove: Being a Collection of Celebrated English, and Scotch Songs, By the best Masters. Set for the Violin,

German Flute, the Common Flute, and Harpsicord. Vol. II. Engraven in a fair Character & Carefully Corrected.

London. Printed for and Sold by I: Walsh . . . 525.

[1734.]

8°. Frontispiece. 'A Table of the Songs' I–IV. pp. 145.
BM. C. 382. Coke. Dundee. Mitchell. NLS.
Issued in parts. No. VII. (1st number of Second Volume.) *Country Journal : or, The Craftsman*, May 18, 1734. No. VIII. *Country Journal : or, The Craftsman*, June 22, 1734. No. IX. *Country Journal : or, The Craftsman*, July 20, 1734. No. X. *Country Journal : or, The Craftsman*, Aug. 31, 1734. No. XI. *London Evening-Post*, Sept. 10–12, 1734. No. XII (Which compleats the Second Volume.) *Country Journal : or, The Craftsman*, Oct. 26, 1734.

261. The British Musical Miscellany; or, the Delightful Grove: Being a Collection of Celebrated English, and Scotch Songs, By the best Masters. Set for the Violin, German Flute, the Common Flute, and Harpsicord. Vol. III. Engraven in a fair Character, and Carefully Corrected.

London. Printed for & sold by I. Walsh . . . N°. 542.

[1735.]

8°. Frontispiece. 'A Table of the Songs' I–IV. pp. 145.
BM. C. 382. Coke. Dundee. Mitchell. NLS.
Issued in parts. No. XIII. *Country Journal: or, The Craftsman*, Nov. 30, 1734. No. XIV. *Country Journal: or, The Craftsman*, Dec. 28, 1734. No. XV, *Country Journal: or, The Craftsman*, Feb. 1, 1735. No. XVI. *London Evening-Post*, Feb. 27–March 1, 1735. No. XVII. *Daily Journal*, April 1, 1735, No. XVIII. *London Evening-Post*, April 22–24, 1735. (Which compleats the Third Vol. With an Index.)

262. The British Musical Miscellany; or, the Delightful Grove: Being a Collection of Celebrated English, and Scotch Songs, By the best Masters. Set for the Violin, German Flute, the Common Flute, and Harpsicord. Vol. IV. Engraven in a fair Character, and Carefully Corrected.

London. Printed for & sold by I. Walsh . . . N°. 571.

[1735.]

8°. Frontispiece. 'A Table of the Songs' I–IV. pp. 145.
BM. C. 382. Coke. Dundee. Mitchell. NLS.
Issued in parts. No. XIX. *London Evening-Post*, May 31–June 3, 1735. No. XX. *Country Journal: or, The Craftsman*, June 28, 1735. No. XXI. *London Evening-Post*, July 29–31, 1735. No. XXII. *Country Journal: or, The Craftsman*, August 30, 1735. No. XXIII. *London Evening-Post*, Sept. 30–Oct. 2, 1735. No. XXIV. *Country Journal: or, The Craftsman*, Nov. 1, 1735. (Just published. Compleats fourth Volume.)

263. The British Musical Miscellany; or, the Delightful Grove: Being a Collection of Celebrated English, and Scotch Songs, By the best Masters. Set for the Violin, German Flute, the Common Flute and Harpsicord. Vol. V. Engraven in a fair Character, and Carefully Corrected.

London. Printed for & Sold by I. Walsh . . .N? 579.

[1736.]
> 8°. Frontispiece. 'A Table of the Songs' I–IV. pp. 145.
> BM. C. 382. Coke. Dundee. Mitchell. NLS.
> Issued in parts. No. XXV. *Country Journal : or, The Craftsman*, Nov. 29, 1735. No. XXVI. *Country Journal : or, The Craftsman*, Jan. 10, 1736. No. XXVII. *Country Journal : or, The Craftsman*, Feb. 7, 1736. (Just published.) No. XXVIII. *Country Journal : or, The Craftsman*, March 20, 1726. (Just published.) No. XXIX. *London Daily Post, and General Advertiser*, April 1, 1736. No. XXX. *London Evening-Post*, May 1–4, 1736. (Compleats the fifth Volume.)

264. The British Musical Miscellany; or, the Delightful Grove: Being a Collection of Celebrated English, and Scotch Songs, By the best Masters. Set for the Violin, German-Flute, the Common Flute, and Harpsicord. Vol. VI. Engraven in a fair Character, & Carefully Corrected.
London. Printed for & Sold by I. Walsh . . . N? 626.

[1737.]
> 8°. Frontispiece. 'A Table of the Songs' I–IV. pp. 144.
> BM. C. 382. Coke. Dundee. Mitchell. NLS.
> Issued in parts. No. XXXI. *Country Journal : or, The Craftsman*, July 24, 1736. No. XXXII. *Country Journal : or, The Craftsman*, Sept. 4, 1736. No. XXXIII. *London Daily Post, and General Advertiser*, Nov. 3, 1736. (Just publish'd.) No. XXXIV. *Country Journal : or, The Craftsman*, Jan. 15, 1737. (Just publish'd.) No. XXXV. ? date. No. XXXVI. ? date. *Country Journal : or, The Craftsman*, Nov. 26, 1737. (In six Volumes.) The six volumes were sold at £1. 11s. 6d. Walsh Cat. 21b and 24a. The British Museum copy of Volume 6 contains a catalogue of 'Vocal Musick. Just Publish'd by I. Walsh in Catherine Street.'

BRITISH ORPHEUS

265. The British Orpheus A Collection of Favourite English Songs Never Before Publish'd Compos'd By Different Authors.
London. Printed for I. Walsh, &c.

London Daily Post, and General Advertiser, Dec. 1, 1741. (By different Authors.) Dec. 29, 1741. (Of whom may be had . . . Compos'd by Mr. Howard, &c.)

> Fol. ff. 1–12. Printed on one side only.
> BM. G. 219.
> Contains songs by Howard, Handel, Holcombe, Carey, Russel, Lampe, John Randall and Leveridge.

266. N? II. The British Orpheus, &c.
London. Printed for I. Walsh, &c.

Daily Advertiser, Sept. 18, 1742. (Of whom may be had.)

> Fol. ff. 13–24. Printed on one side only.
> BM. G. 219.
> Contains songs by Travers, Gladwin, Froude, Vincent, Boyce and Handel. The title-page is the same as the first number with 'N? II.' added.

267. N? III. The British Orpheus, &c.
London. Printed for I. Walsh, &c.

[*c.* 1742.]

Fol. Without foliation. Printed on one side only.
BM. G. 219.
Contains songs by Russel, Stanley, Randel, Arne, Leveridge and Lampe. The title-page is
the same as N? II, altered to 'N? III.' in MS.

268. The British Orpheus A Collection of Favourite English Songs Never Before
Publish'd Compos'd By M͏ͬ Howard &c. Book IV.
London. Printed for I. Walsh, &c.

Daily Advertiser, Feb. 19, 1743. (By Mr. Howard, Mr. Russell, &c.)

Fol. ff. 37–48. Printed on one side only.
BM. G. 219. RCM.
Contains songs by Howard, Russel, Holcombe, Boyce, Carey, Randall, and Savage.

269. The British Orpheus, &c. Book V.

[*c.* 1743.]

Fol.

270. The British Orpheus. Book 6. a Collection of English Songs never before
publish'd by Mr. Howard, and several Eminent Masters, for the Harpsichord,
German Flute, or Violin.
Printed for J. Walsh, &c.

General Advertiser, June 2, 1744.

Fol.

BRIVIO (Giuseppe Ferdinando)

See No. 10. Airs. A Choice Collection of Aires and Duets for two German
Flutes . . . Sig͏ͬ: Brivio, &c.; No. 715. Geminiani (Francesco) and Brivio
(Giuseppe Ferdinando) 6 Solos by Geminiani Brivio, &c.; No. 719 Gianguir;
No. 857. Inconstanza Delusa; Nos. 1393, 1394. Solos. Six Solos for a German
Flute . . . by M͏ͬ Handel . . . Sig͏ͬ Brivio.

BROSCHI (Carlo) *called Farinelli*

All the Songs sung by the celebrated Farinelli.
See No. 557. Delizie dell' Opere. Vol. II.
Farinelli's Celebrated Songs, &c. Collected from Sig͏ͬ Hasse . . . Set for a German
Flute . . . Vol. I.
See No. 771. Hasse (Johann Adolph) [Chamber Airs.]

BROSCHI (RICCARDO)

See No. 769. Hasse (Johann Adolph) The Favourite Songs in the Opera Call'd Artaxerxes.

BURGESS (HENRY) *the Younger*

271. A Collection of English Songs and Cantatas Set to Musick by M.ʳ Henry Burgess Jun.
London. Printed for I. Walsh, &c.

General Advertiser, May 4, 1749.

> Fol. 'A List of the Subscribers.' 2 pp. pp. 22.
> BM. H. 1648. (1.) RCM. Bod.

272. Six Concertos for the Harpsicord or Organ Compos'd by M.ʳ Henry Burgess Jun.ʳ
London. Printed for the Author. Sold by I. Walsh, &c.

Daily Advertiser, March 26, 1743.

> Fol. pp. 2–38.
> BM. g. 251. Durham.

273. Six Concertos, for the Organ and Harpsicord, also for Violins & other Instruments in 5 Parts. Compos'd by M.ʳ Hen. Burgess Jun.ʳ
London Printed for J. Walsh, &c.

Daily Advertiser, Mar. 26, 1743.

> Fol. Parts.
> BM. g. 251.
> Violino primo part contains a list of subscribers.

BURNEY (CHARLES)

274. VI Cornet Pieces with an Introduction for the Diapasons, and a Fugue. Proper for young Organists and Practitioners on the Harpsichord. Compos'd by M.ʳ Charles Burney.
London. Printed for I. Walsh, &c.

London Evening-Post, Nov. 2–5, 1751.

> Obl. fol. pp. 15.
> BM. e. 5. (3.) RCM. Bod. CUL.

BYRON (WILLIAM) *Lord Byron*

275. Lord Biron's Lessons (Harpsicord, Spinnet or Organ). 1s. 0d. N.º 198.
[*c.* 1730.]

Walsh Cat. 18.

Smith 183 ('An Overture and Airs for the Harpsicord') and 498 with Walsh only in the imprint and 'N⁰ 198' added to the title-page.

See also No. 6. Airs. Aires by a Person of Quality.

CALAMITA DE' CUORI

276. The Favourite Songs in the Opera Call'd La Calamita de' Cuori.
London. Printed for I. Walsh, &c.

Public Advertiser, March 5, 1763.

> Fol. Passe-partout title-page. pp. 14.
> BM. G. 760. d. (5.) Gresham. RCM. Rowe.
> Pasticcio. Music by B. Galuppi, J. C. Bach and Cocchi, the last two named in the work. Words by C. Goldoni.
> Pp. 12–14 consist of an 'Aria nel Astarto . . . del Sigʳ Bach'.
> Republished in 'Le Delizie dell' Opere', Vol. X, pp. 51–64.

CALDARA (Antonio)

> *See* No. 1146. Ormisda

CALEDONIAN COUNTRY DANCES

277. Caledonian Country Dances; or a Collection of all the celebrated Scotch Country Dances now in Vogue, with the proper Directions to each Dance, as they are perform'd at Court and publick Entertainments, for the Violin, Hoboy or German Flute, with their Basses for the Bass Violin or Harpsichord. pr. 2s. 6d.
Printed for John Walsh, &c.

Daily Journal, Nov. 21, 1733.

> Obl. 16⁰.
> Cecil Sharp Library. (Wanting title-page. pp. 9–100 only.)
> The title-page may have been similar to that of the second edition.

278. Caledonian Country Dances Being A Collection of all the Celebrated Scotch Country Dances now in Vogue, with the proper Directions to each Dance, As they are perform'd at Court, & publick Entertainments, for the Violin, Hoboy, or German Flute; with their Basses for the Bass Violin, or Harpsicord. 2ᵈ Edition. Engraven in a Fair Character, and carefully Corrected. Price 2ˢ 6ᵈ.
London. Printed for and Sold by I. Walsh . . . N⁰ 493.

Country Journal : or, The Craftsman, Nov. 1, 1735.

> Obl. 16⁰. 'A Table of the Scotch Country Dances'. pp. II–IV (III on verso of title-page), 5–100.
> NLS.
> Walsh Cat. 18: Caledonian Country Dances with Directions. 2s. 6d. N⁰ 493.

279. — 3ᵈ Edition.

London Daily Post, and General Advertiser, Nov. 3, 1736.

> Obl. 16°. 'A Table of the Scotch Country Dances.' pp. II–IV, 5–100.
> Mitchell. NLS.
> The title-page is the same as that of the 2nd edition with '3ᵈ' in the place of '2ᵈ'.

280. Caledonian Country Dances 2ᵈ Book. 2s. 6d.

[*c.* 1736.]

> Walsh Cat. 18.
> Presumably a first edition of the following, No. 281, without 'N⁰ 606' on the title-page.

281. Caledonian Country Dances Book the Second. Being a Collection of all the Celebrated Scotch Country Dances now in Vogue, with the proper Directions to each Dance, as they are perform'd at Court, & publick Entertainments, for the Violin, Hoboy, or German Flute; with their Basses for the Bass Violin, or harpsicord. Engraven in a fair Character and carefully Corrected. Price 2ˢ 6ᵈ

London. Printed for and Sold by I. Walsh . . . N⁰ 606.

Country Journal : or, The Craftsman, Sept. 24, 1737.

> Obl. 16°. 'A Table of the Scotch Country Dances'. pp. II–IV, 13–100.
> Cecil Sharp Library. Mitchell. NLS.
> Walsh Cat. 18: 'Caledonian Country Dances. 2ᵈ Book. 2s. 6d.'

282. Caledonian Country Dances Book the Third Being a Collection of all the Celebrated Scotch Country Dances now in Vogue, with the proper Directions to each Dance, as they are perform'd at Court & publick Entertainments. for the Harpsicord, Violin, Hoboy or German Flute.

London. Printed for I. Walsh . . . Price 2ˢ 6ᵈ

[*c.* 1740.]

> Obl. 16°. 'A Table of the Scotch Country Dances'. pp. II–IV, 13–100.
> Mitchell. NLS.

283. — Caledonian Dances. . . . 4 Books [i.e. Vol. I].

London Evening-Post, Dec. 13–15, 1744.

284. Caledonian Country Dances Book the Fourth. Being a Collection of all the Celebrated Scotch Country Dances now in Vogue, with the Proper Directions to each Dance, as they are perform'd at Court, and Publick Entertainments. for the Harpsicord, Violin, Hoboy, or German Flute.

London. Printed for I. Walsh   Price 2s. 6d. . . . 2ᵈ Edition.

[*c.* 1745.]

> Obl. 16°. 'A Table of the Scotch Country Dances'. pp. II–IV, 5–100.
> Mitchell. NLS.

F

285. Caledonian Country Dances Being a Collection of all the Celebrated Scotch and English Country Dances now in Vogue, with Proper Directions to each Dance For the Harpsicord, Violin, Hoboy, or German Flute. Vol. II. Part I.
London. Printed for I. Walsh, &c.

General Advertiser, Dec. 24, 1748.

> Obl. 16°. Table (pp. 2–4), 5–100.
> NLS. Glen 35. (2.) (Wanting pp. 11–26, nos. 271–286 and pp. 99, 100, nos. 359, 360.)
> *General Advertiser*, Oct. 5, 1749. (Caledonian Dances . . . in 5 Books. i.e. Vol. I and Vol. II. Pt. 1.)

286. A Sixth Set of Caledonian Dances . . . Vol. II. Part 2.

General Advertiser, Sept. 13, 1751. (Just publish'd. Price 2s. 6d.)

287. — Vol. II. Part 3.
[*c.* 1755.]

288. Caledonian Dances, containing the present favourite Scotch and English Country Dances . . . Vol. 2. Part 4.

Public Advertiser, Jan. 20, 1757; Dec. 26, 1760. (In 8 books.)

289. Select Scotch and English Country Dances for the Harpsichord, Violin, or for Flute in Nine Books, each 2s. 6d.

Public Advertiser, Sept. 7, 1761.

290. A Choice Collection of the newest and best Country Dances . . . Book 9. Price 2s. 6d.

Public Advertiser, Dec. 15, 1762.

> Walsh Cat. 27: 'Caledonian Dances. 9 Books. each 2s. 6d.'
> Randall Cat.: 'Caledonian Dances, or a select set of English and Scotch Country Dances, 9 Books each 2s. 6d.'

CALFURNIA

The Favourite Songs in the Opera call'd Calphurnia.
See No. 199. Bononcini (Giovanni)

CAMILLA

Songs In The New Opera Call'd Camilla.
See No. 182. Bononcini (Antonio Maria)

CAMPIONI (CARLO ANTONIO)

291. Divertimento da Camera. Six Duets for a Violin & Violoncello or Harpsichord. Compos'd by Sig^r Carlo Antonio Campioni Opera VII.
London. Printed for I. Walsh, &c.

Public Advertiser, Jan. 22, 1765.

> Obl. fol. pp. 2–30.
> BM. e. 2. (1.) Cardiff.
> Randall Cat.: 'Campioni's Duets (for two Violoncellos). Op. 7. 5s. od.'

292. Six Sonatas for two Violins with a Thorough Bass for the Harpsicord or Violoncello Compos'd by Sig^r Carlo Antonio Campion.
London. Printed for I. Walsh, &c.

Public Advertiser, Oct. 1, 1756.

> Fol. 3 parts.
> BM. g. 274. (1.) CUL.
> With 'N° XXXI' at the top of the title-page.

293. — Another issue, with the name given as 'Campioni'.

[*c.* 1756.]

> Fol. 3 parts.
> BM. h. 5. (1.) Oriel College, Oxford.

294. — Another issue, with 'Opera Prima' added to the title-page.

[*c.* 1760.]

> Fol. 3 parts.
> RM. 17. d. 3. (5.)
> 'Prima' is in MS. Without 'N° XXXI'.

295. — Another issue, with 'Opera I' added to the title-page.

[*c.* 1765.]

> Fol. 3 parts.
> BM. g. 273. g. (2.).
> Without 'N° XXXI'
> Walsh Cat. 27: 'Campioni's Trios. Op. 1. 5s. od.'

296. A 2^d Set of Six Sonatas for two Violins with a Thorough Bass for the Harpsicord or Violoncello. Compos'd by Sig^r Carlo Antonio Campioni.
London. Printed for I. Walsh, &c.

Public Advertiser, Feb. 1, 1758.

> Fol. 3 parts.
> BM. h. 5. (2.) Rowe

297. — Another issue. Six Sonatas for two Violins with a Thorough Bass for the Harpsicord or Violoncello. Compos'd by Sig.ʳ Carlo Antonio Campioni. Opera 2.ᵈᵃ

London. Printed for I. Walsh, &c.

[*c.* 1760.]

> Fol. 3 parts.
> RM. 17. d. 3. (6.)
> '2ᵈᵃ is in MS.

298. — Another issue, with 'Opera II' added to the title-page.

[*c.* 1765.]

> Fol. 3 parts.
> BM. g. 273. (2.) London University. Oriel College, Oxford. Rowe.
> 'II' has been altered from 'I' in MS.
> Walsh Cat. 27: 'Campioni's Trios. Op. 2. 5s. od.'

299. Six Sonatas for Two Violins with a Thorough Bass for the Harpsicord or Violoncello Compos'd by Sig.ʳ Carlo Antonio Campioni. Opera III.

London. Printed for I: Walsh, &c.

Public Advertiser, Jan. 3, 1759.

> Fol. 3 parts.
> BM. g. 273. (3.) RAM. CUL. Oriel College, Oxford. Rowe.
> 'III' has been altered from 'I' in MS.

300. — Another issue, with Opera 3ᶻᵃ on the title-page.

[*c.* 1759.]

> Fol. 3 parts.
> RM. 17. d. 3. (7.)
> '3ᶻᵃ' has been added in MS.
> Walsh Cat. 27: 'Campioni's Trios. Op. 3. 5s. od.'

301. A 4.ᵗʰ Set of Six Sonatas for two Violins with a Thorough Bass for the Harpsicord or Violoncello Compos'd by Sig.ʳ Carlo Antonio Campioni Opera IV.

London. Printed for I. Walsh, &c.

Public Advertiser, Oct. 8, 1762.

> Fol. 3 parts.
> BM. g. 242. (3.)

302. — Another issue. Six Sonatas for two Violins with a Thorough Bass for the Harpsicord or Violoncello. Compos'd by Sig.ʳ Carlo Antonio Campioni. Opera IV.

London. Printed for I: Walsh, &c.

[*c.* 1762.]

Fol. 3 parts.
BM. g. 273. (4.) RM 17. d. 3. (8.)
'IV' has been altered from 'I' in MS.

303. — Another issue, with 'Opera IV' on the title-page.

[*c.* 1765.]

Fol. 3 parts.
BM. g. 273. f. (4.) (Wanting Violin I part.)
Walsh Cat. 27: 'Campioni's Trios. Op. 4. 5s. od.'

304. Six Sonatas for two Violins with a Thorough Bass for the Harpsicord or Violoncello . . . Opera Quinta.
London. Printed for I. Walsh, &c.

[*c.* 1760.]

Fol. 3 parts.
Oriel College, Oxford.

305. Six Sonatas for Two Violins with a Thorough Bass for the Harpsicord or Violoncello Compos'd by Sigᴿ Carlo Antonio Campioni. Opera V.
London. Printed for I. Walsh, &c.

[*c.* 1763.]

Fol. 3 parts.
RM. 17. d. 3. (9.)

306. — Another issue.

[*c.* 1765.]

Fol. 3 parts.
BM. g. 273. a. RM. 17. d. 5. (9.)
Walsh Cat. 27: 'Campioni's Trios. Op. 5. 5s. od.'

307. Six Sonatas for two German Flutes or Violins, with a Bass for the Harpsicord or Violoncello. Compos'd By Sigᴿ Carlo Antonio Campioni. Opera V.
London. Printed for I. Walsh, &c.

[*c.* 1765.]

Fol. 3 parts.
Rowe.

308. Six Sonatas for Two Violins with a Thorough Bass for the Harpsicord or Violoncello Compos'd by Sigᴿ Carlo Antonio Campioni. Opera VI.
London. Printed for I. Walsh, &c.

Public Advertiser, Sept. 13, 1765.

Fol. 3 parts.
BM. g. 273. (5.) RM. 17. d. 3. (10.) RM. 17. d. 5. (10.) CUL. Rowe.
'VI' has been altered from 'V' in MS.
Walsh Cat. 27: 'Campioni's Trios. Op. 6. 5s. od.'

309. Six Sonatas or Duets for two Violins Compos'd by Sigʳ Carlo Antonio Campioni. Op. VIII.
London. Printed for I. Walsh, &c.

[*c.* 1765.]

Fol. 2 parts.
BM. g. 218. d. (2.)
Randall Cat.: 'Campioni's Duets. Op. 8. 4s. od.'

CAMPIONI (Carlo Antonio) and CHABRAN (Charles)

310. Six Favourite Solos for a Violin with a Bass for the Violoncello and Harpsicord Compos'd by Sigʳ Campioni, & Sigʳ Chabran. Price 5ˢ
London. Printed for I. Walsh, &c.

[*c.* 1760.]

Fol. pp. 2–35.
BM. g. 273. b.
Walsh Cat. 27: 'Campioni, Chabran Solos (for a Violin and Harpsicord). 5s. od.'

CANTATAS

311. XII Cantatas in English for a Voice and a Thorough Bass for the Harpsicord being a curious Collection of the Compositions of Several Authors.
London Printed for I: Walsh . . . & Inº & Ioseph Hare, &c.

Post Boy, Feb. 28–March 2, 1722 [1723]. (Twelve Cantato's in English, &c.)

Large fol. 'A Table of the Cantatas', &c. pp. 29.
RAM.
Another issue of Smith 584.

312. — With Walsh only in the imprint and 'Nº 293' added to the title-page.

[*c.* 1730.]

Walsh Cat. 18: '12 Cantatas by several Authors. 4s. od. Nº 293.'

313. Three New English Cantatas, set to Musick for a Voice, Violins and Violincello; with a Thorough Bass for the Harpsicord.
London: Sold by J. Walsh . . . and John Simpson . . . [Price Three Shillings.]

London Daily Post, and General Advertiser, Jan. 6, 1739; Jan 18, 1739. (Set to Musick by Mr. Worgan.)

Fol. pp. 26.

BM. H. 2815. a. (2.) RCM.

'Compos'd by M.ʳ Ja.ˢ Worgan Organist of S.ᵗ Dunstans in yᵉ East & S.ᵗ Botolph Ald.' has been added to the title-page in MS.

CANZONETS

314. N.º V Canzonets For two Voices, German Flutes or Guitars. Being a Collection of the most favourite French Songs. Book II. Price 2.ˢ N.B. The first Volume contains One Hundred French Songs, Price 10.ˢ 6.ᵈ

London: Printed for I. Walsh, &c.

[*c.* 1755.]

Obl. fol. pp. 13.

BM. D. 230. b.

For Book I, *see* No. 382. Cloes (Nicolas) One Hundred French Songs, &c. For Book III, *see* Addenda. Canzonets. N.º VII Canzonets for a Voice. German Flute or Guitar. Being a Collection of the most favourite French Songs. Book III, &c.

CANZONIERE

315. Del Canzoniere d' Orazio di Giovan Gualberto Bottarelli. Ode XII. Messe in musica da più renomati Professori Inglesi. Dedicate al Signor Guise Luogotenente generale dell' Armata di S.M.B.

Public Advertiser, Dec. 4, 1758. (Twelve Odes of Horace, translated in Italian. Set to Music by the following eminent Masters, Dr. Boyce, Mr. Arne, Mr. Worgan, Mr. Howard, Mr. Heron and Mr. Defesch. Printed for J. Walsh.)

Fol. Dedication. pp. 60.

Two previous editions were issued in 1757, without any name in the imprint. (Edizone Seconda. BM. G. 242. (3.))

CAPORALE (Andrea) and GALLIARD (Johann Ernst)

316. Caparali and Galliard's Solos (For 2 Violoncellos). 10s. 6d.

[*c.* 1746.]

Walsh Cat. 25.

This presumably refers to 'XII Solos for the Violoncello, VI of Sig.ʳ Caporale; & VI Compos'd by M.ʳ Galliard. Most Humbly Dedicated to His Royal Highness The Prince of Wales 1746. London Printed for John Johnson', &c. (BM. e. 277. (1.) obl. fol. pp. 2–24, 1–24.)

CAPUA (Rinaldo da)

See No. 394. Commedia in Commedia; No. 719. Gianguir; No. 1129. Nerone.

CARBONELLI (Giovanni Stefano)

317. Sonate da Camera a Violino, e Violone, o Cembalo, &c.

Daily Post, March 3, 1729. (Twelve Solo's for a Violin, &c. Publish'd by the Author. Sold by John Walsh, &c.)

> Fol. pp. 65.
> BM. h. 348. RCM. BUL. CUL. Fitz. Rowe. Tenbury.
> Walsh Cat. 18: 'Carbonelli's Solos. 10s. 0d.'

CARCANI (Giuseppe)

318. Six Sonatas in Three Parts for Two Violins with a Thorough Bass for the Harpsicord or Violoncello Compos'd by Sigr Carcani &c.
> London. Printed for I. Walsh, &c.

Public Advertiser, June 7, 1753. (Also just published. Six Sonatas . . . By Sig. Carcani, and other eminent Italian Masters.)

> Fol. 3 parts.
> BM. h. 2851. d. (3.) Rowe.
> Contains Trios by Carcani, Giuseppe Almerighi, Giulini, Breunich and two anonymous compositions.

CAREY (Henry)

319. Songs in Cephalus and Procris. 1s. 6d.

  [*c.* 1731.]

> Walsh Cat. 18.
> Carey is not named in the Walsh catalogue, which probably refers to an edition advertised by T. Cobb under Carey's name, *Daily Post*, Feb. 16, 1731. (BM. G. 220. (3.))

320. The Tunes, Airs and Dances in the Entertainment call'd Cephalus and Procris, as they are perform'd at the Theatre Royal in Drury-Lane; the Tunes for the Violin, and several of them proper for the German Flute and Common Flute. Price 6d.
> Printed for and sold by John Walsh . . . and Joseph Hare, &c.

Daily Post, Nov. 3, 1730.

> Walsh Cat. 18: 'The Tunes in Cephalus and Procris. (Violin). 6d. No 134.' Carey is not named in the catalogue or notice.

321. Songs in the Contrivances. 3s. 6d.

  [*c.* 1730.]

> Walsh Cat. 18. Carey is not named in the catalogue.
> Editions were published under Carey's name by W. Mears 1729, and others (BM. 11775. c. 11, &c.) and the notice may refer to one of these

322. The Songs Duett and Dialogue in the Contrivances wth their Symphonies & Basses as performed at ye Theatre-Royal in Covent Garden Together with ye Symphony & Song-Part Transposed for ye German or Common Flute and ye Duett for 2 Flutes The words & music by Mr Carey.

London Printed for J. Cox, &c.

[1764.]

> Fol. pp. 11.
> BM. G. 220. (1.)
> This copy bears the manuscript note 'Printed for I. Walsh—64' after the imprint. The work was issued by John Cox *c.* 1755 and was probably purchased by Walsh at the sale of the stock-in-trade of Cox in 1764.

323. Songs in the new Farce call'd The Honest Yorkshire-Man as they are Perform'd at the Theatre in Goodman's Fields. Compos'd by Mr Carey. The Tunes proper for the German Flute, Violin and Common Flute. Price 6^d

London. Printed for and sold by I. Walsh . . . N° 582 [i.e. 583].

London Daily Post, and General Advertiser, Jan. 8, 1736.

> 12°. pp. 21.
> BM. B. 380. (2.)
> Music composed and compiled, and words, by Henry Carey.
> Walsh Cat. 18: 'Honest Yorkshire Man. 6d. N° 583.'

324. Carey's Songs. 2s. 6d. N° 316.

[*c.* 1730.]

> Walsh Cat. 18.
> Not identified.

See Nos. 265, 268. British Orpheus. Books I, IV; No. 749. Harmonia Anglicana . . . by . . . Carey, &c.

CARTER (   )

325. An Ode on the late Earthquakes to which are added a Cantata and Song Sung by Master Thumoth at Ranelagh Gardens Set to Musick by Mr Carter.

London. Printed by William Smith . . . and sold by the author at his House . . . at Mr Walsh's . . . at Mr Johnsons in Cheapside and at all the Musick Shops, &c.

[*c.* 1756.]

> Fol. pp. 11.
> BM. H. 2815. i. (2.)

CASTRUCCI (Pietro)

326. Concerti Grossi Con due Violini e Violoncello obbligati di Concertino e con due altri Violini, Viola e Basso di Concerto grosso da raddoppiarsi ad arbitrio

Dedicati All' Illmo Sig^{re} il Signor Guglielmo Gage Baronetto, e Cavaliero del Bagno e Senatore in Parlamento. Da Pietro Castrucci Opera Terza.
    London Printed for & Sold by Iohn Walsh . . . N° 643.

London Daily Post, and General Advertiser, Nov. 10, 1738. (Revis'd and Recommended by Dr. Pepusch.)

    Fol. Parts.
    BM. g. 237. b. RAM.
    An earlier issue may have appeared without 'N° 643' on the title-page. (Walsh Cat. 18.)

327. — Another issue.

General Evening Post, (London), Jan. 17–19, 1745. (New Editions.)

328. — Another edition.

General Advertiser, Oct. 25, 1749. (New Editions.)

329. Solos for a German Flute, with a Thorough Bass for the Harpsichord, or Bass Violin, by Sig. Pietro. Price 3s.
    Printed for and sold by John Walsh . . . and John and Joseph Hare, &c.

Daily Courant, May 22, 1723.

    Pietro was Pietro Castrucci.
    Walsh Cat. 11*a*: 'Pietro's first Solos for a German Flute and a Bass.'

330. — With Walsh only in the imprint and 'N° 427' added to the title-page.
    [*c.* 1730.]

    Walsh Cat. 18: 'Pietro's Solos. (Solos for a German Flute, Hoboy or Violin with a Thorough Bass for the Harpsicord.) 3s. od. N° 427.'

331. Pietro's Second Solos for a German Flute and a Bass.
    [London. J. Walsh, John and Joseph Hare.]
    [*c.* 1725.]

    Walsh Cat. 11*a*.

332. — With Walsh only in the imprint and 'N° 428' added to the title-page.
    [*c.* 1730.]

    Walsh Cat. 18: 'Pietro's 2d Solos. (Solos for a German Flute, Hoboy, or Violin with a Thorough Bass for the Harpsicord.) 3s. od. N° 428.'

333. XII Solos for a Violin with a Thorough Bass for the Harpsicord or Bass Violin. Compos'd by Pietro Castrucci. [Op. I.]

London Printed for & sold by In? Walsh . . . & In? & Ioseph Hare, &c.

[*c.* 1725.]

>Fol. pp. 2–49.
>BM. g. 237. a.

334. — With Walsh only in the imprint and 'N? 373' added to the title-page.

[*c.* 1730.]

>RCM.
>Walsh Cat. 18: 'Castrucci's Solos (for a Violin and a Bass). 6s. od. N? 373.'

335. Parte Prima Sonate a Violino e Violone o Cimbalo Dedicate alla Serenissima Altezza Reale La Principessa Anna. La Sonata quinta ed Ottaua ad Immitatione di Viola D'amore con il Sordino al Ponticello se Piace. Dà Pietro Castrucci Opera Seconda. (Parte Seconda Preludi Allemande Gighe Gavotte Minuetti e Ciaccona. Printed for I: Walsh.)

Printed for I. Walsh. N? 500.

Daily Journal, Jan. 22, 1734. (Twelve Solo's for a Violin, &c.)

>Fol. Illustrated title-page. pp. 2–11, 13–35, 37–39, 41–49, 51–65. Catalogue of 'New Musick and Editions of Musick Lately Printed for Iohn Walsh' on verso of p. 65. (Walsh Cat. 16a.)
>BM. g. 237. (*See* Frontispiece.)

336. — Another issue, without 'N? 500' on the title-page and without the catalogue.

[*c.* 1740.]

>RM. 16. c. 10.

See also No. 716. Geminiani (Francesco) and Castrucci (Pietro) XII Solos for a German Flute, &c.; No. 717. Geminiani (Francesco) and Castrucci (Pietro) Six Sonatas or Solos . . . for a Flute, &c.

CASTRUCCI (Prospero)

337. Sonate a Violino solo e Basso di Prospero Castrucci.

London. Printed for I. Walsh in Catherine Street in the Strand All' Eccellenza di Guglielmo Capel Conte d'Essex, Viceconte Maiden, Barone Capel di Hadham, Cavaliero della Giarrettiera, e Lord della Camera di S.M.B.

[*c.* 1745.]

>Fol. pp. 1–9, blank, 10–21, blank, 22–26.
>CUL.
>A reissue of the edition with the imprint 'Londra MDCCXXXIX.' (BM. g. 237. c.)
>Walsh Cat. 24a: 'Prospero Castrucci's Solos. 5s. od.'
>Walsh Cat. 25.

CATCH CLUB

338. The Catch Club or Merry Companions being a Choice Collection of the most Diverting Catches for Three and Four Voices Compos'd by the most Eminent Masters of the Age.

London Printed for I: Walsh . . . and In? and Ioseph Hare, &c.

[*c.* 1725.]

Obl. 4°.

339. The Catch Club or Merry Companions being a Choice Collection of the most Diverting Catches for Three and Four Voices Compos'd by the late Mr. Henry Purcell Dr. Blow &c. 1st part. price 2ˢ 6ᵈ

London Printed for I: Walsh . . . N? 297.

The Second Book of the Catch Club or Merry Companions being a Choice Collection of the most Diverting Catches for Three and Four Voices Compos'd by the late Mr. Henry Purcell Dr. Blow &c. 2ᵈ part. price 2ˢ 6ᵈ N? 298.

London. Printed for and Sold by I. Walsh, &c.

Daily Post, March 15, 1733. (Where may be had.)

    Obl. 4°. 2 parts. 'An Alphabetical Table', &c. pp. 48, each part.
    BM. B. 355. BUC gives Hereford and Rowe (not examined).
    On the title-page of part 1 the words 'the late Mr. Henry Purcell Dr. Blow &c.' have been substituted for 'the most Eminent Masters of the Age,' which appears on No. 338, and the names of John and Joseph Hare have been erased from the imprint.

340. — Another edition. Same title-pages as No. 338.

[*c.* 1740.]

    Obl. 4° 2 parts.
    BM. B. 355. a. RCM.
    With 'An Alphabetical Table' of part 1 on the verso of the title-page.
    Several pages of both parts have been re-engraved.
    Walsh Cat. 18, p. 12: 'Hen? Purcell's works. Two Books of Celebrated Catches. 5s. od. N? 298.'
    Walsh Cat. 18, p. 27: 'Vocal Musick. 2 Books of Catches. 5s. od. N? 297.'

341. The Catch Club or Merry Companions. A Collection of Favourite Catches for Three and Four Voices Compos'd by Mr Henry Purcell, Dr Blow, and the most Eminent Authors. Book I.

London. Printed for I. Walsh, &c.

— Book II.

Public Advertiser, Feb. 23, 1762.

    Obl. fol. pp. 1–59. (Continuous pagination.)
    BM. E. 137. d. (Wanting title-page of Book II.) CUL. Manchester.
    An enlarged edition of No. 340, containing 200 Catches in place of 152 in the smaller edition.

342. The Catch Club or Merry Companions. A Collection of Favourite Catches for Three and Four Voices Compos'd by M.ͬ Henry Purcell, D.ͬ Blow, and the most Eminent Authors. Selected by C. I. F. Lampe.
London. Printed for I. Walsh, &c.

[*c.* 1765.]

Obl. fol. 'A Table of the Catches'. pp. 29.
BM. E. 155. Mitchell. Others in BUC, not examined.
The same title-page as No. 341, but with 'Selected by C. I. F. Lampe' in the place of 'Book I'. The contents are the same as Book I, No. 341, 112 Catches.

343. Catche.ͦ for Flutes or A Collection of the best Catches contriv'd and fitted for 1:2:3: or 4 Flutes . . . y.ͤ whole fairly Engraven and carefully Corrected.
Printed for J. Walsh, &c.

[*c.* 1730.]

Obl. 8°. ff. 24. Printed on one side only.
Walsh Cat. 18: 'Catches for the Flute. 2s. od. N.ͦ 15.'
Smith 395 (BM. b. 171. a. (1.)) with Walsh only in the imprint and 'N.ͦ 15' added to the title-page.

CATO

344. The Favourite Songs in the Opera call'd Cato.
London Printed for and sold by I: Walsh, &c.

Daily Journal, Nov. 25, 1732.

Fol. Passe-partout title-page. ff. 20. Printed on one side only.
B.M. H. 130. a.
Pasticcio, music probably from Hasse's opera 'Catone in Utica', with recitatives by Handel.
Words by Metastasio, English words by Samuel Humphreys. One number included in 'Le Delizie dell' Opere', Vol. II, pp. 222–4.

345. — With 'N.ͦ 286' added to the title-page.

[*c.* 1732.]

Walsh Cat. 18: 'Favourite Songs in Cato. 2s. 6d. N.ͦ 286.'

CAVALARI (Francesco)

346. Six Solos for a German Flute or Violin with a Thorough Bass for the Harpsicord or Violoncello. Compos'd by Sig.ͬ Francesco Cavalari.
London. Printed for I. Walsh, &c.

[*c.* 1750.]

Fol. pp. 2–4, blank, 6–10, blank, 12–16, blank, 18–22, blank, 24–28, blank, 30–36.
BM. g. 270. l. (2.) Rowe.

CECERE (Carlo)

347. Twenty Four Duets for Two German Flutes or Violins Compos'd by Sig^r Carlo Cecere of Naples.
  London. Printed for I. Walsh, &c.

  Public Advertiser, Feb. 27, 1761.

  > Fol. pp. 19.
  > BM. g. 280. (5.) Rowe.

CEPHALUS and PROCRIS

  > *See* No. 319. Carey (Henry) Songs in Cephalus and Procris; No. 320. Carey (Henry) The Tunes, Airs and Dances in . . . Cephalus and Procris, &c.

CERVETTO (Giacobbe) *the Elder*

348. Twelve Solos for a Violoncello With a Thorough Bass for the Harpsicord. Dedicated to S. A. S. E. Monseigneur l'Elector Palatin, Duc de Bavière Juliers, Clèves et Berg, Prince de Meurs, Marquis de Berg-op-Zoom. &c. Composed by Sig^r Cervetto Opera Seconda.
  London. Printed for I. Walsh, &c.

  [*c.* 1750.]

  > Obl. fol. Dedication. pp. 57.
  > BM. e. 278. a.
  > A reissue of the edition with the imprint 'Londra Printed for the Author and sold at all the Music-Shops' and with 'Opera Seconda' added to the title-page, but without the list of subscribers.

349. Six Sonatas or Trios For three Violoncellos or two Violins and a Bass Dedicated to Signora Leonora Saluadori Composed by Giacob Baseui detto Ceruetto. Printed for I. Walsh, &c.

  London Daily Post, and General Advertiser, April 1, 1741. (Cervetto's new Sonatas for two Violins and a Bass or three Violoncello's.)

  > Fol. Parts.
  > BM. g. 274. d. (2.) RAM.
  > Walsh Cat. 18: 'Cervetto's Sonatas. 4s. od.'

CESARINI (Carlo Francesco)

  See No. 971. Love's Triumph.

CHABOUD (Pierre)

350. Solos for a German Flute a Hoboy or Violin with a Thorough Bass for the Harpsicord or Bass Violin being all Choice pieces by ye greatest Authors and fitted to the German Flute by Sig^r Pietro Chaboud. Note the following Pieces

may be had where these are sold Instructions for Learners on the German Flute. Lully's Lessons for yͤ German Flute Schichards 10ᵗʰ and 20ᵗʰ Operas for the German Flute.

London Printed for I: Walsh . . . and Inͦ & Ioseph Hare, &c.

[*c.* 1725.]
Fol. pp. 24.
BM. g. 422. j. (3.)

351. Solos for a German Flute a Hoboy or Violin with a Thorough Bass for the Harpsicord or Bass Violin. Being all Choice pieces by the greatest Authors and fitted to the German Flute by Sigͬ Pietro Chaboud. Parte Secondo. Note the following Pieces may be had where these are sold Instructions for Learners on the German Flute Lully's Lessons for the German Flute Schichards 10ᵗʰ & 20ᵗʰ Operas & Pietro's 1ˢᵗ Book for the German Flute.

London Printed for I: Walsh . . . and Inͦ and Ioseph Hare, &c.

[*c.* 1725.]
Fol. pp. 25.
BM. g. 422. j. (3.)

CHABRAN (CHARLES)

See No. 310. Campioni (Carlo Antonio) and Chabran (Charles) Six Favourite Solos for a Violin with a Bass, &c.

CHAPLET

The Chaplet, being a Collection of Twelve English Songs.
See No. 738. Greene (Maurice)

CHARKE (RICHARD)

352. Medley Overture in 4 Parts.
Printed for and sold by John Walsh, &c.

Country Journal: or, The Craftsman, Dec. 25, 1736. (Medley Overtures by Arne, Lampe, Charke and Prelure, in Four Parts—Just publish'd.)

Fol.
Walsh Cat. 18, under 2 Violins and a Bass: 'Medley Overtures by Arne . . . each 6d.'
Subsequently issued in a collection, 'Six Medley or Comic Overtures', 1763. (BM. g. 100. c.) (*See* No. 1160. Overtures.)

CHINZER (GIOVANNI)

353. Six Sonatas or Trios for Two German Flutes or Two Violins and a Bass Compos'd by Sigͬ Giovanni Chinzer.

London. Printed for I. Walsh, &c.

General Advertiser, Jan. 9, 1750.

>Fol. 3 parts.
>BM. g. 241. (3.) RM. 17. d. 2. (13.)

CHURCH (JOHN)

354. An Introduction to Psalmody Containing usefull Instructions for Young Beginners explain'd in a familiar and easie manner, by way of Dialogue. By Iohn Church a member of the Collegiate Church of St Peters Westminster, and Gentleman in Ordinary of His Majesty's Chapel Royal. To which is added a select Number of ye best Psalm Tunes extant in three and four Parts; as they are now sung in Parish-Churches & other places of Divine Worship. Also a Collection, containing some Hymns Compos'd by Dr Willm Croft, & some Anthems and Hymns by Mr Tho: Ravenscroft and the Author, for one two and three Voices, &c.

London Printed for I. Walsh . . . and I^no and Ioseph Hare, &c.

[1723.]

>8°. pp. 122.
>BM. B. 834. Hirsch IV. 1481. Royal School of Church Music, Croydon. Cardiff. NLS. Rowe.

355. — With Walsh only in the imprint and 'N.° 208' added to the title-page.

Daily Journal, Nov. 25, 1730.

>Walsh Cat. 18: 'Church's Psalmody. 3s. od. N.° 208.'

CIAMPI (LEGRENZIO VINCENZO)

356. The Favourite Songs in the Opera Call'd Adriano in Siria.
London. Printed for I. Walsh, &c.

General Advertiser, March 16, 1750.

>Fol. pp. 2–22.
>First Edition Bookshop Cat. 43. No. 19.

357. The Favourite Songs in the Opera Call'd Adriano in Siria Sig Ciampi Price 2/6.
London. Printed for I. Walsh, &c.

[c. 1755.]

>Fol. pp. 2–22 (bottom centre).
>RCM.
>'Adriano in Siria Sig Ciampi Price 2/6' is in MS. With additional top centre pagination 75–95 from 'Le Delizie dell' Opere', Vol. VI.

358. Arie 6. Composte dal Sig.ʳ Vincenzo Ciampi. To which are added Some Favourite Songs from the late Italian Comic Operas.
London. Printed for I. Walsh, &c.

Whitehall Evening-Post, April 23–25, 1754. (Six New Italian Songs.)

Fol. pp. 2–37.
BM. H. 348. d. (7.) RCM.
Also contains songs by Bernasconi and Galuppi.
Republished in 'Le Delizie dell' Opere', Vol. VII, pp. 148–83.

359. Arie 8. Composta dal Sig.ʳ Vincenzo Ciampi.
London. Printed for I. Walsh, &c.

London Evening-Post, March 19–21, 1751. (Of whom may be had. Eight new Italian Songs.)

Fol. pp. 2–33.
BM. H. 1652. w. (19.) Gresham.
Walsh Cat. 25: 'Ciampi's 8 Songs. 5s. od.'

360. The Favourite Songs in the Opera Call'd Bertoldo By Sig.ʳ Ciampi.
London. Printed for I. Walsh, &c.

Public Advertiser, Jan. 11, 1755.

Fol. Passe-partout title-page. pp. 20.
BM. H. 348. e. (8.) Gresham. RCM. Rowe.
Text altered from Carlo Goldoni.

361. N.º I. The Favourite Songs in the Opera Call'd Bertoldo By Ciampi.
London. Printed for I. Walsh, &c.

Public Advertiser, Jan. 29, 1762.

Fol. Passe-partout title-page. pp. 2–12.
RCM. Gresham.
'By Ciampi' is in MS. Bound up with this work is a duet from 'Il Mercato di Malmantile' by Galuppi, pp. 31–34.
Republished in 'Le Delizie dell' Opere', Vol. X, pp. 182–192, 29–32 (with Duet from 'Il Mercato di Malmantile').

362. The Favourite Songs in the Opera Call'd Bertoldo By Sig.ʳ Ciampi. N.º 2.
London. Printed by I. Walsh, &c.

Public Advertiser, Jan. 29, 1762.

Fol. Passe-partout title-page. pp. 1–10 (bottom centre), 11–17 (top centre), 18–20 (bottom centre).
RCM.
'N.º 2' is in MS. With additional top centre pagination 128–147 from 'Le Delizie dell' Opere', Vol. VII. The title-page bears the note in contemporary MS. 'This number of the

G   81

Songs in Bertoldo was published originally in 1749, and republished with the preceding number in 1762.'
    Randall Cat.: 'Bertoldi, 2 Collections, Ciampi, each 2s. 6d.'

363. Six Concertos in Six Parts for three Violins, a Tenor with a Bass for the Harpsicord or Violoncello Compos'd by Sig.ʳ Vincenzo Ciampi. Opera Sexta.
    London. Printed for I. Walsh, &c.

Public Advertiser, Feb. 13, 1754.

> Fol. 6 parts.
> BM. g. 643. a.

364. Six Concertos for the Organ or Harpsicord with Instrumental Parts for Violins &c. Compos'd by Signor Vincenzo Ciampi. Opera Settima.
    London. Printed for I. Walsh, &c.

Whitehall Evening-Post, Jan. 6–8, 1756.

> Fol. pp. 2–40.
> BM. g. 643. CUL. (Organ or Harpsicord part only in each.)

365. The Favourite Songs in the Opera Call'd Didone By Sig.ʳ Ciampi.
    London. Printed for I. Walsh, &c.

Public Advertiser, Jan. 30, 1754.

> Fol. Passe-partout title-page. pp. 24.
> BM. H. 348. e. (7.)

366. — With a slightly different title-page, three operas added to list.

> [*c.* 1754.]
> Fol. Passe-partout title-page. pp. 24.
> BM. G. 201. (2.)

367. The Favourite Songs in the Opera Call'd Didone By Sig.ʳ Ciampi 1754.
    London. Printed for I. Walsh, &c.

> [*c.* 1760.]
> Fol. Passe-partout title-page. pp. 1–24 (top corner).
> RCM.
> '1754' is in MS. With additional top centre pagination 183–206 from 'Le Delizie dell' Opere', Vol. VIII.

368. The Favourite Songs in the Opera Call'd Il Negligente.
    London. Printed for I. Walsh, &c.

General Advertiser, Dec. 21, 1749.

> Fol. Passe-partout title-page. pp. 2–24.
> Gresham. RCM. Rowe.
> Republished in 'Le Delizie dell' Opere', Vol. VI, pp. 96–118.

369. A Tenth favourite Opera Overture, for Violins and French Horns: Compos'd by Sig. Vincenzo Ciampi. Price 2s.
Printed for J. Walsh, &c.

Public Advertiser, April 6, 1764.

Fol. Parts.
Subsequently issued in a collection as No. 4 of 'Six Overtures in 8 Parts . . . Compos'd by Sig.ʳ Bach Jomelli Galuppi Perez Sixth Collection.' (BM. g. 212. a. 1764. *See* No. 1158.) Other numbers in this series are under J. C. Bach, B. Galuppi, D. Perez and N. Jomelli.

370. Six Solos for a Violin with a Bass for the Harpsicord or Violoncello Compos'd by Sig.ʳ Vincenzo Ciampi. Opera Quinta.
London. Printed for I. Walsh, &c.

[*c.* 1753.]
Fol. pp. 1–19, blank, 21–28.
BM. g. 223. y. (1.)
With 'N.º XXXV' printed at the top of the title-page.

371. Sonate per Cembalo Composte da Vincenzo Ciampi.
London. Printed for I. Walsh, &c.

London Evening-Post, Oct. 26–29, 1751. (Six Sonatas or Lessons.)

Obl. fol. pp. 27.
BM. e. 5. k. (1.) Rowe. Tenbury.

372. Six Sonatas for two Violins or German Flutes with a Thorough Bass for the Harpsichord. Composed by Sig.ʳ Vincenzo Ciampi. Opera Secondo.
London. Printed for I. Walsh, &c.

[*c.* 1755.]
Fol. Parts.
RCM.

373. Six Sonatas for two Violins or German Flutes with a Thorough Bass for the Harpsichord Composed by Sig.ʳ Vincenzo Ciampi. [Op. 3.]
London. Printed for I. Walsh, &c.

[*c.* 1755.]
Fol. 3 parts.
RAM.

374. Six Sonatas for two Violins or German Flutes with a Thorough Bass for the Harpsichord. Composed by Sig.ʳ Vincenzo Ciampi. [Op. 4.]
London. Printed for I. Walsh, &c.

[*c.* 1757.]
Fol. Parts.
RCM.

375. The Favourite Songs in the Opera Call'd Trionfo di Camilla.
London. Printed for I. Walsh, &c.

General Advertiser, April 20, 1750.

Fol. Passe-partout title-page. pp. 2–23.
Rowe.
Words by S. Stampiglia.

See also Nos. 565, 566. Delizie dell' Opere. Vols. X, XI; No. 1419. The Summer's
Tale . . . Music by . . . Ciampi, &c.; No. 1452. Tolomeo.

CIRO

376. The favourite Songs in the Opera call'd Cyrus.
London Printed for & sold by I: Walsh . . . & In? & Ioseph Hare, &c.

[1721.]

Fol. Passe-partout title-page. ff. 14. Printed on one side only.
BM. H. 230. f. (3.) (Wanting the title-page.) RCM. Rowe.
Music attributed to Giovanni Bononcini, and to Ariosti (Burney).
Walsh Cat. 18, under Bononcini's works as: 'The Favourite Songs in the Operas of Cyrus
& Arsaces. 3s. od. N? 253.' This was a later issue (*c.* 1730) with Walsh only in the imprint
and 'N? 253' added to the title-page.
'Arsaces' 'Arsace' was an altered version of Orlandini's 'Amore e Maestà' with additional
music by F. Amadei. (Loewenberg.)
See also No. 205 Bononcini (Giovanni)

CIRO RICONOSCIUTO

377. The Favourite Songs in the Opera Call'd Ciro Reconosciuto. [1st Set.]
London. Printed for I. Walsh, &c.
— 2ᵈ Set.

Public Advertiser, Feb. 13, 1759; April 4, 1759. (In 2 cols.)

Fol. Passe-partout title-pages. pp. 1–21, 22–43.
BM. G. 206. RM. 13. c. 20. (4.) RCM.
'2ᵈ Set' is in MS.
Attributed to Gioacchino Cocchi.
Republished in 'Le Delizie dell' Opere', Vol. IX, pp. 49–92.
Randall Cat.: 'Ciro Riconosciuto, 2 Collections, Cocchi, each 2s. 6d.'

CLARKE (JEREMIAH)

378. I will love Thee O Lord. An Anthem.
[J. Walsh?]

[*c.* 1731.]

BM. Add. MSS. 30931, ff. 125–9.
Five leaves printed on one side only each headed 'Divine Harmony', probably intended
to form part of a Third Collection of that work. *See* Nos. 1544, 1545. Weldon (John)

CLAYTON (THOMAS)

379. Songs in the Opera Call'd Arsinoe Queen of Cyprus.
London Printed for & Sould by I: Walsh, &c.

[*c.* 1730.]

Fol. pp. 49.
Music by Thomas Clayton whose name does not appear on the title-page.
Walsh Cat. 18: 'The Opera of Arsinoe. 9s. od. N? 239.'
Walsh Cat. 15*b*: 'Opera of Arsinoe. (With Symphonies.) 9s. od.'
Smith 220 and 600 with Walsh only in the imprint and 'N? 239' added to the title-page.
Words from the Italian of Tomaso Stanzani.

380. Songs in the New Opera Call'd Rosamond as they are perform'd at the Theatre Royall Compos'd by M? Tho. Clayton.
London Printed for I. Walsh, &c.

[*c.* 1730.]

Fol. pp. 47.
Walsh Cat. 18: 'The Opera of Rosamond. 9s. od. N? 240.'
Smith 247 (BM. H. 105.) with Walsh only in the imprint and 'N? 240' added to the title-page.
Words by Joseph Addison.

CLEMENZA DI TITO

381. The Favourite Songs in the Opera Call'd La Clemenza di Tito.
London. Printed for I. Walsh, &c.

Public Advertiser, Feb. 16, 1760.

Fol. Passe-partout title-page. pp. 2–19
BM. G. 206. a. (2.) RM. 13. c. 20. (5.) RCM. London University. DAM.
Pasticiccio, mainly by G. Cocchi.

CLOES (NICOLAS)

382. One Hundred French Songs Set for a Voice, German Flute, Violin, Harpsicord and Pandola. Dedicated to Their Royal Highnesses The Prince and Princess of Wales, By their most Obedient Humble Servant Nicolas Cloes.
London. Printed for I. Walsh, &c.

General Advertiser, Nov. 6, 1749.

Obl. 8°. 'Table'. pp. 108.
BM. B. 361.
This was Book I of 'Canzonets for two Voices,' &c. (*See* No. 314.)

383. — Another issue.

[*c.* 1752.]

BM. A. 1107.
With the words 'By their most Obedient Humble Servant Nicolas Cloes' erased from the plate of the title-page.

CLOTILDA

384. Songs In The New Opera, Call'd Clotilda The Songs done in Italian and English as they are Perform'd at yᵉ Queens Theatre the whole Carefully Corected. Sold by I: Walsh, &c.

[*c.* 1730.]

Fol. pp. 52.
Walsh Cat. 18: 'The Opera of Clotilda. 9s. 0d. N⁰ 238.'
Smith 296 (BM. H. 328.) with Walsh only in the imprint and 'N⁰ 238' added to the title-page.
Music by Francesco Conti and others. Words by Giovanni Battista Neri.

385. The Most Celebrated Aires & Duets In the Opera of Clotilda: Curiously fitted and Contriv'd for two Flutes: With their Symphonys introduc'd in a Compleat manʳ The whole fairly Engraven, &c.
Printed for J. Walsh, &c.

[*c.* 1730.]

Fol. 2 parts.
Walsh Cat. 18: 'Clotilda Aires. 3s. 0d. N⁰ 78.'
Smith 326 with Walsh only in the imprint and 'N⁰ 78' added to the title-page.
Music by Francesco Conti and others.

386. Phyrrus and Clotilda Aires (Single Flute). 2s. 0d.

[*c.* 1730.]

Walsh Cat. 18.
Smith 338 and 339, and assumed to refer to separate issues of each opera, and which probably consisted of the First Flute parts of the editions for Two Flutes, with new title-pages, with Walsh only in the imprint. (*See* Nos. 385 and 1211.)

COBSTON ( )

See No. 882. Jupiter and Europa a Masque of Song's, &c.

COCCHI (GIOACCHINO)

387. Six Duettos For two Voices with Accompanyments for Violins or German Flutes Compos'd by Sigʳ Gio. Cocchi. Opera II.
London. Printed for I. Walsh, &c.

Public Advertiser, May 14, 1764.

Obl. fol. pp. 2–38.
BM. E. 65. Hirsch. IV. 3. (3.) RAM.

388. Six Duets for two Violoncello's Compos'd by Sigʳ Gio: Cocchi. Opera Terza.

    London. Printed for I. Walsh, &c.

    Public Advertiser, May 14, 1764.

> Fol. pp. 2–15.
> BM. g. 225. b. (2.) Cardiff.

389. The Favourite Songs in the Opera Call'd La Famiglia in Scompiglio. Price 4ˢ

    London. Printed for I. Walsh, &c.

    Public Advertiser, April 20, 1762.

> Fol. Passe-partout title-page. pp. 1–13, blank, 14–22, blank, 31–34 (bottom centre).
> Gresham. RCM.
> Consists of the two Collections originally issued at 2ˢ each.
> '4ˢ' altered from '2ˢ' in MS. With additional pagination 77–89 on pp. 1–13.
> Pp. 1–22 republished in 'Le Delizie dell' Opere', Vol. X, pp. 123–45. Cocchi's name
appears at the top of the items in this work.

390. The Favourite Songs in the Opera Call'd Issipile.

    London. Printed for I. Walsh, &c.

    Public Advertiser, April 5, 1758.

> Fol. Passe-partout title-page. pp. 21.
> BM. G. 179. a. (1.) RCM. DAM.
> Cocchi's name appears at the top of the items in the work.
> Randall Cat.: 'Issipile. Cocchi. 2s. 6d.'
> Republished in 'Le Delizie dell' Opere', Vol. VIII, pp. 65–85.

391. Six Sonatas for the Harpsichord with accompanyments for two Violins, and a Violoncello. Compos'd by Sig. Gio. Cocchi. Op. 4. Price 10s. 6d.

    Printed and sold at the late Mr. J. Walsh's in Catherine street, in the Strand.

    Public Advertiser, May 17, 1766.

392. The Favourite Songs in the Opera Call'd Tito Manlio By Sigʳ Cocchi.

    London. Printed for I. Walsh, &c.

    Public Advertiser, March 5, 1761.

> Fol. Passe-partout title-page. pp. 19.
> BM. G. 206. i. (1.) Mitchell.
> Republished in 'Le Delizie dell' Opere', Vol. XI, pp. 80–98.

393. The Favourite Songs in the Opera Call'd Zenobia.

    London. Printed for I. Walsh, &c.

    Public Advertiser, Feb. 6, 1758.

> Fol. Passe-partout title-page. pp. 2–20.
> BM. G. 202; G. 179. a. (2.) RM. 13. c. 22. (11.) RCM. DAM.

The BM. copy (G. 202) has in addition 13 pages of an unidentified work from which the pagination has been erased.

Cocchi's name appears at the top of the items in this work.

Randall Cat.: 'Zenobia. Cocchi. 2s. 6d.'

Republished in 'Le Delizie dell' Opere', Vol. VIII, pp. 33–64.

See also No. 33. Alessandro nelle Indie; No. 38. Antigona; No. 45. Arianna e Teseo; No. 105. Attalo; No. 276. Calamita de' Cuori; No. 377. Ciro Ricono-sciuto; No. 381. Clemenza di Tito; No. 522. Creso; Nos. 565, 566. Delizie dell' Opere. Vols. X, XI; No. 567. Demetrio; No. 672. Galuppi (Baldassare) The Favourite Songs in . . . Il Filosofo di Campagna; No. 1129. Nerone; No. 1154. Overtures. Six Favourite Overtures . . . by Sig.ʳ Cocchi, &c.; No. 1193. Perez (Davidde) and Cocchi (Gioacchino) The Favourite Songs in . . Farnace; Nos. 1419, 1420. The Summer's Tale . . . Music by . . . Cocchi, &c.; No. 1452. Tolomeo; No. 1474. Tutore e la Pupilla; No. 1526. Vologeso.

COCK

A Cock and a Bull. [Song.]

See No. 1451. To. To take a good part, the squeeze of a hand, &c.

COFFARELLO (   )

See No. 105. Attalo

COLLECTION

A Collection of Melodies for the Psalms of David, According to the version of Christopher Smart, &c.

See No. 1233. Psalms

COMEDIA IN COMEDIA

See No. 394. Commedia in Commedia

COMIC TUNES

The Celebrated Comic Tunes to the Opera Dances, &c.

See No. 787. Hasse (Johann Adolph)

COMICAL SONGS

See Songs

COMMEDIA IN COMMEDIA

394. The Favourite Songs in the Opera Call'd La Comedia in Comedia. London. Printed for I. Walsh, &c.

General Advertiser, Jan. 6, 1749.

Fol. Passe-partout title-page. pp. 2–21.
BM. G. 805. r. (2.) RCM. Pendlebury. Rowe.
The music is by Rinaldo da Capua. Includes a song by Pietro Pulli in 'Orazio'
Republished in 'Le Delizie dell' Opere', Vol. VI, pp. 173–92.

COMPLEAT COUNTRY DANCING MASTER

See Country Dancing Master.

CONCERTO

395. (Recommended to all Musical Societies and Lovers of Musick) Numb. III
of a Select Concerto for Violins, German Flutes and other Instruments In Seven
Parts. By a very eminent Italian Author. Never before printed. To be continued
Monthly. With a Concerto from the Works of the best Authors. At 1s. 6d. each.
Printed for John Walsh, &c.

London Evening-Post, April 4–6, 1734. (Where may be had.)

This refers to the Concerto III 'Geminiani, N° 2. 502' in 'Select Harmony. Third Collection'.

No. 1 of this series was by Giacomo Facco, Nos. 2–4 were by Geminiani and Nos. 5 and
6 anonymous.
See No. 1362. Select Harmony.

CONFORTI or CONFORTO (Nicolò)

See No. 38. Antigona.

CONTI (Francesco)

See No. 384. Clotilda; No. 891. The Lady's Banquet 3ᵈ Book; No. 1146.
Ormisda.

CONTRIVANCES

Songs in the Contrivances.

See No. 321. Carey (Henry)

COOK (Henry)

See No. 751. Harmonia Anglicana. Book III.

COOKE (Benjamin)

See No. 1233. Psalms

CORBET ( )

See Corbett (William)

CORBETT (WILLIAM)

396. Le Bizzarie Universali a Quatro cio Due Violini, Viola e Basso Continuo Concerto's, in four Parts For two Violins, Tenor & Thrō Base for yᵉ Harpsicord, Humillissimo Dedicato a Sua Maesta Christianissima Composed by William Corbett, Delitante on all the new Gusto's in his Travels thro' Italy Opera VIII. NB. These Concertos may be play'd in 3 parts, 2 Hautboys, Flutes or German-Flutes. Entr'ed in the Hall according to Act of Parliament.
    London: Printed for the Author & sold at yᵉ shops.

Mist's Weekly Journal, June 15, 1728. (Mr. W. Corbet's Bizzaria's or Concerto's ... The Subscribers may have their Books, by sending the Rest of their Money to Mr. J. Walsh ... and Mr. Tho. Corbett ... where they are sold ... Price a Guinea.)
        Fol. Parts.
        BM. h. 51. Bod.

Fog's Weekly Journal, June 14, 1729: 'Corbett's Twelve Concertos for Violins, Hautboys, or German Flutes. Printed for and sold by John Walsh ... and Joseph Hare', &c.
        Walsh Cat. 18: '12 Concertos for all Instruments. £1. 1s. 0d.'

397. Six Sonatas for 2 Violins and a Bass. Op: 1ᵐᵃ 6s. 0d.
    [*c.* 1730.]
        Fol. Parts.
        Walsh Cat. 18.
        Smith 324 with Walsh only in the imprint.
        Not identified.

398. Six Sonatas for two Flutes and a Bass consisting of Preludes Allemands Corants Sarabands and Jiggs Composed by William Corbett Opera Secunda, &c.
    London. Printed for I. Walsh, &c.
    [*c.* 1730.]
        Fol. Parts.
        Walsh Cat. 18: 'Six Sonatas for 2 Flutes and a Bass. Op: 2da. 4s. 0d. Nº 84.'
        Smith 172 with Walsh only in the imprint and 'Nº 84' added to the title-page.

399. Six Sonatas with an Overture and Aires in 4 Parts for a Trumpet, Violin's and Hautboys Flute de Allmain Bassoons or Harpsicord Compos'd by William Corbett Opera Terza Note that all these Sonatas are to be Play'd wᵗʰ 3 Flutes & a Bass in yᵉ French Kay [*sic*] 3 notes Higher.
    [*c.* 1730.]
        Fol. 4 parts.
        Smith 285 (BM. h. 50. a.) with Walsh only in the imprint.
        Walsh Cat. 18: 'Six Sonatas for variety of Instruments. Opera Terza. 6s. 0d.'

400. Six Sonatas for 2 German Flutes and a Bass. Opera 4ta 4s. od. N° 80.

[*c.* 1730.]

> Walsh Cat. 18.
> Walsh Cat. 24*a*: 'Corbet's Sonatas (for 2 Ger^n Flutes or 2 Violins and a Bass).' Op. 4ta. 4s. od.
> Presumably may refer to an issue of Corbett's 'Six Sonata's a 3° for Two Violins & Thro = bass . . . Opera Quarta', published by L. Pippard. (BM. h. 50. (1, 2.) *See* Smith 324 and 244.

401. 5 Sets of Tunes made for several Plays for 2 Violins and a Bass. 7s. 6d.

[*c.* 1730.]

> Fol. Parts.
> Walsh Cat. 18.
> A collection of previously issued music for plays, not identified, but probably all included in Smith.

See also No. 750. Harmonia Anglicana. Book II.

CORDANS (BARTHOLOMEO)

See No. 1146. Ormisda

CORELLI (ARCANGELO)

402. The Score of the Four Operas, Containing 48 Sonatas Compos'd by Arcangelo Corelli. For two Violins and a Bass. N.B. The First and Third Opera being Compos'd for a Violoncello and Thorough Bass, of which the Variation being but little, they are put on the same Stave for the greater Facility in reading. These Compositions as they are now Printed in Score, are of great advantage to all Students, and Practitioners in Musick, they also make compleat Lessons for the Harpsicord. The whole Revis'd and Carefully Corrected By Dr. Pepusch. Vol. I.

London. Printed for & Sold by I: Walsh . . . N° 550.

The Score of the Twelve Concertos, Compos'd by Arcangelo Corelli. For two Violins and a Violoncello, with two Violins more, a Tenor, and Thorough Bass for Ripieno Parts, which may be Doubled at pleasure. These Compositions, as they are now Printed in Score, are of great advantage to all Students and Practitioners in Musick. The whole Revis'd & Carefully Corrected By Dr. Pepusch. Vol. II.

London. Printed for & Sold by I. Walsh. . . N° 551.

Country Journal : or, The Craftsman, May 17, 1735.

> Vol. I. Fol. Portrait of Corelli. 'H. Howard Pinx. V^{dr} Gucht Sculp.' pp. 44, 34, 54, 43.
> Vol. II. Fol. Portrait of Corelli. 'H. Howard Pinx. V^{dr} Gucht Sculp.' pp. 171.
> BM. g. 39. b. (1.) Hirsch III. 161. (Vol. I.) Hirsch III. 159. (Vol. II.)
> RCM and others in BUC not examined.

403. — Another edition.

London Daily Post, and General Advertiser, Oct. 20, 1740. (This Day are publish'd.); Dec. 11, 1740. 'A Second Edition', &c. (Of whom may be had.)

> Walsh Cat. 18: 'Sonatas and Concertos in Score. £2. 2s. od. № 551.'
> Walsh Cat. 25: 'Corelli's 48 Sonatas in Score. £1. 1s. od.'
> Benjamin Cooke published an edition of the Sonatas and Concertos in two volumes,
> edited by Dr. Pepusch, with portrait of Corelli by J. Cole. (*Daily Post,* April 7, 28, 1732.)

404. Concerti Grossi Con duoi Violini, e Violoncello di Concertino obligati, e
duoi altri Violini, Viola, e Basso di Concerto Grosso, ad arbitrio, che si potranno
radoppiare; Da Arcangelo Corelli di Fusignano. Opera sesta. XII Great Concertos,
or Sonatas, for two Violins and a Violoncello: or for two Violins more, a Tenor,
and a Thorough-Bass: which may be doubled at Pleasure. being the Sixth and last
work of Arcangelo Corelli. Note all the other Works of this author may be had
where this is sold.

London Printed for I. Walsh . . . № 370.

[*c.* 1730.]

> Fol. Parts. Portrait of Corelli. 'H. Howard pinx. W. Sherwin Sculp!' in Violino primo del
> concertino part.
> Hirsch III. 158. RCM. LX. E. 2. (1.) Others in BUC not examined.
> Smith 466 with Walsh only in the imprint and 'N! 370' added to the title-page.

405. — Another edition, with same title-page as No. 404, but with some plates
re-engraved.

[*c.* 1740.]

> Fol. Parts. Portrait of Corelli. 'H: Howard Pinx. V^dr Gucht Sculp.' in Violino primo del
> concertino part.
> BM. g. 45. c. (1.) RCM. LX. D. 3. (1.)
> Walsh Cat. 18: '12 Grand Concertos for Violins in 7 Parts Opera Sexta. 15s. od. № 370.'
> Roger and Le Cene previously published the work at Amsterdam (BM. f. 17.) and
> Henry Ribotteau, successor to Vaillant, advertised the work, *Post Man,* Dec. 30, 1714–Jan. 1,
> 1715.
> In competition with Walsh, Benjamin Cooke advertised an edition engraved by Thomas
> Cross, with a print of Corelli by J. Cole. (*Daily Post,* June 24, 25, 1728. Where may be had.)

406. — Another edition, with the same title-page as No. 405, but with more plates
re-engraved.

General Evening Post, Jan. 17–19, 1745. (New edition.)

> RM. 17. a. 3.

407. — Another edition.

General Advertiser, Oct. 25, 1749. (New edition.)

For 'The Score of the Twelve Concertos'. *See* No. 402. The Score of the Four Operas . . . Vol I . . . the Score of the Twelve Concertos Vol. II.

408. Corelli's XII Concertos [Op. 6] Transpos'd for Flutes viz a Fifth a Sixth a Consort and Voice Flute The proper Flute being nam'd to each Concerto and so adapted to the Parts that they perform in Consort with the Violins and other Instruments Throughout the Whole being the first of this Kind yet Publish'd.

London. Printed for and sold by I: Walsh . . . and In̊ & Ioseph Hare, &c.

Daily Post, Dec. 22, 1725. (Just publish'd.)

> Fol. Parts.
> RM. 17. f. 17. (Violoncello del Concertino part only.)

409. — With Walsh only in the imprint and 'N̊ 89' added to the title-page.

[*c.* 1730.]

> Mitchell. (Imperfect.)
> Walsh Cat. 18: '12 Concertos for 2 Flutes and a Bass contriv'd to play in Consort with the Violins. 8s. od. N̊ 89.'

410. Six Concertos for two Flutes and a Bass with a Through Bass for the Harpsicord Neatly Transpos'd from yᵉ great Concertos of Arcangelo Corelli Note all the Works of this Author may be had where this is sold.

London Printed for and sold by I: Walsh . . . N̊ 480.

[*c.* 1730.]

> Fol. Parts.
> Smith 580 (BM. i. 2. a.) with Walsh only in the imprint and 'N̊ 480' added to the title-page.
> Walsh Cat. 18: 'Corelli's 6 Concertos Transpos'd by Schickard. 4s. od.' (Refers presumably to this work.)

411. Correlli's 12 Concertos (for two Flutes). 6s. od.

> Walsh Cat. 15*b*. [*c.* 1733.]
> Walsh Cat. 16*a*: 'Corelli's Concertos for Flutes.' [*c.* 1733.]
> May refer to work in Walsh Cat. 18: 'Corelli His 2d and 4th Opera of Sonatas for two Flutes and a Bass 6s. od. N̊ 86.' *See* No. 418: 'Six Sonatas for two Flutes and a Bass' and No. 426: Six Setts of Airs for two Flutes and a Bass.'

412. Arcangelo Corelli Opera Prima XII Sonatas of three parts for two Violins and a Bass with a Through Bass for yᵉ Organ Harpsicord or Arch Lute Engrav'd from yᵉ Score and Carefully Corected by yᵉ best Italian Masters. Note there are five Operas of this Author's Engrav'd (wᶜʰ may be had Single or in one Volume) being all that are as yet Publish'd.

London Printed for I. Walsh . . . N̊ 364.

[*c.* 1730.]

Fol. Parts.

BM. g. 45. j. (2.) RCM. LVIII. E. 15. (With portrait 'H. Howard pinx. W. Sherwin Sculp!') Others in BUC not examined.

Smith 181, 477, and 596 with Walsh only in the imprint and 'N?. 364' added to the title-page. RAM. copy without 'N?. 364' or portrait.

413. — Another edition. Music re-engraved.

[*c.* 1740.]

Hirsch III. 160. (1.) RM. 17. a. 4. (1.) (With portrait of Corelli by Van der Gucht after Howard in the Violino primo part.) RCM. LVIII. E. 14. Others in BUC not examined.

Walsh Cat. 18: 'Four Operas consisting of 48 Sonatas for 2 Violins and a Bass. £1. 1s. od. N?. 367.'

414. — Another issue.

[*c.* 1760.]

BM. g. 45. k. (1) (Violino Primo part only.)

In competition with Walsh, Benjamin Cooke published Op. 1–4 with a portrait of Corelli engraved by I. (James) Cole. (*Daily Post*, June 24, 25, 1728. Where may be had.)

415. Arcangelo Corelli Opera Secunda XII Sonatas of three parts for two Violins and a Bass with a Through Bass for ye Organ Harpsicord or Arch Lute Engrav'd from ye Score and Carefully Corected by ye best Italian Masters. Note. there are five Operas of this Author Engrav'd wch may be had Single or in one Volume being all that are as yet Publishd.

London Printed for I Walsh . . . N?. 365.

[*c.* 1730.]

Fol. Parts.

BM. g. 45. j. (3.) RCM. LVIII. E. 15. (With portrait, 'H. Howard pinx. W. Sherwin Sculp!, Others in BUC not examined.

Smith 181, 477, and 596 with Walsh only in the imprint and 'N?. 365 'added to the title-page. RAM. copy without 'N?. 365' or portrait.

416. — Another edition. Music re-engraved.

[*c.* 1740.]

Hirsch III. 160. (2.) RM. 17. a. 4. (2.) RCM. LVIII. E. 14. (With portrait of Corelli by Van der Gucht after Howard.)

Walsh Cat. 18: 'Four Operas consisting of 48 Sonatas for 2 Violins and a Bass. £1. 1s. od. N?. 367.'

417. — Another issue.

[*c.* 1760.]

BM. g. 45. k. (2.) (Violino Primo part only.)

Title-page adapted from that of Opera Prima by a label with 'Second' in MS. pasted over 'Prima'.

In competition with Walsh, Benjamin Cooke published Op. 1–4 with a portrait of Corelli engraved by I. (James) Cole. (*Daily Post*, June 24, 25, 1728. Where may be had.)

418. Six Sonatas for two Flutes and a Bass by Arcangelo Corelli Collected out of yᵉ Choicest of his Works and Carefully Transpos'd and Contriv'd for two Flutes and a Bass the whole fairly Engraven Note this is the 2ᵈ Collection.
London Printed for I. Walsh . . . N° 86.

[*c.* 1730.]

Fol. Parts.
Walsh Cat. 18: 'Corelli. His 2d and 4th Operas of Sonatas for two Flutes and a Bass. 6s. od. N° 86.' *See* No. 426.
Smith 255 (BM. K. 5. c. 9. (1.)) with Walsh only in the imprint and 'N° 86' added to the title-page.
This work consists of Sonatas 2, 5, 6, 7, 1, and 4 of Op. 2.

419. Arcangelo Corelli Opera Terza XII Sonatas of three parts for two Violins and a Bass with a Through Bass for yᵉ Organ Harpsicord or Arch Lute Engrav'd from yᵉ Score and Carefully Corected by yᵉ best Italian Masters Note. there are five Operas of this Author's Engrav'd (wᶜʰ: may be had Single or in one Volume) being all that are as yet Publishd.
London Printed for I. Walsh . . . N° 366.

[*c.* 1730.]

Fol. Parts.
BM. g. 45. j. (4.) RCM. LVIII. E. 15. (With portrait, 'H. Howard pinx. W. Sherwin Sculp?') Others in BUC not examined.
Smith 181, 477, and 596 with Walsh only in the imprint and 'N° 366' added to the title-page. RAM. copy without 'N° 366' or portrait.

420. — Another edition. Music re-engraved.

[*c.* 1740.]

Hirsch III. 160. (3.) RM. 17. a. 4. (3.) RCM. LVIII. E. 14. (With portrait of Corelli by Van der Gucht after Howard.)
Walsh Cat. 18: 'Four Operas consisting of 48 Sonatas for 2 Violins and a Bass. £1. 1s. od. N° 367.'

421. — Another issue.

[*c.* 1760.]

BM. g. 45. k. (5.) (Violino Primo part only.)
In competition with Walsh, Benjamin Cooke published Op. 1–4 with a portrait of Corelli engraved by I. (James) Cole. (*Daily Post*, June 24, 25, 1728. Where may be had.)

422. Concerti Grossi Con Due Violini Viola e Violoncello di Concertino obligati,

e Due altri Violini e Basso di Concerto Grosso. Composti delli Sei Sonate del Opera Terza D' Arcangelo Corelli Per Francesco Geminiani. N.B. The Works of this Author may be had where these are sold, viz. 12 Solos for a Violin and Bass, 12 Concertos for Violins in 7 Parts, and Corelli's 12 Solos made into Concertos.

London. Printed for and Sold by I. Walsh . . . N̥ 569.

Country Journal, Nov. 22, 1735. (Just Published.)

> Fol. Parts.
> RM. 17. f. 16. BM. h. 205. a. (1.) (Violoncello part only.) RCM. Others in BUC not examined.
> Nos. 1, 3, 4, 9, 10, and 11 of Sonatas, Op. 3.
> Walsh Cat. 18: 'Corellis 6 Sonatas made Concertos in 7 Parts. 6s. od. 'N̥ 569.'

423. Arcangelo Corelli Opera Quarta XII Sonatas of three parts for two Violins and a Bass with a Through Bass for yᵉ Organ Harpsicord or Arch Lute Engrav'd from yᵉ Score and Carefully Corected by yᵉ best Italian Masters Note there are five Operas of this Author Engrav'd wᶜʰ may be had Single or in one Volume being all that are as yet Publishd.

London Printed for I Walsh . . . N̥ 367.

[*c.* 1730.]

> Fol. Parts.
> BM. g. 45. j. (5.) RCM. LVIII. E. 15. (With portrait, 'H. Howard pinx. W. Sherwin Sculp!') Others in BUC not examined.
> Smith 181, 477, and 596 with Walsh only in the imprint and 'N̥ 367' added to the title-page. RAM. copy without 'N̥ 367' or portrait.

424. — Another edition. Music re-engraved.

[*c.* 1740.]

> Hirsch III. 160. (4.) RM. 17. a. 4. (4.) RCM. LVIII. E. 14. (With portrait of Corelli by Van der Gucht after Howard.)
> Walsh Cat. 18: 'Four Operas consisting of 48 Sonatas for 2 Violins and a Bass. £1. 1s. od. N̥ 367.

425. — Another issue.

[*c.* 1760.]

> BM. g. 45. k. (7.) (Violino Primo part only.)
> In competition with Walsh, Benjamin Cooke published Op. 1–4 with a portrait of Corelli engraved by I. (James) Cole. (*Daily Post*, June 24, 25, 1728. Where may be had.)

426. Six Setts of Airs for two Flutes and a Bass by Arcangelo Correlli, being the Choicest of his Preludes, Allmands, Sarabands, Corants, Minuets, and Jiggs. Collected out of his Several Opera's Transpos'd and fitted to yᵉ Flute with yᵉ Aprobation of our Eminent Masters, pr. 3s.

London Printed for I. Walsh . . . N̥ 86.

[*c.* 1730.]

Obl. fol. Parts.

This work consists of arrangements of Sonatas from Op. 4.

Smith 107. Title from Rowe earlier edition and Inglefield. (Leighton Buzzard.) Presumably reissued with Walsh only in the imprint and 'N.º 86' added to the title-page.

Walsh Cat. 18: 'Corelli. His 2d and 4th Operas of Sonatas for two Flutes and a Bass. 6s. od. N.º 86.' (*See* No. 418.)

427. Parte Prima Sonate a Violino e Violone o Cimbalo dedicate all altezza serenissima Electorale di Sofia Charlotta Electrice di Brandenburgo, Principessa di Brunswich, et Luneburgo, Duchessa di Prusia, e di Magdeburgo, Cleves, Giuliers, Berga, Stetino, Pomerania, Cassubia, e Devandali in Silesia, C Rossen, Burgravia, di Norimberg, Principessa di Halberstatt, Minden, e Camin, Contessa di Hohenzollern, e Ravensburg, Ravenstein, Lauenburge, Buttau. Da Archangelo Corelli da Fusignano Opera Quinta. (Parte Seconda Preludii Allemande Correnti Gighe Sarabande Gavotte e Follia Da Archangelo Corelli.) [All in capitals.]

Sold by Iohn Walsh . . . at the Harp and Hautboy in Katherine Street near Somerset House in the Strand London.

London Gazette, August 26–29, 1700. (Twelve Sonnata's in Two Parts: The First Part, Solo's for a Violin, a Bass Violin, Viol, and Harpsichord, The Second, Preludes, Almands, Corants, Sarabands, and Jigs, with the Spanish Folly . . . being his Fifth and Last Opera, &c.)

Obl. fol. 2 parts. Dedication (p. 2), pp. 3–70.

BM. d. 73. g.

This appears to be of 'The first Impression' by Walsh with title-page as in the following item (No. 428) but no illustrated frontispiece. Smith 31.

The earlier editions from Smith are included here as the whole subject is complicated and references not easily identified in some cases. Some copies of the various issues in BUC not examined or included.

428. Parte Prima Sonate a Violino e Violone o Cimbalo, &c. (Parte Seconda Preludii, &c.)

Sold by Iohn Walsh . . . London.

Flying Post, Sept. 3–5, 17–19; *Post Boy*, Sept. 19–21, 1700. (The Frontispiece being now finish'd exactly from the Roman Copy, will be given gratis to those Gentlemen who have bought of the first Impression.)

Obl. fol. 2 parts. Frontispiece (by P. P. Bouche after Antonio Meloni with title 'XII Sonatas by Arcangelo Corelli His V Opera'.) Dedication (p. 2), pp. 3–70.

Rowe. Others in BUC not examined.

A second impression of No. 427, with the illustrated frontispiece which did not appear with the 'first Impression'. Smith 31.

429. XII Sonata's or Solos for a Violin a Bass Violin or Harpsicord Compos'd by Arcangelo Corelli. His fifth Opera. This Edition has yᵉ advantage of haveing yᵉ

Graces to all yᵉ Adagio's and other places where the Author thought proper. by Arcangelo Corelli. There is likewise Engraven his first, second, third and fourth Opera's being all the works of that Author yet extant.

London. Printed for J. Walsh . . . & J. Hare, &c.

[*c.* 1711.]

Fol. pp. 1–61, [p. 62] 'The Second Part Containing Preludes, Allemands, Corants, Jiggs, Sarabands, Gavots, & yᵉ Follia. by Arcangelo Corelli. Printed for J. Walsh.', pp. 63–92.

BM. g. 45. g.

Haas Cat. No. 28, 68: With Howard portrait, engraved by Sherwin.

Smith 400.

Walsh advertisements cover Nos. 427 and 428 but it is frequently not clear which of the two editions is referred to or whether the notices are re-advertisements, or indicate reissues or new editions. The following details are from various Walsh catalogues.

Walsh Cat. 9*a*: '12 Solos (for a Violin & a Bass) by Corelli. 5s. od.'

Walsh Cat. 11*a*: 'Corelli's twelve Solos for a Violin and a Bass. Opera Quinta.'

Walsh Cat. 15*a*: '12 Solos by Corelli (for a Violin & a Bass) 5s. od.'

Walsh Cat. 16*a*: 'Corelli's Solos (for a Violin and a Bass) 5s. od.'

Walsh Cat. 21: 'Corelli's 12 Solos (for a Violin and Bass) 5s. od.'

Walsh Cat. 24*a*: 'Corelli's Solos, (for a Violin or [i.e. and] Harpsicord) 2d Edition. 6s. od.'

Randall Cat. 'Corelli's 12 Solos (for a Violin and Harpsicord). 6s. od.'

430. XII Sonata's or Solo's for a Violin a Bass Violin or Harpsicord . . . His fifth Opera, &c.

London. Printed for I. Walsh . . .Nº 369.

[*c.* 1730.]

Fol. pp. 61 [62], 39–68.

Bod. (Wanting portrait.) Durham (BUC).

Walsh Cat. 18: '12 Solos for a Violin and a Bass Opera 5ta. 5s. od. Nº 369.'

First Edition Bookshop Cat. 43, Nos. 214, 215.

With portrait of Corelli by Howard, engraved by Sherwin. Hare's name erased from the title-page.

431. XII Solos for a Violin with a Thorough Bass for the Harpsicord or Violoncello Compos'd by Arcangelo Corelli Opera Quinta. N.B. These Solos are Printed from a curious Edition Publish'd at Rome by the Author. (The Second Part Containing Preludes, Allemands, Corants, Jiggs, Sarabands, Gavots, & yᵉ Follia. by Arcangelo Corelli Printed for J. Walsh.)

London. Printed for and Sold by I. Walsh, &c.

London Daily Post, and General Advertiser, Dec. 11, 1740.

Fol. Portrait of Corelli, 'H. Howard Pinx. Vᵈʳ Gucht Sculp.' pp. 68. Title-page of the second part on verso of p. 37.

BM. g. 93. b. (2.) Hirsch III. 163. RCM. LVIII. E. 20. a.

432. XII Solos. For a Violin with a Thorough Bass for the Harpsicord or Violoncello. Op. 5.

London. Printed for and sold by I. Walsh, &c.

[*c.* 1740.]

> With portrait of Corelli by Howard, engraved by Sherwin.
> Fol. pp. (?).
> The First Edition Bookshop Cat. 43, No. 216.

433. Concerti Grossi Con Due Violini Viola e Violoncello di Concertino obligati, e Due altri Violini e Basso di Concerto Grosso da Francesco Geminiani Composti delli Sei Soli della prima parte dell' Opera Quinta D' Arcangelo Corelli.
Note. all the Works of this Author may be had where these are sold.

London Printed for and sold by I: Walsh . . . and Ioseph Hare, &c.

Daily Courant, Sept. 21, 1726.

> Fol. Parts.
> BM. g. 45. i. (Alto Viola part only.)

434. — With Walsh only in the imprint and 'N.º 376' added to the title-page.

> [*c.* 1732.]

> RAM. BM. g. 45. y. (2.) (Violino primo del concertino, Violino secondo del concertino,
> Alto viola, Violoncello (wanting title-page) only.)
> Walsh Cat. 18: (Under Geminiani.) 'Twelve Concertos made out of Corelli's Solos for
> Violins in 7 Parts. £1. 1s. od. N.º 377.'

435. Concerti Grossi Con Due Violini Viola e Violoncello di Concertino obligati,
e Due altri Violini e Basso di Concerto Grosso da Francesco Geminiani. Composti
delli Sei Soli della Prima parte dell' Opera Quinta D' Arcangelo Corelli.

London. Printed for I. Walsh . . . where may be had Just Publish'd by M.ʳ Geminiani, &c.

Country Journal: or, The Craftsman, Oct. 26, 1734. (A New edition, printed on
fine Dutch Paper of, Corelli's 12 Solos made into Concerto's by Sig. Geminiani,
for Violins 7 Parts.)

> BM. g. 45. c. (2.) RM. 17. f. 22. (Violino primo ripieno, Violino primo del concertino,
> Bass ripieno only.)

436. Concerti Grossi . . . Opera Quinta D'Arcangelo Corelli.

London. Printed for I. Walsh . . . Of whom may be had The Works of M.ʳ
Handel, Geminiani, &c.

General Evening Post. (London), Jan. 17–19, 1745. (New editions.)

> RM. 17. a. 3. (2.) RM. 17. f. 22. (Violino primo ripieno, Violino secondo ripieno only.)
> Fitz.
> Other editions were published by William Smith and John Barrett (BM. g. 45. m. *Daily
> Post*, Aug. 10, 1726.) and by Benjamin Cooke, engraved by Thomas Cross. William Smith

advertised (*Daily Post*, Sept. 28, 1726.) 'There being lately printed two false and spurious Editions of the Solo's of Corelli, turn'd into Concerto's by Mr. Geminiani and sold at half a Guinea a Set. These are to give Notice, that the true original Copies corrected and publish'd by the Author's own Hand, are to be sold at the same Price by William Smith (Printer of the said Books) . . . and J. Barret . . . N.B. The other Editions are very false and incorrect.'

437. Concerti Grossi Con due Violini, Viola e Violoncello di Concertini Obligati, e due altri Violini e Basso di Concerto Grosso Quali Contengono Preludii Allemande Correnti Gigue Sarabande Gavotte e Follia Composti della Seconda Parte del Opera Quinta d'Arcangelo Corelli per Francesco Geminiani. N.B. Where these are sold may be had the first Six Solos of Corelli made into Concertos by Geminiani. and Twelve celebrated Solos by the same Author for a Violin and a Bass.

London. Printed for and sold by I: Walsh . . . and Ios: Hare, &c.

Country Journal: or, The Craftsman, Nov. 1, 1729.

> Fol. Parts.
> BM. g. 45. h. (Violino Primo del Concerto Grosso, Violino Secondo del Concerto Grosso and Basso del Concerto Grosso only.)
> William Smith advertised 'That there is now Printing by Subscription at One Guinea per Set, the second Part of the Solo's of Corelli, turn'd into Concertos, in seven Parts, by Mr. Geminiani, and will be ready . . . by Michaelmas next.' (*Daily Journal*, July 17, 1727.)

438. — With Walsh only in the imprint and 'N⁰ 377' added to the title-page.

[*c.* 1732].

> RAM. BM. g. 45. y. (2.) (Violino primo del concertino, Violino secondo del concertino, Alto viola, Violoncello del concertino only.)
> Walsh Cat. 18: (Under Geminiani.) 'Twelve Concertos made out of Corelli's Solos for Violins in 7 Parts. £1. 1s. 0d. N⁰ 377.'

439. Concerti Grossi Con Due Violini Viola e Violoncello di Concertino obligati, e Due altri Violini e Basso di Concerto Grosso da Francesco Geminiani. Composti delli Sei Soli della Seconda parte dell' Opera Quinta D' Arcangelo Corelli.

London. Printed for I. Walsh . . . where may be had Just Publish'd by Mʳ Geminiani, &c.

Country Journal: or, The Craftsman, Oct. 26, 1734. (A New edition, printed on fine Dutch Paper of, Corelli's 12 Solos made into Concerto's by Sig. Geminiani, for Violins 7 Parts.)

> BM. g. 45. c. (2.) RM. 17. a. 3. (2.) RM. 17. f. 22. (Violino primo del concertino, Violino primo del concerto grosso, Violino secondo del concerto grosso, Basso del concerto grosso only.) Fitz.

440. Concerti Grossi . . . Seconda parte dell' Opera Quinta D' Arcangelo Corelli.

London. Printed for I. Walsh . . . Of whom may be had The Works of Mʳ Handel, Geminiani, &c.

General Evening Post. (*London*), Jan. 17–19, 1745. (New editions.)

Other copies of Geminiani's Concertos from Corelli's Opera Quinta in BUC not examined.

441. Two Concerto'$ being the first & eleventh Solos of y^e late Arcangello Corelli. as they are made into Concerto's by Mr Obadiah Shuttleworth. Ingrav'd by T. Cross.

London, Printed & Sold by Joseph Hare, &c.

Daily Post, Oct. 3, 1729. (Where may be had. Printed for, and sold by Joseph Hare . . . John Walsh . . . and John Young, &c.)

> Fol. Passe-partout title-page. 3 parts.
> BM. h. 202. c. York Minster.
> These are arrangements of Op. 5, Nos. 1 and 11.

442. Six Solos for a Flute and a Bass By Archangelo Corelli Being The second part of his Fifth Opera Containing Preludes Allmands Corrants Iiggs Sarabands Gavotts with the Spanish Folly The whole exactly Transpos'd and made fitt for a Flute and A Bass with the aprobation of severall Eminent Masters.

Printed for and Sold by I: Walsh . . . and I: Hare, &c.

[*c.* 1730.]

> Obl. fol. Parts.
> Smith 85 (BM. e. 682) with Walsh only in the imprint and 'N° 111' added to the title-page as in Smith 85.
> Walsh Cat. 18: 'Six Solos for a Flute and a Bass Opera 5ta 4s. od. 'N° 111.'

Sonate a Violino e Violone o Cimbalo. Opera Quinta.

> *See also* No. 1207. Pez (Johann Christoph) A Second Collection of Sonatas . . . to which is added . . . Solo's out of the First Part of Corelli's Fifth Opera, &c.

443. Sonata's for two Violins a Violoncello and Thorough Bass for the Harpsicord or Organ by Arcangelo Corelli being his Posthumous Work. N:B: Where these are sold may be had all Corelli's works Consisting of Seven Operas Correct & neatly Engraven.

London Printed for & sold by I: Walsh . . . N° 371.

[*c.* 1733.]

> Fol. Parts.
> Mitchell. (1st and 2nd Violin parts only.)
> Reissue of Smith 551 and 561 with Walsh only in the imprint and 'N° 371' added to the title-page.
> Walsh Cat. 18: 'Six Sonatas for 2 Violins and a Bass Opera 7ma Being his Posthumous Work. 6s. od. N° 371.'

See also No. 10. Airs. A Choice Collection of Aires and Duets for two German

Flutes . . . from the Works of . . . Arcan⁰: Corelli, &c.; No. 1392. Solos. Six Solos by several Authors.

CORIOLANO

Coriolanus for a Flute. (Opera of Coriolanus.)
  See Nos. 48, 49. Ariosti (Attilio)

COSTANZA (Giovanni Battista)

  See No. 1226 Porpora (Nicolo Antonio) and Costanza (Giovanni Battista) Six Sonatas for two Violoncello's, &c.

COUNTRY DANCES

Annual Sets of 24 from 1721 to 1766, followed by miscellaneous collections. There is no standard ruling whereby the sizes can be accurately given in the many cases where the paper has been cut to suit the purpose required, and therefore the sizes given as obl. 12⁰ or obl. 8⁰, &c. must not be taken too literally.
  Collections of 24 Country Dances were issued every year, usually published in the year prior to the year given on the title-page. Those published before 1721 are given in Smith.

Twenty four new Country Dances for the Year 1721.
  See No. 887. Kynaston (Nathaniel)

Twenty four new Country Dances for the Year 1722.
  See No. 166. Birkhead (   ) and Egerton (   )

444. Twenty four new Country Dances, for 1723, with new Tunes or Figures to each Dance: the Dances perform'd at the most publick Places, as Epsom, Richmond, Tunbridge and Bath: the publick Balls and Assemblies. Price 6d.
  Printed for and sold by John Walsh . . . and John and Joseph Hare, &c.
  Post-Boy, Nov. 8–10, 1722. (Just publish'd.)

445. Twenty four Country Dances for the Year 1724.
  [J. Walsh and John and Joseph Hare.]
  [1723.]
  Details not available.

446. Twenty four Country Dances for the Year 1725.
  [J. Walsh and John and Joseph Hare.]
  [1724.]
  Details not available.

447. Twenty Four Country Dances for the Year 1726 With New Tunes and Figures or Directions to each Dance The Dances perform'd at the most Publick places as Epsom, Richmond, Tunbridge and Bath. at the Balls and Assemblies. price 6ᵈ Note. The true Genuin Dances will be Publish'd every Year in this Volume and Character.

London Printed for & Sold by I: Walsh . . . and Iⁿ & Ioseph Hare, &c.

[1725.]

Obl. 12°. pp. 24.
Dublin.

448. Twenty Four Country Dances for the Year 1727 With New Tunes and Figures or Directions to each Dance The Dances perform'd at the most Publick places as Epsom Richmond, Tunbridge and Bath. at the Balls and Assemblies. price 6ᵈ Note. The true Genuin Dances will be Publish'd every Year in this Volume and Character.

London Printed for and Sold by I. Walsh . . . & Ioseph Hare.

Daily Post, Dec. 8, 1726. (Just publish'd.)

Obl. 12°. ff. 24. Printed on one side only.
Dublin.

449. Twenty four Country Dances for the Year 1728, with choice and proper Figures to each Dance, the Tunes proper for a Violin or Hautboy, and several within Compass of the Flute. Price 6d.

Printed for, and sold by John Walsh . . . and Ioseph Hare, &c.

Mist's Weekly Journal, Dec. 9, 1727. (Just published.)

450. Twenty-four Country Dances for the Year 1729, with proper Tunes and Figures, or Directions to each Dance. The Dances perform'd at Court and publick Entertainments, the Tunes proper for the Violin and Hoboy, and several of them within the Compass of the Flute. Price 6d.

Printed for and sold by John Walsh . . . and Joseph Hare, &c.

Country Journal: or, The Craftsman, May 3, 1729.

451. Twenty Four Country Dances for the Year 1730 With proper Tunes and Figures or Directions to each Dance The Dances perform'd at Court and Publick Entertainments—The Tunes proper for the Violin and Hoboy and several of them within the compass of the Flute Note. The true Genuin Dances will be Publish'd every Year in this Volume & Character Price 6ᵈ

London. Printed for & sold by Iohn Walsh . . . Ioseph Hare . . . and Iohn Young, &c.

Country Journal: or, The Craftsman, Dec. 6, 1729. (Just published.)

Obl. 12°. pp. 24.
Dublin.

452. Twenty Four Country Dances for the Year 1731 With proper Tunes and Figures or Directions to each Dance The Dances perform'd at Court and Publick Entertainments—The Tunes proper for the Violin and Hoboy and several of them within the compass of the Flute Note. The true Genuin Dances will be Publish'd every Year in this Volume & Character Price 6ᵈ

London. Printed for & sold by Iohn Walsh . . . Ioseph Hare . . . and Iohn Young, &c.

Daily Journal, Dec. 1, 1730.

Obl. 12°. pp. 24.
Dublin.

453. Twenty Four Country Dances for the Year 1732 With proper Tunes and Figures or Directions to each Dance The Dances perform'd at Court and Publick Entertainments The Tunes proper for the Compass of the Flute. Note. The true Genuin Dances will be Publish'd every Year in this Volume and character Price 6ᵈ

London. Printed for and Sold by Iohn Walsh . . . and may be had of I. Hare . . . and I. Young, &c.

Country Journal: or, The Craftsman, Dec. 4, 1731.

Obl. 8°. 'A Table of the Dances'. No pagination.
Cecil Sharp Library.

454. Twenty-four Country Dances for the Year 1733, with Proper Tunes and Figures, or Directions to each Dance. The Dances perform'd at Court and publick Entertainments. The Tunes proper for the Violin, german Flute or Hoboy, and several within the Compass of the common Flute. Price 6d.

Printed for and sold by John Walsh, &c.

Country Journal: or, The Craftsman, Dec. 9, 1732.

455. Twenty four Country Dances for the Year 1734, with proper Tunes, Figures, and Directions to each Dance; the Dances perform'd at Court and Publick Entertainments: the Tunes proper for the Violin, German Flute, or Hautboy and several of them within Compass of the Flute. Price 6d.

Printed for John Walsh, &c.

Fog's Weekly Journal, Dec. 22, 1733.

456. Twenty-four Country Dances for the Year 1735, with proper Tunes and

Figures or Directions to each Dance as they are performed at Court, for the Violin, German Flute or Hoboy. Price 6d.

  Printed for John Walsh, &c.

  Country Journal : or, The Craftsman, Nov. 16, 1734.

457. Twenty Four Country Dances for the Year 1736. With Proper Tunes, Figures, or Directions to each Dance. The Dances Perform'd at Court and Publick Entertainments. The Tunes proper for the Violin, German Flute, or Hoboy, and several of them within the compass of the Flute. Note. The true Genuin Dances will be publish'd every Year in this Volume and Character. Price 6ᵈ

  London. Printed for and Sold by I. Walsh . . . Nᵒ. 570.

  Country Journal: or, The Craftsman, Nov. 1, 1735.

    Obl. 8ᵒ. No pagination.

    Cecil Sharp Library.

458. Twenty-four Country Dances for the Year 1737. With proper Tunes, Figures or Directions to each Dance, as they are perform'd at Court and publick Assemblies. Price 6d.

  Printed for and sold by John Walsh, &c.

  London Daily Post, and General Advertiser, Nov. 3, 1736.

459. Twenty-four Country Dances for the Year 1738, with proper Tunes and Figures, or Directions to each Dance for the Violin, &c. Price 6d.

  Printed for John Walsh, &c.

  London Evening-Post, Oct. 18–20, 1737.

460. Twenty four Country Dances for 1739, with proper Tunes and Directions to each Dance. Price 6d.

  Printed for and sold by John Walsh, &c.

  London Daily Post, and General Advertiser, Nov. 8, 1738.

461. Twenty-four Country Dances for the Year 1740, with proper Tunes and Directions to each Dance. (Price 6d.)

  Printed for and Sold by John Walsh, &c.

  London Daily Post, and General Advertiser, Oct. 31, 1739.

462. Twenty four Country Dances for the Year 1741. Price 6d.

  Printed for J. Walsh, &c.

  London Daily Post, and General Advertiser, Oct. 16, 1740.

463. Twenty Four Country Dances for the Year 1742. With Proper Tunes, Figures, or Directions to each Dance. The Dances Perform'd at Court, and Publick Entertainments. The Tunes proper for the Violin, German Flute, or Hoboy. and several of them within the compass of the Flute.

 London. Printed for and Sold by I. Walsh, &c.

London Daily Post, and General Advertiser, Oct. 21, 1741.

 Obl. 8°.
 NLS. Glen 18. (1.) (Wanting Nos. 13–16.)

464. Twenty-four Country Dances for the Year 1743, with proper Tunes and Direction to each Dance. (Price 6d.)
 Printed for J. Walsh, &c.

Daily Advertiser, Oct. 19, 1742.

465. Twenty four Country Dances, with proper Tunes and Directions to each Dance, for the Year 1744.
 Printed for J. Walsh, &c.

Daily Advertiser, Oct. 17, 1743.

466. Twenty Four Country Dances for the Year 1745. With proper Tunes Figures, or Directions to each Dance. The Dances Perform'd at Court and Publick Entertainments. The Tunes proper for the Violin, German Flute, or Hoboy and several of them within the compass of the Flute. Note. The true Genuin Dances will be Publish'd every Year in this Volume and character. Price 6^d

 London. Printed for and sold by I. Walsh, &c.

London Evening Post, Oct. 13–16, 1744.

 Obl. 8°.
 BM. a. 10. a. (1.) (Wanting Nos. 21–24.)

467. Twenty-four Country Dances for the Year 1746, with new Tunes and Directions to each Dance, for the Violin or Hautboy. Price 6d.
 Printed for J. Walsh, &c.

 General Evening Post (London), Oct. 24–26, 1745. (Just publish'd.)

468. Twenty-four Country Dances for the Year 1747. Price 6^d
 Printed for J. Walsh, &c.

 General Advertiser, Nov. 1, 1746.

469. Twenty Four Country Dances for the Year 1748 With Proper Tunes, Figures, or Directions to each Dance. The Dances Perform'd at Court, and Publick Entertainments. The Tunes proper for the Violin, German Flute, or Hoboy. and

several of them within the compass of the Flute. Note. The true Genuin Dances will be Publish'd every Year in this Volume and Character; Price 6.ᵈ
London. Printed for I. Walsh, &c.

General Advertiser, Oct. 6, 1747.

Obl. 8°.
BM. a. 10. a. (2.)

470. Twenty four Country Dances for the Year 1749, with Directions to each Dance, set for the Violin, German Flute, or Hautboy. Price 6d.
Printed for J. Walsh, &c.

London Evening-Post, Oct. 6–8, 1748.

471. Twenty Four Country Dances for the Year 1750 With Proper Tunes and Directions to each Dance. Set for the Violin, German Flute or Hoboy. The Dances Perform'd at Court & all Publick Entertainments. Price 6ᵈ.
London. Printed for I. Walsh, &c.

General Advertiser, Oct. 5, 1749.

Obl. 8°.
BM. a. 10. a. (3.) (Wanting the last leaf, dances 21–24.) NLS. Glen 18. (2.)

472. Twenty Four Country Dances for the Year 1751 With Proper Tunes and Directions to each Dance. Set for the Violin, German Flute, or Hoboy. The Dances Perform'd at Court & all Publick Entertainments. Price 6ᵈ
London. Printed for I. Walsh, &c.

General Advertiser, Oct. 6, 1750.

Obl. 8°. pp. 12.
Dublin.

473. Twenty-four Country Dances, for the Year 1752. Price 6d.
Printed for J. Walsh, &c.

London Evening-Post, Sept. 28–Oct. 1, 1751.

BUC gives a copy at Dublin (Obl. 8°. pp. 12) but it is without title-page so cannot be definitely identified.

474. Twenty-four New Country Dances for the Year, 1753. Price 6d.
Printed for J. Walsh, &c.

General Advertiser, Oct. 5, 1752.

BUC gives a copy at Dublin (Obl. 8°. pp. 12) but it is without title-page so cannot be definitely identified.

475. Twenty-four new Country Dances for the Year 1754, with Proper Tunes and Directions to each Dance. Price 6d.
  Printed for J. Walsh, &c.

  London Evening-Post, Sept. 25–27, 1753.

476. Twenty four new Country Dances for the Year 1755. Price 6d.
  Printed for J. Walsh, &c.

  London Evening-Post, Sept. 17–19, 1754.

477. Twenty-four new Country Dances for the Year 1756, for the Violin, German Flute, or Hautboy, with Directions. Price 6d.
  Printed for J. Walsh, &c.

  London Evening-Post, Sept. 18–20, 1755.

478. Twenty-four Country Dances, for the Year 1757; with New Tunes and Directions to each Dance; as perform'd at Court, and all polite Assemblies, for the Violin, German Flute or Hautboy. Price 6d.
  Printed for J. Walsh, &c.

  Whitehall Evening-Post, Sept. 16–18, 1756.

479. Twenty-four New Country Dances, for the Year 1758. Price 6d.
  Printed for J. Walsh, &c.

  London Evening-Post, Sept. 13–15, 1757.

480. Twenty-four new Country Dances for the Year 1758, Price 6d.
  Printed for J. Walsh, &c.

  Public Advertiser, Sept. 15, 1758.

481. Twenty four Country Dances, for the Year 1760. Price 6d.
  Printed for J. Walsh, &c.

  London Evening-Post, Sept. 6–8, 1759.

482. Twenty-four new Country Dances for 1761. Price 6d.
  Printed for J. Walsh, &c.

  London Evening-Post, Sept. 2–4, 1760.

483. Twenty-four Country Dances for the Year 1762. Price 6d.
  Printed for J. Walsh, &c.

  Public Advertiser, Sept. 7, 1761.

484. Twenty Four Country Dances for the Year 1763 With Proper Tunes and

Directions to each Dance. Set for the Violin, german Flute or Hoboy. The Dances Perform'd at Court and all Publick Entertainments. Price 6ᵈ.

London. Printed for I. Walsh, &c.

Public Advertiser, Sept. 1, 1762.

> Obl. 8°. No pagination.
> Cecil Sharp Library. (Wanting Nos. 1–4.)

485. Twenty Four Country Dances for the Year 1764 With Proper Tunes & Directions to each Dance. Set for the Violin, German Flute or Hoboy. The Dances perform'd at Court and all Publick Entertainments. Price 6d.

London. Printed for I. Walsh, &c.

Public Advertiser, Aug. 31, 1763.

> Obl. 8°. No pagination.
> Cecil Sharp Library. (Wanting Nos. 9–24.)

486. Twenty Four Country Dances for the Year 1765 With Proper Tunes and Directions to each Dance. Set for the Violin, German Flute, or Hoboy. The Dances Perform'd at Court & all Publick Entertainments. Price 6ᵈ.

London. Printed for I. Walsh, &c.

Public Advertiser, Sept. 7, 1764.

> Obl. 8°.
> BM. a. 10. a. (4.) (At the end is bound up the last leaf (Nos. 21–24) of another of Walsh's sets of Dances.)

487. Twenty four new Country Dances for the Year 1766, with proper Tunes and Directions to each Dance, for the Violin, Hautboy, or German Flute, Price 6d.

Printed for J. Walsh, &c.

Public Advertiser, Aug. 20, 1765.

Country Dances.

Miscellaneous Collections (chronological order).

488. Country Dances for the Flute, &c.

London. John Walsh and Joseph Hare.

[*c.* 1727.]

> No details available; entered because of 'A Second Book'. (No. 490.)

489. Country Dances for the Flute. 2s. od. Nᵒ. 12.

[*c.* 1730.]

> Reissue of No. 488. with Walsh only in the imprint and 'Nᵒ. 12' added to the title-page.
> Walsh Cat. 18.

490. A Second Book of Country Dances for the Flute; being a Collection of 104 of the choicest Country Dances both old and new. Transposed & fitted for the Flute. The whole carefully corrected; Price 1s. 6d.
   Printed for, and sold by John Walsh . . . and Joseph Hare, &c.

   Country Journal: or, The Craftsman, Jan. 20, 1728.

491. — With Walsh only in the imprint and 'N⁰ 13' added to the title-page.
   [*c.* 1730.]
      Walsh Cat. 18: 'Country Dances for the Flute 2d Book. 1s. 6d. N⁰ 13.'

492. 24 Country Dances (German Flute). 6d. N⁰ 487.
   [*c.* 1730.]
      Walsh Cat. 18.
      Not identified. May be one of the yearly sets of 24.

493. Thirty New and Choice Country Dances Set for the Harpsicord or Spinnet The Dances Perform'd at Court and publick Entertainments Being a delightful and Entertaining Collection.
   London Printed for and sold by Iohn Walsh, &c.

   Country Journal: or, The Craftsman, Oct. 2, 1731.
      Obl. fol. 'A Table of the Dances', &c. ff. 3–13. Printed on one side only
      BM. e. 5. r. (2.)

494. — With 'N⁰ 194' added to the title-page.
      Walsh Cat. 18: '30 Choice Country Dances for the Harpsicord. 1s. 6d. N⁰ 194.'

495. A Second Collection of Thirty new and choice Country-Dances, set for the Harpsichord or Spinet. The Dances perform'd at Court and publick Entertainments: being a delightful and entertaining Collection, carefully corrected. Price 1s. 6d.
   Printed for John Walsh, &c.

   Country Journal: or, The Craftsman, May 20, 1732.
      Walsh Cat. 18: 'A Second Collection of Country Dances. 1s. 6d. N⁰ 195.'

496. The third Book of Country Dances for the Flute: Being a Collection of all the celebrated Scotch Country Dances now in Vogue, transpos'd and fitted for the Flute. The whole carefully corrected, price 1s. 6d.
   Printed for John Walsh, &c.

   Country Journal: or, The Craftsman, Oct. 20, 1733.
      Walsh Cat. 18: 'Country Dances for the Flute 3d Book. 1s. 6d. N⁰ 491.'

497. Country Dances Selected As Perform'd at Court and all Publick Assemblies and Entertainments. For the Harpsicord, Violin, German Flute. or Hoboy with proper Directions to each Dance. Part I Price 6d.
London. Printed for I. Walsh, &c.

[*c.* 1760.]
Obl. 16º. ff. 2–11 (in MS.). Printed on one side only.
NLS. (Glen 35. (1.)

498. — Part II.
[*c.* 1760.]
Obl. 16º. ff. 12–23, with 1–12 at bottom centre. Printed on one side only.
NLS. (Glen 35. (1.).)
I has been altered in MS. on title-page to II.

499. 12 Country-Dances for the Harpsicord. 6d.
Printed for J. Walsh, &c.
Public Advertiser, Dec. 13, 1764. (Of whom may be had.)

500. Country Dances selected, as performed at Court, and all public Assemblies, for the Harpsicord and Violin. Price 1s. 6d.
Printed and sold at the late Mr. J. Walsh's, &c.
Public Advertiser, June 25, 1766.
May refer to the issue by Randall & Abell. (Obl. 8º. pp. 32.) Cecil Sharp Library.

See also Caledonian Country Dances.

COUNTRY DANCING MASTER

501. The Compleat Country Dancing-Master: containing Great Variety of Dances, both Old and New; particularly Those perform'd at the several Masquerades: Together with All the Choicest and most Noted Country-Dances, Perform'd at Court, the Theatres, and Publick Balls; With their Proper Tunes, and Figures (or Directions) to each Dance: The Tunes fitted to the Violin, or Haut-boy, and most of 'em within the Compass of the Flute. Note, There is contain'd in this Volume, all the Dances generally us'd, and more correct than the former Editions; printed in the London Capital Character, far exceeding any other of the Common Press.
London, Printed by H. Meere, for J. Walsh . . . and J. Hare, &c.
Post-Boy, April 13–15, 1721. (There is lately publish'd a new edition of the 1st and 2d great Dance-Books.)
Another edition of Smith 533 with presumably the same title-page as the earlier edition. (BM. a. 4. (1.) Obl. 12º. Frontispiece. 'An Explanation of the several Characters us'd', &c. pp. 364.)

502. — With Walsh only in the imprint and 'N? 157' added to the title-page. [*c.* 1730.]

> Walsh Cat. 18: 'First Great Book of Country Dances Engrav'd: Bound 3s. od. N? 157.'

503. The Second Book of the Compleat Country Dancing-Master: containing Great Variety of Dances, both Old and New; particularly Those perform'd at the several Masquerades: Together with All the Choicest and most Noted Country-Dances, Perform'd at Court, the Theatres, and publick Balls; With their proper Tunes, and Figures (or Directions) to each Dance: The Tunes fitted to the Violin, or Hautboy, and most of 'em within the Compass of the Flute. Note, In this, and the first Book, are contain'd all the Dances generally used and more correct than the former Editions; printed in the London Capital Character, far exceeding any other of the Common Press.

London, Printed by H. Meere, for J. Walsh . . . and J. Hare, &c.

Post-Boy, April 13–15, 1721. (There is lately publish'd a new edition of the 1st and 2d great Dance-Books.)

> Another edition of Smith 558, with presumably the same title-page as the earlier edition (BM. a. 4. (2.) Obl. 12°. Frontispiece. 'An Explanation of the several Characters us'd,' &c. An Alphabetical Table of all the Dances. [pp. 4], pp. 376.)

504. — With Walsh only in the imprint and 'N? 158' added to the title-page. [*c.* 1730.]

> Walsh Cat. 18: 'Second Great Book of Country Dances bound. 3s. 6d. N? 158.'

505. [The Third Book of the Compleat Country Dancing Master, &c.] [Printed for and sold by J. Walsh . . . N? 159.]

[*c.* 1730.]

> No copy traced; details uncertain.
> Walsh Cat. 18: 'Third Great Book of Country Dances Bound. 3s. 6d. N? 159.'

506. The Compleat Country Dancing-Master: Containing Great Variety of Dances, both Old & New; Particularly those perform'd at the several Masquerades: Together with All the Choicest and most Noted Country-Dances perform'd at Court, the Theatres, and Publick Balls: With their Proper Tunes, and Figures (or Directions) to each Dance. The Tunes fitted to the Violin, or Hautboy and most of them within the Compass of the German Flute & Common Flute. Engraven in a fair Character, and Carefully corrected. Note, There is contain'd in this Volume all the Dances generally us'd and more correct than yᵉ former Editions.

London. Printed for and Sold by Iohn Walsh . . . MDCCXXXI. Price bound 3s. 6d.

Daily Post, Nov. 3, 1731. (The Compleat Country Dancing Master, containing 300 of the most Celebrated Country Dances.)

Obl. 12°. 'An Explanation of the Several Characters us'd in this Book.' 'An Alphabetical Table of all the Dances.' [ff. 4]. ff. 150. Printed on one side only, with two tunes side by side on each page.
B.M. a. 4. a.

507. A new Edition of the compleat Country Dancing Master.
Printed for and sold by John Walsh, &c.

Country Journal: or, The Craftsman, Oct. 14, 1732.

508. The Compleat Country Dancing Master, Containing 300 Celebrated Scotch and English Country Dances, perform'd at Court, the Theatre and publick Balls.
Printed for and sold by John Walsh, &c.

Fog's Weekly Journal, April 21, 1733.

509. The Compleat Country Dancing-Master . . . The 3ᵈ Edition, &c.
London. Printed for & sold by I. Walsh . . . MDCCXXXV. Price 3s. 6d. Bound. Nº 157.

Country Journal: or, The Craftsman, Nov. 1, 1735. (In three vols.)

Obl. 12°. 'An Explanation of the several Characters us'd in this Book. An Alphabetical Table of all the Dances. ff. II–VI.+ 75 leaves (printed on both sides, irregular pagination 1–150, Dances 151–300, Two Dances side by side on each page.) End of First Volume.
BM. a. 4. d.

510. The Third Book of the Compleat Country Dancing Master . . . Second Edition.
Printed for and sold by John Walsh, &c.

Country Journal: or, The Craftsman, Oct. 16, 1736.

511. — The Compleat Country Dancing Master . . . In Three Vol. Third Edition.
Printed for and sold by John Walsh, &c.

London Daily Post, and General Advertiser, Nov. 3, 1736. (*See also* No. 509.)

512. A Fourth Volume of, The Compleat Country Dancing-Master, Containing all the Country Dances in Vogue for ten years last past. Price bound 3s. 6d.
Printed for J. Walsh, &c.

London Evening-Post, Oct. 20–22, 1747.

Obl. 12°.

513. 'The Compleat Country Dancing Master, containing upwards of 1000 choice

Country-Dances, with Directions to each Dance, for the Violin, Hoboy &c. in 5 Vol.ˢ each 3s. 6d.

> [*c.* 1755.]
>> Obl. 12º.
>>
>> Walsh Cat. 25.

514. The Compleat Country Dancing Master, containing upwards of 1200 Old and New Country Dances Bound in 6 Volumes. Each 3ˢ 6ᵈ

> Advertised on title-page of 'Country Dances Selected . . . Part I . . . Of whom may be had', &c. (*c.* 1760.) (NLS Glen 35. (1.))

515. The New Country Dancing-Master 3ᵈ Book being a choice Collection of Country Dances Perform'd at the Theatre, at Schools and publick Balls; with Directions to each Dance. The Tunes Airy and Pleasant for the Violin or Hoboy and most of them within the compass of the Flute. Price 2ˢ 6ᵈ

> London. Printed for and sold by I: Walsh . . . and Ioseph Hare, &c.

> *London Journal*, Dec. 21, 1728. (New Musick lately published.)

>> Obl. 12º. 'An alphabetical Table', &c. [ff. 3.] ff. 160. Printed on one side only.
>> BM. a. 8.
>> The first book is listed in Smith (No. 193. 1706). A copy of the second book is at Perth (BUC. *c.* 1711.)

COURTEVILLE (Raphael)

516. Sonatas of two Parts, Composed and Purposley Contrived for two Flutes. By Mʳ Raphael Courtivill.

> London Printed and Sold by I: Walsh . . . Nº 68.

> [*c.* 1730.]
>> Obl. fol. Parts.
>> Walsh Cat. 18.
>> Smith 77 (BM. c. 105. a. (3.) with Walsh only in the imprint and 'Nº 68' added to the title-page.

517. Six Sonata's of 2 parts for 2 Violins, Composed by Mr. Courtivil, price 3s.

> Printed for and Sold by J. Walsh . . . Nº 372.

> [*c.* 1730.]
>> Parts.
>> Walsh Cat. 18.
>> Smith 98 with Walsh only in the imprint and 'Nº 372' added to the title-page.

COURTIVILL

> *See* Courteville (Raphael)

COX (Robert)

518. Mr. Cox's Aires (for a Single Flute). 1s. 0d. N.º 54.

[*c.* 1730.]

Walsh Cat. 18.
Composer probably Robert Cox.
Smith 607 with Walsh only in the imprint and 'N.º 54' added to the title-page.
May be the same work as: 'Cox's Aires for a Single Violin' advertised in Walsh Cat. 11*a.*

CRESO (CRŒSUS)

519. Songs in the Opera of Crœsus as they are Perform'd at y.ᵉ Queens Theatre.
London Printed for J: Walsh, &c.

[*c.* 1730.]

Fol. 'A Table of the Songs', &c. ff. 3–51. Printed on one side only.
Walsh Cat. 18: 'The Opera of Crœsus. 9s. 0d. N.º 235'.
Pasticcio. Smith 446 (BM. H. 323.) with Walsh only in the imprint and 'N.º 235' added to the title-page.

520. Opera of Crœsus for the Flute. 1s. 6d. N.º 20.

[*c.* 1730.]

Walsh Cat. 18.
Smith 455 with Walsh only in the imprint and 'N.º 20' added to the title-page.

521. Opera of Crœsus (for 2 Flutes). 2s. 0d. N.º 59.

[*c.* 1730.]

Walsh Cat. 18.
Smith 454 with Walsh only in the imprint and 'N.º 59' added to the title-page

Crœsus. Overture.

See No. 220. Bononcini (Giovanni) and (Antonio Maria) and others. Bononcini's Six Overtures for Violins in the Operas of . . . Crœsus, &c.

522. The Favourite Songs in the Opera Call'd Creso.
London: Printed for I. Walsh, &c.

Public Advertiser, April 27, 1758.

Fol. Passe-partout title-page. pp. 2–21.
BM. G. 206. a. (3.) RCM. DAM.
Pasticcio, different work from No. 519. Composers named are Abos, Potenza, Bertoni, and Cocchi.
Republished in 'Le Delizie dell' Opere', Vol. VIII, pp. 86–105.

CRISPO

The favourite Songs in the Opera call'd Crispus.

See No. 203. Bononcini (Giovanni)

CROFT (WILLIAM)

523. Musica Sacra: or, Select Anthems in Score, consisting of 2, 3, 4, 5, 6, 7 and 8 Parts: To which is added, The Burial-Service as it is now occasionally perform'd in Westminster-Abbey. Compos'd by Dr. William Croft, Organist, Composer, and Master of the Children of His Majesty's Chapel-Royal, and Organist of St. Peter's Westminster. Vol. I.

London, Printed for and sold by John Walsh . . . and John and Joseph Hare, &c.
— Vol. II.
London, Printed for and sold by John Walsh . . . and Joseph Hare, &c.

[1724, 25.]

Fol. Vol. I. Portrait of Croft. Dedication. Licence. 'Preface', pp. 4. 'Names of the Subscribers', &c. pp. 2. 'A Table of the Anthems', &c. pp. 184.

Vol. II. Dedication. 'A Table of the Anthems', &c. pp. 155.

BM. Mad. Soc. 33. Other copies in BUC not examined.

524. — A reissue. 2 vols.

[*c.* 1730.] *Country Journal: or, The Craftsman*, July 17, 1731. (Lately printed.)

Fol. Vol. I. Portrait of Croft. Dedication. Licence. Preface, pp. 4. 'A Table of the Anthems', &c. pp. 184. Vol. II. Dedication. 'A Table of the Anthems', &c. with N⁰ 211 at foot of page. pp. 155.

BM. H. 875. (Without Dedication, Vol. II.) RM. 14. d. 1. (Without Licence and Preface, Vol. I.) Other copies in BUC not examined.

Walsh Cat. 18: 'Bound in 2 vol. £2. 12s. 6d. N⁰ 211.'

525. — Another issue. 2 vols.

London Daily Post, and General Advertiser, Oct. 20, 1740.

Walsh Cat. 25: 'Dʳ Croft's 30 Select Anthems. £2. 2s. 0d.'
Walsh Cat. 27: 'Dʳ Croft's Anthems. £2. 2s. 0d.'

526. Musicus Apparatus Accadimicus. £1. 1s. 0d. N⁰ 215.

[*c.* 1730.]

Walsh Cat. 18.

Presumably refers to copies of 'Musicus Apparatus Academicus, Being a Composition of Two Odes With Vocal & Instrumental Musick Perform'd in the Theatre at Oxford . . . July the 13th 1713, &c. London. Printed for the Author . . . at his House . . . At Mʳˢ Turner the Old Post Office in Russell-street. Covent Garden. And at Richᵈ Mears . . . in Sᵗ Pauls Church Yard.' [1720.] (BM. G. 329. 2 parts. fol. pp. 1–64, 1–27.) This work was not published by Walsh, but was sold by various music dealers.

Walsh advertised it in later catalogues, 1733, &c. and in Cat. 20a. (*c.* 1743) as 'Just Publish'd'.

527. Six Solos for a Flute and a Bass, 3s. 0d. N⁰ 124.

[*c.* 1730.]

Walsh Cat. 18.

Not identified.

528. Six Sonatas of two Parts Purposely made and Contrived for Two Flutes Compos'd by M.ʳ William Croft, &c.
   London Printed for I. Walsh, &c.

   [*c.* 1730.]
   > Obl. fol. Parts.
   > Walsh Cat. 18: 'Six Sonatas for 2 Flutes. 3s. 0d. N.º 69.'
   > Smith 144 (BM. c. 105. a. (1.)) with Walsh only in the imprint and 'N.º 69' added to the title-page.

529. 5 Sets of Tunes made for several Plays for 2 Violins and a Bass. 7s. 0d.

   [*c.* 1730.]
   > Walsh Cat. 18.
   > A collection of previously issued music for plays, not identified, but probably all included in Smith and BUC.
   > *See also* No. 354. Church (John) An Introduction to Psalmody . . . containing some Hymns Compos'd by D.ʳ Will.ᵐ Croft, &c.

CUCKOW SOLO

530. The Cuckow Solo (for a Flute and a Bass). 6d.

   [*c.* 1730.]
   > Walsh Cat. 18.
   > Not identified or otherwise advertised.

CYRUS

The Favourite Songs in the Opera call'd Cyrus.
   See No. 376. Ciro.

DANCES

531. 20 Books of Figure Dances by M.ʳ Issacc [i.e. Isaac]. £1. 10s. 0d. N.º 163.

   [*c.* 1730.]
   > Walsh Cat. 18.
   > Presumably reissues of some works noted in Smith 116, 145, 170, 196, 207, 234, 269, 270, 280, 343, 374, 375, 383, 399, 404–15, 439, 444, and 462.

532. All the Dances that are Printed in Characters. Each Dance. 5s. 0d.

   [*c.* 1730.]
   > Walsh Cat. 18.
   > Randall Cat.: 'Single Dances in Characters by Isaac &c. each 5s. 0d.'

DARIO

The Favourite Songs in the Opera call'd Darius.
   See No. 50. Ariosti (Attilio)

DAVIS (Thomas)

533. Davis's Solos. (German Flute, Hoboy or Violin and a Bass.)

[1744.]

Fol.
Walsh Cats. 18, 21: 'Davis's Solos'.
An edition of 'Twelve original Solos for the German Flute, by Mr. Thomas Davis. Printed for Henry Waylett', &c. was advertised in *The Daily Advertiser,* March 14, 1744. Issued in two collections of 'Six Solos'. First collection, pp. 24, BM. g. 418. c. (1.). A Second Collection. Sonata VII–XII, pp. 22, BM. g. 203. Waylett's edition was presumably the one advertised and sold by Walsh. No edition with Walsh imprint has been traced. The item is a late addition to Cat. 18. In later Walsh catalogues the price is given as 2s. od.

DECEMBER MASK

534. The December Mask, being a Choice Collection of English Songs. 2s. 6d. N⁰ 313.

[*c.* 1730.]

Walsh Cat. 18.
Not identified. Probably refers to an issue of 'The Monthly Mask of Vocal Music'.
See No. 1103.

DEFESCH (Willem)

535. VIII Concerto's in seven parts. Six For two Violins, a Tenor Violin and a Violoncello, with Two other Violins, and Thorough Bass, for yᵉ Harpsicord. One for a German Flute, wᵗʰ all the other Instruments, and one with Two German Flutes, Two Violins, Tenor Violin, Violoncello, and Thorough Bass for the Harpsicord. Dedicated to His Royal Highness the Prince of Wales by Wᵐ Defesch.
London, Printed for I. Walsh, &c.

Daily Advertiser, Nov. 24, 1742. (Printed for J. Walsh. Of whom may be had, Price 10s. od.)

Fol. 8 parts.
RAM.
Printed from the plates of an earlier edition with the same title-page which had the addition of 'Opera the Tenth' after Defesch and was without an imprint, advertised in *The London Daily Post, and General Advertiser,* April 30, 1741. 'This Day . . . will be publish'd. Will be sold at Mr. De Fesch's Lodgings at Mr. Baron's, an Upholster, on the Pav'd Stones in St. Martin's-Lane.' (BM. g. 36. RAM. With dedication and list of subscribers, 2 pp.)

536. — Another issue.

General Evening Post, Jan. 17–19, 1745. (New editions.)

537. — 2d. edition.

General Advertiser, April 2, 1746.

538. — Another issue.

General Advertiser, Oct. 25, 1749. (New editions.)

539. Defesch's Duets for two German Flutes. Op. 9.

> Walsh Cat. 27: 'Defesch's Duets. 2 Sets. each 3s. od.'
> Randall Cat: 'Defech's Duets, Op. 9, Op. 11.'
> No Walsh copy of Op. 9 known. May refer to 'VI Sonatas for two German Flutes . . .
> Op. IX' published by J. Simpson. [1743.] (BM. g. 280. i. (1.))

540. Thirty Duets for two German Flutes Consisting of Variety of Aires in different Movements Compos'd for the Improvement of Young Practitioners on the German Flute By Willem Defesch. Opera XI. Price 3.ˢ
NB. Several of these Aires are proper for a German Flute & Violin.
London. Printed for I. Walsh, &c.

General Advertiser, March 16, 1747.

> Fol. pp. 20.
> BM. g. 280. i. (2.)
> Walsh Cat. 27: 'Defesch's Duets. 2 Sets. each 3s. od.'
> Randall Cat.: 'Defech's Duets. Op. 9, Op. 11.'

541. VI English Songs With Violins and German Flutes, and a Through Bass for the Harpsicord. Sung by Miss Falkner at Mary-Bone Gardens. Set to Musick by W: Defesch Price 1ˢ & 6ᵈ.
London Printed for and Sold by the Author . . . And at Mr Walsh's, &c.

[*c.* 1748.]

> Fol. pp. 9.
> BM. G. 427. (7.)

542. Six new English Songs for the Year 1749 Fitted for the Violin & German Flute with a Thorough Bass for the Harpsicord Sung by Miss Falkner and Mr Baker at Maryle-bon Gardens Set to Musick by Wᵐ Defesch.
London printed for the Author . . . at Mr Walsh's, &c.

[*c.* 1749.]

> Fol. ff. 6. Printed on one side only.
> BM. G. 800. m. (15.)

543. Twelve Sonatas for Two German Flutes, or Two Violins; With a Bass for the Violoncello or Harpsicord. By Willem Defesch. Opera XII.
London. Printed for I. Walsh, &c.

General Advertiser, Oct. 29, 1748.

> Fol. 3 parts.
> BM. g. 241. (4.) RM. 17. d. 2. (12.) RAM. RCM. Bod. OUL. Oriel College, Oxford.

544. VI Sonatas, for a Violoncello Solo with a Thorough Bass for the Harpsichord. Dedicated to His Grace Peregrine Duke of Ancaster. and Kesteren. Hereditary Lord great Chamberlain of England &c. &c. &c. . . . By William Defesch. Opera XIII.

London. Printed for I. Walsh, &c.

Public Advertiser, Nov. 2, 1757.

> Fol. pp. 24.
> BM. g. 225. b. (3.) RCM. Rowe.
> Another edition from the same plates originally issued without an imprint, *c.* 1750. (BM. g. 510. (1.).) Manchester.

545. Defesch's Solos. 5s. od. (For 2 Violoncellos.)

[*c.* 1757.]

> Walsh Cat. 27.
> This appears to refer to No. 544, 'VI Sonatas . . . Opera XIII.'
> Randall Cat.: 'Defesch's Solos (for two Violoncellos), Op. 13. 5s. od.'

546. Mr Defesch's Songs Sung at Marybon-Gardens.
Printed for I. Walsh.

London Evening-Post, Sept. 27–29, 1753. (Defesch's New Songs, sung by Mrs. Chambers, at Marybon Gardens. Price 1s.)

> Fol. ff. 12. Printed on one side only.
> BM. G. 316. a. (17.)
> With illustrated title-page engraved by M. Van der Gucht for Saggione's 'Temple of Love'. Smith 222. Pl. 17. Contains two songs by T. A. Arne.

DELIGHTFUL MUSICAL COMPANION

547. The Delightful Musical Companion. 10s. 6d.

[*c.* 1730.]

> Walsh Cat. 18.
> Not identified, but probably refers to copies of Peter Fraser's publication 'The Delightfull Musical Companion for Gentlemen and Ladies', issued in 1726. (Vol. I. BM. C. 370.) In the proposals for this work (*Daily Post*, Feb. 13, 1725) Peter Fraser, the publisher, stated 'If any of the subscribers please to enclose or signify their favourite Songs in a Penny-Post Letter to Mr. Walsh, it shall be inserted.'

548. The Delightful Musical Companion, or select Duets for two German Flutes or Violins Compos'd by Mr. Handel and other eminent Authors.
London. Printed for J. Walsh, &c.

Daily Advertiser, Jan. 31, Feb. 10, 1744.

> 8°. pp. 24.
> Rowe.
> The only composer named is Handel.

549. A second Set of celebrated Duets for two German Flutes, call'd The Delightful Musical Companion, by Mr. Handel, Hasse, Arne and Howard. Price 1s. 6d.

General Advertiser, April 27, 1744.

8°.

No copy known with this title. For contents, &c. *see* complete edition in two vols. (No. 553.)

London Evening-Post, June 23–26, 1744: 'Two Sets of Select Duets for two German Flutes, by Mr. Howard and Mr. Arne, called The Delightful Musical Companion.'

550. A third Set of select Duets for two German Flutes, call'd The Delightful Musical Companion, by the best Masters.

Printed for J. Walsh, &c.

Daily Advertiser, July 28, 1744. (Just publish'd.)

8°.

No copy known with this title. For contents, &c., *see* complete edition in two vols. (No. 553.)

551. A fourth Set of select Duets or Sonatas for two German Flutes, by the best Italian Masters, call'd The Delightful Musical Companion.

Printed for J. Walsh, &c.

Daily Advertiser, Sept. 29, 1744. (Just published.)

8°.

No copy known with this title. For contents, &c., *see* complete edition in two vols. (No. 553.)

552. Five Sets of Duets or Sonatas for two German Flutes call'd The Delightful Musical Companion, compos'd in an easy Taste by Sig. Hasse, and others. Each 1s. 6d.

Printed for J. Walsh, &c.

Daily Advertiser, August 6, 1745.

8°.

No copy known of the Fifth Set with original title-page.

For contents, &c., *see* complete edition in two vols. (No. 553.)

Sets 6–8 of the Duets were published *c.* 1745–7, but no newspaper advertisements of them as separate works have been traced.

553. Hasse &c. Select Duets For two German Flutes or Violins Call'd The Delightfull Musical Companion. Vol. I.

London. Printed for I. Walsh, &c.

— Vol. II.

[*c.* 1747.]

8°.

BM. d. 139. RCM. (Vol. I.) Coke.

Containing the eight previously issued sets or parts with the collective title-page as issued for Vol. II and as altered for Vol. I by erasure on the paper. The two volumes were sold complete at 12s. od. or in 8 books or parts at 1s. 6d. each.

In the BM. copy, each part has the title-page of the volume as above with the part number added in MS. to parts 2–4 of each volume.

No newspaper advertisement traced of the collected edition, but Walsh advertised in Cat. 24*a* as 'Hasse's Duets, Vol. 1st, 4 Books, each 1s. 6d. Hasse's Duets, Vol. 2d. 4 Books, each 1s. 6d.', and in Cat. 25 as 'Hasse's Duets, 2 Vols 12s. od.' Hasse's name on the title-page and in the advertisements suggests that the sets of unnamed 'Sonatas' and 'Duets' were by him.

DELIZIE DELL'OPERE

This series is a collected edition of various sets of Favourite Songs out of Italian Operas and other collections of songs which also appear under their respective headings in this bibliography.

The series was republished by William Randall as Vols. I–XIV (BM. G. 159), *c*. 1776, from the Walsh plates with illustrated passe-partout title-pages of Vols. I–X and XII as used for Vols. X and XI of the Walsh edition and title-pages of Vols. XI, XIII, and XIV as used for Vols. IV–IX of the Walsh edition, with the volume numbers in MS. The contents of the Randall volumes and the order of some of the items differ from those of the original Walsh edition. Vols. I and II (Randall) consist mostly of different works from Walsh; the contents of pp. 1–185 of Vols. IX and XIII are the same; the contents of pp. 65–191 of Vol. X and pp. 1–32, 51–134, 140–50 of Vol. XIV are the same, and large portions of Vols. XI and XII are identical. Copies of 'A Catalogue of Vocal and Instrumental Music, For the year 1776. Printed for, and sold by William Randall', &c., are bound up with Vols. I–X. These Randall issues are not included separately under the entries for the works in this bibliography but are all listed separately in W. Barclay Squire's 'Catalogue of Printed Music published between 1487 and 1800 now in the British Museum' (1912).

The title-pages of the volumes give 'Delizie dell Opere' but the work was generally advertised as 'Delizie dell' Opere' and this form has been used in this bibliography for entries of separate works in the series.

554. Le Delizie dell' Opere. Vol. 1.

[*c*. 1730.]

Fol. Frontispiece. A Table of the Favourite Songs, &c. pp. 226.

Walsh Cat. 18: 'Bononcini's Works. Le Delizie Dell' Opere Vol. I. containing the Favourite Songs out of all his Operas. £1. 1s. od. N? 337.

A reissue of '2ᵈ Book Apollo's Feast', &c. (No. 41) with Walsh only in the imprint and N? 337 added to the title-page.

555. [Another issue.] Le Delizie dell Opere. Being a Collection of all the Favourite Songs in Score, Collected from the Operas Compos'd by Pescetti Hasse Porpora Vinci Veracini Bononcini. [Vol. I.]

London. Printed for I. Walsh, &c.

[*c*. 1745.]

Fol. Illustrated passe-partout title-page. 'A Table of the Celebrated 'Songs', &c. pp. 226. RCM.

556. [Another issue.] Le Delizie dell Opere. Being a Collection of all the Favourite Songs in Score, Collected from the Operas Compos'd by Lampugnani Hasse Pergolisi [*sic*] Porpora Pescetti Terradellas Vinci Galuppi Veracini Leo Bononcini Count S͏ᵗ Germain Vol. I.

London. Printed for I. Walsh, &c.

[*c.* 1750.]

> Fol. Illustrated passe-partout title-page. pp. 226.
> Rowe.
> 'I' is in MS.
> Contains songs from: 'Aquilio'; 'Artaxerxes', A. Ariosti; 'Astartus', G. Bononcini; 'Calfurnia', G. Bononcini; 'Coriolanus', A. Ariosti; 'Crispus', G. Bononcini; 'Darius', A. Ariosti; 'Elpidia', L. Vinci; 'Erminia', G. Bononcini; 'Griselda', G. Bononcini; 'Pharnaces', G. Bononcini; 'Vespasian', A. Ariosti.

557. Le Delizie dell Opere. Being a Collection of all the Favourite Songs in Score, Collected from the Operas Compos'd by Pescetti Hasse Porpora Vinci Veracini Bononcini To which is Prefixt the Famous Salve Regina by Sigͬ Hasse. Vol. II. N.B. This Volume contains all the Songs Sung by the Celebrated Farinelli.

London. Printed for I. Walsh, &c.

London Daily Post, and General Advertiser, Jan. 15, 1740.

> Fol. Illustrated passe-partout title-page. 'A Table of the Songs', &c. pp. 232.
> RCM. Reid.
> Contains songs from: 'The Famous Salve Regina', J. A. Hasse; 'Diana and Endymion', G. B. Pescetti; 'Partenio', F. M. Veracini; 'Demetrius', G. B. Pescetti; 'Sabrina'; 'Vello d'Oro' (La Conquista del Vello d'Oro), G. B. Pescetti; 'Siroe', J. A. Hasse; 'Orfeo'; 'Aeneas' (Enea nel Lazio), N. A. Porpora; 'Adriano', F. M. Veracini; 'Artaxerxes', J. A. Hasse; 'Polytheme', N. A. Porpora; 'Ariadne', N. A. Porpora; 'Arbaces'; 'Ormisda'; 'Astyanax', G. Bononcini; 'Cato'; 'Venceslaus'; 'Elisa' and 'Lucius Verus', A. Ariosti.
> Walsh Cat. 18: 'Hasse. Le Delizie dell' Opere, being the favourite Airs from all his Operas in Score Vol. 2d. £1. 1s. od.'

558. Le Delizie dell Opere. Being a Collection of the Favourite Songs in Score Collected from all the Operas Compos'd by Sigͬ Galuppi. Vol. III.

London. Printed for I. Walsh, &c.

Daily Advertiser, Dec. 10, 1742. (Le Delizie dell' Opere. 3 vol.)

> Fol. Illustrated passe-partout title-page. 'A Table of the Songs', &c. pp. 2–198.
> RCM.
> Contains songs from: 'Nel Trionfo della Continenza'; 'Antigono'; 'Sirbaces'; 'Enrico'; 'Scipione in Cartagine'; 'Penelope', all by B. Galuppi; and 'Alessandro in Persia.'

559. Le Delizie dell Opere. Being a Collection of all the Favourite Songs in Score, Collected from the Operas Compos'd by Lampugnani Hasse Pergolisi [*sic*] Porpora Pescetti Terradellas Vinci Galuppi Veracini Leo Bononcini Count S͏ᵗ Germain Vol. IV.

London. Printed for I. Walsh, &c.

General Advertiser, Feb. 11, 1746. (Le Delizie dell' Opere. . . 4 v. Just published.)

> Fol. Illustrated passe-partout title-page. 'A Table of all the Songs', &c. pp. 2–201.
> Rowe.
> 'IV' is in MS.
> Contains songs from: 'L'Inconstanza Delusa'; 'Alceste', G. B. Lampugnani; 'Alfonso', G. B. Lampugnani; 'Artamene', C. W. von Gluck; 'Rosalinda', F. M. Veracini; 'Alexander in India', G. B. Lampugnani; 'Merode'; 'Olimpia'; 'Temistocle', N. A. Porpora; 'Alexander in Persia'; 'Penelope', B. Galuppi; and 'Scipione in Cartagine', B. Galuppi.

560. Le Delizie dell Opere . . . Vol. V.

London. Printed for I. Walsh, &c.

General Advertiser, Nov. 22, 1748. (Le Delizie dell' Opere, Vol. 5 . . . Index of all the Songs in the first five Volumes.); Oct. 24, 1749. (5 vol.)

> Fol. Illustrated passe-partout title-page as Vol. IV with 'V' in MS. 'A Table of the Songs', &c. pp. 2–204.
> RM. 13. c. 18. RCM. (Two copies, one with 'Tables' of Vols. I–V.) Rowe.
> Contains songs from: 'Stabat Mater', G. B. Pergolesi; 'Dudici Arie e Due Duetto', D. M. B. Terradellas; 'Semiramide', J. A. Hasse; 'Dido,' J. A. Hasse; 'L' Ingratitudine Punita'; 'Mitridate', D. M. B. Terradellas; 'Bellerofonte', D. M. B. Terradellas; and 'Phaeton', P. D. Paradies.

561. Le Delizie dell Opere . . . Vol. VI.

London. Printed for I. Walsh, &c.

Public Advertiser, Dec. 8, 1753. (Le Delizie del Opere . . . in 6 v.)

> Fol. Illustrated passe-partout title-page as Vol. IV with 'VI' in MS. 'A Table of the Songs', &c. pp. 209.
> RCM.
> Contains songs from: 'L'Olimpiade'; 'Nerone'; 'Attilio Regolo', N. Jomelli; 'La Caduta de' Giganti', C. W. von Gluck; 'Adriano in Siria', L. V. Ciampi; 'Il Negligente', L. V. Ciampi; 'Don Calascione'; 'Tre Cicisbei ridicoli'; 'Orazio' and 'La Commedia in Commedia'.

562. Le Delizie dell Opere . . . Vol. VII.

London. Printed for I. Walsh, &c.

[*c.* 1755.]

> Fol. Illustrated passe-partout title-page as Vol. IV with 'VII' in MS. 'A Table of the Songs', &c. pp. 203.
> RCM.
> Contains songs from: 'Ezio', D. Perez; 'Ezio' with 'Ipermestra', J. A. Hasse, &c.; 'Ricimero', B. Galuppi; 'Siroe', G. B. Lampugnani; 'Bertoldo', L. V. Ciampi; Arie 6, L. V. Ciampi; and 'Annibale in Capua'.

563. Le Delizie dell Opere . . . Vol. VIII.

London. Printed for I. Walsh, &c.

Public Advertiser, Dec. 4, 1758. (Of whom may be had Le Delizie del Opera. . . in 8 volumes.)

Fol. Illustrated passe-partout title-page as Vol. IV with 'VIII' in MS. 'A Table of the Songs', &c. pp. 206.
RCM.
Contains songs from: 'Demetrio'; 'Zenobia', G. Cocchi; 'Issipile', G. Cocchi; 'Creso'; Arie 6, L. Vinci; 'Il Demofoonte'; 'Tito Manlio'; 'Andromaca', N. Jomelli; and 'Didone', L. V. Ciampi.

564. Le Delizie dell Opere . . . Vol. IX.
London. Printed for I. Walsh, &c.

[*c.* 1760.]

Fol. Illustrated passe-partout title-page as Vol. IV with 'IX' in MS. 'A Table of the Songs', &c. pp. 201.
RCM.
Contains songs from: 'Vologeso'; 'Farnace', D. Perez and G. Cocchi; 'Ciro Riconosciuto'; 'Attalo'; 'L'Olimpiade'; 'Attilio Regolo', N. Jomelli; 'Nerone'; 'La Caduta de Giganti', C. W. von Gluck; and 'Solimano'.

565. Le Delizie dell Opere. Being a Collection of all the Favourite Songs in Score, Collected from the Operas Compos'd by Bach Perez Cocchi Ciampi Jomelli Giardini Galuppi Vinci Pergolesi Leo Lampugnani Terradellas Hasse Porpora C. S.t Germain Pescetti Veracini Bononcini. Vol. X.
London. Printed for I. Walsh, &c.

[*c.* 1763.]

Fol. Illustrated passe-partout title-page. 'A Table of the Songs', &c. pp. 2–195.
RCM.
'X' is in MS.
Contains songs from: 'Il Tutore e la Pupilla'; 'Le Pescatrici'; 'La Calamita de' Cuori'; 'Il Filosofo di Campagna', B. Galuppi (with two arias from 'Il Mondo nella Luna'); 'Il Mondo nella Luna', B. Galuppi; 'La Famiglia in Scompiglio', G. Cocchi; 'Il Mercato di Malmantile'; 'Bertoldo', L. V. Ciampi (with a duet from 'Il Mercato di Malmantile', B. Galuppi); and 'Tolomeo'.

566. Le Delizie dell Opere . . . Vol. XI.
London. Printed for I. Walsh, &c.

Public Advertiser, Feb. 18, 1764. (Le Delizie del Opera; the favourite Songs from all the Operas for 20 Years up to Zanaida, in 12 [or rather, 11] Vols.); May 14, 1764. (11 Vols.)

Fol. Illustrated passe-partout title-page as Vol. X with 'XI' in MS. 'A Table of the Songs', &c. pp. 207.
RCM.
Contains songs from: 'Zanaida', J. C. Bach; 'Orione', J. C. Bach; 'Alessandro nelle Indie'; 'Tito Manlio', G. Cocchi; 'Antigona'; 'Tolomeo'; 'Arianna e Teseo'; 'Attilio Regolo', N. Jomelli; 'Didone Abbandonata', D. Perez, and 'Arminio', D. Perez.
Walsh Cat. 27: 'Le Delizie Del Opere, being the Favourite Songs from all the Italian Operas. 11 Vol.s each £1. 1s. 0d.'

DEMETRIO

567. The Favourite Songs in the Opera Call'd Demetrio.
London. Printed for I. Walsh, &c.

Public Advertiser, Dec. 2, 1757; Feb. 6, 1758. (A Second Set of favourite Songs in Demetrio.)

> Fol. Passe-partout title-page. pp. 2–21, 1–11.
> BM. G. 205. RM. 13. c. 20. (6.) (1st Collection only.)
> Pasticcio. The only composer named is Cocchi.
> Republished in 'Le Delizie dell' Opere', Vol. VIII, pp. 2–32.

568. The Favourite Songs in the Opera Call'd Demetrio Price $\frac{s}{5}$/.
London. Printed for I. Walsh, &c.

[*c*. 1760.]

> Fol. pp. 2–21, 2 blanks, 1–24.
> RCM.
> 'Demetrio Price $\frac{s}{5}$/.' is in MS.
> Randall Cat.: 'Demetrio, 2 Collect. each 2s. 6d. Cocchi'.

DEMOFOONTE

569. The Favourite Songs in the Opera Call'd Demofoonte, &c.
London. Printed for I. Walsh, &c.

Public Advertiser, Dec. 24, 1755.

> Fol. Passe-partout title-page. pp. 2–21.
> BM. G. 201. (1.) RM. 13. c. 20. (8.) London University. RAM. RCM.
> Pasticcio. Words by Pietro Metastasio.
> Republished in 'Le Delizie dell' Opere', Vol. VIII, pp. 124–43.

DEMOIVRE (Daniel)

570. A Set of Aires for a single Flute. Op: Primo. 1s. 6d. N⁰ 8.

[*c*. 1730.]

> Walsh Cat. 18.
> Presumably Smith 53 ('Lessons for a Single Flute') with Walsh only in the imprint and 'N⁰ 8' added to the title-page.
> Walsh Cat. 11*a*: 'Demoivers Aires for a Single Flute. Opera Prima.'

571. A Set of Aires for 2 Flutes Opera Seconda. 2s. od. N⁰ 107.

[*c*. 1730.]

> Walsh Cat. 18.
> Not identified. *See* No. 572.

572. Solos for a Flute and a Bass. Opera Seconda.

[*c*. 1730.]

Walsh Cat. 11a.
Probably Smith 148 ('Aires for a Flute and a Bass . . .yᵉ 2ᵈ Collection', &c. BM. b. 1.
Obl. 4°)..
Not in Walsh Cat. 18, where No. 571 appears as 'Opera Seconda'.

573. Aires made on purpose for a Flute as Allemands, Gavotts, Sarabands, Minuets
and Jiggs . . . 3ᵈ Collection.
Printed for J. Walsh, &c.

[c. 1730.]

Obl. 4°. ff. 14. Printed on one side only.
Walsh Cat. 11a: 'Demoivres Solos for a Flute and a Bass. Opera Terza.'
Walsh Cat. 18: 'A Set of Aires for a Flute and a Bass Op: Terza. 1s. 6d. Nº 9.'
Smith 473 (Demoivrs 3d Book of curious Airs for a single Flute) with Walsh only in the
imprint and 'Nº 9' added to the title-page. Title from earlier edition Durham Cathedral
Library. BUC.

DE SANTI (Giovanni)

See Santi (Giovanni de)

DESNOYER (   )

See No. 1068. Minuets For His Majesty's Birth Day . . . 1747; No. 1070. Minuet
Perform'd at Court . . . 1749.

DEVIL TO PAY

574. Songs in the Devil to Pay; or, the Wives Metamorphos'd as they are per-
form'd at the Theatre Royal in Drury Lane. The Tunes Proper for the German
Flute, Violin, and Common Flute. Price 6d.
London. Printed and Sold at the Musick Shops. Nº 301.

[1732.]

BM. A. 869. a. (3.) Manchester.
Walsh Cat. 18: 'The Devil to Pay . . . 6d. Nº 301.'

575. The Devil to Pay. as Perform'd at the Theatres. For the Harpsicord Violin or
German Flute Price 1ˢ 6ᵈ
London. Printed for I. Walsh, &c.

[c. 1740.]

8°. pp. 16.
Mitchell. (2.)

DIEUPART (Charles)

576. Select Lessons for the Harpsicord or Spinnett as Allemands Sarabands Corants

Gavots Minuets and Jiggs Compos'd by M.ʳ Dieupart Plac'd on five lines in yᵉ English Cliff Engraven in a fair Caracter. N.º 175.
London. Printed for I. Walsh . . . I. Hare, &c.

[*c.* 1730.]

> Obl. fol. pp. 16.
> Fitz.
> Smith 179 with 'N.º 175' added to the title-page.
> Walsh Cat. 18: 'Dieupart's Lessons (Harpsicord, Spinnet or Organ). 2s. 6d. N.º 175.'

577. Six Sonatas for a Flute and a Through Bass Compos'd by M.ʳ Dieupart Humbly Inscrib'd to the R.ᵗ Hon.ᵇˡᵉ Lady Essex Finch.
London Printed for I: Walsh . . . N.º 115.

[*c.* 1730.]

> Fol. pp. 2–32.
> Smith 508 (Rowe) with Walsh only in the imprint and 'N.º 115' added to the title-page.
> Walsh Cat. 18: 'Solos (for a Flute and a Bass). 5s. 0d. N.º 115.'

DIVINE COMPANION

578. Divine Companion. 4s. 0d. N.º 214.

[*c.* 1730.]

> Walsh Cat. 18.
> Walsh Cat. 15*a*: 'The Divine Companion'.
> Presumably refers to copies of the work originally issued for Henry Playford in 1701 (BM. B. 655) which Walsh was selling.

DIVINE HARMONY

Divine Harmony (Divine Harmony The 2.ᵈ Collection.)
 See Nos. 1544, 1545. Weldon (John)

DIVISION FLUTE

579. The First Part of The Division Flute Containing a Collection of Divisions upon Several Excellent Grounds for the Flute being Very Improveing and Delight-full to all Lovers of that Instrument the whole Fairly Engraven.
London Printed for I. Walsh . . . N.º 17.

[*c.* 1730.]

> Fol. 'A Table', &c. ff. 16. Printed on one side only.
> Walsh Cat. 18: 'Grounds and Divisions 1st Book. (Single Flute.) 2s. 6d. N.º 17.'
> Smith 184 (BM. h. 250. *c.* (1.)) with Walsh only in the imprint and 'N.º 17' added to the title-page.

580. The Second Part of the Division Flute Containing The Newest Divisions

upon The Choicest Grounds for the Flute as also Several Excellent Preludes Chacon's and Cibells by The best Masters The whole Fairly Engraven. price 2ˢ 6ᵈ

> London Printed for I. Walsh . . . Nᵒ 18.

[*c.* 1730.]

> Fol. ff. 16. Printed on one side only.
> Walsh Cat. 18: 'Grounds and Divisions 2d Book. (Single Flute.) 2s. 6d. Nᵒ 18.'
> Smith 278 (BM. h. 250. c. (1*)) with Walsh only in the imprint and 'Nᵒ 18' added to the title-page.

DIVISION VIOLIN

581. The First Part of the Division Violin Containing A Collection of Divisions upon Several Excellent Grounds for the Violin The Sixth Edition, &c.

> London Printed for I. Walsh . . . Nᵒ 161.

[*c.* 1730.]

> Obl. 4°. pp. 58.
> Walsh Cat. 18: 'Grounds and Divisions 1st Book. 2s. 6d. Nᵒ 161.'
> Smith 167 (RCM.) of which this is a reissue or another edition with Walsh only in the imprint and 'Nᵒ 161' added to the title-page.

582. The Second Part of the Division Violin Containing the newest Divisions upon Grounds for the Violin . . . the Fourth Edition, &c.

> London Printed for I. Walsh . . . Nᵒ 162.

[*c.* 1730.]

> Obl. 4°. pp. 51.
> Walsh Cat. 18: 'Grounds and Divisions 2d. Book. 2s. 6d. Nᵒ 162.'
> Smith 174 (RCM.), of which this is a reissue or another edition with Walsh only in the imprint and 'Nᵒ 162' added to the title-page.

DOCTOR FAUSTUS

Comic Tunes in Dr. Faustus, by Samuel Arnold.

> *See* No. 748. Harlequin Sorcerer.

583. Dᵣ Faustus or the Necromancer a Masque of Song's as they were perform'd at the Theatre in Lincolns Inn Fields Publish'd for February. Price 1ˢ [By J. E. Galliard.]

> London Printed for and Sold by I: Walsh . . . and Inᵒ & Ioseph Hare, &c.

[*c.* 1723.]

> Fol. ff. 1–8 and 2 unnumbered folios. Printed on one side only.
> BM. Add. MSS. 31588, f. 140. RCM.

584. The Masks of Apollo and Daphne and Dᵣ Faustus. 2s. od. Nᵒ 309.

[*c.* 1730.]

Walsh Cat. 18.

No details are known of this combined edition of the two works, Walsh continued to advertise 'Dr Faustus' separately. (*See* also No. 653.)

DON CALASCIONE

585. The Favourite Songs in the Opera Call'd Don Calascione.
London. Printed for I. Walsh, &c.

General Advertiser, Feb. 2, 1749.

> Fol. Passe-partout title-page. pp. 2–20.
> BM. H. 348. h. (1.) Gresham. RAM. RCM. Pendlebury. Rowe.
> Pasticcio. Partly by G. Latilla.
> Republished with the addition of pp. 11–17 (additional songs) in 'Delizie dell' Opere' Vol. VI, pp. 119–44.

DOTHEL (Nicolas)

586. Six Sonatas in Three Parts for a German Flute, a Violin, with a Thorough Bass for the Harpsicord or Violoncello Compos'd by Sig.^r Nicolas Dothel le Fils.
London. Printed for I. Walsh, &c.

Public Advertiser, July 14, 1761.

> Fol. 3 parts.
> BM. g. 242. (8.) RM. 17. d. 2. (3.) GUL.
> Not listed as such in Walsh Cat. 27 or Randall Cat., but may be identified as one or other of the following two entries.

587. Dothel le Fils Solos. 5s. od. (For a German Flute and Harpsicord.)

> Walsh Cat. 27.
> Randall Cat.

588. Dothel Le Fils Sonatas. 5s. od. (For two German Flutes and a Bass.)

> Walsh Cat. 27.
> Randall Cat.

DRAGHI (Giovanni Baptista)

589. Six Select Sutes of Lessons for the Harpsicord in Six Severall Keys, Consisting of Preludes, Allemands, Corrants, Sarabands, Arietts, Minuets, & Jiggs, Compos'd by Sign Giovanni Baptista Draghi.
London   Printed for I. Walsh . . . and I. Hare . . . and P. Randall . . . N.º 199.

c. [1730.]

> Fol. ff. 35. Printed on one side only.
> Fitz.
> Smith 233 (BM. g. 18.) with 'N.º 199' added in MS. to the title-page.
> Walsh Cat. 18: 'Sig.^r Baptist Draghi's Lessons. 5s. od. N.º 199.'

DRINKING SONGS

590. Drinking Songs. 2s. 6d. N⁰ 323.
— 2d Collection. 2s. 6d. N⁰ 329.

[*c.* 1730.]

Fol.
Walsh Cat. 18.
Walsh Cat. 17*a*: 'Drinking Songs 2 Books. (Just Published.)'
BM. H. 1610. Three collections of single sheet songs with titles in MS.:
(1) A Collection of Drinking Songs.
    Printed for I Walsh in Catherine Street.
(2) A Collection of Drinking Songs Book 2ᵈ
(3) Drinking Songs 2ᵈ
All without foliation or indexes. No. 3 consists of duplicates of numbers in Nos. 1 and 2

DUBOURGH (MATTHEW)

See No. 10 Airs. A Choice Collection of Aires and Duets for two German Flutes . . . To which is added a favourite Trumpet Tune of Mr Dubourg's, &c.; Nos. 1068, 1069. Minuets For His Majesty's Birthday . . . 1747 (1748); No. 1124. Musica Bellicosa . . . to which is added Geminiani's and Dubourg's Serenading Trumpet-tunes, &c.

DUETS

Duets or Canzonets for two Voices or Two German Flutes . . . Compos'd by . . . Hasse, &c.
See Nos. 808–10, 815. Hasse (Johann Adolph)

591. Forty select Duets, Ariettas and Minuets for two Guittars or Mandavines, by the best Masters, Price 3s.
Printed for J. Walsh, &c.

Public Advertiser, June 22, 1757.

Walsh Cat. 27: 'Forty Select Ariets. 3s. od. (For the Guitar.)'
Randall Cat.: 'Forty select Airs. 3s. od. (For the Guittar.)'

DUNN (JOHN)

See No. 1419. Summer's Tale.

DU PHLY (   )

592. A Collection of Lessons for the Harpsicord Compos'd by Mr Du Phly. London. Printed for I. Walsh, &c.

Public Advertiser, Dec. 18, 1764.

Obl. fol. pp. 2–29.
RM. 16. a. 14. (5.) RCM.

DUPUIS (Thomas Sanders)

See No. 38. Antigona

D'URFEY (Thomas)

593. Durfey's Songs. 5s. od. N.º 322.

[*c.* 1730.]

> Fol.?
> Walsh Cat. 18.
> Walsh Cat. 15a.
> Smith 358 ('A Collection of Comical Songs', &c.) and Walsh Cat. 9a: 'Durfey's Songs. 2s. od.' may refer to an earlier edition; otherwise not identified.
> Walsh Cat. 17a, as: 'Just Publish'd.'

ECCLES (John)

594. The Tunes in Cato for 2 Violins and a Bass. 2s. od.

[*c.* 1730.]

> Walsh Cat. 18.
> Not identified.
> May be for the Tragedy by Joseph Addison, or for the Opera of 'Cato', an anonymous work. (*See* No. 344. Cato.)

595. A Collection of Songs for One Two and Three Voices Together with such Symphonys for Violins or Flutes As were by the Author design'd for any of Them; and a Thorough-Bass to Each Song Figur'd for an Organ Harpsicord or Theorbo-Lute. Compos'd by Mr Iohn Eccles, Master of Her Majesty's Musick.
London Printed for I. Walsh . . . N.º 317.

[*c.* 1730.]

> Fol. Dedication. 'A Table of the Songs', &c. pp. 165.
> Walsh Cat. 18: 'A General Collection of all His Songs. £1. 5s. od. N.º 317.'
> Smith 156 (BM. G. 300) with Walsh only in the imprint and 'N.º 317' added to the title-page.

596. The Iudgment of Paris or the Prize Music as it was perform'd Before the Nobility and Gentry in Dorsett Garden as also att the Theatre Compos'd by Mr I: Eccles Master of Her Majesti's Music The Words by Mr Congreve.
London Printed for I. Walsh . . . N.º 328.

[*c.* 1730.]

> Fol. Dedication pp. 71.
> Walsh Cat. 18: 'The Judgment of Paris. 7s. od. N.º 328.'
> Smith 102 (BM. H. 111. Without illustrated title-page. Hirsch II. 226. With illustrated title-page) with Walsh only in the imprint and 'N.º 328' added to the title-page.

597. Eight Sets of Tunes for 2 Violins and a Bass made for several Plays. 12s. od.
[*c.* 1730.]

    Walsh Cat. 18: 'Eccles's Works.'
    A collection of previously issued music for plays, not identified, but probably all included in Smith.

See also No. 751. Harmonia Anglicana. Book III.

EGERTON ( )

    See No. 166. Birkhead ( ) and Egerton ( ) Twenty four new Country Dances for the year 1722, &c.

ELISA

598. The favourite Songs in the new Opera Call'd Elisa as also the additional Songs in the Opera of Rodelinda Compos'd by Mr Handel as they are perform'd at the King's Theatre for the Royal Accademy.
London Printed for and sold by Ino Walsh ... and Ioseph Hare, &c.

    [*c.* 1726.]

    Large fol. Passe-partout title-page. 'A Table of the Favourite Songs', &c. ff. 22. Printed on one side only.
    Rowe. NLS. (Without title-page.)

599. — Favourite Songs in Elisa. 2s. 6d. No 252.

    [*c.* 1730.]

    With Walsh only in the imprint and 'No 252' added to the title-page.
    Walsh Cat. 18.
    Contains 6 songs from 'Elisa' (pasticcio, attributed to Porpora by Chrysander) and 4 additional songs and one duet from 'Rodelinda'. One number included in 'Le Delizie dell' Opere', Vol. II, p. 229.

ELLWAY (Thomas)

    See No. 750. Harmonia Anglicana. Book II.

ELPIDIA

The Favourite Songs in the Opera call'd Elpidia.

    See No. 1508. Vinci (Leonardo)

ENGLISH HARMONY REVIVED

    See No. 749. Harmonia Anglicana or English Harmony Reviv'd, &c.

ENGLISH SONGS

600. A Collection of English Songs; with a Thorough Bass for the Harpsichord: Set to Musick by an eminent Author.

Printed for John Walsh, &c.

Universal Spectator, and Weekly Journal, May 13, 1732.

> This refers to a Handel collection. (*See* Smith. Handel. A Descriptive Catalogue. p. 176.)

601. Twelve English Songs sung by Miss Stevenson and Miss Falkner, &c. at Vauxhall and Marybon Gardens. Pr. 1s. 6d.

Printed for J. Walsh, &c.

London Evening-Post, Oct. 6–8, 1748.

602. N⁰ I A favourite Collection of English Songs Sung by Mʳ Beard, Miss Young &c. at Ranelagh Gardens. 1757.

Printed for I. Walsh, &c.

London Evening-Post, May 19–21, 1757.

> Fol. pp. 11.
> BM. H. 2815. a. (14.); G. 323. (3.) Hirsch M. 1386. RCM. Dundee. Leeds.
> The only composer named is Mr. Arne.
> *Public Advertiser,* July 8, 1757. (A Favourite Collection of English Songs sung at the **Public** Gardens. 1757.) May refer to the same work.
> Presumably Randall Cat.: 'Ranelagh and Vauxhall Songs, 3 Books, each 1s. 6d.'

See also Arne (Michael) for other collections.

603. N⁰ II. A favourite Collection of English Songs, &c.

> Fol.

[*c.* 1757.]

> Presumably Randall Cat.: 'Ranelagh and Vauxhall Songs, 3 Books, each 1s. 6d.'

604. N⁰ III A favourite Collection of English Songs Sung by Mʳ Beard, Miss Young &c. at Ranelagh Gardens. 1758.

Printed for I. Walsh, &c.

[1758.]

> Fol. pp. 11.
> BM. H. 1652. w. (23.)
> 'III' has been altered from 'I' in MS.
> The only composer named is Arne.
> Presumably Randall Cat.: 'Ranelagh and Vauxhall Songs, 3 Books, each 1s. 6d.'

See also Arne (Michael) for other collections.

605. The favourite English Songs, sung at Ranelagh and Vauxhall-Gardens. In Six Books.

Printed for J. Walsh, &c.

London Evening-Post, August 10–12, 1758.

> Not identified. The advertisement may refer to works recorded above and under **Arne** (Michael)

ENTERTAINMENTS

606. All the Entertainments Bound. 4s. od.

> [*c.* 1730.]
>> Walsh Cat. 18.
>> Not identified. Probably a collection of previously published music for plays or other dramatic works, various issues of which are probably included in Smith.

ERMINIA

The Favourite Songs in the Opera of Erminia.

> *See* No. 207. Bononcini (Giovanni)

ESSEX (JOHN)

607. The Dancing Master by Mr Essex. £1. 1s. od.

> [*c.* 1730.]
>> Walsh Cat. 18.
>> Presumably Smith 348 and 478 'For the Further Improvement of Dancing A Treatise of Chorography . . . Translated from the French of Monr Feuillet . . . Compos'd and Writt in Characters by John Essex', with Walsh only in the imprint.

> For further details *see* Smith 348 and 478.

> *See also* No. 925. Latour (   ) A Collection of Minuets, Rigadoons, & French Dances . . . Compos'd by Mr Essex.

ETEARCO

608. Songs in the Opera of Etearco as they are Perform'd at ye Queens Theatre. London Printed for J: Walsh . . . No 243.

> [*c.* 1730.]
>> Fol. Illustrated title-page. 'A Table of the Songs', &c. pp. 70.
>> Walsh Cat. 18: 'The Opera of Etearco. 9s. od. No 243. (With Symphonys for 2 Viols & Bass.)'
>> Pasticcio. Words adapted from Silvio Stampiglia.
>> Smith 384 (BM. I. 354. b.) with Walsh only in the imprint and 'No 243' added to the title-page.

EZIO

609. The Favourite Songs in the Opera Call'd Ezio [by J. A. Hasse &c.] With some Songs [by J. A. Hasse and G. B. Lampugnani] in Ipermestra never before Printed. London. Printed for I. Walsh, &c.

> *Public Advertiser*, April 28, 1755. (The Favourite Songs in Ezio by Sig. Hasse, with some Songs in Ipermestra, never before printed, Price 2s. 6d.)

>> Fol. Passe-partout title-page. pp. 1–7 (bottom centre), 1–4 (top corner), 1–12 (bottom centre), 1–21 (bottom centre).

BM. G. 173. Gresham. RCM. Coke. DAM.

Republished in 'Le Delizie dell' Opere', Vol. VII, pp. 41–47, 91–127. Pp. 1–21 of this work were previously published separately with the title 'The Favourite Songs in the Opera Call'd Ipermestra'. (No. 860.)

FABRIO ( )

610. Six Sonatas or Duets for two German Flutes or Violins Compos'd by Sig.ʳ Fabrio.

London. Printed for I. Walsh, &c.

Public Advertiser, June 18, 1762.

> Fol. pp. 2–21.
> BM. g. 70. g. (9.)

FACCO (Giacomo)

611. N.º 1. A Select Concerto for Violins and other Instruments in 6 Parts chose from the Works of Giacomo Facco. To be continued Monthly with a well chosen Concerto from the Works of the most Eminent Italian Authors at 1.ˢ 6.ᵈ each Publish'd for Jan.ʸ 1734.

Printed for I: Walsh in Catherine Street. where may be had just Publish'd 6 Concertos by Geminiani in 7 Parts Opera Terza.

London Evening-Post, Feb. 14–16, 1734. (Where may be had just publish'd. Price 1s. 6d.)

> Fol. 6 parts.
> BM. h. 141. f.
> The title is printed only at the top of the Violino Primo Principale part. The number '501' is at the bottom of each page of music.
> Afterwards issued as Concerto VI of 'Select Harmony Third Collection'. (*See* No. 1362.)

FAIRBANK ( )

> *See* Nos. 759, 761. Harpsichord Master. VIIIᵗʰ (Xᵗʰ) Book; No. 925, Latour
> ( ) A Collection of Minuets . . . Compos'd by . . . M.ʳ Fairbank, &c.

FAMIGLIA IN SCOMPIGLIO

The Favourite Songs in The Opera Call'd La Famiglia in Scompiglia

> *See* No. 389. Cocchi (Gioacchino)

FARINELLI (Carlo Broschi)

> *See* Broschi (Carlo) *called Farinelli*

FARNACE

The favourite Songs in the Opera call'd Pharnaces.

    See No. 209. Bononcini (Giovanni)

The Favourite Songs in the Opera Call'd Farnace.

    See No. 1193. Perez (Davidde) and Cocchi (Gioacchino)

FEDELLI (GIUSEPPE) called *Saggione*

612. Songs in the New Opera, Call'd The Temple of Love Compos'd by Signr Gioseppe Fedelli Saggione.
    Sold by I: Walsh . . . Nº 241.

    [*c.* 1730.]

        Fol. ff. or pp. 32.
        Smith 222 (BM. H. 124. (2.)) with Walsh only in the imprint and 'Nº 241 added to the title-page.
        Walsh Cat. 18: 'The Opera of Temple of Love. 9s. od, Nº 241.'

FEO (FRANCESCO)

    See No. 1009. Meraspe

FERRARI (DOMENICO)

    See No. 1128. Nardini (Pietro) and Ferrari (Domenico) Six Sonatas or Duets for Two Violins . . . Opera Seconda.

FESCH (WILLEM DE)

    See Defesch (Willem)

FESTING (MICHAEL CHRISTIAN)

613. Minuets with their Basses For Her Majesty Queen Caroline's Birth Day 1733 as they were performed at the Ball at Court. The Tunes proper for the Violin german Flute or Harpsicord. Compos'd by Mr. M. C. Festing. &c. Price 6ᵈ Note. where these are Sold may be had 2 Vol. of choice Minuets and Rigadoons, and 3 Vol. of the most celebrated Old and New Country Dances.
    London. Printed for and Sold by I: Walsh . . . Nº 166.

    Daily Post, March 15, 1733.

        Obl. 12º. ff. 9. Printed on one side only.
        Hirsch IV. 1596.
        Walsh Cat. 18: 'Festing's Minuets (Violin). 6ᵈ Nº 166.'

614. Minuets with their Basses For Her Majesty Queen Caroline's Birth Day 1734 as they were perform'd at the Ball at Court The Tunes proper for the Violin Ger-

man Flute or Harpsicord Compos'd by Mr. M. C. Festing. &c. Price 6ᵈ 2ᵈ Book.
Note. where these are Sold may be had 2 Vol. of choice Minuets and Rigadoons, &c.
London. Printed for and Sold by I: Walsh . . . Nº 166.

> [1734.]
>> Obl. 12º. ff. 12. Printed on one side only.
>> BM. a. 26. q. (9.)
>> Walsh Cat. 18: 'Festing's Minuets. 2ᵈ Book. (Violin.) Nº 512.'

615. Minuets with their Basses, For His Majesty's Birth Day. as they were perform'd at the Ball at Court. The Tunes proper for the Violin, German Flute or
Harpsicord. Compos'd by Mʳ Festing, and other Eminent Authors. Price 6ᵈ 3ᵈ
Book. 1735. Note. where these are sold may be had 2 Volumes of choice Minuets
and Rigadoons, &c.

> London. Printed for and sold by I: Walsh . . . Nº 526.

> *Country Journal: or, The Craftsman*, Nov. 9, 1734. (Minuets . . . for his Majesty's
Birth-Day . . . Published for the Year 1735.)

>> Obl. 12º. ff. [2], 3, 1–6. Printed on one side only.
>> BM. a. 26. q. (8.)
>> Walsh Cat. 18: 'Festing's Minuets 3ᵈ Book. (Violin.) Nº 527.'
>> The 4ᵗʰ Book and subsequent books appeared anonymously. (*See* Nos. 1053–1056, 1058,
>> 1059.)

616. Festing's Solos (for a Violin and a Bass). £1. 1s. od.

> [c. 1733.]
>> Walsh Cat. 18.
>> This may refer to 'Twelve Solo's for a Violin and Thorough Bass . . . Opera Prima. Lon-
>> don: Printed by William Smith . . . and sold only by the Author . . . MDCCXXX. price
>> One Guinea.' (BM. g. 951. b. Fol.)
>> This work was published by subscription and Walsh may have acquired surplus copies for
>> sale.

> *See also* No. 969. Love in a Village . . . Music by . . . Festing, &c.; No. 1061.
> Minuets. Select Minuets . . . Compos'd by . . . Mʳ M. C. Festing, &c.

FEUILLET (Raoul Auger)

617. Orchesography; or, The Art of Dancing by Characters, and Demonstrative
Figures, wherein the whole Art is explained with complete Tables of all Steps used
in Dancing; and Rules for the Motions of the Arms, & whereby any Person, who
understands Dancing, may of himself learn all manner of Dances; being an exact and
just Translation from the French of Monsieur Feuillet. By John Weaver. Dancing
Master. The 2d Edition. NB. To this edition is added the Rigadoon the Louvre,
and the Britagne in Characters; with the Contents or Index. The whole engraven.

Printed for and sold by John Walsh . . . and John and Joseph Hare, &c.

Post-Boy, Feb. 10–13, 1721 [i.e. 1722].

4°.
BM. 7907. i. 5. (Destroyed.)
See Smith 343*a*.

618. — With Walsh only in the imprint and 'N⁰ 160' added to the title-page.

[*c.* 1730.]

Walsh Cat. 18: 'Weaver's Art of Dancing. 12s. 0d. N⁰ 160.'

FILOSOFO DI CAMPAGNA

The Favourite Songs in The Opera Call'd Il Filosofo di Campagna.

See No. 672. Galuppi (Baldassare)

FINGER (GOTTFRIED)

619. Aires for 2 Violins. 3s. 0d. N⁰ 375.

[*c.* 1730.]

Walsh Cat. 18.
Smith 142*a* ('Six Sonatas for two Violins') and 609 ('Fingers Aires for two Violins') with Walsh only in the imprint and 'N⁰ 375' added to the title-page.

620. Six Solos for a Flute and a Bass. 4s. 0d. N⁰ 108.

[*c.* 1730.]

Walsh Cat. 18.
Not definitely identified, but may be Smith 82*a* ('VI Sonatas or Solo's. Three for a Violin & Three for a Flute wth a Thorough Bass', &c. Copy in possession of Richard Newton, Henley-in-Arden).

621. Six Solos for a Violin and a Bass. 4s. 0d. N⁰ 374.

[*c.* 1730.]

Walsh Cat. 18.
Not identified, presumably another edition of some earlier work, see reference under Smith 82*a*.

622. 12 Sonatas for 2 Violins and a Bass. 6s. 0d. N⁰ 468.

[*c.* 1730.]

Walsh Cat. 18.
Smith 177 ('Mr. Fingers 12 Sonata's in 4 parts') with Walsh only in the imprint and 'N⁰ 468' added to the title-page. The work was Op. 1 (Sonatæ XII, &c.) first published in London without publisher's name, 1688. (BM. K. i. 15.)

623. Six Sonata's of two Parts, For Two Flute's Composed by M̲ᵣ Finger Opera Secunda.
London Printed for I. Walsh . . . N̲° 67.

[*c.* 1730.]

Obl. fol. Parts.
Walsh Cat. 18: 'Six Sonatas for 2 Flutes. 3s. od. N̲° 67.'
Smith 99 (BM. c. 105. a. (2.) with Walsh only in the imprint and 'N̲° 67' added to the title-page.

624. Six Sets of Tunes for 2 Violins and a Bass made for several Plays. 9s. od.

[*c.* 1730.]

Walsh Cat. 18.
A collection of previously issued music for plays, not identified, but probably all included in Smith.

FINGER (Gottfried) and PURCELL (Daniel)

625. Six Sonatas or Solos for the Flute with a Through Bass for the Harpsichord, Compos'd by M̲ᵣ G. Finger and M̲ᵣ D. Purcell.
London Printed for J. Walsh, &c.

[*c.* 1733.]

Fol. pp. 17.
Walsh Cat. 15b: 'Fingers & Purcells Solos' (for a Flute & a Bass). 4s. od.
Smith 329 (BM. h. 17. (2.)) with Walsh only in imprint.

626. Fingers & Purcels Solos (for a Violin & a Bass). 4s. od.

[*c.* 1733.]

Walsh Cat. 15a.
Smith 277e, with Walsh only in the imprint.
Details of title-page not known.
Probably another edition of No. 625.

FINI (Michele)

See No. 1144. Orazio

FISCHIETTI (Domenico)

See No. 1010. Mercato di Malmantile

FLACKTON (William)

627. A Cantata And several Songs Set to Musick by William Flackton.
London Printed for the Author & sold by J. Simpson . . . J. Walsh . . . and M̲ʳˢ Wamsley, &c.

London Evening-Post, Jan. 6–8, 1747.

> Fol. pp. 11.
> BM. G. 427. (5.)

628. The Chace. Selected from the Celebrated Poem of William Somervile, Esq.ʳ Set to Musick For a Voice, Accompanied with a French Horn, Two Violins, a Tenor, & Thorough Bass For the Harpsicord. To which is added, Rosalinda; With several other Songs in Score. By William Flackton.

London Printed for the Author, & sold by M.ʳ Walsh . . . M.ʳ Wamsley . . . and M.ʳ Simpson, &c.

> *Daily Advertiser,* May 21, 1743. (Just publish'd.)

> > Fol. pp. 32. 'Philips Sculp.ᵗ' at foot of p. 32.
> > BM. H. 1650. c. (2.) RAM. Rowe.

> *Daily Advertiser,* Dec. 25, 1744. (This Day is publish'd.) This may be a readvertisement or refer to a new issue.

629. Six Sonatas for the Harpsichord or Organ, composed by Mr. William Flackton, of Canterbury. Price 4s.

Sold by Mr. Walsh . . . and John Johnson, &c.

> *Public Advertiser,* March 8, 1760.

630. Six Sonatas for Two Violins and a Violoncello or Harpsicord by William Flackton.

London. Printed for the Author, & sold by M.ʳ Walsh . . . and M.ʳ Johnson . . . price 5s. MDCCLVIII.

> *Whitehall Evening-Post,* Dec. 1–3, 1757. (This day is published, Price 5s.)

> > Fol. 3 parts.
> > BM. g. 409. f. (1.)
> > [Op. 1. Grove.]

FLORA'S OPERA

631. Songs in Flora's Opera or Hob in the Country-Wake as they are perform'd at the Theatre Royal in Lincolns Inn Fields. The tunes Proper for yᵉ German Flute, Violin & Common Flute. Price 6d.

London. Printed for and sold by I: Walsh . . . I: Hare . . . and I: Young . . . N.º 299.

> *Daily Journal,* May 14, 1730.

> > 8°. pp. 20.
> > BM. A. 869. a. (4.); 11772. aaa. 3. (2.)
> > Walsh Cat. 18: 'Floras Opera. 6d. N.º 299.'

FLUTE BOOKS

632. New Violin and Flute Books; with Instructions for Learners for the Year 1728.

> Printed for, and sold by John Walsh . . . and Joseph Hare, &c.

Country Journal: or, The Craftsman, Jan. 20, 1728.

> Presumably a general reference to works recorded elsewhere, which cannot be identified.

FORD, afterwards THICKNESSE (Ann)

633. Eighteen English and Italian Airs and Lessons for the Guitar, with Variations to Three favourite Tunes, &c. (Pr. 10s 6d.) To be had of the Author; of Mr. Davis . . . Mr. Walsh, &c.

Public Advertiser, March 12, 1761.

> Walsh Cat. 27: 'Miss Ford's Instructions for the Guitar.'

FOREIGNER

634. Six Solos for a Violin and Harpsichord, composed by a Foreigner of Distinction.

> Printed for J. Walsh, &c.

Public Advertiser, March 1, 1753.

> Not identified.

FOREST HARMONY

635. Forest Harmony, or the Musick of the French Horn, as it is perform'd in Field, Park, Forest or Chace; with the proper Notes, Terms and Characters made use of in Field Hunting. To which is added, the choicest Hunting Songs, with proper Notes for the Horn. The whole engraven. Price 1s.

> Printed for and sold by John Walsh . . . and Jos. Hare, &c.

Mist's Weekly Journal, Dec. 24, 1726. (New Musick and Editions of Musick lately published.)

636. — With Walsh only in the imprint and 'N⁰ 138' added to the title-page. [*c.* 1730.]

> Walsh Cat. 18: 'Forrest-Harmony, or the Hunting notes for the French-Horn. 1s. 0d. N⁰ 138.'
>
> This is a different work from Forest Harmony, Books I–IV for two French Horns.

See also No. 856. Hunting Notes.

637. Forest Harmony, a Collection of Marches and Trumpet Tunes (for 2 French Horns or 2 German Flutes). 1s. 6d. [Book I.]
[London. Printed for and Sold by Iohn Walsh.]

[*c.* 1733.]

Obl. 8º.
Walsh Cat. 24*a*.
Walsh Cat. 18, p. 17: 'Forest Harmony 1ˢᵗ & 3ᵈ Books for 2 F. Horns. 3s. 6d.'
Walsh Cat. 18, p. 18: 'Forest Harmony in 3 Books (for 2 German Flutes). 6s. od. Nº 588.'

638. Forrest Harmony, Book the Second: Being a Collection of the most Celebrated Aires, Minuets, and Marches: Together with several Curious Pieces out of the Water Musick [by G. F. Handel], made on purpose for two French Horns, By the Greatest Masters. N.B. These Aires may be play'd on two German Flutes, two Trumpets, or two Violins &c. Price 2ˢ 6ᵈ
London. Printed for and Sold by Iohn Walsh . . . Nº 460.

Daily Post, June 12, 1733.

Obl. 8º. ff. 2–47. Printed on one side only.
BM. b. 4. (Imperfect. ff. 39–47 in facsimile.) NLS. BH. 226.
Walsh Cat. 18: 'Forest Harmony 2d Collⁿ or 60 Aires for French Horns. 2s. 6d. Nº 460.'
Walsh Cat. 24*a*: 'Forest Harmony, 2d Book, containing 68 Marches and Trumpet Tunes. (for 2 French Horns or 2 German Flutes). 2s. 6d.'

639. Forest Harmony Book the Third. Being a Collection of Celebrated Aires, Minuets, Marches, and Musett's made on purpose for two French Horns, N.B. These Aires are proper for two German Flutes, two Trumpets or two Violins.
London. Printed for & Sold by I. Walsh . . . Nº 581.

London Daily Post, and General Advertiser, May 19, 1736.

Obl. 8º. ff. 22. Printed on one side only.
NLS. BH. 227.
Walsh Cat. 18, p. 17: 'Forest Harmony 1ˢᵗ & 3ᵈ Books for 2 F. Horns. 3s. 6d.' p. 18: 'Forest Harmony in 3 Books (for 2 German Flutes). 6s. od. Nº 588.'
Book I is without any number in Walsh Cat. 18; Book II as 'Nº 460'. Nº 588 (or rather 581) applies to Book III, which was sold at 2s. od.
Walsh Cat. 24a: Forest Harmony, 3d Book. 2s. od.

640. Forest Harmony. Book IV. Being a Collection of Airs, Minuets and Marches, made on purpose for two French Horns, compos'd by Antonio Bennegger. Price 1s. 6d.
Printed for J. Walsh, &c.

Daily Advertiser, Dec. 20, 1744.

Obl. 8º.
Walsh Cat. 24*a*: 'Musick for 2 French Horns or 2 German Flutes. Forest Harmony, a Collection of Marches and Trumpet Tunes. 1s. 6d. [Book I.] Forest Harmony, 2d Book, con-

taining 68 Marches and Trumpet Tunes. 2s. 6d. Forest Harmony, 3d Book. 2s. od.—Do. 4th Book, Trumpet Tunes. 1s. 6d.'

Walsh Cat. 25: 'Forest Harmony. 4 Books. 2 F. H. 7s. 6d.'

FORZA D'AMORE

The Favourite Songs in the Opera call'd La Forza d'Amore.

See No. 1165. Paradies (Pietro Domenico)

FREDERICK II, *King of Prussia*

See No. 1396. SOLOS. Six Solos for a German Flute or Violin . . . Compos'd by Several Eminent Authors, &c.

FRENCH AND ITALIAN CANZONETS

Twenty French and Italian Canzonets, for a Guitar, German Flute, Voice, or Harpsichord.

See No. 812. Hasse (Johann Adolph) [Duets or Canzonets.] Number VII.

FRENCH DANCES

641. A Collection of the choicest French Dances, consisting of Minuets, Rigadoons, Sarabands, Jiggs, Entries, Paspies, Chacoons, Gavots and Brawls, in all 250: Together with the Birth Day Figure Dances perform'd at Court; as also several of the late Masquerade Dances. Note, The Tunes are proper for the Violin or Hoboy, and most of them in the Compass of the Flute, &c.

Printed for J. Walsh . . . Nº 146.

[*c.* 1730.]

Walsh Cat. 18: 'French Dances and Minuets. 1st Book Bound. (Violin.) 2s. 6d. Nº 146.'
No details of the first book have been traced. Title from Smith 514 (Second Book). This is presumably a reissue with Walsh only in the imprint and 'Nº 146' added to the title-page.

642. A Collection of the choicest French Dances, consisting of Minuets, Rigadoons, Sarabands, Jiggs, Entries, Paspies, Chacoons, Gavots and Brawls, in all 250: Together with the Birth Day Figure Dances perform'd at Court; as also several of the late Masquerade Dances.

Note, The tunes are proper for the Violin or Hoboy, and most of them in the Compass of the Flute, Second Book, price bound 2s. 6d.

Printed for J. Walsh . . . Nº 147.

[*c.* 1730.]

Walsh Cat. 18: 'French Dances and Minuets. 2d Book Bound. (Violin.) 2s. 6d. Nº 147.'
Smith 514 with Walsh only in the imprint and 'Nº 147' added to the title-page.

643. For the Flute A Collection of all the Choicest French Dances Perform'd at Court the Theatres and Publick Balls together with the newest & most Celle-brated Minuets Rigadoons & Paspys Several of them Forreign & Danc'd at most of the Princes Courts in Europe, compleatly fitted to the Flute, being the first of the kind for that Instrument. Fairly Engraven & Carefully Corected.
London. Printed for J. Walsh . . . N? 10.

[*c.* 1730.]

Obl. 8°. 'A Table of the French Dances', &c. ff. 30. Printed on one side only.
Walsh Cat. 18: 'French Dances for the Flute. 1s. 6d. N? 10.'
Smith 352 (BM. a. 26. i. (2.)) of which this is presumably a reissue with Walsh only in the imprint and 'N? 10' added to the title-page.

FRENCH SONGS

644. A Collection of French Songs. 6d.

[*c.* 1730.]

Walsh Cat. 18.
Not identified.

See also No. 314. Canzonets; No. 382. Cloes (Nicolas); and Addenda.

FRITZ (GASPARO)

645. Sei Sonate a Quatro Stromenti a Violino Primo, Secondo, Alto Viola, Cem-balo o Violoncello. Dedicate A. S. E. Francesis Opera prima.
London. Printed for the Author. MDCCXLII. Price One Guinea.

[1742.]

Fol. 4 parts.
BM. g. 266. a.

646. — Reissued by Walsh, with the same title-page.

Daily Advertiser, Jan. 5, 1744. (Printed for J. Walsh, &c. Of whom may be had, just publish'd. Sonatas for two Violins and a Bass, Compos'd by Gasparo Fritz.)

Fol. 5 parts (2 copies of Basso part).
Hirsch III. 208.
This copy contains a Walsh Catalogue No. 21b at the end of the Violino Primo part.

647. Six Solos for a Violin with a Bass for the Violoncello and Harpsicord. Com-pos'd by Sig^r Gasparo Fritz. Opera Seconda.
London. Printed for I. Walsh, &c.

Public Advertiser, Aug. 1, 1764.

Fol. pp. 2–23.
BM. g. 266.

648. Six Sonatas for two Violins with a Through Bass for the Harpsicord or Violoncello Compos'd by Sig.ʳ Gasparo Fritz. Opera Terza.
London. Printed for I. Walsh, &c.

Public Advertiser, April 24, 1765.

Fol. Parts.
Rowe.

649. Sei Sonate a Due Violini Del Sig.ʳ Gasparo Fritz.
London Printed for I. Walsh, &c.

Public Advertiser, Dec. 4, 1759.

Fol. 2 parts.
BM. g. 266. b. Rowe.
Randall Cat.: 'Gasparo Fritz Duets (for two Violins). 3s. od.'

See also No. 1396. Six Solos for a German Flute or Violin with a Thorough Bass . . . Compos'd by Several Eminent Authors, &c.

FROUDE ( )
See No. 266. British Orpheus. No. II.

GALEOTTI (STEFANO)
650. Six Sonatas For Two Violoncellos with a Through Bass for the Harpsicord Compos'd by Sig.ʳ. Stefano Galeotti.
London. Printed for I. Walsh, &c.

Public Advertiser, May 12, 1763.

Fol. 3 parts.
BM. g. 242. (11.)

651. Six Sonatas or Trios for two Violins or a German Flute & Violin with a Bass for the Violoncello or Harpsichord Compos'd by Sig.ʳ Stefano Galeotti. Op: 2.ª
London. Printed for I. Walsh, &c.

Public Advertiser, May 16, 1763.

Fol. 2 parts.
RM. 17. d. 6. (8.)
Walsh Cat. 27: 'Galeottis Sonatas (for two German Flutes and a Bass). Op. 2. 5s. od.'

GALLIARD (JOHANN ERNST)
652. Songs in the New Entertainment Call'd Apollo & Daphne Compos'd by M.ʳ Galliard and Perform'd by M.ʳ Leveridge M.ʳˢ Barbier & M.ʳˢ Chambers at the Theatre Royall in Lincolns Inn Fields.
London. Printed for and sold by I: Walsh . . . and Ioseph Hare, &c.

[1726.]

Fol. ff. 9. Printed on one side only.
BM. Add. MSS. 31588, f. 130. Birmingham. Rowe.
Words by L. Theobald.

653. The Masks of Apollo and Daphne and Dr Faustus. 2s. od. No 309.

[*c.* 1730.]

With Walsh only in the imprint.
Walsh Cat. 18.
No details known of this combined edition of the two works. (*See also* No. 584.)

654. Apollo and Daphne for a (Single Flute). 6d. No 55.

[*c.* 1730.]

Walsh Cat. 18.

655. The Opera of Calypso. (With Symphonys for 2 Viols & Bass.) 9s. od. No 230.

[*c.* 1730.]

Fol. 'A Table of the Songs', &c. pp. 62.
Walsh Cat. 18.
Smith 426 ('Songs in the Opera of Calypso & Telemachus', &c. BM. G. 223. (1.)) with Walsh only in the imprint and 'No 230' added to the title-page, and the addition of the Symphonys.

656. Opera of Calypso for the Flute. 1s. 6d. No 24.

[*c.* 1730.]

Walsh Cat. 18.
Smith 428 with Walsh only in the imprint and 'No 24' added to the title-page.

Dr Faustus or the Necromancer

See Nos. 583, 653. Doctor Faustus

657. Six English Cantatas After the Italian manner. Compos'd by Mr Galliard. London Printed for J: Walsh . . . No 291.

[*c.* 1733.]

Fol. Illustrated passe-partout title-page (Smith, illustration 22). pp. 28.
BM. G. 223. (2.) RCM. (2 copies)
Words by John Hughes, William Congreve, and Matthew Prior.
Smith 495 with Walsh only in the imprint and 'No 291' added to the title-page.
Walsh Cat. 18: 'Six Cantatas . . . 4s. od. No 291.'

658. — Another edition. Mr. Galliards VI Cantatas.

[*c.* 1735.]

Fol. Illustrated passe-partout title-page with the title in MS. pp. 28.
Rowe.

147

659. Twelve English Songs, entirely new, for the Harpsichord, Violin, &c. Compos'd by Mr. Galliard.
  Printed for J. Walsh, &c.

  London Daily Post, and General Advertiser, Oct. 21, 1741.

  Walsh Cat. 18: 'Twelve English Songs. 1s. 6d.'

660. The Hymn of Adam and Eve, Out of the Fifth Book of Milton's Paradise-Lost; Set to Musick by Mr Galliard.
  Printed for I. Walsh, &c. J. Pine im; & Sculp.

  General Evening Post, May 14–16, 1745. (A Second edition of.)

  Obl. 4°. Illustrated title-page. pp. 30. 'Engraven by Tho: Atkins' at foot of p. 30.
  Hirsch III. 759. (Original date 1728 erased.) Others in BUC not examined.
  First published without imprint but with date 1728. (*Country Journal: or, The Craftsman*, June 8, 1728.) Subscriptions were taken by Joseph Hare, Mich. Rawlins, and the Author. This edition, not by Walsh, was presumably the one listed in Walsh Cat. 18: '7s. 6d.'

The Rape of Proserpine. Entertainment.

  See No. 1200. Perseus and Andromeda. The Comic Tunes in the Entertainments of Perseus & Andromeda and the Rape of Proserpine, &c.; No. 1273. Rape of Prosperpine, Tunes, Aires and Dances in the Rape of Proserpine.

Tunes in the Royal Chace, or Merlin's Cave.

  See No. 1291. Royal Chace

661. Six Solos for two Violoncellos by Mr. Galliard.
  Printed for and sold by J. Walsh, &c.

  London Daily Post, and General Advertiser, Dec. 11, 1740. (Of whom may be had.)

  Walsh Cat. 21: 'Gaillard . . . Solos for two Violoncellos. 4s. 0d.'

662. — Another edition.

  General Advertiser, Nov. 28, 1747. (Just publish'd for two Violoncellos . . . Galliard's Solos.)

663. Sonata A Flauto Solo e Basso Continuo Composees par Monsieur Galliard Opera prima.
  Sur l'Edition d Amsterdam par Etienne Roger. No 114.

  [*c.* 1730.]

  Fol. pp. 21.
  BM. g. 422. (2.) Issued anonymously by Walsh (No 114 engraved). RCM. (No 114 in MS.)
  Walsh Cat. 18: 'Six Celebrated Solos for a Flute and a Bass. 5s. 0d. No 114.'
  Smith 610 (BM. g. 280. b. (3.)) with 'No 114' added to the title-page.

664. Six Sonatas for the Bassoon or Violoncello with a Thorough Bass for the Harpsicord. Compos'd by Mʳ Galliard.

London. Printed for, & Sold by Iohn Walsh . . . Nọ 382.

Daily Post, May 1, 1733.

Fol. pp. 27.
BM. f. 515.
Walsh Cat. 18: 'Six Solos for a Bassoon or Violoncello. 4s. od. Nọ 382.'

665. — Without 'Nọ 382' on the title-page.

[*c.* 1740.]

Fol. pp. 27.
RM. 16. d. 2. (1.) In BUC other copies of one or other of these editions, not checked.

See also No. 316. Caporale (Andrea) and Galliard (Johann Ernst) Caparali and Galliard's Solos, &c.; No. 749. Harmonia Anglicana . . . by . . . Galliard Book I; No. 882. Jupiter and Europa; No. 891. The Lady's Banquet 3ᵈ Book, &c.

GALLO (ALBERTO)

666. Twelve Sinfonie or Sonatas in 4 Parts. For Two Violins, a Tenor, with a Bass for the Violoncello & Harpsicord. Compos'd in an easy and Pleasing Stile by Sigʳ Alberto Gallo. Opera 2 ᵈᵃ

Public Advertiser, Sept. 17, 1754.

Fol. 4 parts.
BM. g. 420. r. (3.) RAM. Bod.
With 'Numb. XXVIII' of a series of symphonies or sonatas printed at the top of the title-page.

667. Six Sonatas for two German Flutes or Violins, with a Bass for the Harpsicord or Violoncello. Compos'd by Sigʳ Gallo.

London. Printed for J. Walsh, &c.

London Evening-Post; Public Advertiser, March 12, 1754. (Sig. Gallo's Trios, &c.)

Fol. Parts.
Rowe.
With 'Numb: XXIII' of a series of symphonies or sonatas printed at the top of the title-page.

668. — A reissue or re-advertisement.

Public Advertiser, Feb. 23, 1765. (Six Sonatas for two German Flutes, &c.)

GALUPPI (BALDASSARE)

669. The Favourite Songs in the Opera Call'd Antigono By Sig.r Galuppi.
London. Printed for I. Walsh, &c.
— 2.d Coll.n

General Advertiser, May 22, 1746; June 9, 1746. (Two collections.)

Fol. Passe-partout title-pages. pp. 2–22, 23–44.
BM. G. 191. (1.) RAM. RCM.
'2.d Coll.n' is in MS.
Words by Metastasio.
Republished in 'Le Delizie dell' Opere', Vol. III, pp. 35–74.

670. The Favourite Songs in the Opera Call'd Enrico By Sig.r Galuppi.
London. Printed for I. Walsh, &c.

Daily Advertiser, Jan. 15, 1743. (Of whom may be had.) *London Daily Post, and General Advertiser*, Jan. 29, 1743. (A Second Set of Favourite Songs in . . . Enrico.)

Fol. Passe-partout title-page.
BM. G. 190. (2.) (Book 1. pp. 25.) Others in BUC. not examined.

671. — Another edition.

Public Advertiser, Dec. 8, 1753.

Fol. Passe-partout title-page. pp. 1–20, 26–28, 32–46 (bottom centre).
BM. H. 348. c. (8.) RCM. (Second Set.) Gresham. Rowe.
With additional top centre pagination 89–126 from 'Le Delizie dell' Opere', Vol. III.
Words by Francesco Vanneschi.

672. The Favourite Songs in the Opera Call'd Il Filosofo di Campagna.
London. Printed for I. Walsh, &c.
— 2.d Set.

Public Advertiser, Jan. 28, 1761; Feb. 10, 1761. (A Second Set.)

Fol. Passe-partout title-pages. pp. 1–18, 19–37.
BM. H. 348. c. (7.) RM. 13. c. 21. (8.) RCM. Gresham. Bod. DAM. Michell. Pendlebury. Rowe.
'2.d Set' is in MS.
Pp. 32–37 consist of two arias from 'Il Mondo nella Luna', one each by G. Cocchi and B. Galuppi.
Words by Carlo Goldoni.
Randall Cat.: 'Il Filosofo, 2 Colln. each 2s. 6d.'
Republished in 'Le Delizie dell' Opere', Vol. X, pp. 65–102.

673. The Favourite Songs in the Opera Call'd Il Mondo nella Luna By Sig.r Galuppi.
London. Printed for I. Walsh, &c.

Public Advertiser, Dec. 11, 1760.

> Fol. Passe-partout title-page. pp. 2–20.
> BM. G. 760. g. (1.) RCM. Other copies in BUC. not examined.
> Words by Carlo Goldoni.

674. — Another edition.

[*c.* 1760.]

> Fol. Passe-partout title-page. pp. 2–20. (Songs in different order.)
> RM. 13. c. 21. (13.)
> Republished in 'Le Delizie dell' Opere', Vol. X, pp. 103–121.

675. Number VII. Price 2s. A Favourite Overture for Violins, French Horns &c. in 8 Parts. Compos'd by Sig. Galuppi.
Printed for J. Walsh, &c.

Public Advertiser, Jan. 2, 1764.

> Fol. Parts.
> Issued in a collection as No. 6 of 'Six Favourite Opera Overtures Set for the Harpsicord or Organ Compos'd by Sigʳ Bach. &c.' (BM. e. 12. (2.) 1763.) (*See* No. 127.)
> Also as No. 1 of 'Six Overtures in 8 Parts . . . Compos'd by Sigʳ Bach Jomelli Galuppi Perez Sixth Collection.' (BM. g. 212. a. 1764.) (*See* No. 1158.)
> Other numbers in this series are under J. C. Bach, L. V. Ciampi, D. Perez, and N. Jomelli.

676. The Favourite Songs in the Opera Call'd Penelope Compos'd by Sigʳ Galuppi. Nº II.
London. Printed for I. Walsh, &c.

[**1741.**]

> Fol. Passe-partout title-page. pp. 2–22.
> BM. G. 191. (2.) Gresham.
> Words by Paolo Antonio Rolli.

677. — Another edition.

Public Advertiser, Dec. 19, 1754.

> Fol. Passe-partout title-page. pp. 2–19, 15–17 (bottom centre).
> BM. H. 1648. d. (6.)
> With additional top centre pagination 163–80 on pp. 2–19 and 194–6 on pp. 15–17 respectively from 'Le Delizie dell' Opere', Vols. III and IV.

678. The Favourite Songs in the Opera Call'd Ricimero By Sigʳ Galuppi.
London. Printed for I. Walsh, &c.

Public Advertiser, March 22, 1755.

> Fol. Passe-partout title-page. pp. 1–3, 1–19.
> BM. H. 2815. j. (3.) RM. 13. c. 22. (3.) (Wanting the title-page.) RCM. Gresham. DAM. Euing.

Words by Francesco Silvani.
The first three pages contain an aria by Leo.
Republished in 'Le Delizie dell' Opere', Vol. VII, pp. 48–69.

679. The Favourite Songs in the Opera Call'd Scipione in Cartagine. Compos'd by Sigʳ Galuppi.
London. Printed for I. Walsh, &c.
— 2ᵈ Collⁿ

[*c.* 1742.]

> Fol. Passe-partout title-pages. pp. 21, 22–40.
> BM. G. 190. (1.) Rowe.
> '2ᵈ Collⁿ' is in MS.
> Words by Francesco Vanneschi.
> Republished in 'Le Delizie dell' Opere', Vol. III, pp. 127–62 and Vol. IV, pp. 199–201.

680. The Favourite Songs in the Opera Call'd Sirbaces. By Sigʳ Galuppi, &c.
London. Printed for I. Walsh, &c.

London Daily Post, and General Advertiser, May 7, 1743.

> Fol. Passe-partout title-page. pp. 2–24.
> BM. G. 190. (3.)
> Words by — Stampa.
> A selection was included in 'Le Delizie dell' Opere', Vol. III, pp. 75–88.

681. Sonate per Cembalo Composte da Sigʳ Galuppi.
London. Printed for I. Walsh, &c.

Whitehall Evening-Post, April 20–22, 1756. (Six Sonatas or Lessons.)

> Obl. fol. pp. 2–19, blank, 21–27.
> BM. e. 430. (1.) RCM. Manchester.

682. Sonate per Cembalo Composte dal Sigʳ Galuppi. Opera Primo.
London. Printed for I. Walsh, &c.

Public Advertiser, Jan. 1, 1760. (Of whom may be had.)

> Fol. pp. 2–21, blank, 23–29.
> RM. 16. a. 14. (2.) RCM. Other copies in BUC not examined.
> 'Primo' is in MS.
> Another edition of No. 681 with an extra movement in Sonata I (pp. 4–5).
> Randall Cat.: 'Galuppi's Lessons, Op. 1, 5s. od.'

683. Sonate per Cembalo Composte dal Sigʳ Galuppi. Opera 2ᵈᵃ.
London. Printed for I. Walsh, &c.

Public Advertiser, Oct. 11, 1759. (A Second Sett of six Sonatas.)

> Obl. fol. pp. 2–30.
> BM. e. 430. (2.) RM. 16. a. 14. (3.) Rowe.
> '2ᵈᵃ' is in MS.
> Randall Cat.: 'Galuppi's Lessons, Op. 2, 5s. od.'

684. The Favourite Songs in the Opera Call'd Il Trionfo della Continenza By Sig.r Galuppi.

London. Printed for I. Walsh, &c.

General Advertiser, Feb. 15, 1746; March 1, 1746. (A Second Set.)

Fol. Passe-partout title-page. pp. 2–23.
BM. G. 191. (3.) (First Set only.) London University. RAM.

685. — 2.d Coll.n

Fol. Passe-partout title-page. pp. 24–42.
BM. G. 811. e. (1.)
'2.d Coll.n' is in MS.
Words by Agostino Piovene.
A selection was included in 'Le Delizie dell' Opere', Vol. III, pp. 2–34.

See also No. 38. Antigona; No. 45. Arianna e Teseo; No. 127. Bach (Johann Christian) Six Favourite Opera Overtures, &c.; No. 276. Calamita de' Cuori; No. 358. Ciampi (Legrenzio Vincenzo) Arie 6; No. 360. Ciampi (Legrenzio Vincenzo) the Favourite Songs in . . . Bertoldo. (Duet from Il Mercato di Malmantile); Nos. 556, 558–66. Delizie dell' Opere. Vols. I, III–XI; Nos. 775–85. Hasse (Johann Adolph) Galuppi's (Galuppi), Hasse . . . Chamber Aires, &c.; No. 815. Hasse (Johann Adolph) N.o X Duets or Canzonets, &c.; No. 969. Love in a Village . . . Music by . . . Galuppi, &c., No. 1010. Mercato di Malmantile; No. 1129. Nerone; No. 1138. Olimpiade; Nos. 1151–4, 1158, 1159. Overtures; No. 1188. Perez (Davidde) The Favourite Songs in . . . La Didone Abbandonata; No. 1419. Summer's Tale; No. 1452. Tolomeo.

GARDINI (JOANNES DE)

See Jardini

GARTH (JOHN)

686. Six Concertos, For the Violoncello, with Four Violins, one Alto Viola, and Basso Ripieno, Dedicated to His Royal Highness the Duke of York, by John Garth. Engrav'd by W.m Clark, S.t Ann's Lane.

Printed for the Author and Sold by John Johnson . . . J. Walsh . . . London.

Public Advertiser, April 16, 1760. ('Printed for Author, and sold by J. Johnson . . . J. Walsh . . . and T. Smith in Piccadilly', &c.)

Fol. 7 parts.
BM. g. 246. a.

GASPARINI OR GASPERINI

See Visconti (Gasparo) commonly called Gasparini or Gasperini

GASPARINI (FRANCESCO)

687. [Amleto.] Songs in the Opera of Hamlet as they are perform'd at yᵉ Queens Theatre. [By F. Gasparini.]
     London Printed for J: Walsh . . . Nº 245.

   [*c.* 1730.]

> Fol. Passe-partout title-page. pp. 73.
> Words altered from Apostolo Zeno and Pietro Pariata.
> Walsh Cat. 18: 'The Opera of Hamlet. (With Symphonys for 2 Violˢ & Bass.) 9s. od Nº 245.'
> Smith 422 (BM. 114.(1.)) with Walsh only in the imprint, 'Nº 245' added to the title-page, and the Symphonys included.
> Produced as 'Amleto'.

688. Songs in the Opera of Antiochus as they are Perform'd at yᵉ Queens Theatre. [By F. Gasparini.]
     London Printed for J: Walsh . . . Nº 244.

   [*c.* 1730.]

> Fol. Passe-partout title-page. pp. 69.
> Walsh Cat. 18: 'The Opera of Antiochus. (With Symphonys for 2 Violˢ & Bass.) 9s. od. Nº 244.'
> Smith 417 (BM. H. 298.) with Walsh only in the imprint, 'Nº 244' added to the title-page and the Symphonies included.
> Words by Apostolo Zeno.

689. The Song Tunes for yᵉ Flute in the Opera's of Antiochus & Hamlet. Fairly Engraven & Carefully Corected, Price 1ˢ 6ᵈ
     London, Printed for J. Walsh . . . Nº 19.

   [*c.* 1730.]

> Obl. 4º. pp. 20.
> Walsh Cat. 18: 'Antiochus and Hamlet for the Flute. 1s. 6d. Nº 19.'
> Smith 437 (BM. a. 209. a. (7.)) with Walsh only in the imprint and 'Nº 19' added to the title-page.

   See also No. 7 Airs. Aires by 8 Masters (for 2 Flutes); No. 971. Love's Triumph; No. 1443. Thomyris.

GEMINIANI (FRANCESCO)

690. Concerti Gosssi con Due Violini, Violoncello, e Viola di Concertino obligati, e due altri Violini e Basso di Concerto grosso ad arbitrio il IV. V. e VI. si potranno suonar con due Flauti traversieri, o due Violini con Violoncello. Dedicati a sua Eccellenza Henrietta, Duchessa di Marlborough. &c. &c. da Francesco Geminiani. Opera Seconda.

London. Printed for the Author, and sold by I. Walsh . . . Nº [Blank.]

[1732.]

Fol. Parts.
BM. g. 38. b. (1.) RCM. LX. D. 3. (4.) (With '72: F. G—' in MS. after Nº) RCM. LX.
E. 2. (4.) (With '4: F.G—' in MS. after Nº) Other copies in BUC not examined.
Walsh Cat. 18: '6 Concertos for Violins in 7 Parts Opera 2da. 12s. 6d.'
An advertisement appeared in *The Daily Post*, June 8, 1732, 'This Day is published. Six
Concerto's in Seven Parts. Composed by Mr. Francis Geminiani, (three of which are for the
German Flute) and are to be had at Mr. Hickford's in Panton Street (where Subscriptions
for his Concerts next Year are taken in) and at the Musick Shops, at 12s 6d per set. N.B.
These are not the Concerto's published by Mr. Walsh; but are those which were perform'd
at Mr. Geminiani's Concerts last Winter, and were never before printed.'

691. — Another edition. This Day is Publish'd. By Mr. Kellway, by Order of the
Author. Six Concerto's for Violins, &c. in Seven Parts. Composed by Francesco
Geminiani, Op. 2d. There is a new Adagio added to them by the Author. Note,
These are the Concerto's that were perform'd at his Concert with so much Applause
and have been out of Print above a Year.

Sold by John Walsh . . . and by Mr. Kellway, at Mr. Brigg's, a Coach Painter
in Prince's street, near Leicester Fields.

Country Journal: or, The Craftsman, Oct. 22, 1737.

692. — Another edition.
Printed for and Sold by I. Walsh, &c.

[*c.* 1740.]

Fol. Parts.
Hirsch III. 214. RCM. LX. D. 2. (3.) Other copies in BUC not examined.
Same title-page as first edition (No. 690) except for imprint.

693. — Another edition. Concerti Grossi . . . Da Francesco Geminiani, &c.
London. Printed for & sold by I. Walsh, &c.

General Evening Post, Jan. 17–19, 1745. (New editions. Geminiani's twelve Concertos for Violins &c. seven Parts.) [i.e. Op. 2 and 3.]

Fol. Parts.
RM. 17. a. 3. (3) Other copies in BUC not examined

694. — Another edition.

General Advertiser, Oct. 25, 1749. (Also new editions. Geminiani's 12 Concertos.)
[i.e. Op. 2 and 3.]

695. Concerti Grossi Con Due Violini Viola e Violoncello di Concertino obligati,
e Due altri Violini e Basso di Concerto Grosso Da Francesco Geminiani Opera
Terza. Note, All the Works of this Author may be had where these are Sold.

London. Printed for and Sold by Iohn Walsh, &c.

[*c.* 1730.]

> Fol. Parts.
> BM. g. 38. d. (2.) (Violoncello del Concertino part only.)

696. — With 'N° 379' added to the title-page.

Daily Journal, April 22, 1732.

> Fol. Parts.
> Hirsch III. 215. a. (Wanting the title-page of the Basso ripieno part which has been sup-
> plied in MS.) RCM. LX. E. 2. (5.); LX. D. 3. (5.) CUL.
> Walsh Cat. 18: 'Six Concertos for Violins in 7 Parts Op: Terza. 10s. 6d. N° 379.'

697. Concerti Grossi . . . Opera Terza. N.B. All the Works of this Author may be
had where these are Sold.

London. Printed for I. Walsh, &c.

[*c.* 1740.]

> Fol. Parts.
> BM. g. 38. b. (2.) RCM. LX. D. 2. (4.) Other copies in BUC (*c.* 1735) not examined.

698. Concerti Grossi . . . Opera Terza. NB. All the Works of this Author may be
had where these are sold.

London. Printed for I. Walsh, &c.

General Evening Post, Jan. 17–19, 1745. (New editions. Geminiani's twelve Concertos for Violins &c. seven Parts.) [i.e. Op. 2 and 3.]

> Fol. Parts.
> RM. 17. a. 3. (4.)

699. — Another edition.

General Advertiser, Oct. 25, 1749. (Also new editions Geminiani's 12 Concertos
&c.)

700. Concerti Grossi . . . Opera Terza. NB. All the Works of this Author may be
had where these are sold.

London. Printed for I. Walsh, &c.

[*c.* 1760.]

> Fol. Parts.
> BM. g. 38. d. (3.) (Violino primo concertino, Violino secondo concertino, Alto Viola
> parts only.) LCO. (Not examined.)

Concerti Grossi Con Due Violini Viola e Violoncello di Concertino obligati, e Due altri Violini e Basso di Concerto Grosso. Composti delli sei Sonate del Opera Terza D' Arcangello Corelli Per Francesco Geminiani.

See No. 422. Corelli (Arcangelo)

Concerti Grossi Con Due Violini Viola e Violoncello di Concertino obligati, e Due altri Violini e Basso di Concerto Grosso da Francesco Geminiani Composti delli Sei Soli della prima parte dell' Opera Quinta D'Arcangelo Corelli.

See No. 433. Corelli (Arcangelo)

Concerti Grossi Con due Violini, Viola e Violoncello di Concertini obligati, e Due altri Violini e Basso di Concerto Grosso Quali Contengono Preludii Allemande Correnti Gigue Sarabande Gavotte e Follia Composti della Seconda Parte del Opera Quinta d'Arcangelo Corelli per Francesco Geminiani.

See Nos. 437–40. Corelli (Arcangelo)

701. No. II. A Select Concerto. For Violin & other Instruments in Seven Parts.
Printed for I. Walsh, &c. Feb., 1734.

London Evening-Post, Feb. 28–March 2, 1734. (Where may be had, just publish'd.)

Fol. Parts.
First Edition Bookshop Cat. 43, No. 233, 1953.
Afterwards issued in 'Select Harmony Third Collection', as Concerto III, 'Geminiani Nº 2. 502'. (*See* No. 1362.)

702. No. III. A Select Concerto.
Printed for I. Walsh, &c.

London Evening-Post, April 4–6, 1734. (Where may be had, just published. Numb. III of a select Concerto for Violins, German Flutes and other Instruments. In Seven Parts. By a very eminent Italian Author. Never before printed.)

Fol. Parts.
Afterwards issued in 'Select Harmony Third Collection', as Concerto IV, 'Geminiani Nº 3. 503'. (*See* No. 1362.)

703. No. IV. Select Concerto.
Printed for I. Walsh, &c.

[1734.]

Fol. Parts.
Afterwards issued in 'Select Harmony Third Collection', as Concerto II, 'Geminiani Nº 4. 504'. (*See* No. 1362.)

704. Six Concertos in eight Parts for Violins, &c. compos'd by Mr. Geminiani.
Sold by Mr. Walsh ... Mr. Walmsley ... & Mr. Simpson, &c.

London Daily Post, and General Advertiser, May 20, 1743.

This probably refers to 'Concerti Grossi a due Violini, due Viole e Violoncello obligati con due altri Violini, e Basso di Ripieno Composti e dedicati All' Altezza Reale di Federico Prencipe Di Vallia da Francesco Geminiani.

'Londra MDCCXLIII, a spese dell' Autore. Questi Concerti sono composti dalle Sonate a Violino e Basso dell Opera IV.' (BM. i. 10. c. Fol. Frontispiece. Parts.)

705. Sept. 1, 1747. In January next will absolutely be published, Six Grand Concertos, compos'd By Mr. Geminiani . . . Subscriptions will be taken in . . . at Mr. Walsh's . . . Mrs. Walmsley . . . Mr. Johnson . . . and Mr. Simpson's, &c.

General Advertiser, Sept. 3, 1747.

This presumably refers to 'Concerti Grossi Composti a 3, 4, 5, 6, 7, 8 Parti Reali, per essere eseguiti da due Violini, Viola e Violoncello di Concertino, e due altri Violini, Viola, e Basso di Ripieno, à quali vi sono annessi due Flauti Traversieri, e Bassone. da F. Geminiani Dedicati alla Celebre Accademia della buona ed Antica Musica Op VII . . . Londra. MDCCXLVIII.' (BM. g. 38. b. (3.) Fol. Parts.)

706. A Book of Lessons for the Harpsichord.

General Advertiser, Sept. 3, 1747. (At Mr. Walsh's . . . may be had . . . A New Edition.)

Walsh Cat. 24a: 'Geminiani's Lessons (for the Harpsiᵈ).'
Walsh Cat. 25: 'Geminiani's Lessons (Harpsicord). £1. 1. 0.'
The notices refer to 'Pièces de clavecin, tirées des differens ouvrages de Mr. F. Geminiani adaptées par luy même à cet instrument. Londres, 1743.' (RAM. Rowe. Fol. pp. 38.)

707. XII Solos for a Violin with a Thorough Bass for the Harpsicord or Bass Violin Compos'd by Francesco Geminiani. [Op. 1.]
London. Printed for and Sold by J. Walsh . . . N⁰ 378.
[*c.* 1730.]

Fol. pp. 35.
Bod. CUL. Fitz. Manchester. Pendlebury.
Smith 570 with Walsh only in the imprint and 'N⁰ 378' added to the title-page.
Walsh Cat. 18: 'Twelve Grand Solos for a Voilin and a Bass Opera Prima. 6s. od. N⁰ 378.'

708. — Another edition.

General Advertiser, Sept. 3, 1747. (At Mr. Walsh's . . . may be had A new Edition of Twelve Solos for a Violin and Bass. Op. 1.)

709. Six Solos for Two Violoncellos. Also the same transpos'd for a Violin and Bass.

General Advertiser, Sept. 3, 1747. (At Mr. Walsh's . . . may be had . . . A New edition.)

Not identified.

710. Sonatas of three Parts for two Violins a Violoncello and Thorough Bass made out of Geminiani's Solos Dedicated to Hewer Edgeley Hewer Esq.ʳ By Francesco Barsanti.

London. Printed for and sold by I: Walsh . . . and Joseph Hare, &c.

[*c.* 1728.]

Fol. Parts.
Leeds.
From Op. 1. Nos. 7–12.
Walsh Cat. 11*b*: 'Barsanti's Sonatas for 2 Violins and a Bass. Opera 2.ᵈᵃ'

711. — With Walsh only in the imprint and 'N.º 354' added to the title-page.

[*c.* 1730.]

Fol. Parts.
BM. g. 274. (7.)
Walsh Cat. 18: 'Barsanti. Six Sonatas for 2 Violins and a Bass Opera seconda made from Geminiani's Solos. 5s. od. N.º 354.'

712. Sonatas of three Parts. For Two Violins with a Thorough Bass for the Harpsicord or Violoncello made from the Solos of Francesco Geminiani.

London. Printed for I. Walsh, &c.

[*c.* 1742.]

Fol. Parts.
BM. g. 409. c. (3.) RM. 17. a. 4. (5.) RM. 17. d. 6. (2.) RAM. Fitz. Rowe.
This is another issue of No. 711 with a different title-page.

713. Proposals for printing by Subscription, Twelve Sonatas, compos'd by Mr. Francis Geminiani, for the Violin and Bass . . . That the copies shall be of two Sorts, one printed on large, the other on small paper . . . Subscriptions are taken in by Mr. John Walsh . . . Mr. John Simpson . . . and Mr. Wamsley, &c.

London Evening-Post, Feb. 15–17, 1737.

This notice presumably refers to 'Sonate a Violino e Basso, composte da Francesco Geminiani . . . Opera IV. London, MDCCXXXIX.' (BM. i. 10. a. (2.) Fol. Licence. pp. 48.) Advertised in *The London Daily Post, and General Advertiser*, Wednesday, April 18, 1739. Next Monday will be published, Twelve Sonata's for a Violin, with a Thorough Bass for the Harpsichord, or Bass Violin. Composed by Sig. Francesco Geminiani. The Subscribers to which Work are desired to send to Mr. Kelway's near Dupuis's Coffee-house in Conduit Street, &c.

714. — Another edition.

General Advertiser, Sept. 3, 1747. (At Mr. Walsh's . . . may be had . . . A New Edition . . . Twelve Solos for a Violin and Bass. Op. 4.)

Walsh Cat. 24*a*: 'Geminiani's 12 Solos (for a Violin or Harpsichord) Op. 4ta.'
Walsh Cat. 25: 'Geminiani's 12 Solos. Op. 4.ᵃ'
No copy known with English title.

See also Nos. 11, 13. Airs. Select Airs or Duets for two German Flutes . . . By . . . Geminiani . . . 2d Book. (A Fourth Book . . . By . . . Geminiani, &c.); No. 890. The Lady's Banquet Second Book; No. 936. Lessons. Select Lessons . . . by . . . Geminiani, &c.; No. 969. Love in a Village . . . Music by . . . Geminiani, &c.; No. 981. Mancini (Francesco) XII Solos for a Violin . . . Revis'd . . . by M.ʳ Geminiani; No. 1124 Musica Bellicosa . . . to which is added Geminiani's . . . Trumpet-tunes, &c.; No. 1362. Select Harmony Third Collection . . . Compos'd by Sig.ʳ Geminiani, &c.; No. 1393. Solos. Six Solos Four for German Flute . . . by M.ʳ Handel . . . Sig.ʳ Brivio.

GEMINIANI (Francesco) AND BRIVIO (Giuseppe Ferdinando)

715. 6 Solos by Geminiani Brivio and other Authors. (German Flute Hoboy or Violin with a Thorough Bass for the Harpsicord.) 3s. od. N.º 398.

[*c.* 1731.]

Walsh Cat. 18.
This refers to 'Six Solos Four for a German Flute and a Bass and two for a Violin with a Thorough Bass . . . Compos'd by M.ʳ Handel Sig.ʳ Geminiani . . . Printed for and sold by I: Walsh, &c. (BM. h. 2140. d. (3.) Fol. pp. 20.) With Walsh only in the imprint and 'N.º 398' added to the title-page. (Smith, 'Handel. A Descriptive Catalogue', &c., p. 241.)

GEMINIANI (Francesco) AND CASTRUCCI (Pietro)

716. XII Solos for a German Flute, Violin or Harpsichord.

[*c.* 1743.]

Fol. pp. 24.
Walsh Cat. 21: 'Geminiani and Castrucci's 12 Solos (for a German Flute Hoboy or Violin and a Bass). 6.ˢ od.'
Walsh Cat. 24*a*: 'Geminiani and Castrucci's Solos (for a Germ.ⁿ Flute Violin or Harpsicord). 6s. od.'
H. Reeve's Cat. 118, 1936.
This may refer to an edition of 'Geminiani e Castrucci: 12 Sonate a Flauto traversi. o Violino o Hautbois e Basso continuo delle Compositioni. Amsterdam a Spesa di Michele Carlo Cene.' (Eitner. Quellen-Lexikon.)

717. Six Sonatas or Solos Contriv'd & fitted for a Flute and a Bass Collected out of the Last new Solos Compos'd by M.ʳ Geminiani & Castrucci. Engraven & carefully Corrected, &c.
London Printed for and Sold by I: Walsh and I: Hare . . . N.º 102.

[*c.* 1730.]

Fol. pp. 27.
Smith 611, title-page as above from Rowe copy, with Walsh only in the imprint and 'N.º 102' added to the title-page.
Walsh Cat. 18: 'Geminiani and Castrucci's Solos (for a Flute and a Bass). 5s. od. N.º 102.'

GERARD (JAMES)

718. Six Sonatas for two German Flutes, or Violins . . . Composed by James Gerard.
  Printed for the Author, and sold at Mr. Walsh's, &c.

  Public Advertiser, March 2, 1753.

  > May refer to the work printed for J. Johnson. (BM. g. 502. (3.) Fol. pp. 19.)

GIANGUIR

719. The Favourite Songs in the Opera Call'd Gianguir.
  London. Printed for I. Walsh, &c.

  Daily Advertiser, Nov. 25, 1742.

  > Fol. Passe-partout title-page. pp. 2–25.
  > Rowe.
  > Pasticcio. Music by Hasse, Lampugnani, Brivio and Sig. Rinaldo [i.e. Rinaldo da Capua].
  > Walsh Cat. 25: 'Gianguir by Hasse.'
  > Walsh Cat. 28; 'Gianguir, Hasse.'

GIARDINI (FELICE)

  See Nos. 565, 566. Delizie dell' Opere. Vols. X, XI; No. 969. Love in a Village . . . Music by . . . Giardini, &c.; Nos. 1419, 1420. The Summer's Tale . . . Music by . . . Giardini, &c.

GIULINI (   )

  See No. 318. Carcani (Giuseppe) Six Sonatas in Three Parts, &c.

GLADWIN (THOMAS)

  See No. 266. British Orpheus. No. II.

GLOVER (   )

  See No. 1061. Minuets. Select Minuets Collected From the Operas, &c.

GLUCK (CHRISTOPH WILLIBALD VON)

720. The Favourite Songs in the Opera Call'd Artamene By Sig^r Gluck.
  London. Printed for I. Walsh, &c.

  General Advertiser, March 17, 1746.

  > Fol. Passe-partout title-page. pp. 2–19.
  > BM. G. 194. (1.) Hirsch IV. 1566. RAM. RCM. Liverpool. Rowe.
  > Words by B. Vitturi, altered by F. Vanneschi. (Loewenberg.)
  > Republished in 'Le Delizie dell' Opere', Vol. IV, pp. 75–92.

721. The Favourite Songs in the Opera Call'd La Caduta de' Giganti By Sigᵣ Gluck.

London. Printed for I. Walsh, &c.

General Advertiser, Feb. 15, 1746.

> Fol. Passe-partout title-page. pp. 2–23.
> Hirsch IV. 1567. RAM. DAM.
> Words by F. Vanneschi.
> Republished in 'Le Delizie dell' Opere', Vol. VI, pp. 69–74, 193–209, Vol. IX, pp. 164–85, and Vol. XI, pp. 161–70.

See also No. 780. Hasse (Johanne Adolph) [Chamber Airs. Vol. II, Pt. III.]

GORTON (WILLIAM)

722. Catechitical Questions in Musick by Mᵣ W. Gorton. 6d.

[*c.* 1730 or earlier.]

> Walsh Cat. 18.
> Presumably copy of or reissue of 'Catechetical Questions in Musick, containing a hundred and seventy Questions, fairly answered and made plain to the meanest capacity . . . London, Printed by W. Pearson for the Author, 1704.' (Library of Congress, Washington.)

GRANO (GIOVANNI BATTISTA)

723. Solos for a German Flute a Hoboy or Violin with a Thorough Bass for the Harpsicord or Bass Violin Compos'd by Iohn Baptist Grano. Note. the following pieces may be had where these are sold. Instructions for Learners on the German Flute. 6 Solos by several Authors 4 Collections of Mᵣ Handel's Opera Airs Lampe's Solos and Pietro's 2 books of Solos all for a German Flute and a Bass. and Loeillets Sonatas for two German Flutes.

London. Printed for and sold by I: Walsh . . . and Ioseph Hare, &c.

Country Journal: or, The Craftsman, April 20, 1728.

> Fol. pp. 24.
> BM. g. 422. j. (4.)

724. — With Walsh only in the imprint and 'Nᵒ 381' added to the title-page.

[*c.* 1730.]

> Walsh Cat. 18: 'Grano's Solos. 3s. od. Nᵒ 381.'

See also No. 10. Airs. A Choice Collection of Aires and Duets for two German Flutes . . . Mr. Grano, &c.

GRANOM (LEWIS CHRISTIAN AUSTIN)

725. Twelve Solos for a German Flute or Harpsichord, and Six Sonatas for two German Flutes and a Bass. Compos'd by Lewis C. A. Granom, Esq; Price of each 10s. 6d.

Printed for the Author; and sold by J. Walsh, &c.

Daily Advertiser, Dec. 9, 1742.

John Simpson issued editions of these works. (1.) XII Solos for a German Flute with a Thorough Bass for the Harpsicord or Violoncello . . . Opera Prima. [*c.* 1745.] (BM. g. 280. i. (4.)) (2.) Six Sonatas for two German Flutes or two Violins with a Thorough Bass for the Harpsicord or Violoncello . . . Opera Seconda. [1746.] (B.M. g. 274. g. (2.))

See also No. 1419. Summer's Tale.

GRAUN (CARL HEINRICH) OR (JOHANN GOTTLIEB)

See No. 1154. Overtures. Six Favourite Overtures . . . For Violins . . . by Sig.ʳ Cocchi, &c.

GRAUN (JOHANN GOTTLIEB)

726. Eight Sonatas for two German Flutes or Violins with a Bass for the Violoncello or Harpsicord Compos'd by Sig.ʳ Graun Musician in ordinary to the King of Prussia.

London. Printed for I. Walsh, &c.

Whitehall Evening-Post, Jan. 27–30, 1759.

Fol. 2. parts.
BM. g. 270. u. (8.) (Primo part only.); Hirsch M. 1468. (5.) (Imperfect; wanting title-page and all after p. 8 of the primo part, and the bass part.) CUL. GUL.

GRAUN (JOHANN GOTTLIEB) AND AGRELL (JOHANN JOACHIM)

727. Six Concertos for the Harpsicord or Organ Compos'd by Sig.ʳ Graun and Agrell. Opera 2 ᵈᵃ

London. Printed for I. Walsh, &c.

Public Advertiser, Nov. 25, 1762.

Fol. pp. 2–32, blank, 34–48.
BM. g. 972. Rowe.

GRAVES (JAMES)

728. Graves's Songs. 2s. 6d. N.º 318.

[*c.* 1730.]

Walsh Cat. 18.
Smith 528 ('A Collection of Songs,' &c.), with Walsh only in the imprint and 'N.º 318' added to the title-page.
Walsh Cat. 17a [*c.* 1737]: 'Just Publish'd.' Refers to above or a new edition.

GREENE (MAURICE)

729. Forty Select Anthems in Score, composed For 1, 2, 3, 4, 5, 6, 7, and 8 Voices. By Dr. Maurice Greene, Organist and Composer to His Majesty's Chapels Royal, &c. Vol. I.
London: Printed for, and Sold by J. Walsh, &c. [Without date.]

— Volume Second.
London: Printed for, and Sold by J. Walsh, &c. M.DCC.XLIII.

Country Journal: or, The Craftsman, Jan. 15, 1743. (This day are publish'd.) *Daily Advertiser*, Jan. 13, (Thursday), 1743. (On Saturday will be publish'd.)

Large fol. Vol. I. Dedication. Privilege dated 27 Feb. 1741–2. 'A List of the Subscribers' [pp. 3]. 'A Table of the Anthems.' pp. 138. Vol. II. 'A Table of the Anthems.' pp. 155.
BM. Mad. Soc. 34. (With a 'Catalogue of Divine Musick, Just publish'd.')
RM. 14. d. 19. Many others in BUC not examined.

730. — Another issue. Volume First. (Volume Second.)
London: Printed for and Sold by J. Walsh . . . M.DCC.XLIII.

Large fol. Vol. 1. Dedication. Privilege dated 27 Feb. 1741–2. 'A List of the Subscribers' [pp. 3.] 'A Table of the Anthems.' pp. 138. Vol. 2. 'A Table of the Anthems.' pp. 155.
BM. H. 3099. RM. 14. d. 20. (Without list of Subscribers.) RCM. Smith.

731. — Another edition. Vol. I. (Vol. II.)
London: Printed for, and Sold by J. Walsh, &c.

General Evening Post (London), May 14–16, 1745. (A Second Edition of.)

Large fol. Vol. 1. Dedication. 'A Table of the Anthems.' pp. 138. Vol. 2. 'A Table of the Anthems.' pp. 155.
BM. I. 232. a.

732. — Third edition.

Public Advertiser, April 6, 1753. (Dr. Greene's forty select Anthems in Score, revised by the Author. Third Edition.)

733. — Another edition.

Public Advertiser, Dec. 24, 1761.

734. Six Solo Anthems Perform'd before His Majesty at the Chapel Royal for a Voice alone with a Thorough Bass for the Harpsicord or Organ Composed by D.r Greene.
London. Printed for I. Walsh, &c.

London Evening-Post, Sept. 24–26, 1747.

Large fol. pp. 2–34 (top centre). With additional top corner pagination 11–15 on pp. 2–6, 26–32 on pp. 7–13, 16–25 on pp. 14–23, 105–9 on pp. 24–28, 125–30 on pp. 29–34.

BM. I. 232. d. RCM. Birmingham. CUL.
From the plates of his 'Forty Select Anthems'.
Randall Cat.: 'Dr. Green's 6 Solo Anthems, taken out of his 40 select Anthems. 5s. od.'

735. A Cantata and Four English Songs. Set to Musick by Dᵣ Greene. Book 1 [in MS.].
— Book 2ᵈ [in MS.].
London. Printed for I. Walsh, &c.

Daily Advertiser, Jan. 7, 1745. *General Advertiser*, July 5, 1746. (Book the Second.)

Book 1. Fol. Licence. pp. 2–7, blank, 8–12. Book 2. Fol. Licence verso of title-page. pp. 13.
BM. G. 427. (4.); G. 426.(4.) (Book I.)RAM. RCM. Bod. OUF. Others in BUC not examined.

736. A Cantata and English Songs Set to Musick by Dᵣ Greene. Book II.
London. Printed for I. Walsh, &c.

[c. 1750.]

Fol. pp. 15.
BM. Mad. Soc. 58. (10.) RCM. Birmingham.
Another edition of Book 2 of 'A Cantata and Four English Songs'. The cantata has been partly re-engraved and extended from pp. 6–13 in the original to pp. 1–10.

737. Catches and Canons for Three and Four Voices. To which is added A Collection of Songs for Two and Three Voices With a Through Bass for the Harpsicord. Compos'd By Dᵣ Greene.
London. Printed for I. Walsh, &c.

General Advertiser, Dec. 12, 1747.

Obl. fol. Preface. 'The Reader', &c. pp. 2–41.
BM. D. 393. (2.) RAM. RCM. Rowe. Others in BUC not examined.
Walsh Cat. 25: 'Dr. Greene's Catches and two Part Songs. 5s. od.'

738. The Chaplet, being a Collection of Twelve English Songs. MDCCXXXVIII. [By Maurice Greene.]
Printed for In. Walsh, &c.

London Daily Post, and General Advertiser, March 13, 1738.

8°. pp. 38.
RM. 8. b. 14. John Rylands Library, Manchester.
Walsh Cat. 18: 'The Chaplet. A Collⁿ of Songs by Dr. Greene. 2s. 6d.' RM. copy contains a catalogue of 'Vocal Musick Just Publish'd by I. Walsh in Catherine Street.'

739. A Collection of Lessons for the Harpsicord compos'd by Dr Greene. 2nd Book.
London. Printed for I. Walsh, &c.

[c. 1755.]

Obl. fol. pp. 2–24.
Fitz.
Randall Cat.: 'Dr. Greene's easy Lessons. 2d Set 3s.od.'
The First Book may be: 'Six Overtures for the Harpsicord', &c. (No. 740.)

740. Six Overtures for the Harpsicord or Spinnet Compos'd by D.ʳ Maurice Greene. Being proper Pieces for the Improvement of the Hand.
Printed for I. Walsh, &c.

General Evening Post. (*London*), Oct. 24–26, 1745. (Six Overtures for the Harpsichord or Organ.)

Fol. pp. 2–33.
Hirsch IV. 1606. a. Tenbury.

741. Six Overtures for Violins, German Flutes, Hoboys &c. in Seven Parts Compos'd By D.ʳ Maurice Greene.
London. Printed for I. Walsh, &c.

General Advertiser, April 22, 1745.

Fol. Parts.
BM. g. 99. (With licence.) RM. 17. d. 4. (7.) (Without licence.) RAM. Manchester.

742. — New edition.

General Advertiser, Oct. 25, 1749. (New editions, &c.)

743. Spensers Amoretti Set To Music by D.ʳ Greene.
Printed for In.º Walsh, &c.

London Daily Post, and General Advertiser, March 28, 1739; May 18, 1739. (Where may be had . . . The Second Edition.)

Obl. fol. Illustrated title-page. Dedication. pp. 47, blank, Index.
RM. 8. d. 5. BM. D. 393. (1.) (Wanting p. 47 and Index.) Hirsch III. 782 (With Index on verso of p. 47.) Others in BUC not examined.
Walsh Cat. 18: 'Spenser's Amoretti . . . 5s. od.'
No advertisements traced of the third edition.

744. — The 4th Edition.

London Daily Post, and General Advertiser, Jan. 15, 1740. (Just publish'd.)

See also No. 749. Harmonia Anglicana. Harmonia Anglicana . . . D.ʳ Greene, &c.
No. 1061. Minuets. Selected Minuets . . . Compos'd by . . . D.ʳ Greene, &c.

GROENEMANN (Johann Albert)

See Nos. 175, 176 Blavet (Michel) Six Sonatas or Duets, for two German Flutes. By Mr. Blavet, Sig. Groneman, &c.

GUERINI (Francesco)

745. Guerini's Sonatas (for 2 German Flutes and a Bass).
[*c*. 1752.]

> Walsh Cat. 25.
> Not identified.
> Not in Walsh Cat. 27 or Randall.

H., A.

746. Twelve Italian Canzonets. To which is added a Collection of English Songs.
Compos'd by A. H.
London. Printed for I. Walsh, &c.

Public Advertiser, May 7, 1753. (Twelve Italian Canzonets, with some English Ballads, never before printed, by Mr. Holcombe.)

> Obl. fol. pp. 2–20.
> BM. D. 836. jj. (4.) RCM
> *See also*: No. 839. Holcombe (A.); No. 862. Italian Canzonets; and Addenda.

HAMLET

Songs in the Opera of Hamlet.

> *See* No. 687. Gasparini (Francesco) [Amleto.]

HANDEL (George Frideric)

Works by Handel published by Walsh are not included in this Bibliography but are listed in 'Handel. A Descriptive Catalogue of the Early Editions by William C. Smith' (Cassell & Co. 1960). The following references are to the miscellaneous works that include Handel items or extracts.

> *See* No. 10. Airs. A Choice Collection of Aires and Duets for two German Flutes Collected from the Works of . . . Mr. Handel, &c.; Nos. 11–13. Airs. Select Aires or Duets for two German Flutes . . . By . . . Handel, &c. . . .2d (3ᵈ, Fourth) Book; No. 41. 2ᵈ Book Apollo's Feast, &c.; No. 253; The British Miscellany, &c. (In which are inserted the favourite Songs in the Pastoral called The Spring: The Music by Mr. Handel, &c.); Nos. 265, 266. The British Orpheus, &c.; Nos. 344, 345. Cato. The Favourite Songs in the Opera call'd Cato; Nos. 548, 549. The Delightful Musical Companion, or select Duets for two German Flutes . . . by Mr. Handel, &c. (A Second Set, &c.); Nos. 598, 599. Elisa. The favourite Songs in the new Opera Call'd Elisa as also the additional Songs in the Opera of Rodelinda Compos'd by Mʳ Handel, &c.; No. 600. English Songs. A Collection of, &c.; No. 638. Forest Harmony. Forrest Harmony, Book the Second . . . with . . . Pieces out of the Water Musick, &c.; No. 715. Geminiani (Francesco) and Brivio (Giuseppe Ferdinando) 6 Solos by Geminiani Brivio and other Authors; No. 749. Harmonia

Anglicana . . . by . . . M.ʳ Handel, &c.; Nos. 888–95. The Lady's Banquet First (–Sixth) Book, &c.; No. 898. Lady's Entertainment. the Ladies Entertainment 5th Book . . . To which is prefix'd the celebrated Organ Concerto [Op. 4. No. 2] Composed by Mr. Handel; No. 902. Lampe (Johann Friedrich) Medley Overture in 4 parts; No. 907. Lampe (Johann Friedrich) and Howard (Samuel) The Vocal Musical Mask; No. 936. Lessons. Select Lessons . . . Aires by Mr. Handel, &c.; Nos. 969, 970. Love in a Village . . . Music by Handel, &c. Nos. 1028, 1029, 1034, 1039, 1042–5, 1061, 1066, 1082, 1085. Minuets; No. 1102. The Monthly Mask of Vocal Music; Nos. 1125, 1126. Muzio Scevola. The favourite Songs in the Opera call'd Muzio Scævola; No. 1146. Ormisda. The Favourite Songs in the Opera call'd Ormisda; No. 1148. Orpheus and Eurydice; the Comic Tunes in, &c.; Nos. 1265, 1266. The Quarterly Collection of Vocal Music; No. 1364. Select Harmony Fourth Collection. Six Concertos . . . Compos'd by M.ʳ Handel, &c.; No. 1388. Solimano. The Favourite Songs in the Opera Call'd Solimano; No. 1393. Six Solos. Four for a German Flute . . . Compos'd by M.ʳ Handel, &c.; No. 1534. Warlike Music. Second Book . . . Compos'd by M.ʳ Handel, &c.; Addenda. The Harpsichord Master.

HARLEQUIN RESTORED

747. The Tunes in Harlequin Restor'd or Taste Alamode.
[London. Printed for John Walsh.]

London Daily Post, and General Advertiser, April 23, 1736.

> Obl. fol. ff. 3 Without pagination or title-page. Printed on one side only.
> BM. e. 5. k. (2.)
> Attributed to T. A. Arne.

HARLEQUIN SORCERER

748. The Comic Tunes in the Celebrated Entertainment Call'd Harlequin Sorcerer as it is Perform'd at the Theatre-Royal in Covent Garden. For the Harpsicord, Violin, &c.
London. Printed for I. Walsh, &c.

London Evening-Post, Feb. 25–27, 1752.

> Obl. fol. pp. 21.
> BM. e. 5. f. (5.) RCM.
> Harlequin Sorcerer was composed and arranged by Thomas A. Arne. This work also contains 'Comic Tunes in Dr. Faustus' (pp. 17–21) by Samuel Arnold.

HARMONIA ANGLICANA

749. Harmonia Anglicana or English Harmony Reviv'd. A Collection of the most Favourite Two, Three and Four Part Songs and Dialogues Set to Musick by

Hen: Purcell Dᵣ Blow Mᵣ Handel Dᵣ Boyce Dᵣ Arne Dᵣ Greene Weldon Leveridge Carey Galliard Book I.
London. Printed for I. Walsh, &c.

[*c.* 1745.]

Fol. pp. 30, with other irregular pagination.
BM. G. 103. b. Bod.
Also contains a composition by Bedford Aldrich.
Walsh Cat. 24*a*. 'English Harmony Reviv'd, a Collⁿ of Songs for one 2, 3 & 4 Voices. 4s. od.'

750. — Book II.

[*c.* 1755.]

Fol. pp. 31–60, with other irregular pagination.
BM. G. 103. b.
'II' altered from 'I' in MS.
Also contains compositions by William Corbett, Dan. Purcell and Tho. Ellway.

751. — Book III.

[*c.* 1760.]

Fol. pp. 61–90, with other irregular pagination.
BM. G. 103. b.
'III' altered from 'I' in MS.
Also contains compositions by John Eccles, Mr. Hayden and Mr. Cook.

752. — Book IV.

[*c.* 1764.]

Fol.
Public Advertiser, Sept. 19, 1764. (Of whom may be had English Harmony Reviv'd . . . by Purcell, Blow, Handel, Boyce, in four Books each 3s.)

HARMONIA MUNDI

753. Harmonia Mundi Consisting of Six Favourite Sonata's Collected out of the Choisest Works of Six Most Eminent Authors viz Signᵣ Torelli . . . Mᵣ H. Purcell . . . Signᵣ Bassani . . . Mᵣ Pepusch . . . Signᵣ Albinoni . . . Signᵣ Pez . . . the first Collection Engraven & Carefully Corected.
London Printed for I. Walsh . . . and I. Hare, &c.

[*c.* 1727.]

Fol. Parts. Violino Primo, Violino Secondo, Basso Continuo (Violino Basso).
Walsh Cat. 11*a*: 'Harmonia Mundi, being Six Celebrated Sonatas by the Greatest Masters for Violins in 4 Parts.'
Smith 257 (BM. g. 419.), with Randell omitted from the imprint.

754. — With Walsh only in the imprint and 'N.º 383' added to the title-page.

[*c.* 1730.]

> Walsh Cat. 18: 'Harmonia Mundi being 6 Sonatas by several Authors for 2 Violins and a Bass. 5s. od. N.º 383.'

755. Harmonia Mundi. The 2.ᵈ Collection. Being VI Concertos in Six Parts For Violins and other Instruments. Collected out of the Choicest Works of the most Eminent Authors viz Vivaldi Tessarini Albinoni Alberti never before Printed.

London Printed for and sold by I: Walsh . . . and Ioseph Hare, &c.

County Journal: or, The Craftsman, Dec. 21, 1728.

> Fol. 6 parts.
> BM. g. 419. a.
> Walsh Cat. 11*a*: 'Harmonia Mundi the Second Collection or Six Sonatas . . . for Violins in 7 Parts.'
> Smith 364, with Walsh and Hare only in the imprint.

756. — With Walsh only in the imprint and 'N.º 384' added to the title-page.

[*c.* 1730.]

> Walsh Cat. 18: 'Harmonia Mundi 2d Collection being Six Concertos by Alberti Vivaldi and Tessarini (for Violins). 7s. od. N.º 384.'

HARMONIA SACRA

757. Harmonia Sacra. £1. 1s. od. N.º 213.

[*c.* 1730.]

> Walsh Cat. 18.
> No copy traced with a Walsh imprint. This may refer to 'Harmonia Sacra; or Divine Hymns and Dialogues', printed for Henry Playford in two books, 1688, 1693, &c. (BM. G. 84. (1.) &c. Fol.)
> Walsh advertised the work in various catalogues: in 15*a* at £1. 1. 0, in 24*a* as 'Harmonia Sacra Divine Hymns by Purcell, Blow, &c. 2 Books each 5s. od.'

HARPSICHORD MASTER

758. The Harpsichord-Master: The Seventh Book. Containing plain and easy Instructions for learners on the Harpsichord or Spinnet; with a complete Explanation of Graces, and the true manner of fingering the Keys. Together with a Collection of Aires and Lessons proper for Learners, and the favourite Song Tunes, Minuets, Rigadoons, and Jiggs, now in use. All fairly engraven; price 2s.

Printed for and sold by J. Walsh . . . and J. Hare, &c.

Post-Boy, Jan. 12–14, 1721.

> Obl. fol.
> For books 1–6 see Smith 14, 27, 59, 403, 471, and 566.

759. The Harpsichord Master VIIIth Book Containing Plain & easy Instructions for Learners on the Harpsichord or Spinnet with a Compleat Explanation of Graces, & the true man.^r of Fingering ye Keys, also an exact method of tuneing the Harpsichord & Spinnet, being of material use to all as play thereon, together with a Collection of Aires and Lessons proper for Learners & the favourite Song-tunes Minuets Rigadoons and Iiggs now in Use. all fairly Engraven. Price 2.^s 1722, &c.
London. Printed for I Walsh . . . & I Hare, &c.

> 1722.
> Obl. fol. ff. 13. Printed on one side only, except for 3 on verso of 2.
> BM. d. 38.
> Composers named: Vanbrughe, Fairbank.

760. The Harpsichord Master IXth. Book, &c.
London. Printed for I Walsh . . . & I Hare, &c.

> [c. 1724.]
> Obl. fol.
> No copy or advertisement traced.

761. The Harpsichord Master X^th Book . . . Price 2.^s 1725.
London. Printed for I Walsh . . . and I Hare, &c.

> Obl. fol. ff. 16. Printed on one side only, except for 3 on verso of 2. Title-page same as the 'VIIIth Book' except for number and date.
> BM. d. 38. a.
> Composer named: Fairbanks.

762. The Harpsichord Master XIth Book . . . Price 2.^s 1726.
London. Printed for I. Walsh . . . and I. Hare, &c.

> Obl. fol. ff. 16. Printed on one side only, except for 3 on verso of 2. Title-page same as 'X^th' Book except for number and date.
> Bod.

763. The Harpsichord Master XIIth Book . . . Price 2.^s 1727.
London. Printed for I Walsh . . . & I Hare, &c.

> Obl. fol. ff. 16. Printed on one side only, except for 3 on verso of 2. Title-page same as 'X^th' Book except for number, date and additions to list of works.
> BM. d. 38. b.

764. The Harpsichord Master XIIIth Book . . . Price 2.^s 1728.
London. Printed for I Walsh . . . & I Hare, &c.

> Obl. fol. ff. 16. Printed on one side only, except for 3 on verso of 2. Title-page same as 'XIIth' Book, except for number and date.
> BM. d. 38. c.
> Composer named: Bitti.

765. The Harpsichord Master XIVth Book . . . Price 2ˢ 1734. N° 186.
London. Printed for I Walsh, &c.

> Obl. fol. f. 1, 'A Scale of the Gamut.' f. 2, 'Rules for Graces'. 'A Table of the Dances'
> (not foliated). Printed on one side only. Title-page same as 'XIIIth' Book, except for number
> and date, Hare omitted from imprint, and addition of 'N° 186.' (*See also*: Addenda.)
> BM. d. 38. e.
> Walsh Cat. 18: 'Musick for the Harpsichord . . . Books for Learners. 2s. od. N° 186.'

HARPSICORD BOOK

> *See* No. 1132. New Harpsicord Book

HART (PHILIP)

766. Hart's Hymn from Milton. 5s. od.

[*c.* 1735.]

> Walsh Cat. 18.
> Presumably refers to 'The Morning Hymn: From the Fifth Book of Milton's Paradise
> Lost. Set to Musick By Philip Hart. Ingrav'd by Tho. Cross, for ye author.' Published 1729,
> (BM. G. 505. Fol. pp. (2). 34), or another edition, Printed for the Author, *c.* 1729. (RCM.)

767. Hart's Melodies for the Organ. 6d. N° 567.

[*c.* 1735.]

> Walsh Cat. 18.
> Walsh Cat. 20*a*: 'Hart's Psalms or Melodies.'
> Walsh Cat. 24*a*: 'Hart's Psalm Tunes (Voluntarys and Fugues for ye Organ and Harp^d) 6d.'
> Presumably a reissue of 'Melodies proper to be sung to any of ye Versions of the Psalms
> of David', &c. Published by Phil. Hart in 1716 (*The Post-Man*, July 17–19), with imprint
> Printed and Sold at the Musick-Shops London. (BM. a. 120. 12°. pp. 2–24.)

HARTLEY (JAMES)

768. Six Sonatas For Two Violins or German Flutes & a Bass. Composed (for his
Amusement) by James Hartley Gent: Late an Officer in His Majesties IX Regi-
ment of Foot. Revised, Corrected and approved of by Thomas Augustine Arne
Gent: Price 5ˢ
London Printed for the Author and Sold at the Music Shops.

Public Advertiser, June 3, 1758. (On the 7th or 9th of this Instant will be published
Six Sonatas . . . Subscriptions taken in at Mr. Walsh's . . . Mr. Johnson's, &c.)

> Fol. 3 parts.
> BM. g. 100. b. RAM.
> Engraved by William Smith.

HASSE (JOHANN ADOLPH)

769. The Favourite Songs in the Opera Call'd Artaxerxes. By Sig^r Hasse.
London. Printed for and Sold by I. Walsh, &c.

London Evening-Post, March 27–29, 1735.

> Fol. Passe-partout title-page. pp. 2–16 (bottom centre), 17 (top corner) and 3 pp. without pagination.
> BM. G. 173. a. Manchester. Rowe.
> Words by Apostolo Zeno. According to Burney some of the songs in this work were composed by Riccardo Broschi.

770. — With 'N.º 540' added to the title-page.

> [*c.* 1735.]
> Walsh Cat. 18: 'Artaxerxes by Sig.ʳ Hasse. 2s. 6d. N.º 540.'
> Republished in 'Le Delizie dell' Opere', Vol. II, pp. 146–63, 187.

6 Cantatas for a Voice and Harpsi.ᵈ 5s. od.

> *See* No. 816. Hasse (Johann Adolph) Six Italian Cantatas, &c.

Catone in Utica.

> *See* No. 344. Cato

771. [Chamber Airs.] Farinelli's Celebrated Songs &c. Collected from Sig.ʳ Hasse, Porpora, Vinci, and Veracini's Operas Set for a German Flute Violin or Harpsicord. Vol. I. [Part I.]

> London: Printed for and Sold by J. Walsh . . . N.º 602.

> *Country Journal: or, The Craftsman*, Jan. 15, 1737.

> > Fol. 'A Table of the Songs contain'd in the first Volume' [Pt. 1–7], &c. pp. 2–25.
> > BM. g. 444.
> > Part 1, not indicated on the title-page. The Table was issued in 1744.
> > Walsh Cat. 18: 'Farinelli's Songs for a Ger.ⁿ Flute. 3s. od.'

772. — Vol. I. Part 2.ᵈ

> *London Daily Post, and General Advertiser*, April 28, 1740. (A Second Collection of Chamber Airs . . . collected from the Operas compos'd by Pescetti, Hasse, and Vinci, &c.); May 7, 1740. (Sonatas or Chamber Airs . . . Vol. I. Part 2.)

> > Fol. pp. 2–25.
> > BM. g. 444.
> > Title-page as Part 1, with 'Part 2.ᵈ' added in MS.
> > Walsh Cat. 18: 'Hasse. Airs for a German Flute and a Bass. 6s. od, [Part. 1 and 2.]

773. Hasse, Vinci, Veracini & Pescetti's Chamber Aires For a German Flute Violin or Harpsicord. Being the most Celebrated Songs & Ariets Collected out of all their late Operas. Vol. I. Part 3.ᵈ

> London. Printed for I. Walsh, &c.

> [*c.* 1741.]

Fol. pp. 2–25.
BM. g. 444.
'Part 3.ᵈ' added in MS.
Walsh Cat. 21: 'Hasse and Vinci's Airs 3 Sets. 9s. od.'

774. — Vol. I. Part 4.

Daily Advertiser, Sept. 18, 1742. (Of whom may be had. Hasse and Galuppi's Airs for a German Flute and Bass, from all the Operas perform'd last Winter, in four Books.)

Fol. pp. 2–25.
BM. g. 444.
Title-page as Part 3, with 'Part 4' added in MS.

775. Galuppi's, Hasse, Vinci, Lampugnani, Veracini & Pescetti's Chamber Aires For a German Flute Violin or Harpsicord. Being the most Celebrated Songs & Ariets Collected out of all their late Operas. Vol. I. Part V.
London. Printed for I. Walsh, &c.

Daily Advertiser, March 5, 1743. (Galuppi's Airs in the Opera of Enrico, &c.)

Fol. pp. 2–25.
BM. g. 444.
'Galuppi's,' and 'Part V' added in MS.

776. Galuppi, Hasse, Vinci, Lampugnani, Veracini & Pescetti's Chamber Aires For a German Flute Violin or Harpsicord. Being the most Celebrated Songs & Ariets Collected out of all their late Operas. Vol. I. Part 6.ᵗʰ
London. Printed for I. Walsh, &c.

Daily Advertiser; General Advertiser, June 25, 1744. (The celebrated Airs in the Opera Alceste, &c. Set for a German Flute and Bass. Vol. I. Part VI.)

Fol. pp. 2–24.
BM. g. 444.
'Part 6.ᵗʰ' added in MS.

777. Galuppi, Hasse, Vinci, Lampugnani, Veracini & Pescetti's Chamber Aires . . . Vol. I. Part 7. London. Printed for I. Walsh, &c.

General Advertiser, July 4, 1744. (Which completes the First Volume, Lampugnani's Second Set of celebrated Airs in Alceste, &c. set for a German Flute and Bass Part VII. With an Index to the whole.)

Fol. pp. 2–10, blank, 12–23.
BM. g. 444.
Title-page as Part 6, with 'Part 7' added in MS.

General Evening Post, Oct. 12–15, 1745. (Hasse and Lampugnani's Airs 7 Collections. Just Publish'd.)

778. — Vol. II. [Part I.]

General Advertiser, April 16, 1746. (The celebrated Airs in the Opera of Artamene, &c. set for a German Flute and a Bass. Vol. II. Part I.)

> Fol. 'A Table of the Songs contain'd in the Second Volume', &c. [Pt. 1–7.] pp. 2–25.
> BM. g. 444.
> Title-page as No. 777.
> 'II' altered from 'I' in MS. Part 1, not indicated on the title-page.
> The Table was issued in 1750.

779. — Vol. II. Part 2ᵈ

General Advertiser, March 2, 1747. (The favourite Airs set for a German Flute
and a Bass, from all the Operas perform'd this Year. Vol. II. Part I. [i.e. II.];
March 5, 1747. (The favourite Airs . . . in the Operas of Phaeton, Mithridate, &c.
Vol. II. Part II.)

> Fol. pp. 2–25.
> BM. g. 444.
> Title-page as No. 777.
> 'II' altered from 'I' and 'Part 2ᵈ' added in MS.

780. — Vol. II. Part 3. (Contains Airs by Terradellas, Gluck and Galuppi.)

> [*c.* 1747.]
> Fol. pp. 2–21.
> BM. g. 444.
> Title-page as No. 777.
> 'II' altered from 'I' and 'Part 3' added in MS.

781. — Vol. II. Part 4.

General Advertiser, June 21, 1748. (Hasse's favourite Airs in the Opera of Dido set
for a German Flute and a Bass. Vol. II. Part 4.)

> Fol. pp. 70–90.
> BM. g. 444.
> Title-page as No. 777.
> 'II' altered from 'I' and 'Part 4' added in MS.

782. — Vol. II. Part 5. (Contains Airs by Hasse, Lampugnani and Terradellas.)

> [*c.* 1748.]
> Fol. pp. 92–111.
> BM. g. 444.
> Title-page as No. 777.
> 'II' altered from 'I' and 'Part 5' added in MS.

783. — Vol. II. Part 6th

General Advertiser, July 11, 1749. (The Celebrated Airs in the late Comic Operas, set for a German Flute and a Bass. V. 2. p. 6. Pr. 6s.)

    Fol. pp. 112–30.
    BM. g. 444.
    Title-page as No. 777.
    'II' altered from 'I' and 'Part 6th' added in MS.

784. — Vol. II. Part 7th

General Advertiser, July 3, 1750. (With an Index which completes the Second Volume. The favourite Songs in all the Operas perform'd last Winter, set for a German Flute and a Bass, Vol. 2 part 7.) *London Evening Post*, July 5–7, 1750. (The celebrated Aires, &c.)

    Fol. pp. 132–51.
    BM. g. 444.
    Title-page as No. 777.
    'II' altered from 'I' and 'Part 7th' added in MS.

785. Galuppi, Hasse, Vinci, Lampugnani, Veracini and Pescetti's Chamber Aires... Vol. I.
    Printed for I. Walsh, &c. [*c.* 1755.]

    Fol.
    RM. 17. f. 19. Another edition of Vol. I, Parts 1–7 without separate title-pages.
    Walsh Cat. 25: 'Hasse, Galuppi, and Vinci's Aires from Operas in 2 Vol^s Each £1. 1s. 0d. (for a German Flute and Harpsicord).'
    Walsh Cat. 27: 'Galuppi and Hasse's Airs. 2 Vol. each £1. 1s. 0d. (For a German Flute & Bass.)'
    Randall Cat.: 'Hasse, Galuppi, and Vinci's Chamber Airs, from the Operas, 2 vols. each £1. 1s. 0d. N.B. These Airs may be had in 14 Collections, each 3s. 0d.'
    Other copies under 'Songs' in BUC not examined.

786. The Comic Tunes &c, to the Celebrated Dances Perform'd at Both Theatres By Sig^r & Sig^{ra} Fausan, Mons. Desnoyer and Sig^{ra} Barberini. Mons. & Madem. Michel. For the Harpsicord, Violin, or German Flute. Compos'd by Sig^r Hasse. &c. Price 1^s 6^d Book I. (II.) (III.) (IV.)
    London. Printed for I. Walsh, &c.

    With an outer illustrated title-page:—Hasse's Comic Tunes To the Opera and Theatre Dances. Vol. I.
    Printed for I. Walsh, &c.

    Issued in 4 sets or books. *London Daily Post, and General Advertiser*, Feb. 28, 1741; March 7, 1741; March 14, 1741; March 21, 1741. (Which compleats all the comic Tunes.); April 1, 1741. (In four books.)

    Obl. 8º. ff. 2–93. Printed on one side only. Containing the four sets or books.
    BM. a. 149. (With inner title-page of Book I only, with price '1^s' altered to '7^s' in MS.)

RM. 15. g. 3. (With inner title-page of Book I only, price unaltered.) CUL. (Book I. With inner title-page only.) Rowe. (With inner title-page of Book I only.) Bod. (Books I–III. With inner title-pages only.)

Walsh Cat. 18: 'Comic Dance Tunes of Fausan & Barberini. 6s. od.'

Walsh Cat. 21: 'Hasse's Comic Dance Tunes. 6s. od.'

787. The Celebrated Comic Tunes to the Opera Dances, as Perform'd at the King's Theatre in the Hay Market. To which is added, Several of the most Celebrated Dances Perform'd at both Theatres. By Sig.^r Sodi Sig.^{ra} Auretti &c. Never before Printed. For the Harpsicord, Violin, or German Flute. Compos'd by the most Eminent Italian Authors. Vol. II. Part I. Price 1.^s 6.^d &c.

London. Printed for I. Walsh, &c.

With an outer illustrated title-page: Hasse's Comic Tunes To the Opera and Theatre Dances. Vol. II. [Altered from 'I' in MS.]

Printed for I. Walsh, &c.

Issued in 4 sets or parts. Part I. [Sept. 1742.] *Daily Advertiser*, Sept. 29, 1742. (A Second Set.); April 26, 1743. (Vol. II. Part III.); Oct. 3, 1743. (Vol. II. Part IV.)

Obl. 8°. ff. 2–85. Printed on one side only. Containing the four sets or parts.

BM. a. 149. (With inner title-page of Part I only; imperfect.) RM. 15. g. 3. (Title-page with, 'Vol. II', only.)

788. The Comic Tunes to all the Late Opera Dances as Perform'd by Sig.^a Auretti, Sodi, Campioni &c. at the Kings Theatre in the Hay Market. Set for the German Flute, Violin, or Harpsicord. Compos'd by Sig.^r Hasse, and ỹ most Eminent Italian Authors. Vol. III.

With an outer illustrated title-page: Hasse's Comic Tunes To the Opera and Theatre Dances. Vol. III. [Altered from 'I' in MS.]

Printed for I. Walsh, &c.

Issued in 4 sets or parts. *Daily Advertiser*, July 18, 1744; August 4, 1744; August 28, 1744; Sept. 5, 1744.

Obl. 8°. ff. 76. Printed on one side only.

BM. a. 149. (With outer title-page only.) RM. 15. g. 3. (With inner title-page only.)

789. The Comic Tunes to all the Late Opera Dances As Perform'd by Sig.^a Violetta, Salamon Nardi, Valenti & Michels, at the King's Theatre in the Hay Market. Set for the German Flute, Violin, or Harpsicord. Compos'd by Sig.^r Hasse, Pasquali, and ỹ most Eminent Italian Authors. Vol. IV.

London. Printed for I. Walsh, &c.

With an outer illustrated title-page: Hasse's Comic Tunes To the Opera and Theatre Dances. Vol. IV. [Altered from 'I' in MS.]

Printed for I. Walsh, &c.

Issued in 4 sets or parts. *General Advertiser*, June 14, 1746; June 21, 1746; June 28, 1746; July 12, 1746.

> Obl. 8°. pp. 96.
> BM. a. 149. (With outer title-page only.) RM. 15. g. 3. (Both title-pages.)
> Bod. (With inner title-page only.)

790. The Comic Tunes to all the Late Opera Dances As Perform'd by Sig. Auretti's, Nardi, Sodi, Valenti &c. at the King's Theatre in the Hay Market. Set for the Harpsicord, Violin, or German Flute. Compos'd by Sigᵣ Hasse, Pasquali, and the most Eminent Italian Authors. Vol. V.

> London. Printed for I. Walsh, &c.

With an outer illustrated title-page: Hasse's Comic Tunes To the Opera and Theatre Dances. Vol. V. [Altered from 'I' in MS.]

> Printed for I. Walsh, &c.

Issued in 4 sets or parts. *General Advertiser*, June 6, 1747; June 18, 1747; June 23, 1747; June 27, 1747.

> Obl. 8°. pp. 84.
> BM. a. 149. RM. 15. g. 3. Bod. (With inner title-page only.)
> Walsh Cat. 24*a*: 'Hasse's Comic Tunes to the Opera and Theatre Dances in 4 vol. each Volume Bound 7s. 6d.'
> Walsh Cat. 24*c*: 'In 5 vol.'

General Advertiser, Oct. 24, 1748. (5 vol.)

791. The Comic Tunes to all the Late Opera Dances As Perform'd by Sigᵃ Bugiani, Maranesi, Conti, Nieri, etc. at the Kings Theatre in the Hay Market. Set for the German Flute, Violin or Harpsicord. Compos'd by Sigᵣ Hasse, and ẙ most Eminent Italian Authors. Vol. VI.

> London. Printed for I. Walsh, &c.

With an outer illustrated title-page: Hasse's Comic Tunes to the Opera and Theatre Dances. Vol. VI. [Altered from I in MS.]

> Printed for I. Walsh, &c.

Issued in 2 parts. *Public Advertiser*, May 27, 1755. (The Comic Tunes to the Opera Dances for the Harpsichord, &c. Price 1s. 6d.); May 8, 1758. (The Comic Tunes to the Opera Dances, performed this year, for the Harpsichord, German Flute or Violin. Price Three Shillings.)

> Obl. 8°. pp. 80.
> Dundee. (With inner title-page only.)

791a. The Comic Tunes to all the Late Opera Dances [space] As Perform'd at the King's Theatre in the Hay Market. Set for the German Flute, Violin, or Harpsicord. Composed by Sigᵣ Hasse, and yᵉ most Eminent Italian Authors. Vol. VI.

London. Printed for I. Walsh, &c.

With an outer illustrated title-page: Hasse's Comic Tunes To the Opera and Theatre Dances. Vol. VI. [Altered from I in MS.]

Printed for I. Walsh, &c.

Public Advertiser, March 6, 1758. (The Comic Tunes to this Year's Opera Dances ... Price 3s.) Assumed to refer to this edition.

> Obl. 8º. pp. 80.
> BM. a. 149. a. (With both title-pages, wanting pp. 35, 36.) The inner title-page adapted from that of Vol. III (No. 788) by deletion and minor alterations.

792. The Comic Tunes to all the Late Opera Dances [space] As Perform'd at the Kings Theatre in the Hay Market. Set for the German Flute, Violin, or Harpsicord. Compos'd by Sigʳ Hasse, and ỹ most Eminent Italian Authors. Vol. VII. [Altered from VI in MS.]

London. Printed for I. Walsh, &c.

With an outer illustrated title-page: Hasse's Comic Tunes To the Opera and Theatre Dances. Vol. VII. [Altered from I in MS.]

Printed for I. Walsh, &c.

Issued in 2 sets. *Public Advertiser*, April 5, 1759. (The Comic Tunes to the Opera Dances 1759 ... Pr. 2s.); May 8, 1759. (A Second Set of the Comic Tunes ... Pr. 2s.)

> Obl. 8º. pp. 88.
> BM. a. 149. (With outer title-page only.) Bod. (With inner title-page only.) Dundee. (With inner title-page only.)

793. Hasse's Comic Tunes To the Opera and Theatre Dances. Vol. VIII. [Altered from I in MS.]

Printed for I. Walsh, &c.

Issued in 2 parts, *Public Advertiser*, June 2, 1760. (The Comic Tunes to this Year's Opera Dances ... Price 2s.); June 27, 1760. (Comic Dances ... Vol. 8. Price 2s.); May 27, 1761. (The Comic Tunes to this Year's Opera Dances ... Price 2s.); June 2, 1761. (In two Collections.)

> Obl. 8º. pp. 72.
> BM. a. 149. (Without inner title-page.)

793a. The Comic Tunes to all the late Opera Dances as Perform'd at the Kings Theatre in the Hay Market for the Harpsicord German Flute or Violin. or Guitar. Compos'd by Sigʳ Agus. Vol. VIII. Part 2. ['Vol. VIII' altered from 'VI' in MS. and 'Part 2' is in MS.] 1761. Price 2ˢ

London. Printed for I. Walsh, &c.

> Obl. 8º. pp. 24. (Consisting of pp. 25–48 of the complete volume, No. 793.)
> BM. a. 149. b. Pendlebury.

794. [Comic Tunes.] The Opera Dances for the Year 1762. Part First, for the Harpsichord, German Flute, or Guitar.
  Printed for J. Walsh, &c.

Public Advertiser, May 1, 1762; May 18, 1762. (Vol. IX.)

795. [Comic Tunes.] A Second Set of Opera Dances for the Year 1762, with the favourite Minuet for the Harpsicord, German Flute, or Guitar.
  Printed for J. Walsh, &c.

Public Advertiser, May 26, 1762.

> Randall Cat.: 'Hasse's Comic Tunes to the Opera and Theatre Dances, in 8 vols. each 6s. od. — Vol. 9, part 1st and 2d, each 2s.od.'

796. Twelve Concertos in Six Parts, For a German Flute, Two Violins, a Tenor, with a Thorough Bass for the Harpsicord or Violoncello. Compos'd by Signor Giovanni Adolffo Hasse. Opera Terza.
  London. Printed for I. Walsh, &c.

London Daily Post, and General Advertiser, Feb. 19, 1741. (Of whom may be had.)

> Fol. 5 parts.
> Details of title-page uncertain, taken from No. 798.
> Walsh Cat. 18: '12 Concertos for German Flutes and Violins in 6 Parts. Opera 3ª 15s. od.'

797. — Another edition.

General Evening Post (London), Jan. 17–19, 1745. (New editions. Hasse's eighteen Concertos for German Flutes, Violins, &c. [i.e. Op. 3 and Op. 4.])

798. Twelve Concertos in Six Parts, For a German Flute, Two Violins, a Tenor, with a Thorough Bass for the Harpsicord or Violoncello. Compos'd by Signor Giovanni Adolffo Hasse. Opera Terza.
  London. Printed for I. Walsh, &c.

[*c.* 1749.] *General Advertiser*, Oct. 25, 1749. (New editions . . . Hasse Concertos, &c.)

> Fol. 5 parts.
> BM. g. 979. a. (1.) RM. 26. b. 2. (6.) RAM. Others copies in BUC not examined.

799. Six Concertos For Violins, French Horns or Hoboys, &c. with a Thorough Bass for ẙ Harpsicord or Violoncello. in Eight Parts. Compos'd by Giovanni Adolffo Hasse. Opera Quarta.

London. Printed for I. Walsh ... N° 683.

London Daily Post, and General Advertiser, Sept. 17, 1741. (In a few days.) Oct. 24, 1741. (This day is publish'd.)

Fol. 6 parts.
BM. g. 979. b. RM. 26. b. 2. (7.) Other copies in BUC not examined.
Walsh Cat. 18: '6 Concertos for French Horns. Op. 4ª 6s. od.'
'No. 683' also given to Howard's 'Musical Companion.' (No. 846.)

800. — Another edition.

General Evening Post (London), Jan. 17–19, 1745. (New editions. Hasse's eighteen Concertos for German Flutes, Violins, &c. [i.e. Op. 3 and Op. 4].)

801. — Another edition.

General Advertiser, Oct. 25, 1749. (New editions ... Hasse Concertos, &c.)

802. Six Concertos Set for the Harpsicord or Organ Compos'd by Signor Giovanni Adolffo Hasse. [Op. 4.]
London. Printed for I. Walsh, &c.

[*c.* 1743.]

Fol. pp. 42.
BM. f. 517. RM. 17. e. 5. (1.) RM. 16. d. 11. RAM. Fitz. Rowe. Tenbury (2).
Walsh Cat. 21: 'Hasse's Organ Concertos. 4s. od.'

803. Hasse's Celebrated Concerto for the Harpsichord.
Printed for I. Walsh. &c.

[*c.* 1745.]

Fol. pp. 2–6.
Tenbury (2 copies).
Concerto Op. 4. No. 1.

804. Six Concertos in Six Parts. For a German Flute, Two Violins, a Tenor, with a Thorough Bass for the Harpsichord or Violoncello. Compos'd by Signor Giovanni Adolffo Hasse. Opera Sexta.
London. Printed for I. Walsh, &c.

General Evening Post (London), Dec. 3–5, 1745.

Fol. 5 parts.
BM. g. 979. a. (2.) RM. 26. b. 2. (8.) RAM. Oriel College, Oxford.

Le Delizie dell' Opere, being the favourite Airs from all his Operas in Score Vol. 2d £1. 1s. od. (Hasse's Works. Walsh Cat. 18.)

See No. 557. Delizie dell' Opere. Vol. II.

805. The Favourite Songs in the Opera Call'd Dido By Sig.ʳ Hasse.
London. Printed for I. Walsh, &c.

London Evening-Post, April 21–23, 1748. (Of whom may be had.)

> Fol. Passe-partout title-page. pp. 2–17, blank, 70–74 (top centre pagination, with 40–44 bottom centre).
> BM. G. 206. b. (2.) Gresham. RCM. Rowe.
> Republished in 'Le Delizie dell' Opere', Vol. V, pp. 93–112.

806. Twelve Duets or Canzonets for Two German Flutes or Voices compos'd by Sig.ʳ Hasse &c. To which is added The favourite Song of Sig.ʳᵃ Galli.
London. Printed for I. Walsh, &c.

General Advertiser, Sept. 9, 1748. (Of whom may be had.)

> Obl. fol. pp. 13.
> BM. E. 525. (2.) Cardiff. Manchester. Reid. Rowe.
> Walsh Cat 25: 'Hasse's 12 Canzonets or Duets. 2s. od.'

807. — 2nd Set.

[*c.* 1752–5.]

> No advertisement traced.

808. A 3.ᵈ Set of XV Duets or Canzonets for two Voices or Two German Flutes and a Bass Compos'd by Sig.ʳ Jomelli, Hasse, and the most Eminent Italian Masters.
London. Printed for I. Walsh, &c.

Public Advertiser, Dec. 16, 1755.

> Obl. fol. pp. 12.
> BM. E. 601. k. (5.*) RAM.

809. A 4.ᵗʰ Set of XV Duets or Canzonets for two Voices or Two German Flutes and a Bass Compos'd by Sig.ʳ Jomelli, Hasse, and the most Eminent Italian Masters.
London. Printed for I. Walsh, &c.

Public Advertiser, Nov. 15, 1757.

> Obl. fol. pp. 2–13.
> BM. E. 270. y. (5.) RAM.

810. N.º V. Duets or Canzonets for two Voices or Two German Flutes and a Bass Compos'd by Sig.ʳ Jomelli, Hasse, and the most Eminent Italian Masters.
London. Printed for I. Walsh, &c.

Public Advertiser, April 18, 1759. (A fifth and Sixth Book of Duets... Printed for J. Walsh, &c.)

> Obl. fol. pp. 12.
> RAM.

811. — 6th Set.
Public Advertiser, April 18, 1759. (A fifth and Sixth Book of Duets... Printed for J. Walsh, &c.) (*See* Addenda.)

812. Number VII. Twenty French and Italian Canzonets, for a Guitar, German Flute, Voice, or Harpsichord, Price 2s.
Printed for J. Walsh, &c.
Public Advertiser, July 3, 1760. (*See* Addenda.)

813. Number VIII. A Favourite Collection of Canzonets or Duets for Voices, German Flutes, or Guittars, by Sig. Jomelli, Hasse, Pergolesi.
Printed for J. Walsh, &c.
Public Advertiser, July 28, 1761.

814. N⁰ IX. Duets or Canzonets for two Voices Guitars or Two German Flutes and a Bass Compos'd by Sigʳ Jomelli, Hasse, and the most Eminent Italian Masters.
London. Printed for I. Walsh, &c.
Public Advertiser, Sept. 18, 1762. (A Ninth and Tenth Set of Italian Canzonets or Duets, &c.)
> Obl. fol. pp. 12–22.
> BM. E. 601. k. (4★.)
> 'IX' is in MS.

815. N⁰ X Duets or Canzonets for two Voices Guitars or Two German Flutes and a Bass Compos'd by Sigʳ Jomelli, and the most Eminent Italian Masters.
London. Printed for I. Walsh, &c.
Public Advertiser, Sept. 18, 1762. (A Ninth and Tenth Set of Italian Canzonets or Duets, &c.).
> Obl. fol. pp. 11.
> BM. E. 601. k. (5.)
> 'X' is in MS.
> Randall Cat.: 'Vocal Music. Italian. Hasse, Galuppi, and Jomelli's Canzonets, 10 books, each 2s. od.'

Farinelli's Celebrated Songs, &c.
See No. 771. Hasse (Johann Adolph) [Chamber Airs.]

816. Six Italian Cantatas for a Voice Accompany'd with a Harpsicord or Violoncello Compos'd by Sigʳ Gio. Adolffo Hasse.
London. Printed for I. Walsh, &c.

London Evening-Post, April 11–13, 1751. (Of whom may be had.)

> Obl. fol. pp. 2–30.
> BM. E. 525. d; E. 525 c. (2.) (Without title-page.)
> Walsh Cat. 25: 'Hasse's 6 Cantatas for a Voice and Harpsi.ᵈ 5s. od.,

Opera Dances.

> *See* Nos. 794, 795. Hasse (Johann Adolph) The Comic Tunes, &c.

817. The Famous Salve Regina Compos'd by Sigʳ Hasse.
London Printed for and sould by I: Walsh, &c.

> *London Daily Post, and General Advertiser*, Jan. 15, 1740. (Just publish'd . . . The Famous Salve Regina, sung by Sig Corestina [i.e. Carestini], set by Hasse.)

> Fol. Passe-partout title-page, Collins frame. pp. 14.
> Hirsch IV. 791. RM. 14. f. 14. (4.) RCM. CUL. Fitz. Rowe.
> Walsh Cat. 18: 'The Celebrated Salve Regina.'
> Republished in 'Le Delizie dell' Opere', Vol. II, pp. 1–14.

Hasse &c. Select Duets For two German Flutes or Violins Call'd The Delightful Musical Companion.

> *See* No. 553. Delightful Musical Companion.

818. The Favourite Songs in the Opera Call'd Semiramide. By Sigʳ Hasse.
London. Printed for I. Walsh, &c.

General Advertiser, May 17, 1748.

> Fol. Passe-partout title-page. pp. 2–18.
> Rowe.
> Contains six songs, one by Lampugnani.
> Libretto by Metastasio.

819. The Favourite Songs in the Opera Called La Semiramide Riconosciuta 2/6.
London. Printed for I. Walsh, &c.

[*c.* 1765.]

> Fol. pp. 5–16, 2–4 (bottom centre).
> RCM.
> 'Called La Semiramide Riconosciuta' is in MS. on a label pasted on to the title-page. '2/6' is in MS. With additional top centre pagination 81–92 and 130–2 on pp. 5–16 and 2–4 respectively from 'Le Delizie dell' Opere', Vol. V.
> Contains five songs, one by Lampugnani.

820. The Favourite Songs in the Opera Call'd Siroe by Sigʳ Hasse. Nº 274.
London. Printed for and Sold by I. Walsh, &c.

London Daily Post, and General Advertiser, Dec. 14, 1736.

Fol. Passe-partout title-page. pp. 2–14, blank, 16–22.
BM. G. 173. b.
'N.º 274' also appears on Handel's 'Siroe'.
Republished in 'Le Delizie dell' Opere', Vol. II, pp. 88–103, 188–91.

821. Solos for a German Flute or Violin With a Through Bass for the Harpsicord or Violoncello Compos'd by Signor Giovanni Adolffo Hasse. Opera Seconda. London. Printed for Iohn Walsh . . . N.º 676.

London Daily Post, and General Advertiser, Oct. 16, 1740. (Just published.)

Fol. pp. 29.
BM. g. 223. y. (2.) RM. 17. f. 20. (1.) CUL. Tenbury (2).
'N.º 676' also appears on 'Handel's Overtures in Score'.

822. Six Solos for a German Flute or Violin with a Through Bass for the Harpsicord or Violoncello Compos'd by Signor Giovanni Adolffo Hasse. Opera Quinta. London. Printed for I. Walsh, &c.

General Advertiser, Nov. 8, 1744.

Fol. pp. 1–7, blank, 9–13, blank, 15–17, blank, 19–25, blank, 27–29, blank, 31–33, blank, 35–37.
RM. 17. f. 20. (2.) BUL. Tenbury (2 copies).

823. Six Sonatas or Trios for two German Flutes or two Violins and a Bass. Compos'd by Signor Giovanni Adolffo Hasse. [Op. 1.] London Printed for and sold by I. Walsh . . . N.º 658.

London Daily Post, and General Advertiser, Nov. 29, 1739. (May be had.)

Fol. 3 parts.
BM. g. 409. (4.) RCM. Cardiff. Manchester. Tenbury.

824. Six Sonatas or Trios . . . Opera Prima. London. Printed for I. Walsh, &c.

[*c.* 1750.]

Fol. 3 parts
BM. g. 979. (1.) BM. g. 241. (6.) RM. 17. d. 6. (6.) RM. 17. d. 2. (1.) RAM. Bod. GUL. Oriel College, Oxford.

825. Sonate per Cembalo composte dal Sig.ʳ Giovanni Hasse Opera VII. London. Printed for I. Walsh, &c.

Public Advertiser, Nov. 8, 1758. (Six Sonatas or Lessons for the Harpsichord.)

Obl. fol. pp. 2–33.
BM. e. 115.
Randall Cat.: 'Hasse's Lessons. 5s. od.'

826. Venetian Ballad's Compos'd by Sigᵣ Hasse And all the Celebrated Italian Masters.
    Printed for Inᵒ Walsh, &c.

Daily Advertiser, Nov. 3, 1742.

    Obl. fol. 'Raccolta di Gondoliere &c.' pp. 37.
    Hirsch III. 796. Others in BUC not examined.
    Illustrated title-page, adapted from that issued with 'Spensers Amoretti Set To Music By Dᵣ Greene', 1739. (No. 743.)

827. — Another issue, with a catalogue of 'Musick Printed for Iohn Walsh', &c. on verso of p. 37.

    [*c.* 1744.]

    Obl. fol. 'Raccolta di Gondoliere, &c.' pp. 37.
    BM. E. 856. (Wanting the title-page.)

828. The First Set of Venetian Ballads For the German Flute, Violin, or Harpsicord. Compos'd by Sigᵣ Hasse, and all the Celebrated Italian Masters.
    London. Printed for I. Walsh, &c.

    [*c.* 1748.]

    Obl. fol. pp. 40.
    BM. E. 525. (1.)
    'The First, is in MS.

829. Venetian Ballad's Compos'd by Sigᵣ Hasse And all the Celebrated Italian Masters.
    Printed for Inᵒ Walsh, &c.

    [*c.* 1750.]

    Obl. fol. 'Raccolta di Gondoliere &c.' on verso of title-page . . . pp. 40.
    BM. E. 525. c. (1.) Hirsch IV. 1682.
    Another edition of the First Set, with illustrated title-page. (Misbound, after Second Set.)

830. A Second Set of Venetian Ballads For the German Flute, Violin, or Harpsicord. Compos'd by Sigᵣ Hasse, and all the Celebrated Italian Masters.
    London. Printed for I. Walsh, &c.

Daily Advertiser, Jan. 5, 1744.

    Obl. fol. pp. 40.
    BM. E. 525. (1.) Hirsch IV. 1682. (Misbound, before First Set.)

831. Nᵒ II. Venetian Ballads For the German Flute, Violin, or Harpsicord. Compos'd by Sigᵣ Hasse, and all the Celebrated Italian Masters.

London. Printed for and sold by I. Walsh, &c.

[*c.* 1750.]

    Obl. fol. pp. 40.
    BM. E. 525. c. (1.)

832. A Third Set of Venetian Ballads For the German Flute, Violin, or Harpsicord. Compos'd by Sig.ʳ Hasse, and all the Celebrated Italian Masters.
London. Printed for I. Walsh, &c.

London Evening-Post, Dec. 8–10, 1748.

    Obl. fol. pp. 39.
    BM. E. 525. (1.)

833. N°. III. Venetian Ballads For the German Flute, Violin, or Harpsicord Compos'd by Sig.ʳ Hasse, and all the Celebrated Italian Masters.

[*c.* 1750.]

    Obl. fol. pp. 39.
    BM. E. 525. c. (1.)
    'III' has been altered from 'II' in MS.
    Composers named in the three books are: Hasse, Auletta, Pergolesi, and Lampugnani.

See also No. 13 Airs. A Fourth Book of Select Aires or Duets, For Two German Flutes . . . By . . . Hasse, &c.; No. 32. Alessandro in Persia; No. 37. Annibale in Capua; No. 44. Arbaces; Nos. 549, 552. Delightful Musical Companion; Nos. 555–7, 559–66. Delizie dell' Opere. Vols. I, II, IV–XI; No. 609. Ezio. No. 719. Gianguir; No. 858. Ingratitudine Punita; No. 860. Ipermestra; No. 937. Lessons. Select Lessons for the Flute. Third Book . . . Minuets & Marches, By . . . Hasse, &c.; No. 1014. Merode; Nos. 1061, 1066, 1082, 1085. Minuets; No. 1129. Nerone; No. 1145, Orfeo; No. 1151. Overtures. Six Overtures in Seven Parts . . . Compos'd by Sig.ʳ Hasse, &c.; No. 1190. Perez (Davidde) The Favourite Songs in the Opera Call'd Ezio . . . 2.ᵈ [With 'Arie nel Penelope by Hasse.']; No. 1314. San Martini (Giovanni Battista) and Hasse (Johann Adolph) Six Concertos in 8 parts, &c.; Nos. 1419, 1420. The Summer's Tale . . . Music by . . . Hasse, &c.

HAYDEN (George)

834. Three Cantatas Compos'd by M.ʳ G: Hayden.
London Printed for & sold by Iohn Walsh, &c.

[*c.* 1730.]

    Fol. Passe-partout title-page. ff. 2–14. Printed on one side only.
    BM. G. 116; G. 116. a.
    Smith 518 with Walsh only in the imprint.

835. — With 'N⁰ 292' added to the title-page.

[*c.* 1731.]

> Walsh Cat. 18: 'Hayden's Cantatas. 2s. od. N⁰ 292.'
> Others in BUC not examined.

See also No. 10 Airs. A Choice Collection of Aires and Duets for two German Flutes . . . Mr. Hayden, &c.; No. 751. Harmonia Anglicana. Book III.

HAYM (Nicolò Francesco)

See No. 1209. Pirro e Demetrio. Songs In The New Opera, Call'd Pyrrhus and Demetrius, &c.

HELLENDAAL (Pieter) *the Elder*

836. Six Grand Concerto's For Violins &c. in Eight Parts Compos'd by Peter Hellendaal Opera Terza.

London Printed for the Author And Sold by M⁺ Walsh, &c.

[1758.]

> Fol. 8 parts. Privilege (dated 25 April 1758).
> BM. g. 260. RCM. Oriel College, Oxford. Rowe.

HERON (Claude)

See No. 315. Canzoniere

HILL ( )

See No. 925. Latour ( ) A Collection of Minuets, Rigadoons, & French Dances Compos'd by M⁺ Latour; No. 1029. Minuets. For the Flute The Newest Minuets, &c.

HILLS (W.)

837. Fifty two Minuets and Rigadoons for Violins; Hautboys and Bassoons; Two Airs with them, and a Paspie, One Hornpipe, Two Jiggs, and a Boree. With a Bass to each of them. All fit for Balls and Dancing Schools. Compos'd by Mr. W. Hills.

[*c.* 1730.]

> Walsh Cat. 18: 'Hills Minuets (Violin) with Basses. 1s. od. N⁰ 151.'
> Smith 341 with Walsh only in the imprint and 'N⁰ 151' added to the title-page.

HINE (William)

838. Hines Anthems and Te Deum. 7s. 6d.

[*c.* 1735.]

> Walsh Cat. 18.
> Presumably refers to 'Harmonia Sacra Glocestriensis. or Select Anthems for, 1, 2, & 3

Voices and a Te-Deum and Jubilate Together with a Voluntary for the Organ. Compos'd by M.' William Hine late Organist of the Cathedral Church at Glocester', which was issued without any imprint, 1731. (BM. H. 1636. Fol. pp. 53.)

HOLCOMBE (A.)

839. Twelve Italian Canzonets, with some English Ballads, never before printed, by Mr. Holcombe.
Printed by J. Walsh, &c.
Public Advertiser, May 7, 1753.
See also No. 746. H., A.; No. 862. Italian Canzonets

HOLCOMBE (Henry)

See Nos. 265, 268. British Orpheus. Books I, IV.

HONEST YORKSHIRE-MAN

See No. 323. Carey (Henry)

HORNPIPES

840. A fourth Book of Hornpipe's In which is that Celebrated Hornpipe Danc'd by M.'s. Vernon in the Beggars Opera Compos'd by D.' Arne For the Harpsicord Violin or German Flute. Price 1.ˢ
London Printed for I. Walsh, &c.
Public Advertiser, Oct. 4, 1760.
> Obl. 8°. ff. 18. printed on one side only.
> BM. a. 5. a.

HOTTETERRE (Jacques) *called Le Romain*

841. The Rudiments or Principles of the German Flute. Explaining after an easy Method every thing necessary for a learner thereon, to a greater nicety than has been ever taught before. Wrote in French by the Sieur Hotteterre le Romain; Monsieur in Ordinary to the late French King; & faithfully translated into English. To which is added a Collection of Familiar Airs for Examples.
London. Printed for and sold by I: Walsh . . . and Ioseph Hare, &c.
Daily Post, Oct. 25, 1729.
> Obl. 8°. ff. 36 with folded charts. Printed on one side only. Last leaf contains 'A Catalogue of choice Musick for the Flute. Printed for I. Walsh.'
> Euing. Library of Congress, Washington, Dayton C. Miller collection.

HOWARD (Samuel)

842. The Overture, Act Tunes, and Songs, in the Entertainment call'd the Amorous Goddess. Compos'd by M.' Howard. for the Harpsicord, German Flute, or Violin.

London. Printed for I. Walsh, &c.

General Advertiser, April 27, 1744; *Daily Advertiser*, April 27, 1744. (Just publish'd.)

> Fol. pp. 16, with p. 11 printed on one side only.
> BM. G. 347. RAM. RCM. Manchester. Tenbury.

843. Mr. Howard's Overture in the Amorous Goddess.
[J. Walsh.]

> [*c.* 1747.]

> Fol. s. sh. 4 parts.
> BM. g. 410. e. (3.) RM. 17. d. 4 (13.) Pendlebury.
> Walsh Cat. 24*a*.
> Subsequently issued in a collection, 'Six Medley or Comic Overtures', 1763. (BM. g. 100. c.) (See No. 1160. Overtures.)

844. A Cantata and English Songs. Set to Musick by Mr Howard.
London. Printed for I. Walsh, &c.

General Advertiser, Nov. 2, 1745.

> Fol. Privilege (dated 21 March 1744). pp. 2–7, blank, 9–13.
> BM. G. 427. (6.) (Wanting pp. 9 and 10.) RCM (2 copies). Leeds. Manchester. Rowe

845. — Reissue.

> [*c.* 1750.]

> Fol. pp. 2–7, blank, 9–13.
> BM. G. 424. hh. (1.) Without privilege.

846. The Musical Companion. A Collection of Twelve English Songs, Set to Musick By Mr Sam! Howard.
London. Printed for I. Walsh . . . N° 683.

London Daily Post, and General Advertiser, Nov. 11, 1740.

> 8°. pp. 25.
> BM. D. 362. Others in BUC not examined.
> 'N° 683' also given to Hasse's Concertos. Op. 4. (No. 799.)

847. — Second edition.

London Daily Post, and General Advertiser, April 1, 1741. (May be had. 'Howard's Twelve English Songs, the Second Edition.')

848. — Book II. not traced.

849. The Musical Companion. A Collection of English Songs compos'd by Mr Samuel Howard. Book III. [I altered to III in MS.]

London. Printed for I. Walsh, &c.

[*c.* 1750.]

Fol. pp. 22 (top centre pagination), followed by an unpaginated leaf.
BM. G. 424. hh. (2.)
With additional top corner pagination 41 on p. 2, 67 on p. 3, 69 on p. 5, 43 on p. 6,
61–64 on pp. 7–10, 68 on p. 14, 57 on p. 17, 39 on p. 18, 2 on p. 19, 4 on p. 20 and 1 on p. 21.

850. The Musical Companion . . . Book IV.

London. Printed for I. Walsh &c.

Gazetteer and London Daily Advertiser, Nov. 2, 1756. (A Collection of English
Songs sung this Year at Ranelagh Gardens. Composed by Mr. Samuel Howard.
Price 3s.) *Public Advertiser*, Nov. 17, 1756. (A Collection of English Songs. Book 4.)

Fol. Privilege (dated 1 March 1744.) pp. 2–21.
BM. G. 347. a. RCM. Others in BUC not examined.

851. [Musical Companion, Book V.] A Collection of Songs sung by Miss Davies
at Vaux Hall Never before Publish'd. Compos'd by Mʳ Samuel Howard. Book V.

London. Printed for I. Walsh, &c.

Public Advertiser, Aug. 11, 1763. (A Collection of New Songs . . . 3s.); Oct. 12,
1763. (The new Songs sung at Vauxhall . . . Book V.)

Fol. pp. 2–19.
BM. G. 800. (14.) Gresham. Rowe.
Randall Cat.: 'Dr. Howard's Songs. Book 1st. 2s. od. Book 2d. 1s. 6d. Book 3d. 3s. od.
Book 4th. 3s. od. Book 5th. 3s. od.'

See also Nos. 265, 268, 269. British Orpheus. Books I, IV, VI; No. 315. Can-
zoniere; No. 549. Delightful Musical Companion. A second Set of celebrated
Duets for two German Flutes . . . by . . . Howard; No. 907. Lampe (Johann
Friedrich) and Howard (Samuel) The Vocal Musical Mask . . . Songs . . . by
. . . Mʳ Howard, &c.; Nos. 969, 970. Love in a Village . . . Music by . . .
Howard, &c.; No. 1233. Psalms; Nos. 1419, 1420. The Summer's Tale
. . . Music by . . . Howard, &c.

HUDSON (JOHN)

See No. 1061. Minuets. Select Minuets Collected From the Operas . . . Compos'd by . . . Mʳ Hudson.

HUMPHRIES (J. S.)

852. XII Sonatas, for two Violins; with a Through Bass for the Harpsichord.
Composed by I: S: Humphries. Opera Prima.

London. Printed for, and sold by I: Walsh, &c.

[*c.* 1736.]

Fol. 3 parts.
BM. g. 291. b. RAM. Smith. Others in BUC not examined.
An edition was issued in 1734 with the imprint 'London Printed for the Author, and Sold by Tho. Cobb.' (BM. g. 291.)

853. — With Walsh imprint and 'N⁰ 563' added to the title-page.
[*c.* 1740.]
Walsh Cat. 18: 'Humphries Sonatas (2 Violins and a Bass). 6s. od. N⁰ 563.'

854. — Another edition.
General Evening Post, Oct. 12–15, 1745. (New editions . . . Humphreys Sonatas. Just Publish'd.)

HUNTING NOTES
855. The Hunting Notes for the Common Horn, 6d.
[*c.* 1730.]
Walsh Cat. 18.

856. The Hunting Notes for the French Horn, with the best Instructions for that Instrument. Price 1s. 6d.
Printed for J. Walsh, &c.
Daily Advertiser, June 22, 1745. (Just publish'd.)
Walsh Cat. 24*a*: 'Instructions for Learners on the French Horn. 1s. 6d.' This is a different work from 'Forest Harmony, or the Musick of the French Horn', &c. (No. 635.)

HURLOTHRUMBO
Songs in Hurlothrumbo.
See Johnson (Samuel)

HYDASPES
Songs in The New Opera, Call'd Hydaspes, &c
See No. 977. Mancini (Francesco)

INCONSTANZA DELUSA
857. The Favourite Songs in the Opera Call'd L'Inconstanza Delusa.
London. Printed for I. Walsh, &c.
General Advertiser, March 11, 1745.
Fol. pp. 2–20.
BM. G. 193. (1.) Gresham. RAM. RCM. Rowe.
Music composed by Count St. Germain and G. F. Brivio.
Walsh Cat. 24*a*: 'L'Inconstanza Delusa, by Count St. Germaine. 2s6d.'
Republished in 'Le Delizie dell' Opere', Vol. IV, pp. 2–20.

INGRATITUDINE PUNITA

858. The Favourite Songs in the Opera Call'd La Ingratitudine Punita. By Sigʳ Hasse, Pergolisi, &c.
London. Printed for I. Walsh, &c.

[*c.* 1748.]

Fol. Passe-partout title-page. pp. 2–21.
RCM. Rowe.
Pasticcio. Composers named are Hasse, Paganelli, Pergolesi, Lampugnani and Pasquali.
Walsh Cat. 25: 'L'Ingratitudine Punita, by Hasse.'
Randall Cat.: 'L'Ingratitudine, Hasse.'
Republished in 'Le Delizie dell' Opere', Vol. V, pp. 113–29.

INSTRUCTIONS

859. Instructions for Learners on yᵉ Mock trumpet. 2 Books. 1s. 6d. Nº 3.

[*c.* 1730.]

Walsh Cat. 18.
These are presumably two of three books reissued with Walsh only in the imprint and 'Nº 3' added to the title-page. *See* Smith 17 ('A Collection of Ayres for the new Instrument call'd the mock Trumpet, with Instructions to play on it', &c.), Smith 21 ('A Second Book for the new Intrument, called, The Mock Trumpet', &c.), Smith 137 ('The 3d Book of the Mock Trumpet', &c.).

IPERMESTRA

860. The Favourite Songs in the Opera Call'd Ipermestra.
London. Printed for I. Walsh, &c.

London Evening-Post, Nov. 28–30, 1754.

Fol. Passe-partout title-page. pp. 21.
BM. H. 348. e. (2.) RM. 13. c. 21. (10.) (Wanting title-page.) Gresham. RCM. DAM. Reid.
Pasticcio. Composers named are Hasse and Lampugnani.
The Songs were afterwards included in the work published with the title, 'The Favourite Songs in the Opera Call'd Ezio with some Songs in Ipermestra.' (No. 609.)

ISAAC ( )

20 Books of Figure Dances by Mʳ Isaacc [Issac].

See No. 531. Dances

ISUM (JOHN)

See No. 1121. Morley (William) and Isum (John) A Collection of New Songs, &c.

ITALIAN AIRS

861. A Select Collection of Italian Aires Set in a Familliar Taste for a German Flute and a Bass. Book III NB. The 1st and 2d Collections are Original Scotch Aires for a German Flute and a Bass.

London. Printed for I. Walsh . . . Price 1ˢ 6ᵈ

General Advertiser, June 20, 1745; *General Evening Post* (*London*), June 20–22, 1745.

> 8°. pp. 24.
> Mitchell.
> Books I and II are 'Original Scotch Aires for a German Flute and a Bass.' (Nos. 1340, 1341, Scotch Airs.)
> > Walsh Cat. 24a: 'Select Scotch and Italian Airs (for a German Flute, Violin or Harpsicord) in 4 Books, each 1s. 6d.'

ITALIAN CANZONETS

862. A 2ᵈ Set Twelve Italian Canzonets.
London. Printed for I. Walsh, &c.

[*c.* 1755.]

> Obl. fol. pp. 14 (top centre).
> RAM.
> 'A 2ᵈ Set' is in MS. With additional top corner pagination, 8 on p. 1, 10–15 on 8–13, 9 on 14.
> *See* also No. 746. H., A.; No. 839. Holcombe (A)

ITALIAN MUSIC

Choice Italian and English Musick for Two Flutes In which is contain'd the Overture of Pyrrhus and Demetrius, &c.

> *See* No. 1214. Pirro e Demetrio.

JARDINI (JOANNES DE)

863. Six Sonatas or Duets for two German Flutes or Violins: Composed by Sig. Joannes de Jardini. Price 4s.
Printed for J. Walsh, &c.

Public Advertiser, May 24, 1764; May 26, 1764. (Sig. Joannes de Gardini.)

> Walsh Cat. 27: 'Jardini's Duets. 4s. od.'
> Randall Cat.: 'Jardini's Duets. 4s. od.'

JIGS

864. A Collection of the most celebrated Jigs, Lancashire Horn-pipes, Scotch and Highland Lilts, Northern Frisks, and Cheshire Rounds. Together with several excellent new Stage Dances by Mr. Duruel, Mr. Cherier, Mr. Cotine and others, being all High Dances, fitted to the Humours of most Countries and People.

London. Printed for J. Walsh ... N⁰ 141.

[*c.* 1730.]

> Smith 164 with Walsh only in the imprint and 'N⁰ 141' added to the title-page.
> Walsh Cat. 18: 'Jiggs and Hornpipes (Violin). 1s. 6d. N⁰ 141.'

865. Jiggs and Hornpipes 2d Book (Violin). 1s. 6d. N⁰ 142.

[*c.* 1730.]

> Walsh Cat. 18.
> Reissue of work in Walsh Cat. 9*a* (Smith Plate 27) with 'N⁰ 142' added to the title-page.

866. The Third Book of The most Celebrated Jiggs, Lancashire Hornpipes, Scotch and Highland Lilts, Northern Frisks, Morris's, and Cheshire Rounds, with Hornpipes the Bagpipe manner. To which is added the Black Joak the White Joak, the Brown, the Red, and the Yellow Joaks. With Variety of Whims and Fancies of diff'rent humour, fitted to the genious and use of Publick Performers. Price 1s. 6d.

London. Printed for and sold by I. Walsh ... and I. Hare, &c.

Daily Journal, August 12, 1730.

> Obl. 12⁰. 'A Table of the Hornpipes', &c. ff. 30. Printed on one side only.

867. — With Walsh only in the imprint and 'N⁰ 143' added to the title-page.

[*c.* 1730.]

> BM. a. 26. q. (11.)
> Manchester. (Wanting ff. 29, 30.)
> Walsh Cat. 18: 'Jiggs and Hornpipes 3d Book (Violin). 1s. 6d. N⁰ 143.'

JOHNSON (SAMUEL)

868. All the Songs, With the Symphonies, in the opera of Hurlothrumbo, as they were perform'd at the Theatre in the Hay-Market, with great applause. price 1s. 6d.

Printed for and sold by John Walsh ... and Joseph Hare, &c.

Fog's Weekly Journal, June 14, 1729.

869. — With Walsh only in the imprint and 'N⁰ 305' added to the title-page.

[*c.* 1730.]

> Walsh Cat. 18: 'Songs in Hurlothrumbo. 1s. 0d. N⁰ 305.'
> An edition of 'The Songs in Hurlothrumbo. Compos'd by Mᵣ Samˡˡ Johnson. London, Printed for y Author, sold by Dan: Wright ... P. Warmsley ... & W. Smith', &c. was issued in 1729. (BM. H. 114. (2.))

JOMELLI (NICOLÒ)

870. The Favourite Songs in the Opera Call'd Andromaca By Sigᵣ Iomelli.

London. Printed for I. Walsh, &c.

Public Advertiser, Nov. 29, 1755.

> Fol. Passe-partout title-page. pp. 2–23.
> RM. 13. c. 19. (2.) RCM.
> Contains a song by Lampugnani.
> Republished in 'Le Delizie dell' Opere', Vol. VIII, pp. 161–82.

871. The Favourite Songs in the Opera Call'd Attilio Regolo By Sigʳ Iomelli.
London. Printed for I. Walsh, &c.

Public Advertiser, May 14, 1754.

> Fol. Passe-partout title-page. pp. 2–21.
> BM. H. 348. e. (4.) London University. RCM. DAM.
> Republished in 'Le Delizie dell' Opere', Vol. VI, pp. 48–67 and IX, pp. 139–58.

872. — Another issue. N⁰ 2 The Favourite Songs in the Opera Call'd Attilio
Regolo. pʳ 2 6.
London. Printed for I. Walsh, &c.

Public Advertiser, June 5, 1762.

> Fol. pp. 2–21.
> BM. H. 327. b.
> 'N⁰ 2' and 'Attilio Regolo. pʳ 2 6' are in MS.
> Another collection of four songs (pp. 10) was published in 'Le Delizie dell' Opere', Vol.
> XI, pp. 161–70.

873. Eleventh favourite Opera Overture in 8 Parts for Violins, French Horns,
&c. By Sig. Jomelli.
Printed for J. Walsh, &c.

Public Advertiser, June 5, 1764. (Eleven favourite Opera Overtures . . . in 8 parts.)

> Fol. Parts.
> Details of title-page uncertain.
> Subsequently issued in a collection as No. 5 of 'Six Overtures in 8 Parts . . . Compos'd by
> Sigʳ Bach Jomelli Galuppi Perez Sixth Collection.' (BM. g. 212. a. 1764.) (*See* No. 1158.)
> Other numbers in this series are under J. C. Bach, B. Galuppi, D. Perez and L. V. Ciampi.

874. Twelfth favourite Opera Overture in 8 Parts for Violins, French Horns, &c.
By Sig. Jomelli.
Printed for J. Walsh, &c.

[1764.]

> Fol. Parts.
> Details of title-page uncertain.
> Subsequently issued in a collection as No. 6 of 'Six Overtures in 8 Parts . . . Compos'd by
> Sigʳ Bach Jomelli Galuppi Perez Sixth Collection.' (BM. g. 212. a. 1764.) (*See* No. 1158.)
> Other numbers in this series are under J. C. Bach, B. Galuppi, D. Perez and L. V. Ciampi.

875. Six Sonatas for two German Flutes or Violins with a Thorough Bass for the Harpsichord or Violoncello Compos'd by Sig.ʳ Nicolo Jomelli.
London. Printed for I. Walsh, &c.

Public Advertiser, Sept. 13, 1753.

Fol. 3 parts.
BM. g. 990. RM. 17. d. 2. (9.) Hirsch III. 330. RCM. Rowe.

See also No. 45 Arianna e Teseo; Nos. 565, 566. Delizie dell' Opere. Vols. X, XI; Nos. 808–10; 813–15. Hasse (Johann Adolph) Duets or Canzonets, &c.; No. 1144. Orazio; Nos. 1153, 1154, 1158, 1159. Overtures; No. 1526. Vologeso.

JONES (   )

See No. 888. Lady's Banquet. First Book.

JONES (JOHN)

876. Easy Lessons for the Harpsichord. Dedicated to the Honourable Mrs. Ingram Composed by John Jones. Organist &c.
To be had of the following Musick-shops, viz. Mr. Welckers ... Mr. Hintz ... Mr. Waylets ... Mr. Oswald ... Mr. Walsh ... and Mrs. Johnsons, &c.

Public Advertiser, Oct. 5, 1761.

Presumably: 'Lessons for the Harpsichord ... Printed for the Author. London, 1761.' 2 vols. obl. fol. (BM. e. 443. RM. 15. i. 1. (2.))

JONES (RICHARD)

877. Suits or Setts of Lessons for the Harpsicord or Spinnet Consisting of great variety of Movements as Preludes Aires Toccats All'mands Jiggs Corrents Borre's Sarabands Gavots Minuets &c. &c. Composed by Mr Richard Jones.
London. Printed for and Sold by I. Walsh ... N.º 196.

Universal Spectator and Weekly Journal May 13, 1732.

Fol. pp. 2–4, blank, 6–8, blank, 10–12, blank, 14–42, blank, 43–58.
BM. K. 7. g. 12. Fitz. Rowe. (Imperfect.)
'N.º 196' is in MS. on BM. copy. Engraved on Fitz. and Rowe.

JOVIAL CREW

878. The Airs & Song Tunes in the Jovial Crew as Perform'd at the Theatre Royal in Covent Garden for the Violin German Flute or Guitar Price 1.ˢ 6.ᵈ
London. Printed for I. Walsh, &c.

[*c.* 1760.]

8º. pp. 16.
BM. e. 340. h. (6.)

JOZZI (Giuseppe)

879. A Collection of Lessons for the Harpsicord compos'd by Sig.ʳ Jozzi S.ᵗ Martini of Milan Alberti Agrell never before Printed. Book I.
  London. Printed for I. Walsh, &c.

  Public Advertiser, Jan. 24, 1761.

> Obl. fol. pp. 29.
> BM. f. 20. RM. 16. a. 6. (1.)

880. A 2.ᵈ Collection of Lessons . . . Book II.

  Public Advertiser, April 3, 1762.

> Obl. fol. pp. 2–28, blank, 30–32.
> Hirsch IV. 3. (2.) RM. 16. a. 6. (1.) RM. 16. a. 14. (6.)
> '2ᵈ' has been inserted in MS. and 'II' has been altered from 'I' in MS.

881. A Collection of Lessons . . . Book III.

  Public Advertiser, Feb. 25, 1764.

> Obl. fol. pp. 27.
> BM. f. 20. RM. 16. a. 6. (1.)
> 'III' has been altered from 'I' in MS.

JUPITER AND EUROPA

882. Jupiter and Europa, a Masque of Song's as they were perform'd at the Theatre in Lincolns Inn Fields. Publish'd for September. Price 6.ᵈ
  London. Printed for and Sold by I: Walsh . . . and In.º & Ioseph Hare, &c.

  [*c.* 1723.]

> Fol. ff. 6 and two unnumbered sheets. Printed on one side only, except 4 and 5 printed on both sides.
> BM. Add. MSS. 31588. fol. 3. (With the basses figured in Galliard's handwriting and another edition of three of the songs inserted.) H. 76. (Without the additional songs.) RCM. (With two Songs from Handel's 'Floridant' inserted.)
> Music by J. E. Galliard, Cobston, and Richard Leveridge.

883. — With Walsh only in the imprint and 'N.º 310' added to the title-page.

  [*c.* 1730.]

> Walsh Cat. 18: 'The Mask of Jupiter and Europa. 6d. N.º 310.'

KELLER (Gottfried)

884. Rules Or a Compleat Method for Attaining to Play a Thorough Bass upon the Harpsicord Organ or Arch Lute by the late M.ʳ Godfry Keller together with Variety of proper Lessons & Fugues and the most Ienuin Examples & Explinations

of yᵉ several Rules Throughout the whole Work to which is added an Exact Scale
for Tuneing the Harpsicord or Spinnet by the same Author.

London Printed for I: Walsh . . . and I: Hare . . . Nº 185.

[*c.* 1730.]

Fol. pp. 15.
BM. K. 2. i. 23.
Smith 511 with 'Nº 185' added to the title-page.
Walsh Cat. 18: 'Keller's Rules for a Thorough Bass. 1s. 6d. Nº 185.'

KEMPTON (Thomas)

See No. 10. Airs. A Choice Collection of Aires and Duets for two German
Flutes . . . Mr. Kempton, &c.

KILBURN (James)

See No. 925. Latour (   ) A Collection of Minuets, Rigadoons, & French
Dances . . . Compos'd by . . . Mʳ Kilburn.

KILMANSECK, *Baron*

See No. 888. Lady's Banquet. First Book.

KLEINKNECHT (Jacob Friedrich)

885. VI Trio's For two German Flutes or two Violins and Bass, Composed by Mʳ
Kleinknecht Musician to his Highness the Duke of Bareuth.

London. Printed for I. Walsh, &c.

Public Advertiser, Dec. 29, 1760.

Fol. 3 parts.
RM. 17. d. 6. (7.)

KREMBERG (Jacob)

886. A Collection of Easy and Familiar Aires for Two Flutes without a Bass to
which is added an Overture and Passacaile for Three Flutes without a Bass the
whole Compos'd by Mʳ Iames Kremberg one of the Gentlemen of Her Majestys
Musick.

London. Printed for I. Walsh . . . Nº 76.

[*c.* 1730.]

Obl. 8º. Parts.
Smith 213 (BM. b. 2.) with Walsh only in the imprint and 'Nº 76' added to the title-page.
Walsh Cat. 18: 'Kremberg's Aires (for 2 Flutes). 2s. 9d. Nº 76.'

KYNASTON (NATHANIEL)

887. Twenty four new Country Dances for the Year 1721, with new Tunes, and new Figures to each Dance; composed by Mr. Nath. Kynaston.
  Printed for and sold by J. Walsh . . . and J. Hare, &c.
  Post-Boy, April 13–15, 1721.

L'ABBÉ (ANTHONY)
  See No. 1039, Minuets

LADIES ENTERTAINMENT

The Ladies Entertainment 5th Book.
  See No. 898. Lady's Entertainment

LADY'S BANQUET

888. The Ladys Banquet First Book; Being a Choice Collection of the newest & most Airy Lessons for the Harpsicord or Spinnet: Together with several Opera Aires, Minuets, & Marches Compos'd by Mʳ: Handel. Perform'd at Court, the Theatres, and Publick Entertainments: being a most delightful Collection, and proper for the Improvement of the Hand on the Harpsicord or Spinnet. All Fairly Engraven. Price 2s. 6d. Nº 171.
  London. Printed for and sold by I: Walsh . . . and I: Hare, &c.
  Country Journal: or, The Craftsman, June 27, 1730.

> Obl. fol. 'A Table of the Lessons, Aires, & Minuets', &c. (with advertisement). pp. 2–21. NLS. BH. 249.
> Contains eight numbers attributed to Handel, consisting of four Minuets, and four Marches from 'Julius Cæsar', 'Richard the 1st,', 'Floridante', an arrangement of 'Si caro, in Admetus' without Handel's name, and nineteen other items the composers of which are only given in two cases: 'Symphony or Overture in Wagner and Abericock' (Mr. Jones) and 'A Minuet by Baron Kilmanseck'. Some of the unidentified numbers may be by Handel.
> Pp. 6–7 and 19 are from plates of the same works as used in 'The Harpsichord Master', Books XII (1727) and XIII (1728) and other pages may have been taken from other books of 'The Harpsichord Master', no complete set of which is available for examination. (Nos. 758–65.)
> Walsh published Books I–III of 'The Ladies (Lady's) Banquet' (1704, 1706, 1720), Books I–II being different works to Books I and II in this series; Book III being reissued in this series. (Smith, Nos. 151, 187, 593.)
> Walsh Cat. 18: 'Ladys Banquet 1st Book. 2s. 6d. Nº 171.

889. The Ladys Banquet First Book; Being a Choice Collection . . . All Fairly Engraven. Nº 171.
  London. Printed for and sold by I: Walsh, &c.

[*c.* 1730–2.] *Daily Post*, July 19, 1732. (Where may be had.)

Obl. fol. 'A Table', &c. (with advertisement). pp. 2–21.
RM. 7. e. 17. (1.)
Similar to preceding except for the deletions from the title-page of price and Hare portion of imprint.

890. The Lady's Banquet Second Book; Being a Choice Collection of the newest, & most Airy Lessons for the Harpsicord or Spinnet, Compos'd by the most Eminent Masters. Together with several Minuets & Marches Perform'd at Court, the Theatres, & Publick Entertainments: Being a most delightfull Collection, and proper for the Improvement of the Hand on the Harpsicord or Spinnet. All Fairly Engraven, Price 3ˢ

London. Printed for and Sold by I: Walsh . . . Nº 217.

Daily Journal, May 25, 1733.

Obl. fol. 'A Table of the Lessons Aires and Song Tunes', &c. pp. 23.
BM. f. 100. (1.) RM. 7. e. 17. (2.)
A different work to Book 2 of 'The Ladys Banquet' advertised by Walsh in 1705. (*See* Smith, No. 187.)
Geminiani is given as the composer of two Minuets, otherwise the contents are anonymous, but may include some unidentified Handel items. Pp. 22–23 (two numbers from 'Astartus' by G. Bononcini) are from plates as used in 'The Harpsichord Master', Book X (1725). (No. 761.)
Walsh Cat.: 'Ladys Banquet 2d Book. 3s. od. Nº 217.'

891. The Ladys Banquet 3ᵈ Book Being a Choice Collection of the Newest & most Airy Lessons for the Harpsicord or Spinnet Together with the most noted Minuets, Jiggs, and French Dances, Perform'd at Court the Theatre and Publick Entertain-ments, all Set by the best Masters. Price 3ˢ &c.

London. Printed for I. Walsh . . . Nº 172.

[*c.* 1732.]

Obl. fol. 'A Table of the Lessons Aires and Song Tunes', &c. pp. 35.
BM. f. 100. (2.) (Wanting title-page). RM. 7. e. 17. (3.)
Presumably similar to the 1720 edition (Smith, No. 593) in every respect except for the deletion of Hare from the imprint and the addition of 'Nº 172' to the title-page. No copy available of the 1720 edition.
Contains fifty-four numbers. The composers as named are Lateur, Conti, Galliard, Van-brughe, and Handel. The Handel items include 'The Royal Guards March' ('Rinaldo'), 'A Trumpet Minuet' and 'A Minuet for the French Horn' both afterwards included in 'The Water Music', Harpsichord edition (*c.* 1743), Minuets from 'Rinaldo' and 'Radamisto' and an arrangement of 'Hò un non sò che nel cor' from 'La Resurrezione' sung in A. Scarlatti's 'Pirro e Demetrio' (1710) and described as 'Song Tune in Pyrrhus'. Other anonymous num-bers may be unidentified Handel items.
Walsh. Cat.: 18. 'Ladys Banquet 3d Book. 3s. od. Nº 172.'

892. The Lady's Banquet Fourth Book, &c.
London. Printed for and Sold by I: Walsh . . . N.º 217.

[*c.* 1734.)

> Obl. fol. pp. 26.
> RM. 7. e. 17. (4.)
> Title-page adapted from that of the Second Book by substituting 'Fourth' for 'Second'.
> Pp. 3–24 are from the plates of two unidentified collections of Country Dances, Marches,
> &c. Pp. 2 and 26 are from 'The Harpsichord Master', Books VIII, X, XII, XIII (1722–8)
> and pp. 1 and 25 may have appeared earlier in some other books of 'The Harpsichord Master'.
> (Nos. 758–65.) The only Handel numbers identified are 'Sgombra dell Anima in Siroe'
> (p. 1) and 'Dimmi cara in Scipio' (p. 2).

893. The Ladys Banquet Fifth Book; Being a Choice Collection of the newest &
most Airy Lessons for the Harpsicord or Spinnet: Together with several Opera
Aires, Minuets, & Marches Compos'd by M.ʳ Handel. Perform'd at Court, the
Theatres, and Publick Entertainments: Being a most delightfull Collection, and
proper for the Improvement of the Hand on the Harpsicord or Spinnet. All fairly
Engraven. Price 3s. N.º 171.
London. Printed for and sold by I: Walsh, &c.

Country Journal: or, The Craftsman, Aug. 23, 1735. (Where may be had The
Lady's Banquet . . . in Six Books.)

> Obl. fol. pp. 2–30.
> BM. f. 45. a. RM. 7. e. 17. (5.)
> Title-page from the same plate as that used for the second issue of the 'First Book' (No. 889),
> 'Fifth' being substituted for 'First'. Pp. 2–15 contain four anonymous unnamed works, very
> boldly engraved, and which consist of the four Handel pieces published by Witvogel (1732).
> They are in this order: 'Capricio', 'Preludio et Allegro', 'Fantasie', and 'Sonata'. (H.G. II.
> Dritte Sammlung, pp. 144–7, 148–9, 133–5, 151–3.) Pp. 16–30 are from old plates differently
> engraved to pp. 2–15, most of which have been identified as used in volumes VIII, X, XII,
> XIII of 'The Harpsichord Master' (1722–8), and the other pages may have been taken from
> other volumes of 'The Harpsichord Master'. The items on pp. 16–30 are all named and are
> mostly arrangements of airs from Handel's 'Admetus', 'Julius Cæsar', 'Ptolomy', 'Rodelinda',
> with works by other composers, Handel's name not being given except on the title-page,
> the only other composers named being Bitte, Vanbrughe, and Pepusch.

894. The Lady's Banquet, Sixth Book. Being a Collection of all the Sarabands,
Jiggs, Gavots, Minuets and Marches Perform'd in all the late Operas, Compos'd by
M.ʳ Handel. Set for the Violin or Harpsicord. Note. All the Works of this Author
may be had where these are sold.
London. Printed for and Sold by I. Walsh . . . Price 3s. N.º 548.

Country Journal: or, The Craftsman, Aug. 23, 1735. (Where may be had The Lady's
Banquet . . . in Six Books.)

> Obl. fol. pp. 2–21.
> BM. f. 60. (2.) RM. 7. e. 17. (6.)

The contents have all been identified as arrangements from 'Terpsicore', 'Il Pastor Fido', 'Alcina', 'Ariadne', 'Oreste', &c. but they appear simply as 'Sarabande', 'Gigue', 'Air', &c.

Walsh Catalogue 18 under Handel: 'Lady's Banquet . . . in 6 Books each 3s. od. N? 548.'

Walsh junior continued to advertise 'Ladies Banquet. 6 Books of Minuets and Opera Dances by M? Handel, &c. Each 3s. od.' and this work also appeared in the catalogues of William and Elizabeth Randall.

895. A Collection of Lessons for the Harpsicord Compos'd by M? Handel 4ᵗʰ Book.

London. Printed for I. Walsh, &c.

Public Advertiser, Jan. 17, 1758. (A Collection of easy Lessons and Airs for the Harpsichord by Dr. Greene and Mr. Handel. In Two Books Each 3s.)

RM. 17. e. 16. (3.) RAM. NLS. BH. 163, 162 (without title-page). Bod. Smith.

Another edition of 'The Lady's Banquet, Sixth Book', with a new title-page, otherwise from the same plates.

Advertised in Randall's Catalogue, 1776, as 'Handel's easy Lessons. 3s. o' but as no copy has been traced with the Randall imprint, the notice is assumed to refer to stock Walsh copies. Also advertised on various works as 'Easy Lessons for the Harpsicord 4 Books'. (*Public Advertiser*, May 31, 1764.) This notice apparently covers the two volumes of 'Suites de Pieces', the 'Fugues' and the 'Collection of Lessons for the Harpsicord 4ᵗʰ Book.'

Walsh advertised on the Full Score of 'Acis and Galatea' (1743) among Handel's works: 'The Dance Tunes from all his Operas', and on 'The Triumph of Time and Truth' (1757) 'A Collection of Dance Tunes. 3s. od.' These notices apparently referred to issues of 'The Lady's Banquet. Sixth Book' and 'A Collection of Lessons. . . . 4th Book'.

LADY'S ENTERTAINMENT

896. The Lady's Entertainment or Banquet of Musick being a Choice Collection of the Newest and most Airy Lessons for the Harpsicord or Spinnet Together with several Excellent Preludes Tocatas and the most favourite Song Tunes in the Opera all Fairly Engraven price 2s. 6d. Note these Lessons are likewise proper for the Lute Harp or Organ by Mr. Ramondon.

London Printed for I. Walsh . . . N? 167.

[*c.* 1730.]

Walsh Cat. 18: 'Ladys Entertainment 1st Book. 2s. 6d. N? 167.'

Smith 275, title from the Cathedral Library, Durham (Fol. ff. 24), with Walsh only in the imprint and 'N? 167' added to the title-page.

897. The 2d Book of The Ladys Entertainment or Banquet of Musick being a Choice Collection of the Newest and most Airy Lessons for the Harpsicord or Spinnet Together with several Excellent Preludes Tocatas and the most favourite Song Tunes in the Opera's all Fairly Engraven price 2s. 6d. Note these Lessons are likewise proper for the Lute Harp or Organ by Mr. Ramondon.

London Printed for I. Walsh . . . N.º 168.

[*c.* 1730.]

> Walsh Cat. 18: 'Ladys Entertainment 2d Book. 2s. 6d. N.º 168.'
> Smith 282. Title from the Cathedral Library, Durham (Fol. ff. 24) with Walsh only in the imprint and 'N.º 168' added to the title-page.

For the 3rd and 4th Books of the Ladys Entertainment

> *See* Nos. 111, 112. Babell (William)

898. The Ladies Entertainment 5th Book. Being a Collection of the most favourite Airs from the last operas, set for the Harpsicord or Spinnet. To which is prefix'd the celebrated Organ Concerto, Composed by Mr. Handel.
Printed for, and sold by John Walsh, &c.

Country Journal: or, The Craftsman, Sept. 2, 1738.

> Fol. pp. 25.
> The Concerto is Op. 4. No. 2. The book also contains six arias from Handel's 'Serse' and two from 'Faramondo' (Deutsch, 'Documentary', p. 466).
> Rowe.

LAMPE (CHARLES JOHN FREDERICK)

> *See* No. 302. Catch Club. The Catch Club or Merry Companions . . . Selected by C. I. F. Lampe.

LAMPE (JOHANN FRIEDRICH)

899. A Cantata and Four English Songs Set to Musick by M.ʳ I. F. Lampe.
London. Printed for I. Walsh, &c.

General Advertiser, Sept. 9, 1748. (A Cantata and English Songs sung at Ranelagh Gardens.)

> Fol. pp. 11.
> BM. G. 221. (5.) RCO. Edinburgh.

900. A Collection of all the Aires, Pastorells, Chacoons, Entre, Jiggs, Minuets, and Musette's in Columbine Courtezan and all the late Entertainments, Compos'd by Mr. Iohn Frederick Lampe. To which is Prefix'd the Original Medley Overture. The whole fitted for a Violin, German Flute & Harpsicord.
London. Printed for and Sold by I. Walsh . . . N.º 568.

London Daily Post, and General Advertiser, Dec. 10, 1735.

> Obl. fol. ff. 15. Printed on one side only.
> BM. c. 60. (1.) Perth.
> Walsh Cat. 18: 'Lampe's Tunes from all the Entertainments. 3s. od. N.º 586 [*sic*].'
> Randall Cat.: 'Lampe's Airs in Columbine Courtezan.'
> (See also No. 902.)

901. Songs and Duetto's in the Burlesque Opera, call'd The Dragon of Wantley, in Score. Compos'd by John Frederick Lampe.
London. Printed for I. Walsh, &c.

[*c.* 1746.]

Fol. pp. XLI.
BM. G. 221. (2.) Edinburgh. Rowe.
This is the same as the edition issued by J. Wilcox in 1738 (BM. F. 5.) with a new title-page.
Randall Cat.: 'Lampe's Dragon of Wantley. 5s. od.'

902. Medley Overture in 4 parts.
Printed for and sold by John Walsh, &c.

Country Journal: or, The Craftsman, Dec. 25, 1736. (Medley Overtures by Arne, Lampe, Charke and Prelure, in Four Parts—Just published.)

Fol. 4 parts.
Walsh Cat. 18 (under 2 Violins and a Bass).
The music of the overture consists mainly of numbers by Handel. Subsequently issued in a collection, 'Six Medley or Comic Overtures', 1763. (BM. g. 100. c.) (*See* No. 1160. Overtures.)
BM. g. 474. a. (14.): 'Lampe's original Medley Overture'. 3 parts, no imprint, same plates as p. 3 of BM. g. 100. c.; contains only a selection from c. 60. (1.): Lampe (J. F.) 'A Collection of all the Aires,' &c. (No. 900.)

903. Pyramus and Thisbe: a Mock-Opera. The Words taken from Shakespeare. as it is Perform'd at the Theatre-Royal in Covent-Garden. Set to Musick by Mr I. F. Lampe.
London. Printed for I. Walsh, &c.

General Evening Post, Feb. 14–16, 1745.

Fol. 'A Table of the Songs', &c. pp., 2–39 (verso blank).
BM. G. 193. (5.); Hirsch II. 504.
From 'Midsummer Night's Dream' as altered in 1716 by Richard Leveridge.

904. — Another edition. Pyramus and Thisbe . . . I. F. Lampe.
London. Printed for I. Walsh, &c.

[*c.* 1746.]

Fol. 'A Table of the Songs', &c. pp. 2–39, with 'Arioso Sung by M^r. Beard' on verso of p. 39.
BM. G. 221. (4.) Others in BUC. not examined.

905. Lampe's Solos for a German Flute.

[*c.* 1727.]

Walsh Cat. 11*a*.
Not identified. (*See* No. 906.)

906. Lampe's Solos. (German Flute, Hoboy or Violin with . . . Harpsicord.) 2s. od. N.° 412.

    [*c.* 1730.]

      Walsh Cat. 18.
      Presumably a later edition of No. 905 with 'N.° 412' added to the title-page.
      Walsh Cat. 14: 'Lampe's Solos (for a Violin & a Bass). 2s. od.'

See also Nos. 265, 267. British Orpheus. Books I, III; No. 1160. Overtures. Six Medley or Comic Overtures, &c.; No. 1419. The Summer's Tale . . . Music by . . . Lampe, &c.

LAMPE (JOHANN FRIEDRICH) AND HOWARD (SAMUEL)

907. The Vocal Musical Mask A Collection of English Songs Never before Printed Set to Musick by M.ʳ Lampe, M.ʳ Howard &c.
London. Printed for I. Walsh, &c.

Daily Advertiser, Dec. 14, 1744.

      Unnumbered Book, probably No. 1, containing: 'The Wish', by Mr. Lampe; 'Why heaves my fond Bosom?' by Mr. Howard; 'Go lovely Rose', by Mr. Lampe; 'The Garland,' by Mr. Weideman; 'Damon's Mistake'; 'Goddess of Ease', by Mr. Boyce, and 'Cease o Judah', by Mr. Handel.
      Fol. ff. 12. Printed on one side only.
      RAM. RCM.

908. — Book II.

    [*c.* 1745.]

909. — Book III.

    [*c.* 1746.]

910. — Book IV.

    [*c.* 1746.]

      Fol. Title-page as [Book I] with 'Book IV' in MS. ff. 12, without foliation. Printed on one side only.
      BM. H. 39. (With additional items in MS.)
      Walsh Cat. 24*a*: 'Vocal Musical Mask, 4 Books of Songs by Mr. Lampe and Mr. Howard, each 1s. 6d.'

911. — Book V.

    [*c.* 1750.]

912. — Book VI.

    [*c.* 1752.]

      Walsh Cat. 25: 'Vocal Musical Mask, a Collection of Songs by Mr. Lampe Mr. Howard. Six Books each 1s. 6d.'

LAMPUGNANI (Giovanni Battista)

913. The Favourite Songs in the Opera Call'd Alceste By Sig.r Lampugnani.
London. Printed for I. Walsh, &c.
— Second Colln.

Daily Advertiser; General Advertiser, May 10, 1744, June 19, 1744. (Second Colln.)

 Fol. Passe-partout title-pages: pp. 2–18, blank, 20–38.
 Rowe. BM. G. 206. a. (4.) (1st Collection.) RCM. (1st Collection. Wanting title-
 page.) Durham. (1st Collection.)
 Republished in 'Le Delizie dell' Opere', Vol. IV, pp. 21–54, 93–94. Gresham.

914. The Favourite Songs in the Opera Call'd Alexander in India By Sig.r Lampugnani.
London. Printed for I. Walsh, &c.

General Advertiser, May 2, 1746.

 Fol. Passe-partout title-page: pp. 2–25.
 BM. G. 811. e. (2.) RAM. RCM. Hall.
 Walsh Cat. 24a: 'Alexander by Lampugnani. 2s. 6d.'
 Walsh Cat. 25: 'Alexander in India. 2s. 6d.'
 Randall Cat.: 'Alexandro nel India. Lampugnani. 2s. 6d.'
 Republished in 'Le Delizie dell' Opere', Vol. IV, pp. 117–40.

915. The Favourite Songs in the Opera Call'd Alfonso By Sig.r Lampugnani.
London. Printed for I. Walsh, &c.

Daily Advertiser, Jan. 14, 1744.

 Fol. pp. 2–21.
 BM. G. 190. (6.) Rowe.
 Republished in 'Le Delizie dell' Opere', Vol. IV, pp. 55–74.

916. The Favourite Songs in the Opera Call'd Siroe By Sig.r Lampugnani.
Printed for I. Walsh, &c.

London Evening-Post, Feb. 6–8, 1755.

 Fol. Passe-partout title-page: pp. 21.
 BM. G. 201. (3.); H. 348. e. (1, 10.) RM. 13. c. 22. (5.) Gresham. DAM. NLS. Pendlebury.
 Bound up with the BM. G. 201. (3.) copy is the publication without imprint with the
 title 'Publish d by particular Desire, The Two favourite Songs in the Opera call'd Siroe, sung
 by Sign.ra. Mingotti.' (pp. 13.) This was published by John Cox at Simpson's Music Shop,
 London, and advertised in the *Public Advertiser*, April 8, 1755. BUC states that some copies
 have a second title-page with the imprint 'Printed by John Cox (for John Walsh)'.
 Republished in 'Le Delizie dell' Opere', Vol. VII, pp. 70–90.

917. Six Sonatas for Two Violins with a Through Bass for the Harpsicord or
Violoncello. Compos'd By Sig.r Gio. Batista Lampugnani. Opera Prima.

London. Printed for & Sold by I. Walsh, &c.

[*c.* 1745.] *General Evening Post*, Feb. 21–23, 1745. (Just publish'd.)

Fol. 3 parts.
BM. g. 420. c. (8.) RM. 17. c. 5. (11.) RAM.
This work is the same as the Six Sonatas published under the names of Lampugnani and San Martini as Opera Prima. (Nos. 918, 919.)

See also No. 32 Alessandro in Persia; No. 37 Annibale in Capua; Nos. 556, 559–66. Delizie dell' Opere. Vols. I, IV–XI; No. 719. Gianguir; Nos. 775–84. Hasse (Johann Adolph) [Chamber Airs.]; Nos. 818, 819. Hasse (Johann Adolph) The Favourite Songs in the Opera Call'd Semiramide; No. 833. Hasse (Johann Adolph) Nº III. Venetian Ballads; No. 858. Ingratitudine Punita; No. 860. Ipermestra; No. 870. Jomelli (Nicolò) The Favourite Songs in the Opera Call'd Andromaca; No. 1009. Meraspe; Nos. 1419, 1420. The Summer's Tale . . . Music by . . . Lampugnani, &c.; No. 1450. Tito Manlio.

LAMPUGNANI (Giovanni Battista) and SAN MARTINI (Giovanni Battista)

918. Six Sonatas for Two Violins with a Through Bass for the Harpsicord or Violoncello. Compos'd by Sigr Gio. Batista Lampugnani and St Martini of Milan. London. Printed for and Sold by I. Walsh, &c.

London Evening-Post, Oct. 2–4, 1744.

Fol. Parts.
RAM. Oriel College, Oxford. Rowe.

919. — Another issue. With 'Opera Prima' on title-page, 'Prima' in MS. on Violino Primo and Violino Secondo parts. It has not been added to the Basso part.

[*c.* 1748.]

BM. g. 480. (1.)
This work is the same as the Six Sonatas published under Lampugnani's name alone as Opera Prima. (No. 917.)

920. Six Sonatas for Two Violins with a Through Bass for the Harpsicord or Violoncello. Compos'd by Sigr Gio. Batista Lampugnani and St Martini of Milan. Opera Seconda.
London. Printed for and Sold by I. Walsh, &c.

General Evening Post (*London*), Nov. 14–16, 1745. (Just publish'd, never before printed. A Second Set of Six Sonatas, &c.)

Fol. 3 parts.
BM. g. 480. (2.) RM. 17. d. 3. (3.) Oriel College, Oxford.
With 'Seconda' in MS. on the title-page of BM. g. 480. (2.) and '2da' on RM. 17. d. 3. (3.)

921. A Second Set of Six Sonatas. For Two Violins with a Through Bass for the Harpsicord or Violoncello. Compos'd By Sig.ʳ Gio. Batista Lampugnani and S.ᵗ Martini of Milan.

London. Printed for and Sold by I. Walsh, &c.

[*c.* 1750.]

> Fol. 3 parts.
> RAM. RCM. Rowe.
> Walsh Cat. 27: 'Lampugnani and Martini of Milan's Sonatas (for two Violins and a Bass). 5 Sets. each 5s. od.'
> Sets 1 and 2 are given above as Opera Prima and Opera Seconda. Set 3 by G. B. San Martini, Broschi and others is under San Martini. (No. 1313.) Set 4 is assumed to be San Martini's Op. Quinta (No. 1308.) and Set 5 has not been identified.

LANGDON (RICHARD)

922. Ten Songs and a Cantata Set to Musick by Richard Langdon Organist of Exeter Cathedral.

London Printed for the Author by J. Johnson in Cheapside.

Public Advertiser, June 1, 1759. (Printed for the Author, and sold by J. Walsh . . . Mr. Johnson . . . and Mr. Waylet, &c.)

> Fol. Dedication, 'To Lady Bampfylde'. 'A List of the Subscribers', 3 pp. pp. 43.
> BM. G. 805. e. (2.) RAM.

LANZETTI (SALVATORE)

923. Six Solos for two Violoncellos or a German Flute and a Bass. Dedicated to his Royal Highness Frederick Prince of Wales. Compos'd by Sig.ʳ Salvatore Lanzetti.

London. Printed for I. Walsh . . . N.º 674.

[*c.* 1740.]

> Fol. pp. 41.
> BM. g. 421. v. (2.)
> Presumably Op. 1.
> Walsh Cat. 18: 'Lanzetti's Solos for 2 Violoncello's 4s. od.'
> Walsh Cat. 24a: 'Lanzetti's Solos (for a Germ.ⁿ Flute Violin or Harpsicord). 4s. od.'

924. Six Solos for two Violoncellos or a German Flute and a Bass. Dedicated to his Royal Highness Frederick Prince of Wales. Compos'd by Sig.ʳ Salvatore Lanzetti. Opera Seconda.

London. Printed for I. Walsh . . . N.º 674.

General Advertiser, Nov. 28, 1747. (Lanzetti's Solos. 2 Bk. Just publish'd for two Violoncellos.)

> Fol. pp. 34.
> BM. g. 270. l. (6.) g. 500. (2.) BUL. Cardiff.

The same title-page as Op. 1 with the addition of 'Opera Seconda'. Contains same works as Benjamin Cooke's original edition (1737) in a different order. (BM. g. 208.)

Walsh Cat. 24a: 'Lanzetti's 6 Solos (for a Germ.ⁿ Flute, Violin or Harpsicord). Op. 2da. 4s. od.'

LATEUR ( )

See Latour ( )

LATILLA (GAETANO)

See No. 585. Don Calascione; No. 1464. Tre Cicisbei Ridicoli. [Two Arias from 'Don Calascione'.]

LATOUR ( )

925. A Collection of Minuets, Rigadoons, & French Dances (Containing 70 in Number) Of two Parts for a Violin & a Bass Being the Newest things Perform'd at Court the Theatres and Publick Balls Compos'd by M.ʳ Latour M.ʳ Fairbank M.ʳ Hill M.ʳ Essex M.ʳ Vincent M.ʳ Kilburn.

London: Printed for I: Walsh . . . & I. Hare, &c.

Post Boy, June 1–3, 1721. (The Prince William, Mr. L'abee's new Dance for his Majesty's Birth Day, 1721. Together with a Collection of the newest Minuets, Rigadoons, and French Dances, &c.)

Obl. 8°. Treble. ff. one unnumbered, 1–26. Bass. ff. one unnumbered, 1–26. Printed on one side only.

BM. a. 26. i. (3.)

See also No. 891. Lady's Banquet. 3.ᵈ Book.

LECLAIR (JEAN MARIE)

926. Solo's for a Violin or German Flute, with a Thorough Bass for the Harpsichord or Bass Violin. Compos'd by Mr. Le Clair, lately come from Italy. Opera Secunda.

Printed for and sold by John Walsh . . . and Joseph Hare, &c.

Country Journal: or, The Craftsman, July 20, 1728.

Walsh Cat. 11 b: 'Leclair's Solos for a German Flute or Violin.'

927. — With Walsh only in the imprint.

[*c.* 1730.]

Walsh Cat. 18; p. 18: 'Leclair's Solos Opera 2da. (for a German Flute, Hoboy or Violin with Harpsicord)' 7s. od.; p. 21: 'Leclair's Solos Opera 2da. (for a Violin and a Bass). 7s. od.'

Walsh Cat. 15a: gives 'Leclair's Solos (for a Violin and a Bass. 2 Vol. 14s. od.' (This refers presumably to Op. 2 and another not identified.

928. Six Solos for a Violin with a Bass for the Harpsicord or Violoncello com-pos'd by M.r Leclair Opera Seconda.
   London. Printed for I. Walsh, &c.

   Whitehall Evening-Post, August 7–9, 1755.

   Fol. pp. 35. With 'Numb. XXXIV' on the title-page.
   BM. g. 220; g. 223. y. (3.) CUL.
   Consists of Nos. 1, 12, 4, 3, 5, and 6 of 'Quatrième Livre de Sonates. Oeuvre IX. Chez l'Auteur, Paris', *c.* 1738. (BM. i. 8.)
   Randall Cat.: 'Leclair's Solos (for a Violin and Harpsichord). Op. 2. 5s. od.'

929. Six Sonatas for two Violins Compos'd by M.r Leclair. [Opera I.]
   London. Printed for I. Walsh, &c.

   General Advertiser, June 20, 1744.
   General Evening Post, Feb. 21–23, 1745. (Leclair Sonatas for two German Flutes or Violins.)

   Fol. 2 parts.
   BM. g. 220. d. Bod. Oriel College, Oxford. Rowe.
   Originally published as 'Sonates à deux violins sans basse. Troisième Oeuvre. Chez l'auteur, Paris, 1730.'

930. Six Sonatas for two Violins Compos'd by M.r Leclair. Opera I.
   London. Printed for I. Walsh, &c.

   [1744.]

   Fol. 2 parts.
   Brussels Conservatory.

931. A 2.d Set of Six Sonatas for two Violins Compos'd by M.r Leclair. Opera Terza.
   London. Printed for I. Walsh, &c.

   Public Advertiser, Jan. 10, 1757. (A Second Set of the Sonatas for two Violins . . . Op. 3.)

   Fol. 2 parts.
   Marc Pincherle, Paris.
   Title-page from the same plate as No. 929. Contents as Leclair's Second Livre de Sonates . . . Oeuvre XII.e, Paris, *c.* 1747. Randall Cat.: 'Leclaire's Sonatas (for two Violins), Op. 3. 5s. od.'

932. Six Sonatas for two Violins with a Through Bass for the Harpsicord or Violon-cello Compos'd by M.r Leclair Op: IV. Price 6.s
   London. Printed for I. Walsh, &c.

   Public Advertiser, Oct. 23, 1764.

   Fol. Parts.
   RCM. CUL.

LEO (LEONARDO)

> *See* No. 32. Alessandro in Persia; Nos. 556, 559–66. Delizie dell' Opere. Vols. I, IV–XI; No. 678. Galuppi (Baldassare) The Favourite Songs in the Opera Call'd Ricimero; No. 1009. Meraspe.

LESSONS

933. Lessons by several Authors. (Harpsicord, Spinnet or Organ.) 1s. 6d. N⁰ 197.

> [*c.* 1730.]
>> Walsh Cat. 18.
>> Smith 210*a* with Walsh only in the imprint and 'N⁰ 197' added to the title-page.

934. Lessons for the German Flute with an Explanation of ye largest Scales extant Easy and Instructive for Learners the Lessons compos'd in ye Several Keys proper for the Instrument.

> London Printed for I: Walsh . . . & I: Hare, &c.

> *Daily Post,* July 22, 1730. ('An easy Book of Lessons for the Flute', &c.)

>> Obl. 8⁰. ff. 21; 2 folded charts of fingerings. Printed on one side only.
>> Library of Congress, Washington. Dayton C. Miller collection.

Select Lessons 1st Book. (Violin.) 1s. 6d. N⁰ 164.

> *See* No. 9. Airs. Select Airs for the Violin, &c. [*c.* 1730.]

935. Select Lessons. 2d Book. (Violin.) 1s. 6d. N⁰ 152.

> [*c.* 1730.]
>> Walsh Cat. 18.
>> Smith 322 with Walsh only in the imprint and 'N⁰ 152' added to the title-page.
>> For the 1st Book, *see* No. 9. Airs. Select Airs for the Violin.

936. Select Lessons, or a choice Collection of easy Aires by Mr. Handel, Geminiani, Bononcini, Baston, &c. for the Flute. Price 1s. 6d.

> Printed for John Walsh, &c.

> *Country Journal: or, The Craftsman,* July 1, 1732.

>> Obl. 12⁰.
>> Walsh Cat. 18: 'Select Lessons 1st Book (Single Flute). 1s. 6d. N⁰ 6.'
>> Smith 321 may be the same work.

937. Select Lessons for a Flute Second Book Containing an excellent Collection of English & Italian Aires, perticulerly the most Favourite Song Tunes in the late Opera's, together with ye choicest Minuets and Rigadoons perform'd at the Balls at Court . . . price 1ˢ 6ᵈ

> London Printed for and sold by I: Walsh . . . N⁰ 7.

> [*c.* 1732.]

Obl. 12°. ff. 10–11, 25–27, 12, 7–23. Printed on one side only.
Coke.
Walsh Cat. 18: 'Select Lessons 2d Book (Single Flute). 1s. 6d.' N⁰ 7.'
Smith 321 may be the same work.

938. Select Lessons for the Flute Third Book. Being a Collection of all the Celebrated Aires Perform'd at Vauxhall and in all Publick Places. Together with the Dance Tunes perform'd at both Theatres, and a Collection of the choicest Opera Aires, Minuets, & Marches, By Mr Handel, Hasse, &c.
London Printed for and sold by I. Walsh, &c.

[*c.* 1733.]

Obl. 12°. ff. 2–28. Printed on one side only.
Coke.
Walsh Cat. 18: 'Select Lessons 3d Book. 1s. 6d.'
Presumably a reissue of a work covered by Smith 619.

A Collection of Lessons for the Harpsicord compos'd by Sigr Jozzi, S Martini of Milan, &c. (Book II, Book III.)

See Nos. 879–81. Jozzi (Giuseppe)

LEVERIDGE (RICHARD)

939. A Collection of Songs by Mr. Leveridge. Price 6 shillings.
London. Printed for & sold by I: Walsh . . . and Ioseph Hare, &c.

[*c.* 1725.]

Fol. Illustrated passe-partout title-page (Day and Murrie, fig. 38, bottom half of illustration cut out). 'A Table of the Songs'. Containing 89 songs formerly issued in single sheets.
W. H. N. Harding, Chicago.

940. — Leveridge's Songs. 6s. od. N⁰ 312.
Printed for and sold by John Walsh, &c.

Daily Journal, May 14, 1730.

Presumably reissue of the above with Walsh only in the imprint and 'N⁰ 312' added to the title-page.
Walsh Cat. 18.
Walsh Cat. 17a. (Just Publish'd. Leveridge's Songs.)
The low price of the work suggests that the Harding copy contains more than the original Walsh collection, and the publisher may have issued various collections from time to time with the same title-page.

See also Nos. 265, 267. British Orpheus. Books I, III; No. 749. Harmonia Anglicana . . . by . . . Leveridge, &c.; No. 882. Jupiter and Europa a Masque of Songs, &c.; No. 903. Lampe (Johann Friedrich) Pyramus and Thisbe, &c.; No. 1400. Songs. Four New and Diverting Songs . . . the Cobbler's End, &c.

LOCATELLI (Pietro Antonio)

941. XII Concertos in Eight Parts, for Violins and other Instruments; with a Through Bass for the Harpsichord. Compos'd by Pietro Locatelli. Opera Prima. London. Printed for and Sold by I. Walsh . . . N.º 600.

London Evening-Post, Dec. 9–11, 1736.

> Fol. 8 parts.
> BM. g. 294. a. RCM.

942. — Reissued later presumably without 'N.º 600' on the title-page.

General Evening Post, Jan. 17–19, 1745. (New editions, &c.)

943. — Another edition.

General Advertiser, Oct. 25, 1749. (New editions, &c.)

944. Solos for a German Flute or Violin with a Through Bass for the Harpsicord or Bass Violin. Compos'd by Pietro Locatelli. Opera Seconda. London. Printed for and Sold by I. Walsh, . . . N.º 603.

Country Journal : or, The Craftsman, Jan. 29, 1737.

> Fol. pp. 2–27.
> BM. g. 280. i. (5.) Bod. Reid. Rowe.
> Consists of Nos. 2, 1, 9, 10, 4, and 7 of 'XII Sonate a flauto traversiere solo e basso . . . Opera seconda. Appresso l'autore, Amsterdam,' 1732. (BM. g. 294. b.)

945. VI Sonatas for two German Flutes or two Violins with a Thorough Bass for the Harpsicord or Violoncello. Compos'd by Sig.ʳ Pietro Locatelli. Opera Terza. London. Printed for I. Walsh, &c.

General Evening Post, April 6–9, 1745.

> Fol. 3 parts.
> BM. g. 241. (5.) RAM. RCM. Bod.
> Originally published as 'Sei Sonate a tre, o due violini, o due flauti traversieri e basso per il cembalo . . . Opera Quinta. Appresso l'autore, Amsterdam,' 1736. (BM. h. 1663.)

946. Six Sonatas or Duets for Two German Flutes or Violins Compos'd by Sig.ʳ Pietro Locatelli Opera Quarta. London. Printed for I. Walsh, &c.

General Advertiser, March 13, 1746. (Just published.)

> Fol. pp. 2–13, blank, 15–27.
> BM. g. 225. a. (2.)

LOEILLET (JEAN BAPTISTE) AND (JOHN)

Jean Baptiste Loeillet and John Loeillet have been considered by some writes as referring to the same person, but from the investigations of Alec Skempton there seems to be good reason for treating them as different composers, as they have been in this bibliography.

In Walsh Cat. 9*b*, the surname is given as 'Lully'. In Walsh Cats. 11*a* and 18, the works listed here under John Loeillet are given as 'Loeillets Works', and those listed under Jean Baptiste Loeillet are given as 'Loeillet of Gant's Works'. Randall Cat. gives 'Loeillet' only throughout.

Readers should consult 'Catalogue thèmatique des œuvres de Jean Baptiste, John et Jacques Loeillet', by Brian Priestman (Revue Belgique du Musicologie, Vol. 6, Fasc. 4, pp. 219–74. 1952. BM. Ac. 5152. b.); 'The Keyboard Works of John Loeillet', by Brian Priestman (The Music Review', May 1955, pp. 89–95) and 'The Instrumental Sonatas of the Loeillets', by Alec Skempton ('Music and Letters', July 1962, pp. 206–17).

LOEILLET (JEAN BAPTISTE)

947. Lully's Lessons for yᵉ German Flute. Advertised on Pierre Chaboud's 'Solos for a German Flute,' &c. (No. 350.) [*c.* 1725.]

> Not identified

948. Sonatas or Solos for a Flute with a Through Bass for the Harpsicord or Bass Violin Compos'd by Jean Luly of Gant. Parte Prima. [Op. 1.]
London, Printed for J. Walsh . . . Nọ 116.

> [*c.* 1730.]
>
> Fol. pp. 53.
> Manchester. (With Nọ 116 in MS.) Rowe. (Without number.)
> Smith 429 with Walsh only in the imprint and 'Nọ 116' added to the title-page in MS.
> Walsh Cat. 9*b*.: 'Lullys 1st Solos (for a Flute and a Bass). 6s. od.'

949. XII Sonatas or Solos for a Flute with a Thorough Bass for the Harpsicord or Bass Violin Compos'd by Jean Baptiste Loeillet de Gant Opera Seconda.
London. Printed for I: Walsh . . . and I: Hare, &c.

> [*c.* 1730.]
>
> Fol. pp. 46.
> Manchester ('Seconda' and Nọ 117' in MS.) Rowe. (3 copies, without 'Nọ 117', 2 with 'Seconda' engraved, 1 with 'Seconda' in MS.)
> 'Seconda' in MS.
> Smith 476 with 'Nọ 117' added to the title-page in MS.
> Walsh Cat. 9*b*.: 'Lullys 2ᵈ Solos (for a Flute & a Bass). 6s. od.'

950. XII Sonatas or Solos for a Flute with a Thorough Bass for the Harpsicord or Bass Violin Compos'd by Jean Baptiste Loeillet de Gant Opera Terza.
London. Printed for I: Walsh . . . and I: Hare . . . Nọ 118.

> [*c.* 1730.]
>
> Large fol. pp. 2–51.
> CUL. Manchester.
> 'Terza' in MS.
> Smith, 556 with 'Nọ 118' added to the title-page in MS.
> Walsh Cat. 9*b*.: 'Lullys 3ᵈ Solos (for a Flute and a Bass). 6s. od.'

951. XII Sonatas or Solos for a Flute with a Thorough Bass for the Harpsicord or Bass Violin Compos'd by Jean Baptiste Loeillett de Gant Opera Quarta.
London Printed for & Sold by I: Walsh . . . and In? & Ioseph Hare, &c.

[*c.* 1725.]

> Fol. pp. 45.
> BM. g. 685. c. Rowe.

952. — With imprint as above and 'N? 119' added in MS. to the title-page.

[*c.* 1730.]

> Fol. pp. 45.
> Manchester.
> Walsh Cat. 15*b*: 'Lullys 4th Solos (for a Flute & a Bass) 6s. od.'
> Walsh Cat. 11*a*: 'Loeillet of Gant his first, second, third & fourth Books of Solos for a Flute and a Bass.'
> Walsh Cat. 18: 'Loeillet of Gant's works. Four Books of Solos for a Flute and a Bass. £1. 4s. od. N? 119.'
> Books I–III were Walsh Nos. 116, 117, and 118. (*See* Nos. 948–50.)

953. Six Sonatas of two Parts made on Purpose for two German Flutes Compos'd by Jean Baptiste Loeillet de Gant.
London Printed for I. Walsh . . . and I. Hare, &c.

Mist's Weekly Journal, Jan. 27, 1728.

> [Op. V. Bk. 2.]
> Fol. 2 parts.

954. — With Walsh only in the imprint and 'N? 411' added to the title-page.

Daily Post, Aug. 6, 1730. (New Musick just publish'd . . . Six Sonatas for two German Flutes, &c.)

> Walsh Cat. 11*a*: 'Loeillet of Gant. His Sonatas for 2 German Flutes.'
> Walsh Cat. 18: 'Loeillet of Gant's works. Six Sonatas for 2 German Flutes. 3s. od. N? 411.'

955. Six Sonata's of two Parts Fitted and Contriv'd for two Flutes. Compos'd by Mr Loeillet of Gant.
London Printed for I: Walsh . . . and I: Hare . . . N? 57.

Daily Post, July 22, 1730. (A Collection of Lessons for two German Flutes, &c.)

> Fol. 2 parts.
> BM. g. 71. e. (9.) Lincoln College, Oxford.
> These Sonatas are arrangements of Op. 1, Nos. 1, 3, and 4, and Op. 2, Nos. 3, 4, and 8.
> Walsh Cat. 9*b*: 'Lullys Sonatas (for two Flutes) 3s. od.'
> Walsh Cat. 11*a*: 'Loeillet of Gant. His Sonatas for two Flutes.'
> Walsh Cat. 18: 'Loeillet of Gant's works. Six Sonatas for 2 Flutes. 3s. od. No. 57.'
> Smith 612 with 'N? 57' added to the title-page.

LOEILLET (JOHN)

956. Sonata's for Variety of Instruments Viz for a Comon Flute a Hoboy or Violin also for two German Flutes with a Bass for the Violoncello and a Thorough Bass for yᵉ Harpsicord Compos'd by Mʳ John Loeillet Opera Prima.

London Printed for and Sold by Inᵒ Walsh . . . and Messiers Inᵒ and Ioseph Hare, &c.

Post-Boy, Jan. 25–27, 1721 (i.e. 1722).

Fol. 4 parts.
BM. g. 685. b. (1.); h. 17. (6.) (Thorough Bass part only.) CUL.

957. — With Walsh only in the imprint and 'Nᵒ 413' added to the title-page.

[*c.* 1730.]

Walsh Cat. 11*a*: 'Loeillets Sonatas for variety of Instruments,' &c.
Walsh Cat. 18: 'Loeillets works. Six Sonatas for variety of Instruments. Opera Prima. 6s. od. Nᵒ 413.'

958. XII Sonatas in three Parts Six of which are for two Violins and a Bass three for two German Flutes and three for a Hautboy & Common Flute with a Bass for the Violoncello and a Thorough Bass for the Harpsicord Compos'd by Mʳ John Loeillet Opera Seconda.

London Printed for and sold by I: Walsh . . . and Inᵒ and Ioseph Hare, &c.

· [*c.* 1725.]

Fol. 3 parts.
BM. g. 685. CUL. Rowe. (Imperfect.)

959. — With Walsh only in the imprint and 'Nᵒ 414' added to the title-page.

[*c.* 1730.]

Walsh Cat. 11*a*: 'Loeillets . . . 2ᵈ Sett of Sonatas for Violins, German Flutes & common Flutes.'
Walsh Cat. 18: 'Loeillets works. Twelve Sonatas for Violins, German Flutes and common Flutes. Opera 2da. 8s. od. Nᵒ 414.'

960. Six Sonatas for two German Flutes with a Thorough Bass for the Harpsicord or Violoncello Compos'd by Mʳ John Loeillet. Opera 4ᵗᵃ

London. Printed for I. Walsh, &c.

[*c.* 1757.]

Fol. 3 parts.
RM. 17. d. 2. (14.)
This work consists of Sonatas 8, 2, 10, 4, 12, and 6 of 'XII Sonatas in three Parts . . . Opera Seconda.' (No. 958.)

961. XII Solos Six for a Common Flute and Six for a German Flute with a Thorough Bass for the Harpsicord or Bass Violin. Humbly Inscrib'd to Charles Edwin Esqr By His most Obedient Humble Servant Iohn L'œillet. Opera Terza.
London. Printed for and sold by I: Walsh . . . and Ios. Hare, &c.

Daily Post, April 19, 1729; *Country Journal: or, The Craftsman*, April 19, 1729.

Fol. pp. 49. (Verso of p. 20 is blank.)
BM. h. 3845. a. Manchester. Rowe.

962. — Another edition. Solos for a German Flute or Violin with a Thorough Bass for the Harpsicord or Bass Violin. Compos'd by Mr Iohn L'œillet. Opera Terza.
London. Printed for and sold by I: Walsh . . . and Ioseph Hare, &c.

Country Journal: or, The Craftsman, August 23, 1729.

Fol. pp. 49. (Verso of p. 20 is blank.)
BM. h. 3845. Hirsch IV. 1630.

963. — With Walsh only in the imprint and 'No 415' added to the title-page.
[c. 1730.]
CUL.
Walsh Cat. 18: 'Loeillets Works. Twelve Solos for a German Flute, Comon, Flute, and Violin, Opera Terza. 6s. od. No 415.'

964. Six Suits of Lessons for the Harpsicord or Spinnet in most of the Key's with Variety of Passages and Variations throughout the Work Compos'd by Mr Iohn Loeillet.
London Printed and Sold by I: Walsh . . . and In & Ioseph Hare, &c.

Post Boy, Jan. 12–15, 1723.

Fol. pp. 55.
BM. g. 685. a.

965. — With Walsh only in the imprint and 'No 188' added to the title-page.
[c. 1730.]
Walsh Cat. 11a: 'Loeillets . . . Lessons for the Harpsicord.'
Walsh Cat. 18: 'Loeillets Works. Six Suits of Lessons for the Harpsicord. 6s. od. No 188.'

LONG (SAMUEL)
See No. 1233. Psalms

LOTTERY

966. Songs in the Lottery as they are perform'd at the Theatre Royal in Drury Lane. The Tunes Proper for the German Flute, Violin, & Common Flute. Price 6d
London. Printed and Sold at the Musick Shops. No 300.
[c. 1732.]

8°. pp. 24.
BM. A. 869. a. (2.)
Engraved throughout.
Walsh Cat. 18: 'The Lottery. 6d. N⁇ 300.'
Probably pirated by Walsh.

LOTTI (Antonio)

See No. 57. Arminio

LOVE IN A RIDDLE

967. Love in a Riddle. For the Flute.
Printed for and sold by John Walsh . . . and Joseph Hare, &c.

Country Journal: or, The Craftsman, July 5, 1729. (Where may be had.)

968. — With Walsh only in the imprint and 'N⁇ 49' added to the title-page
[*c.* 1730.]
Walsh Cat. 18: 'Love in a Riddle. 6d. N⁇ 49.'

LOVE IN A VILLAGE

969. Love in a Village. A Comic Opera As it is Perform'd at the Theatre Royal in Covent Garden. The Music by Handel Boyce Arne Howard Baildon Festing Geminiani Galuppi Giardini Paradies Agus Abos For the Harpsicord, Voice, German Flute, or Violin.
London. Printed for I. Walsh, &c.

Public Advertiser, Dec. 20, 1762. (Songs in the Comic Opera.); Dec. 31, 1762. (A Second Set of Songs.); Jan. 15, 1763. (A Third Set of Songs.); Feb. 5, 1763. (A Fourth Set of Songs . . . which compleats the Opera with an Index to the whole.)

Obl. fol. 'A Table of the Songs'. pp. 2–6, blank, 7–45, blank, 47–62, with 31–35 (top corner) on 2–6.
BM. D. 269. RCM. Hall. Many others in BUC.
Walsh Cat. 27: 'Love in a Village, a Comic Opera. 8s. od.'

970. Love in a Village. A Comic Opera. Set for a German Flute Hoboy or Violin. The Musick by M⁇ Handel, D⁇ Boyce, D⁇ Arne, M⁇ Howard &c. Price 1⁇ 6ᵈ
London. Printed for I. Walsh, &c.

Public Advertiser, Feb. 28, 1763. (Of whom may be had, just published.)

8°. pp. 2–36.
BM. e. 340. h. (2.); D. 269a. (Wanting pp. 5, 6.) Mitchell.

LOVE'S TRIUMPH

971. Songs in the Opera Calld Loves Triumph.
London Printed for & Sold by Iohn Walsh . . . N̥ 237.

[*c.* 1730.]

    Fol.

    Words adapted from the Italian of Cardinal Ottoboni by Peter Anthony Motteux. Music by Carlo Francesco Cesarini, Francesco Gasparini and others.

    Smith 450 (BM. H. 227. Fol. ff. 70. Printed on one side only), of which this is presumably a reissue with Walsh only in the imprint and 'N̥ 237' added to the title-page.

    Walsh Cat. 18: 'The Opera of Love's Triumph. 9s. od. N̥ 237.'

    Walsh Cat. 15*a*: 'Opera of Loves Triumph. 9s. od. (With Symphonys.)'

    See Smith 450 for details of the four title-pages, one of which was used for this issue of which no copy has been traced.

LUCIO VERO

The Favourite Songs in the Opera call'd Lucius Verus.

    See No. 51. Ariosti (Attilio)

LULLY (JEAN BAPTISTE)

    See Loeillet (Jean Baptiste)

LULY (JEAN) *of Gant*

    See Loeillet (Jean Baptiste)

LYRA DAVIDICA

972. Lyra Davidica: or, a Collection of Divine Songs and Hymns, partly New Composed, partly Translated from the High-German, and Latin Hymns: and set to easy and pleasant Tunes, for more General Use. The Musick Engrav'd on Copper Plates, &c.
London Printed for J. Walsh . . . N̥ 209.

Country Journal: or, The Craftsman, July 17, 1731.

    8°. pp. 78.

    Walsh Cat. 18: 'Lyra Davidica. 1s. 6d. N̥ 209.'

    Smith 287 (BM. A. 749.) with Walsh only in the imprint and 'N̥ 209' added to the title-page.

MAASMANN (ALEXANDER)

973. A Compleat Suite of Lessons for the Harpsicord as Overture, Allemand, Saraband, Corant, Gavott, Chacoon, Jigg & Minuett. Compos'd by M̥ Alexander Maas-Mann Prusse.
London Printed for I: Walsh . . . N̥ 177.

[*c.* 1730.]

Fol. pp. 2–12.
Walsh Cat. 18: 'Maasman's Lessons. 2s. od. N.º 177.'
Smith 481 (BM. g. 16.) with Walsh only in the imprint and 'N.º 177' added to the title-page.

MACCHARI ( )

See No. 1144. Orazio

MAHAUT (ANTON)

974. Six Sonatas or Duets for Two German Flutes or Violins Compos'd in a pleasing fine Taste by Sig.ʳ Antonio Mahaut.
London. Printed for I. Walsh, &c.

Public Advertiser, June 25, 1756.

Fol. pp. 1–5, blank, 7–13, blank, 15–17, blank, 19–21.
BM. g. 464. CUL.

975. A 2.ᵈ Set of Six Sonatas or Duets for two German Flutes or Violins Compos'd in a pleasing fine Taste By Sig.ʳ Antonio Mahaut.
London. Printed for I. Walsh, &c.

[*c.* 1758.]

Fol. pp. 22–39.
Rowe.
Pagination continued from the first set. (No. 974.)
Randall Cat.: 'Mahaut's Duets, 2 books, each 3s. od.'

MALDERE (PIERRE VAN)

976. VI Sonatas for Two Violins with a Bass for the Harpsicord or Violoncello. Compos'd by P. van Maldere First Violin to His Serene Highness Prince Charles of Lorrain.
London. Printed for I. Walsh, &c.

Public Advertiser, Jan. 24, 1756.

Fol. 3 parts.
BM. g. 277. RM. 17. c. 5. (2.) Bod. Manchester. Rowe.
With 'N.º XXX' at the top of the title-page.

MALEGIAC, *Cavalier*

See No. 37. Annibale in Capua

MANCINI (FRANCESCO)

977. Songs In The New Opera, Call'd Hydaspes, &c.
Sold by I: Walsh . . . N.º 229.

[*c.* 1730.]

Fol. pp. 72.
Music by F. Mancini.
Smith 354 (BM. I. 282.) of which this is presumably a reissue with Walsh only in the im-
print and 'N⁰ 229' added to the title-page.
Walsh Cat. 18: 'The Opera of Hydaspes. 9s. od. N⁰ 229.'
Walsh Cat. 15a: 'Opera of Hydaspes. 9s. od. (With Symphonies.)'

978. **All The Song Tunes for the Flute In the Last new Opera call'd Hydaspes.**
Fairly Engraven & Carefully Corrected. Price 1ˢ 6ᵈ
London, Printed for J. Walsh . . . N⁰ 23.

[*c.* 1730.]

Obl. 8⁰. Passe-partout title-page.
Music by F. Mancini.
Smith 436 (BM. a. 209. a. (6.) ff. 24.) with Walsh only in the imprint and 'N⁰ 23' added
to the title-page.
Walsh Cat. 18: 'Hydaspes for the Flute. 1s. 6d. N⁰ 23.'

979. **The Most Celebrated Aires and Duets In the Opera of Hydaspes. Curiously**
fitted and Contriv'd for two Flutes and a Bass; With their Symphony Introduc'd in
a Compleat Manner The whole fairly Engrav'd.
London Printed for I: Walsh . . .N⁰ 98.

[*c.* 1730.]

Fol. Parts.
Music by F. Mancini.
Smith 368 (Rowe, Cardiff) with Walsh only in the imprint and 'N⁰ 98' added to the
title-page.
Walsh Cat. 18: 'Aires in Hydaspes (for 2 Flutes and a Bass). 3s. od. N⁰ 98.'

980. **The Instrumental Musick, in the Opera of Hydaspes, for two Violins, with a**
thorow Base; the Song Part fitted to a Hautboy, German Flute or Violin; the Haut-
boy performing the Song-Part, forms a complete Consort, as if a Voice accom-
pany'd.
Printed for J. Walsh, &c.

[*c.* 1730.]

Fol. Parts.
Music by F. Mancini.
Smith 520 (Fitz., imperfect) of which this is presumably a reissue with Walsh only in the
imprint.
Walsh Cat. 11a: 'Hydaspes. Concertos for Violins in five Parts.'
Walsh Cat. 15a: 'Hydaspes Concertos (for Violins). 6s. od.'

Hydaspes. Overture.

See No. 220. Bononcini (Giovanni) and (Antonio Maria) and others.
Bononcini's Six Overtures for Violins . . . in the Operas of . . . Hydaspes, &c.

981. XII Solos for a Violin with a Thorough Bass Dedicated to the Honble John Fleetwood Esq: Consull Genl.l for the Kingdom of Naples. By Sig^ra Francesco Mancini. Which Solos are Proper Lessons for the Harpsicord. carefully Revis'd and Corected by Mr Geminiani.

London. Printed for and sold by I: Walsh . . . and Ios: Hare, &c.

Country Journal: or, The Craftsman, Dec. 23, 1727; *Daily Journal*, Jan. 29, 1730. (Mancini's Solos for a Violin. Op. prima.)

> Large fol. Dedication. pp. 55. With 'Wm Smith Sculp' on p. 55.
> BM. i. 11. Rowe.
> The BM. copy has the words 'Flute or' inserted in the title in MS., and reads 'XII Solos for a Flute or Violin', &c.
> Previously issued by John Barrett and Wm. Smith, 1724. (BM. g. 680.)

982. — With Walsh only in the imprint and 'N⁰ 103' added to the title-page.
[*c.* 1730.]

> Walsh Cat. 18, p. 21: 'Mancini's Solos (for a Violin and a Bass). N⁰ 103. 6s. od.'; p. 25: 'Mancini's Solos (for a Flute and a Bass). N⁰ 103. 6s. od.'

MARCELLO (BENEDETTO)

983. XII Solos for a German Flute or Violin with a Thorough Bass for the Harpsicord or Bass Violin. Compos'd by Sig^r Benneditti Marcello. Opera Primo.

London. Printed for and sold by I: Walsh . . . N⁰ 419.

Daily Post, Oct. 4, 1732.

> Fol. pp. 46.
> BM. g. 1008.
> Walsh Cat. 18: 'Bennditti Marcello's 12 Solos. 6s. od. N⁰ 419.'

984. Six Solos for a Violoncello with a Thorough Bass for the Harpsicord Compos'd by Benedetto Marcello Opera Seconda.

London. Printed for & Sold by Iohn Walsh . . . N⁰ 420.

Country Journal: or, The Craftsman, Oct. 28, 1732.

> Fol. pp. 25.
> BM. g. 500. (4.) BUL. CUL. Cardiff. Manchester.
> Walsh Cat. 18: 'Marcello's Solos for a Violoncello. 4s. od. N⁰ 420.'

985. — Reissue?

London Daily Post, and General Advertiser, Dec. 11, 1740. (Of whom may be had.)

986. — Another edition.

General Advertiser, Nov. 28, 1747. (Just publish'd for two Violoncellos . . . **Marcelli's Solos.**)

MARCHES

987. Marches and Minuets. (Violin.) 1s. 0d. N? 150.

[*c.* 1730.]

> Walsh Cat. 18.
> Not identified.

A Choice Collection of 72 Marches, Minuets, and Trumpet Tunes, &c.

See No. 1044. Minuets.

MARTYN (Bendall)

988. Fourteen Sonatas For Two Violins With a Bass for the Violoncello and a Through Bass for the Harpsichord. Compos'd by Bendall Martyn, Esq!

> London. Printed for I. Walsh, &c.

Public Advertiser, March 13, 1763. (N.B. A few Copies are printed on Imperial Paper for the Curious. Price 1£. 1s.)

> Fol. 3 parts.
> BM. g. 242. (2.) RM. 26. a. 13. (2.) (On Imperial paper.) Fitz. (2.)
> Ordinary price was 15s. 0d.

MASCITTI (Michele)

989. Solos for a Violin With a Thorough Bass for the Harpsicord or Bass Violin Compos'd by Michele Mascitti Opera Prima, &c.

> Printed for and sold by John Walsh . . . and Joseph Hare, &c.

Country Journal: or, The Craftsman, July 19, 1729. (New Musick and Editions of Musick lately published. Five Books of Solos for a Violin and Bass.)

> Reissue of Smith 430. (BM. g. 422. (3.)) Fol. pp. 31.)

990. — With Walsh only in the imprint and 'N? 426' added to the title-page.

[*c.* 1730.]

> Walsh Cat. 18: 'Five Operas of Solos for a Violin and a Bass. 12 Solos in Each. £1. 10s. 0d. N? 426.'

991. Solos for a Violin With a Thorough Bass for the Harpsicord or Bass Violin Compos'd by Michele Mascitti Opera 2ᵈᵃ &c.

> Printed for and sold by John Walsh . . . and Joseph Hare, &c.

Country Journal: or The Craftsman, July 19, 1729. (New Musick and Editions of Musick lately published. Five Books of Solos for a Violin and Bass.)

> Reissue of Smith 431. (Arthur F. Hill collection. Fol. pp. 50.)

992. — With Walsh only in the imprint and 'N⁰ 426' added to the title-page.
[*c.* 1730.]
    Walsh Cat. 18: 'Five Operas of Solos for a Violin and a Bass. 12 Solos in Each. £1. 10s. od.
N⁰ 426.'

993. Solos for a Violin With a Thorough Bass for the Harpsicord or Bass Violin
Compos'd by Michele Mascitti Opera Terza Note there are four excellent pieces
Consisting of Solos by the same Author extant.
    Printed for and sold by John Walsh . . . and Joseph Hare, &c.
    Country Journal: or, The Craftsman, July 19, 1729. (New Musick and Editions of
Musick lately published. Five Books of Solos for a Violin and Bass.)
    Reissue of Smith 432. (Rowe. Fol. pp. 57.) 'Terza' in MS.

994. — With Walsh only in the imprint and 'N⁰ 426' added to the title-page.
[*c.* 1730.]
    Walsh Cat. 18: 'Five Operas of Solos for a Violin and a Bass. 12 Solos in Each. £1. 10s. od.
N⁰ 426.'

995. Solos for a Violin With a Thorough Bass for the Harpsicord or Bass Violin
Compos'd by Michele Mascitti Opera Quarta &c.
    Printed for and sold by John Walsh . . . and Joseph Hare, &c.
    Country Journal: or The Craftsman, July 19, 1729. (New Musick and Editions of
Musick lately published. Five Books of Solos for a Violin and Bass.)
    Reissue of Smith 433. (BM. g. 422. (4.) Fol. pp. 59.) 'Quarta' in MS.

996. — With Walsh only in the imprint and 'N⁰ 426' added to the title-page.
[*c.* 1730.]
    Walsh Cat. 18: 'Five Operas of Solos for a Violin and a Bass. 12 Solos in Each. £1. 10s. od.
N⁰ 426.'

997. Solos for a Violin With a Thorough Bass for the Harpsicord or Bass Violin
Compos'd by Michele Mascitti Opera Sexta.
    Printed for and sold by John Walsh . . . and Joseph Hare, &c.
    Country Journal: or, The Craftsman, July 19, 1729. (New Musick and Editions of
Musick lately published. Five Books of Solos for a Violin and Bass.)
    Reissue of Smith 479. (BM. g. 672. Fol. pp. 58.) 'Sexta' in MS.

998. — With Walsh only in the imprint and 'N⁰ 426' added to the title-page.
[*c.* 1730.]
    Walsh Cat. 18: 'Five Operas of Solos for a Violin and a Bass. 12 Solos in Each. £1. 10s. od.
N⁰ 426.'

999. Sonatas of three Parts, for two Violins & a Bass with a through Bass for yᵉ Organ Harpsicord or arch Lute Compos'd by Michele Mascitti. Opera Quinta. London, Printed for J. Walsh,... Nᵒ 425.

> [*c.* 1730.]
>
>> Fol. Parts.
>> Smith 434 (BM. g. 672. b.) with Walsh only in the imprint and 'Nᵒ 425' added to the title-page.
>> Walsh Cat. 18: 'Six Sonatas for 2 Violins and a Bass. 5s. od. Nᵒ 425.'

MATICE (Nicola)

> *See* Matteis (Nicola)

MATTEIS (Nicola)

1000. Senᵗ Nicola's first and Second Book's of Aire's in 3 Parts Containing Preludes Allemand's Saraband's Corrant's Minuett's and Jigg's with divers Fancye's and Vollentary's in Every Key for two Violins and a Bass The Second Treble never being Printed before is now Engraven from the Authors own Manuscript which renders the whole work Compleat Composed by Nicola Matteis Napolitano Libro Primo ett Secundo. London Printed for I. Walsh... Nᵒ 467.

> [*c.* 1730.]
>
>> Obl. fol. 3 parts.
>> Smith 119 (BM. c. 66.), of which this is presumably a reissue with Walsh only in the imprint and 'Nᵒ 467' added to the title-page. Walsh Cat. 18: 'Nicola Matice's Aires (2 Violins and a Bass). 10s. od. Nᵒ 467.'

1001. Nicola's Trumpet-tune (for a Flute and a Bass). 6d.

> [*c.* 1730.]
>
>> Walsh Cat. 18.
>> Not identified.

MATTEIS (Nicholas)

> *See* No. 1392. Solos. Six Solos by several Authors.

MATTHESON (Johann)

1002. Matthesons Lessons for the Harpsicord.

>> Walsh Cat. 11*a.*
>> Walsh Cat. 18: '12 Suits of Lessons for the Harpsicord. £1. 1s. od.'
>> No Walsh edition traced. May refer to copies of the work Pieces de Clavecin...1714', published by I. D. Fletcher, London (BM. h. 52.), which Walsh had acquired and was selling. It does not appear in later Walsh catalogues.

1003. Six Sonatas of Three Parts Purposely made and Contriv'd for three Flutes Compos'd by Monsier Mattheson Opera Prima.
London Printed for I. Walsh . . . and I. Hare . . . N⁰ 100.

[*c.* 1730.]

    Fol. Parts. Printed on one side only.
    Mitchell. (Flauto Terzo only, ff. 6.)
    'N⁰ 100' in MS.
    Smith 465 with 'N⁰ 100' added to the title-page.
    Walsh Cat. 18: 'Mattheson. Six Sonatas for three Flutes. 3s. od. N⁰ 100.'
    The work consists of Sonatas 3, 5–9, of 'XII Sonates à Deux & Trois Flutes sans Basse . . .
    Premier Ouvrage . . . Amsterdam.' (BM. f. 84.)

MEDLEY OVERTURES

See No. 1160. Overtures

MELANDE (GEORGIO) *pseud.* [i.e. GEORG PHILIPP TELEMANN]

1004. Solos for a Violin with a Thorough Bass for the Harpsicord or Bass Violin. Compos'd by Georgio Melande. Opera prima.
London Printed for & sold by I: Walsh . . . & In⁰ & Ioseph Hare, &c.

Daily Courant, Nov. 19, 1722. (Just published.)

    Fol. pp. 28.
    BM. g. 422. j. (1.) CUL.
    'prima' is in MS.

1005. — With Walsh only in the imprint and 'N⁰ 416' added to the title-page.

[*c.* 1730.]

    Walsh Cat. 18: 'Melande's Solos. 4s. od. N⁰ 416'
    See later edition under No. 1430. Telemann (George Philipp)

1006. Solos for a Violin with a Thorough Bass for the Harpsicord or Bass Violin. Compos'd by Georgio Melande. Opera Seconda.
London Printed for & sold by I: Walsh . . . In⁰ & Ioseph Hare, &c.

[*c.* 1725.]

    Fol. pp. 25.
    BM. g. 422. j. (2.)
    'Seconda' is in MS.

1007. — With Walsh only in the imprint and 'N⁰ 417' added to the title-page.

[*c.* 1730.]

    Walsh Cat. 18: 'Melande's Solos Opera 2da. 4s. od. N⁰ 417.'
    See later edition under No. 1430. Telemann (George Philipp)

MELODIA SACRA

1008. Melodia Sacra. £1. 1s. 0d.

> Walsh Cat. 15a.
> Not identified.

MERASPE

1009. The Favourite Songs in the Opera Call'd Meraspe o l'Olimpiade.
London. Printed for I. Walsh, &c.

[*c.* 1742.]

> Fol. Passe-partout title-page. pp. 2–20.
> BM. H. 348. e. (6.)
> Pasticcio. Composers named are Pergolesi, Scarlatti, Lampugnani, L. Leo, and F. Feo.
> Altered from Metastasio by Rolli.
> Walsh Cat. 25: 'Meraspe. Vinci. 2s. 0d.'
> Randall Cat. as anonymous.

MERCATO DI MALMANTILE

1010. The Favourite Songs in the Opera Call'd Il Mercato p^{ri} 2^s
London. Printed for I. Walsh, &c.

Public Advertiser, Dec. 3, 1761; Dec. 16, 1761. (A Second Set.)

> Fol. pp. 15. (First Set.) pp. 17–30. (Second Set.)
> BM. G. 206. i. (2.) (First Set only.)
> 'Il Mercato p^{ri} 2^s' is in MS. The full title 'Mercato di Malmantile' is given inside the work.
> Composers named are Galuppi and Fischietti.

1011. The Favourite Songs in the Opera Call'd Il Mercato di Malmantile Price 4^s
London. Printed for I. Walsh, &c.

[*c.* 1762.]

> Fol. Passe-partout title-page. pp. 1–15, blank, 17–30 (bottom centre).
> RCM. Gresham.
> 'Price 4^s' is in MS. With additional top centre pagination 117–30 on pp. 17–30.
> Republished with the addition of pp. 31–34 in 'Le Delizie dell' Opere', Vol. X, pp. 147–80.

MERCY (Louis)

1012. Six Solos for a Flute With a Thorough Bass for the Harpsicord or Violoncello. Humbly Dedicated to the Right Honble the Earle of Carnarvan By his most Obedient and Devoted Humble Servant Luis Mercy.
London Printed for I: Walsh . . . and I: Hare . . . N° 112.

[*c.* 1730.]

Fol. Preface. pp. 1–5, blank, 6–10, blank, 11–19, blank, 20–24, blank, 25–28, blank, 29–30.
BM. g. 524. Rowe.
Walsh Cat. 18: 'Mercy's Solos Opera Prima. 4s. 0d. N.° 112.'
Smith 553 with 'N.° 112' added to the title-page in MS.
Described as Opera Prima in the Preface.

1013. Mercy's Solos Opera Seconda (for a Flute and a Bass). 4s. 0d. N.° 113.
[*c.* 1730.]

Walsh Cat. 18.
Smith 613 with 'N.° 113' added to the title-page.

MERODE (Meride)

1014. The Favourite Songs in the Opera[s] call'd Merode & Olimpia as Perform'd at the Theatre in the Hay-Market.
London Printed for and sold by I. Walsh, &c.

London Daily Post, and General Advertiser, April 1, 1740.

Fol. Passe-partout title-page. pp. 2–25. (Merode 2–12, Olimpia 13–25.)
BM. H. 348. g. (1.) Rowe.
Two pasticcios. Composers named in 'Merode', Vinci and Pescetti, and Hasse and Pescetti in 'Olimpia'.
Burney gives the titles as 'Meride e Selinunté' and 'Olimpia in Ebuda'.
Randall Cat.: 'Merode Olympia. 2s. 0d.'
Republished in 'Le Delizie dell' Opere', Vol. IV, pp. 141–51, 152–64, 187–98.

MERRY MUSICIAN

1015. The Merry Musician; or, A Cure for the Spleen: Being A Collection of the most diverting Songs and pleasant Ballads, set to Musick; adapted to every Taste and Humour. Together with a curious Compound of State Pills, to allay the Malady of Malecontents.

> Here Mirth and Musick both appear,
> And Songs diverting, new and rare;
> Biting Satyr, smooth tho' keen,
> The surest Physick for the Spleen,
> By whom, both Age and Youth may be
> From Indolence and Vapours free.

Part I.
London, Printed by H. Meere, for J. Walsh . . . J. Hare . . . 1716. Price Bound 2s. 6d.

12°. 'An Alphabetical Table of the Songs', &c. 4 pp. without pagination. pp. 336.
BM. B. 353.
Smith 485.

1016. The Merry Musician . . . Vol. the First. The Second Edition.
London, Printed for J. Walsh . . . and J. Hare . . . 1730. Price bound 3s.

> 12°. 12 pp. unpaginated. pp. 336.
> Euing.

1017. — With 'N° 333' added to the title-page.

> [*c.* 1731.]

> Walsh Cat. 18: 'The Merry Musician . . . Vol. I. Bound 3s. od. N° 333.'

1018. The Merry Musician; or, a Cure for the Spleen: Being A Collection of the most diverting Songs & pleasant Ballads set to Musick; adapted to every Taste and Humour.

> Harmonious Mirth, & sweetest Lays have long
> Charm'd with soft Notes ÿ beauteous feather'd Throng
> If so, Melodious Strains must surely prove
> Successful to persuade Mankind to Love.
> For Musick fills the Breast with warm desire
> Touches the Heart, and does each Soul inspire.

Vol. II.
London. Printed for and sold by I: Walsh . . . Ios. Hare . . . and I: Young . . . Price Bound 3ˢ

> *Daily Post,* June 15, 1728. (Vol. II. Part I. Price 1s.); Nov. 5, 1728. (Vol. II. Pt. II.) *Country Journal: or, The Craftsman,* Sept. 20, 1729. (Curiously printed in a neat Pocket Volume. Any person that has the first and second Part of the Second Volume . . . may have the Third and Fourth Part separate.)

> 12°. Frontispiece. 'A Table of the Songs', pp. i–iv. pp. 180.
> BM. B. 353.
> Engraved throughout.

1019. — With 'N° 334' added to the title-page.

> [*c.* 1730.]

> 12°. Frontispiece. 'A Table of the Songs', pp. i–iv. pp. 180.
> Euing.
> Walsh Cat. 18: 'The Merry Musician . . . Vol. II. Bound. 3s. od. N° 334.'

1020. Mitchell copy, Walsh and Hare only in the imprint. [*c.* 1732 or later.]

1021. The Merry Musician; or A Cure for the Spleen: Being a Collection of the most diverting Songs and Pleasant Ballads set to the Violin and Flute; adapted to every Taste and Humour.

> Let other Arts in Senseless Matter reign,
> Mimick in Brass, or with mix'd Juices stain;
> Musick the mighty Artist Man, can rule,
> As long as it has Numbers, he a Soul.

Vol. III.

London, Printed for and sold by Iohn Walsh . . . Price Bound 3s. N⁰ 335.

Country Journal: or, The Craftsman, May 23, 1730. (Vol. III. Part I. Price 2s.); June 19, 1731. (The Third Volume.)

> 12⁰. Frontispiece. 'A Table of the Songs', 4 pp. without pagination. pp. 5–188.
> BM. B. 353. Euing.
> Engraved throughout.
> Walsh Cat. 18: 'The Merry Musician . . . Vol. III. Bound. 3s. od. N⁰ 335.'

1022. The Merry Musician; or, A Cure for the Spleen: Being A Collection of the most diverting Songs, and pleasant Ballads, set to the Violin & Flute adapted to every Taste & Humour.

> Here, in this little Magazine,
> The greatest Rarities are seen;
> For Musick has such Pow'rful charms,
> The Valiant Souldier She disarms,
> The Cripple throws his Crutch away,
> And the Morose looks brisk and gay.

Vol. IV.

London. Printed for & Sold by I. Walsh . . . Price Bound 3s.

Country Journal: or, The Craftsman, August 11, 1733.

> 12⁰. Frontispiece. 'A Table of the Songs', 4 pp. without pagination. pp. 176.
> BM. B. 353. Euing. (With 'N⁰ 488' on title-page.)
> Engraved throughout.
> Walsh Cat. 18: 'The Merry Musician . . .Vol. IV. 3s. od. N⁰ 488.'

MEUSEL (GODFREY)

1023. Rural Poetry or A Hymn on the Month of May taken from Milton. To which are added, Several more Pastoral and other Songs taken from Mᵣ Pope's Works, the Spectator &c. &c. Set to Musick by Godfrey Meusel.

London. Printed for the Author, and Sold at Mᵣ Walsh's, &c.

Daily Advertiser, Feb. 22, 1744.

> Fol. pp. 2–33.
> BM. G. 233.

1024. Midas A Comic Opera As it is Perform'd at the Theatre Royal In Covent Garden. For the Harpsichord, Voice, German Flute, Violin, or Guitar.

London. Printed for I. Walsh, &c.

Public Advertiser, March 8, 1764; March 19, 1764. (A Second Set of Songs.);
April 2, 1764. (A Third Set of Songs.); April 9, 1764. (In 4 vols.)

> Obl. fol. 'A Table of the Songs', &c. pp. 2–38, blank, 40–67 (with additional top and bottom paginations).
> BM. D. 272. (3.) Hirsch IV. 1177. RCM. Bod. Fitz. Manchester. Rowe.
> Libretto by Kane O'Hara. Music selected from popular airs.
> BM. copy contains an opening chorus in the handwriting of Dr. Kitchener.
> Walsh Cat. 27: 'Midas, a comic opera. 8s. od.'

1025. Midas A Comic Opera. Set for a German Flute, Violin, or Guitar. Price
1ˢ 6ᵈ Just Publish'd Midas, a Comic Opera. for the Harpsichord and Voice.
London. Printed I. Walsh, &c.

[1764.]

> 8°. pp. 1–16.
> Mitchell.

1026. — N̊ 2.

> 8°. pp. 17–32.
> BM. e. 340. h. (4.) Mitchell.
> 'N̊ 2' is in MS.

MINUETS (arranged chronologically)

> Other collections are under separate composers.
> There is no standard ruling whereby the sizes can be accurately given in the many cases
> where the paper has been cut to suit the purpose required, and therefore the sizes given as
> obl. 12° or obl. 8° must not be taken too literally.

The Newest Minuets, Rigadoons, and French Dances for the Year 1721 ... Compos'd by Mr. Murphy, &c.

> *See* No. 1123. Murphy (   )

1027. New Minuets for the Prince's Birth-Day perform'd at Court.
Sold by John Walsh . . . and John and Joseph Hare, &c.

> *Daily Courant*, April 4, 1722.

1028. Minuets, Rigadoons or French Dances for the Year 1722 Perform'd at the
Balls at Court . . . Together with Several Favourite Minuets by Mr Handell, Mr
Bononcini, and other Eminent Masters. The Tunes proper for the Violin or Hoboy
and many of them within the Compas of the Flute. price 1ˢ N.B. There are lately
Publish'd, &c.

London Printed for and Sold by Iᵒ. Walsh . . . and Iohn and Ioseph Hare, &c.
[1722.]

> Obl. 12°. ff. 21. Printed on one side only.
> Coke.
> One number only given as by Handel.

1029. For the Flute The Newest Minuets Rigadoons & French Dances for the Year 1723 Several of them perform'd at Court on the Prince's Birth Day and also at the most publick Places as Richmond Epsom Tunbridge & Bath at Balls & Assemblies The Tunes proper for ye Violin & Hoboy price 6d. N.B. there are lately Publish'd, &c.

London Printed for I: Walsh . . . & Iᵒ. & Ioseph Hare, &c.

Post-Boy, Dec. 15–18, 1722.

> Obl. 12°. ff. 2–13. Printed on one side only.
> Rowe. Coke. (With 'For the Flute' cut off.)
> Includes the Minuet in 'Muzio Scevola' and one other attributed to Handel, and items by Bononcini, Hill, &c.

1030. A Book of Minuets and Rigadoons for a single Flute, Price 6d.

Printed for and sold by John Walsh . . . and John and Joseph Hare, &c.

Daily Post, Dec. 21, 1722. (Lately published.)

1031. The Newest Minuets Rigadoons and French Dances Perform'd at the Ball at Court On His Majesty's Birth Day 1725 and at the Installation Ball of the Knight's of the Bath The tunes proper for the Violin and Hoboy price [erased].

London. Printed for and Sold by I: Walsh . . . and Iᵒ. & Ioseph Hare, &c.

[1725.]

> Obl. 8°. ff. 12. Printed on one side only.
> RCM.

1032. A choice Collection of Minuets and French Dances for a Flute. Price 6d.

Printed for and sold by John Walsh . . . and Jos. Hare, &c.

Mist's Weekly Journal, Jan. 14, 1727.

1033. A choice Collection of the newest Minuets and Rigadoons for a Violin or Hautboy, with a Bass perform'd at Balls and publick Entertainments for 1727. Price 6d.

Printed for and sold by John Walsh . . . and Jos. Hare, &c.

Mist's Weekly Journal, Jan. 14, 1727.

1034. Minuets for his Majesty K. George IId's Birthday, 1727, as they were perform'd at the Ball at Court. Composed by Mr. Handell. To which is added,

Variety of Minuets, Rigadoons, and French Dances, perform'd at Court and publick Entertainments. The tunes proper for a Violin or Hoboy, and several of them within the Compass of the Flute. Price 6d.

    Printed for, and sold by John Walsh . . . and Joseph Hare, &c.

    Mist's Weekly Journal, Nov. 11, 1727.

1035. A Collection of New Minuets, Airs and French Dances for the Flute, for the Year 1728. Being the choicest Minuets and Rigadoons perform'd at Court, the Theatres, and Publick Entertainments. Composed by the best Masters; Price 6d.

    Printed for, and sold by John Walsh . . . and Joseph Hare, &c.

    Country Journal: or, The Craftsman, Jan. 20, 1728.

1036. Minuets for her Majesty Queen Caroline's Birthday 1728. As they were performed at the Ball at Court, to which is added Variety of Minuets, Rigadoons and French Dances performed at Court and Publick Entertainments, the Tunes proper for the Violin or Hoboy. Price 6d.

    Printed for and sold by John Walsh . . and Joseph Hare, &c.

    Country Journal: or, The Craftsman, March 16, 1728.

1037. Minuets with their Basses for his Majesty's Birth-Day, 1728, as they were perform'd at the Ball at Court. To which is added, Variety of Minuets and French Dances perform'd at Court and Publick Entertainments, the tunes proper for the Violin or Hoboy, and several of them within the Compass of the Flute. Price 6d.

    Printed for and sold by John Walsh . . . and Jos. Hare, &c.

    Daily Post, Nov. 5, 1728.

1038. Minuets with their Basses for his Majesty's Birth-day. Published for the year 1729. Price 6d.

    Printed for and sold by John Walsh . . . and Joseph Hare, &c.

    London Journal, Dec. 21, 1728.

1039. Minuets. An unidentified collection without title-page.

    [*c.* 1728.]

        Obl. 12º. pp. 2–26. Treble.
        NLS. BH. 228.
        Includes two minuets by 'Bononcini', 'Minuets perform'd at Court on her Majestys Birth Day', 'Queen Caroline. A new Dance by Mʳ L'abbe', and six 'Minuets Compos'd by Mʳ Handel'. Bass part was probably issued also, as 'with their Basses' has been erased from p. 19. The Handel items occur as Nos. 3, 29, 1, 27, 12, and 38 in 'A General Collection of Minuets' (BM. K. 8. i. 16 and NLS. BH. 228 with which this work is placed. (No. 1042.)
        May have been issued by Walsh and Joseph Hare, and be identical with No. 1040.

1040. Minuets for her Majesty's Queen Caroline's Birthday, 1729, as they were perform'd at the Ball at Court. To which is added, Variety of Minuets, Rigadoons, and French Dances, performed at Court, and publick Entertainments. The Tunes proper for the Violin or Hautboy. Price 6d.

Printed for John Walsh . . . and Jos. Hare, &c.

Daily Post, March 13, 1729.

See also No. 1039.

1041. A Collection of the newest Minuets for the Flute for 1729. Price 6d.

Printed for, and sold by John Walsh . . . and Joseph Hare, &c.

Country Journal: or, The Craftsman, March 22, 1729.

1042. A General Collection of Minuets made for the Balls at Court The Operas and Masquerades Consisting of Sixty in Number Compos'd by Mr Handel. To which are added Twelve celebrated Marches made on several occasions by the same Author. All curiously fitted for the German Flute or Violin Fairly Engraven and carefully corected. Price 1^s 6^d

London. Printed for & sold by I: Walsh . . . Ios. Hare . . . and I: Young, &c.

Daily Post, April 19, 1729.

Obl. 12°. ff. 36. Printed on one side only.
BM. K. 8. i. 16. NLS. BH. 228.
Some of the Marches have not been identified.
See also No. 1039.

1043. Handel's Minuets and Marches (German Flute). 1s. 6d. N° 135.

[c. 1731.]

Walsh Cat. 18.
No. 1042. with Walsh only in the imprint and 'N° 135' added to the title-page.
Walsh Cat. 15a: 'Handel's Minuets and Marches (Violin). 1s. 6d.'

1044. The Basses to the General Collection of Minuets and Marches Compos'd by Mr Handel. Fairly Engraven and carefully Corected. Price 1^s

London. Printed for and sold by I: Walsh . . . Ios. Hare . . . and I. Young, &c.

Country Journal: or, The Craftsman, May 17, 1729.

Obl. 12°. ff. 24. Printed on one side only.
BM. K. 8. i. 16.

Nos. 1042 and 1044 were advertised by Walsh and Hare as 'A Choice Collection of 72 Marches, Minuets & Trumpet Tunes for the German Flute, Violin and Hautboy with a Thorough Bass . . . Price 2s. 6d.'

(*Daily Post*, July 22, 1730.)

1045. — Reissue of Nos. 1042 and 1044.

> Walsh Cat. 18: '72 Minuets and Marches for a German Flute and a Bass. 2s. 6d. N⁰ 136.'
> With Walsh only in the imprint and 'N⁰ 136' added to the title-page.
> Walsh Cat. 21: 'Handel's Minuets and Marches (for 2 German Flutes or Violins). 2s. 6d.',
> apparently refers to this work.
> Randall Cat.: 'For a single German Flute. Handel's 72 Minuets and Marches 2ˢ 6ᵈ', pre-
> sumably stock copies of the Walsh and Hare editions.

1046. Minuets with their Basses for his Majesty's Birth Day, as they were per-
formed at the Ball at Court. To which is added, Variety of Minuets and French
Dances, perform'd at Court and publick Entertainments; the Tunes proper for the
German Flute or Violin, and several of them within the Compass of the Flute.
  Printed for and sold by John Walsh ... and Joseph Hare, &c.

  Daily Post, Nov. 6, 1729.

1047. Minuets for his Majesty's Birth-Day, as they were perform'd at the Ball at
Court. To which is added Variety of Minuets and Rigadoons Perform'd at Court
and Publick Entertainments, for the Violin or German Flute and several of them
within the Compass of the Common Flute. Price 6d.
  Printed for and sold by John Walsh, &c.

  Daily Journal, Nov. 10, 1730.

1048. A new Minuet Book (for a single Violin). N⁰ 133.
  [*c.* 1730.]
> Walsh Cat. 18.
> Not identified.

1049. 2 Books of Minuets (for a single Violin) with Basses. 2s. 6d. N⁰ 130.
  [*c.* 1730.]
> Walsh Cat. 18.
> Not identified.

1050. Minuets with their Basses for his Majesty's Birth-Day, as they were per-
formed at the Ball at Court. To which is added, Variety of Minuets, Rigadoons and
French Dances, perform'd at Court and publick Entertainments; the tunes proper
for the Violin or German Flute, and several of them within the Compass of the
Flute. Price 6d.
  Printed for and sold by John Walsh, &c.
  Daily Post, Nov. 3, 1731.

1051. Minuets, with their Basses, for his Majesty's Birth Day; as they were perform'd at the Ball at Court. To which is added, variety of Minuets and French

Dances perform'd at Court and publick Entertainments: The Tunes proper for the Violin or German Flute, and several of them within the Compass of the common Flute. Published for the Year 1733. Price 6d.

Printed and sold by John Walsh, &c.

Daily Post, Nov. 8, 1732.

1052. Minuets for the Flute. 6d. N⁰ 47.

> [*c.* 1732.]
>> Walsh Cat. 18.
>> Not identified.

Minuets with their Basses For Her Majesty Queen Caroline's Birth-Day 1733, &c.

See No. 613. Festing (Michael Christian)

Minuets and their Basses For Her Majesty Queen Caroline's Birth-Day 1734 . . . 2ª Book, &c.

See No. 614. Festing (Michael Christian)

Minuets with their Basses, For His Majesty's Birth Day . . . 3ᵈ Book. 1735, &c.

See No. 615. Festing (Michael Christian)

1053. Minuets with their Basses For Her Majesty Queen Caroline's Birth Day. 1735. as they were perform'd at the Ball at Court. The Tunes proper for the Violin, German Flute, or Harpsicord. Price 6ᵈ 4ᵗʰ Book. N.B. Where these are Sold may be had The British Musical Miscellany, &c.

London. Printed for & Sold by I. Walsh . . . N⁰ 537.

London Evening-Post, March 8–11, 1735.

> Obl. 12⁰. pp. 12 (Bottom centre). With additional top corner pagination 1 on p. 1, 4 on p. 2, 2 on p. 3, 5 on p. 4, 3 on p. 5, 6 on p. 6, 1 on p. 7, 2 on p. 9, 3 on p. 11.
> BM. a. 26. q. (7.) (p. 13 unpaginated, probably from another collection).
> Walsh Cat. 18: 'Minuets. 4th Book. (Violin) 6d. N⁰ 537.'
> Books 1–3 are catalogued under Festing (Michael Christian). (Nos. 613–15.)

1054. Minuets with their Basses For His Majesty's Birth Day, as they were Perform'd at the Ball at Court. The Tunes proper for the Violin, German Flute, or Harpsicord. Price 6ᵈ 5ᵗʰ Book. 1736. N.B. Where these are sold may be had The British Musical Miscellany, &c.

London. Printed for & sold by I. Walsh . . . N⁰ 573.

Country Journal: or, The Craftsman, Nov. 8, 1735. (Minuets for his Majesty's Birth-Day . . . Published for 1736. 5th Book.)

Obl. 12°. 9 ff. (not foliated). Printed on one side only.
BM. a. 26. q. (6.)
Books 1–3 are catalogued under Festing (Michael Christian). (Nos. 613–15.) Book 4 under
Minuets. (No. 1053.)

1055. Minuets with their Basses for her Majesty's Birth-Day, 1736, as they were
perform'd at Court. The Tunes proper for the Violin, German Flute or Harpsicord. Price 6d.

Printed for and sold by John Walsh, &c.

Country Journal: or, The Craftsman, March 20, 1736. (Just published.)

Presumably the 6th Book.

1056. Minuets with their Basses For His Majesty's Birth Day, as they were Per-
form'd at the Ball at Court. The Tunes proper for the Violin, German Flute, or
Harpsicord. Price 6.ᵈ 7.ᵗʰ Book. 1737. N.B. Where these are sold may be had The
British Musical Miscellany, &c.

London. Printed for & sold by I. Walsh . . . N.º 573.

London Daily Post, and General Advertiser, Nov. 3, 1736.

Obl. 12°. 3 ff. (not foliated), ff. 1–6. Printed on one side only.
BM. a. 26. q. (4.)

1057. 2 Volumes of choice Minuets and French Dances for the Violin.

[*c.* 1736.]

Walsh Cat. in No. 279, 'Caledonian Country Dances . . . 3ᵈ Edition'. (*General Advertiser,
and General Post*, Nov. 3, 1736.) Mitchell.
Not identified.

1058. Minuets with their Basses For Her Majesty Queen Caroline's Birth Day.
1737. as they were perform'd at the Ball at Court. The Tunes proper for the Violin,
German Flute, or Harpsicord. Price 6.ᵈ 8.ᵗʰ Book. N.B. Where these are Sold may
be had, The British Musical Miscellany, &c.

London. Printed for & Sold by I. Walsh . . . N.º 537.

[1737.]

Obl. 12°. ff. 1–9 (1 not foliated). Printed on one side only.
BM. a. 26. q. (3.) Coke.

1059. Minuets with their Basses For His Majesty's Birth Day, as they were Per-
form'd at the Ball at Court. The Tunes proper for the Violin, German Flute, or
Harpsicord. Price 6.ᵈ 9.ᵗʰ Book. 1738. N.B. Where these are sold may be had The
British Musical Miscellany, &c.

London. Printed for & sold by I. Walsh . . . N⁰ 573.

Country Journal: or, The Craftsman, Nov. 19, 1737.

> Obl. 12°. ff. 9. With additional foliation 1–3 on ff. 4–6.
> BM. a. 26. q. (2.)

1060. Minuets with Basses for his Majesty's Birth Day, publish'd for 1739, for the Violin and Harpsichord. Price 6d.

Printed for and sold by John Walsh, &c.

London Daily Post and General Advertiser, Nov. 8, 1738.

1061. Select Minuets Collected From the Operas, the Balls at Court, the Masquerades, and all Publick Entertainments. For the Harpsicord, Violin, or German Flute. Compos'd by Mʳ Handel Dʳ Greene Mʳ M. C. Festing Mʳ Hudson.

London. Printed for I. Walsh . . . Price Bound 3ˢ 6ᵈ

London Daily Post, and General Advertiser, Oct. 31, 1739.

> Obl. 12°. ff. 2–111. Printed on one side only.
> BM. e. 26. h. NLS. BH. 250 (wanting ff. 102–8). Schœlcher.
> Made up from plates of earlier collections.
> The composers named are Hudson, Glover, Handel, Pescetti, Hasse, Sᵗ Martino, Festing, and Weideman. Five numbers attributed to Handel.
> Walsh Cat. 18: 'Select Minuets. Vol. 1. 3s. 6d.'
> A 'Second Book' was issued in 1745 (No. 1066), a third as part of 3 vols.in 1759 (No. 1082), and 'Vol. IV', 1760 (No. 1085).

1062. Minuets with their Basses, as they were perform'd at the Ball at Court on the Marriage of her Royal Highness the Princess Mary, with his Serene Highness the Prince of Hesse. Price 6d.

Printed for and sold by John Walsh, &c.

London Daily Post, and General Advertiser, May 3, 1740.

1063. Minuets with Basses for his Majesty's Birth-Day, as they were perform'd at Court, &c.

Printed for J. Walsh, &c.

London Daily Post, and General Advertiser, Nov. 3, 1740.

1064. Minuets for his Majesty's Birth-Day, as they were perform'd at Court, for the Violin or Harpsichord. Price 6d.

Printed for J. Walsh, &c.

London Daily Post, and General Advertiser, Nov. 2, 1741.

1065. Price 6d. Minuets for his Majesty's Birth-Day as they are perform'd at Court, publish'd for 1745 for the Harpsichord or Violin.
Printed for J. Walsh, &c.

London Evening-Post, Nov. 1–3, 1744.

1066. Select Minuets Second Book. Collected from the late Operas, the Balls at Court, and Masquerades, and all Publick Entertainments. For the Harpsicord, German Flute, or Violin. By M.ʳ Handel Sig.ʳ S.ᵗ Martini Sig.ʳ Pasquali Sig.ʳ Hasse. To which are added Twenty Six Venetian Tunes.
London. Printed for I. Walsh, &c.

General Advertiser; Daily Advertiser, March 11, 1745. (Just published.)

> Obl. 12°. ff. 2–108. Printed on one side only.
> NLS. BH. 251.
> Walsh Cat. 25: 'Select Minuets . . . in 2 Vol.ˢ Each 3s. 6d.'
> An earlier book was issued in 1739 (No. 1061), a third book as part of 3 vols. in 1759 (No. 1082), and 'Vol. IV' *c.* 1760 (No. 1085).

1067. Minuets for his Majesty's Birth Day, as they were perform'd at Court for the Violin and Harpsichord for the Year 1746.
Printed for J. Walsh, &c.

General Advertiser, Nov. 6, 1745. (Just published.)

1068. Minuets For His Majesty's Birth Day, as they were Perform'd at the Ball at Court. For the Harpsicord, Violin, or German Flute. Price 6.ᵈ 1747.
London. Printed for I. Walsh, &c.

> Obl 8°. ff. 9. Printed on one side only.
> BM. a 26. g. (1.) (Wanting the last leaf.)
> The composers named are:—Desnoyer, Vincent, Junr., Dubourgh, and Weideman.

1069. Minuets For His Majesty's Birth Day, as they were Perform'd at the Ball at Court. For the Harpsicord, Violin or German Flute. Price 6.ᵈ 1748.
London. Printed for I. Walsh, &c.

> Obl. 8°. ff. 9. Printed on one side only.
> BM. a. 26. g. (2.)
> The only composer named is Dubourgh.

1070. Minuets Perform'd at Court, the Masquerades, and all Publick Places. For the Harpsichord, Violin or German Flute for 1749. Price 6.ᵈ
London. Printed for I. Walsh, &c.

General Advertiser, Dec. 6, 1748.

> Obl. 8°. ff. 9. Printed on one side only.
> BM. a. 26. g. (3.); a. 300. (3.)
> The composers named are: Desnoyer and St. Martini.

1071. Minuets Perform'd at Court, the Masquerades, and all Publick Places. For the Harpsicord, Violin, or German Flute for 1750. Price 6ᵈ
London. Printed for I. Walsh, &c.
[1749.]
Obl. 8º. ff. 9. Printed on one side only.
BM. a. 26. g. (5.)

1072. Minuets For His Majesty's Birth Day, as they were Perform'd at the Ball at Court. For the Harpsicord, Violin, or German Flute. Price 6ᵈ 1750.
London. Printed for I. Walsh, &c.
Obl. 8º. ff. 9. Printed on one side only.
BM. a. 26. g. (4.)

1073. Minuets For His Majesty's Birth Day, as they were Perform'd at the Ball at Court. For the Harpsicord, Violin, or German Flute. Price 6ᵈ 1751.
London. Printed for I. Walsh, &c.
General Advertiser, Nov. 19, 1750.
Obl. 8º. ff. 9. Printed on one side only.
BM. a. 26. g. (6.)

1074. Minuets Perform'd at Court, the Masquerades, and all Publick Places. For the Harpsicord, Violin, or German Flute for 1752. Price 6ᵈ
London. Printed for I. Walsh, &c.
[1751.]
Obl. 8º. ff. 9. Printed on one side only.
BM. a. 26. g. (7.); a. 26. e. (1.)

1075. Minuets for His Majesty's Birth-day, as they were performed at Court, for the Harpsichord, Violin &c. Price 6d.
Printed for J. Walsh, &c.
General Advertiser, Nov. 28, 1752.

1076. Minuets For His Majesty's Birth Day, as they were Perform'd at the Ball at Court. For the Harpsicord, Violin, or German Flute. Price 6ᵈ 1753.
London. Printed for I. Walsh, &c.
Public Advertiser, Nov. 16, 1753.
Obl. 8º. ff. 9. Printed on one side only.
BM. a. 26. g. (8.)
The only composer named is Sigr. Palma.

1077. Minuets For His Majesty's Birth Day as they were Perform'd at the Ball at Court. For the Harpsicord, Violin, or German Flute. Price 6ᵈ. 1754.

R   241

London. Printed for I. Walsh, &c.

London Evening-Post, Nov. 9–12, 1754.

> Obl. 8°. ff. 10. Printed on one side only.
> BM. a. 26. g. (9.)

1078. Minuets For His Majesty's Birth Day, as they were Perform'd at the Ball at Court. For the Harpsicord, Violin, or German Flute. Price 6ᵈ 1755.
London. Printed for I. Walsh, &c.

Public Advertiser, Nov. 11, 1755.

> Obl. 8°. ff. 9. Printed on one side only.
> BM. a. 26. g. (10.)

1079. Minuets For His Majesty's Birth Day, as they were Perform'd at the Ball at Court. For the Harpsicord, Violin, or German Flute. Price 6ᵈ 1756.
London. Printed for I. Walsh, &c.

London Evening-Post, Nov. 9–11, 1756.

> Obl. 8°. ff. 9. Printed on one side only.
> BM. a. 26. g. (11.)

1080. Minuets for his Majesty's Birth Day. Price 6d.
Printed for J. Walsh, &c.

London Evening-Post, Nov. 10–12, 1757.

1081. Minuets for his Majesty's Birth-Day. Price 6d.
Printed for J. Walsh, &c.

Public Advertiser, Nov. 11, 1758.

1082. Select Minuets by Mr. Handel, Hasse, &c. for Harpsichord German Flute or Violin, &c. 3 vols.
London. Printed for J. Walsh, &c.

Public Advertiser, Sept. 6, 1759.

> Obl. 12°. 3 vols.
> No copy of the third volume traced. For Vols. I and II *see* Nos. 1061 and 1066.

1083. Minuets for the Harpsichord, German Flute, or Violin. 6d.
Printed for J. Walsh, &c.

Public Advertiser, Nov. 12, 1759.

1084. Minuets For His Majesty's Birth Day, as they were Perform'd at the Ball at Court. For the Harpsicord, Violin, or German Flute. Price 6ᵈ 1760.
London. Printed for I. Walsh, &c.

> Obl. 8°. ff. 2–10. Printed on one side only.
> Mitchell.

1085. Select Minuets. Vol. IV. Collected from the late Operas, the Balls at Court, the Masquerades, and all Publick Entertainments. For the Harpsicord, German Flute, or Violin. By Mʳ Handel Sigʳ Sᵗ Martini Sigʳ Pasquali Sigʳ Hasse & Mʳ Weideman.
London. Printed for I. Walsh . . . Of whom may be had Caledonian Dances . . . in 8 Books, &c.

[*c.* 1760.]

> Obl. 12°. ff. 2–10, 1–10, 1–6, 2–10, 2–9, 2–10, 1–9, 1–9, 2–10, 2–10, 1–9, with blanks. Foliated 11–96 in MS. after the first set.
> Coke.
> A composite work consisting of various sets.
> *Public Advertiser*, June 7, 1765. (Select Minuets for the Harpsicord and German Flute by Mr. Weideman, Sᵗ Martini and Hasse. 4 vols.)
> Randall Cat.: 'For a German Flute . . . Select Minuets, 4 vols. each 3ˢ 6ᵈ'
> The earlier volumes are entered under Nos. 1061, 1066, and 1082.

1086. Minuets for his Majesty's Birth-Day, as they were performed at the Ball at Court for the Harpsichord, German Flute, or Violin, Price 6d.
Printed for J. Walsh, &c.

Public Advertiser, June 6, 1761.

1087. Minuets for Her Majesty's Birth-Day, as they were performed at the Ball at Court, for the Harpsichord, German Flute, or Violin, Price 6d.
Printed for J. Walsh, &c.

Public Advertiser, Jan. 25, 1762.

1088. Minuets for His Majesty's Birth-Day, as they were performed at the Ball at Court, for the Harpsichord, German Flute, or Violin, Price 6d.
Printed for J. Walsh, &c.

Public Advertiser, June 8, 1762.

1089. Minuets for Her Majesty's Birth Day, as they were performed at Court, for the Harpsichord, German Flute, or Violin, Price 6d.
Printed for J. Walsh, &c.

Public Advertiser, Jan. 27, 1763.

1090. Minuets for His Majesty's Birth Day: As they were performed at the Ball at Court, for the Harpsicord, Violin, or German Flute.
Printed for J. Walsh, &c.
Public Advertiser, June 6, 1763.

1091. Minuets for Her Majesty's Birth-Day, as they were performed at the Ball at Court, for the Harpsicord, German Flute, or Violin . . . for 1764.
See No. 1540. Weideman (Charles Frederick)

1092. Minuets for His Majesty's Birth-Day; as they were performed at the Ball at Court; for the Harpsicord, Violin, or German Flute. Price 6d.
Printed for J. Walsh, &c.
Public Advertiser, June 7, 1764.

1093. Minuets for Her Majesty's Birth-Day; as performed at Court; for the Harpsicord, German Flute, or Violin.
Printed for J. Walsh, &c.
Public Advertiser, Jan. 28, 1765.

1094. Minuets for His Majesty's Birth-Day, as performed at the Ball at Court, for the Harpsicord, Violin, or German Flute.
Printed for J. Walsh, &c.
Public Advertiser, June 7, 1765.

1095. Select Minuets for the Harpsicord and German Flute by Mr. Weideman, St. Martini and Hasse. 4 vols.
Public Advertiser, June 7, 1765.
See Nos. 1061, 1066, 1082, 1085, entries for the four vols., 1739, 1745, 1759, and c. 1760.

1096. Minuets for the Year 1766; as performed at the Ball at Court; for the Harpsicord, Violin, &c. Price 6d.
Printed and sold at the late Mr. Walsh's, &c.
Public Advertiser, March 1, 1766.

MINUTI ( )
See No. 1138. Olimpiade

MOCK DOCTOR

1097. Songs in the Mock Doctor. 6d.

[*c.* 1732.]

Walsh Cat. 15*a*.
Not identified. An anonymous edition, 'Printed & Sold at the Musick Shops', was issued
c. 1732. (BM. A. 869. a. (1.))
Walsh Cat. 17*a*: 'Just Publish'd by I. Walsh. Ballad Operas . . . Mock Doctor.'
Randall Cat.: 'Mock Doctor. 6ᵈ'

1098. The Mock Doctor. 1s. 0d. Nº 302.

[*c.* 1732.]

Walsh Cat. 18: 'Vocal Musick. The Mock Doctor.'
Walsh Cat. 24*a*.: 'Polly's Opera and Mock Docʳ each 1s. 0d. (For a Single Flute.)'

MONDONVILLE (Jean Joseph CASSANEA DE)

1099 Six Sonatas or Lessons for the Harpsicord which may be Accompanied with
a Violin or German Flute. Compos'd by Mʳ Mondonville.
London. Printed for I. Walsh, &c.

Public Advertiser, Jan. 18, 1753.

Fol. pp. 1–13, blank, 15–19, blank, 21–23, blank, 25–29, blank, 31–43, blank, 45–51.
BM. g. 79. b. (4.); g. 248. Rowe. Tenbury.
Originally issued as 'Pièces de Clavecin en Sonates . . . Œuvres 3ᵉ Chez l'Auteur, Paris et
Lille'. *c.* 1740. (BM. i. 3. (1.))

1100. — 2nd edition.

Public Advertiser, Oct. 25, 1763. (Mondonville Lessons for the Harpsichord,
with the Accompanyment printed separate, for the Violin and German Flute,
2 edition.)

MONRO (George)

1101. Monro's Songs. 2s. 6d. Nº 332.

[*c.* 1730.]

Walsh Cat. 18.
Walsh Cat. 15*a*, 17*a*: 'Just Publish'd . . . Monro's Songs.'
Not identified. Probably a collection of sheet songs, previously published without im-
prints, many of which are in the British Museum.

MONTHLY MASK OF VOCAL MUSIC

1102. The Monthly Mask of Vocal Music; or the Newest Songs Made for the
Theatre's & other Ocations Publish'd for November Price 6 Pence These Collection's will be Continued Monthly for yᵉ Year 1703.

London Printed for and sold by I. Walsh and I. Hare, &c.

[1702–24.]

Fol.

The first of an important periodical with various illustrated title-pages, which ran from November 1702 to April 1712 at least, after which it ceased until a new series commenced in July 1717, which continued until July 1724. It consists of single songs issued separately at the time or a little earlier, from the same plates, including a number of first editions of Handel items.

No complete set is known, various numbers are scattered about in different libraries, the British Museum having a long range (BM. K. 7. e. 4, 4a) and odd parts are in RAM, RCM, Rowe Library, Cambridge University Library, Durham Cathedral Library, Euing Library, Glasgow, Mitchell Library, Glasgow, Magdalen College, Oxford, and the Bodleian Library.

For more details reference should be made to the entry under Periodical Publications in BUC and to the entries in the Smith, Walsh Bibliography, 1695–1720.

In June 1737 Walsh the younger issued 'The Monthly Mask, or an Entertainment of Musick', which continued irregularly until some time in 1738. (*See* Nos. 1104-1119.)

1103. The December Mask, being a Choice Collection of English Songs. 2s. 6d. Nọ 313.

[*c.* 1730.]

Walsh Cat. 18.

Not identified. Probably a small collection from the first series. (No. 1102.)

MONTHLY MASK, OR AN ENTERTAINMENT OF MUSICK

1104. No. 1. The Monthly Mask, or an Entertainment of Musick Consisting of Six Celebrated Songs, Set for the Violin, German Flute, Com̃on Flute & Harpsi-cord, by ye best Masters. Price 6d.

Printed for I. Walsh, &c.

[1737.]

Fol. Illustrated passe-partout title-page (Smith, Walsh, pl. 17).

W. N. H. Harding, Chicago, A collection of single sheets from various numbers of this work, with the above title-page. (*See* No. 1119.)

1105. — Numb. 2.

Country Journal: or, The Craftsman, July 9, 1737.

Details of title-page of this and subsequent numbers not known.

1106. — No. 3.

[1737.]

1107. — Numb. IV.

Country Journal: or, The Craftsman, July 30, 1737.

1108. — Numb. V.
Country Journal: or, The Craftsman, August 27, 1737.

1109. — Numb. VI.
Country Journal: or, The Craftsman, Sept. 24, 1737.

1110. — No. 7.
[1737.]

1111. — Numb. VIII.
London Evening-Post, Oct. 18–20, 1737.

1112. — Numb. IX.
Country Journal: or The Craftsman, Nov. 5, 1737.

1113. — Numb. X.
Country Journal: or, The Craftsman, Nov. 19, 1737.

1114. — Numb. XI.
Country Journal: or, The Craftsman, Nov. 26, 1737.

1115. — No. XII.
London Evening-Post, Dec. 29–31, 1737.

1116. — No. XIII.
[1738.]

1117. — No. XIV.
[1738.]

1118. — No. XV.
[1738.]

1119. — No. XVI.
[1738.]
    Fol.
    Euing. XV (?) and XVI together, with one title-page, No. XVI.
    'XVI' in MS. Contains 10 numbers, 11 ff., printed on one side only.
    W. N. H. Harding of Chicago has three collections with different contents and title-pages. The first as 'No. 1. The Monthly Mask,' &c. (No. 1104) but with many more items, the second 'The Vocal Musical Mask. A Collection of English Songs'; no imprint but a

Walsh volume containing some numbers from No. 1; and many others (No. 1525*b*); the third 'The Vocal Mask. A Collection of Favourite English Songs. Printed for I. Walsh in Catherine Street', 67 single and 10 folio sheets with title-page, from plate 17, Smith, Walsh Bibliography 1695–1720 (No. 1525*c*.)

MORIGI (ANGELO)

1120. Six Sonatas for Two Violins with a Thorough Bass for the Harpsicord or Violoncello. Compos'd by Angelo Morigi da Rimini.
London. Printed for I. Walsh, &c.

London Daily Advertiser, Oct. 12, 1751.

> Fol. 3 parts.
> BM. g. 278. Manchester. Reid.

MORLEY (WILLIAM) AND ISUM (JOHN)

1121. A Collection of New Songs set to Musick by Mr Wm Morley and Mr Iohn Isum With A Thorough-bass to each Song, All transpos'd for the Flute: and fairly Engraven on Copper Plates. T: Cross sculpt.
London, Printed for the Authors . . . Sold by John Hare . . . John Walsh, &c.

[*c.* 1730.]

> Fol.
> Smith 379 (BM. H. 1601. h. (1.) ff. 22, without foliation), of which this is presumably a reissue with Walsh only in the imprint, or with the original imprint amended.
> Walsh Cat. 18: 'Morley and Issum's Songs. 1s. 6d.'

MUDGE (RICHARD)

1122. Six Concertos in Seven Parts, Five for Four Violins, a Tenor Violin, and Violoncello, with a Thorough Bass for the Harpsicord. and one Concerto for the Organ or Harpsicord, with Instruments Compos'd by Mr Mudge. To which is added, Non Nobis Domine, in 8 Parts.
London. Printed for I. Walsh, &c.

London Evening-Post, June 22–24, 1749.

> Fol. 7 parts.
> BM. g. 254. RCM. Durham. Fitz. Rowe. Tenbury.

MURPHY ( )

1123. The Newest Minuets, Rigadoons, and French Dances for the Year 1721 Perform'd at Court and Publick Entertainment^s Compos'd by Mr. Murphy To which is added the Ball Dances perform'd at Schools. The Tunes proper for the Violin Hoboy or Flute Price 6^d Note there are lately Publish'd, &c.

London Printed for J: Walsh . . . and J. Hare at the Viol & Flute, &c.

Post-Boy, Jan. 19–21, 1721. (Just publish'd.)

> Obl. 12°. ff. 12. Printed on one side only.
> Coke.

MUSICA BELLICOSA

1124. Musica Bellicosa. Or, Warlike Music. Being a Choice Collection of Sixty-eight Marches and Trumpet-tunes for the German Flute Violin & Hautboy with a Through Bass to the whole. to which is added Geminiani's and Dubourg's Seranading Trumpet-tunes and a Scale of the Gamut for the Bassoon. being the most Correct Edition Extant.   Price 2s.

London. Printed for and sold by I. Walsh . . . N⁰ 449.

Country Journal: or, The Craftsman, Sept. 5, 1730. (Warlike Musick: Or A Choice Collection of Sixty-eight Marches and Trumpet-Tunes . . . The whole carefully corrected. Price 1s. Printed for and sold by J. Walsh . . . and J. Hare, &c.)

> Obl. 4°. German Flute Violin or Hautboy Primo. ff. 24. 'A Scale of notes on the Bassoon' on folding sheet. Bass. ff. 24. Printed on one side only. 2 parts.
> RCM. Cardiff (imperfect).
> Walsh Cat. 18: '68 Marches and Trumpet tunes for a German Flute and a Bass. 2s. 0d. N⁰ 449.'
> Walsh Cat. 15a: '68 Marches & Trumpet Tunes (for a German Flute, Hoboy, or Violin with a Bass)'. 2s. 0d.
> Walsh Cat. 16c: 'Warlike Music (for 2 German Flutes).' 2s. 0d.
> Walsh Cat. 21: 'Warlike Musick (for 2 German Flutes or Violins). 2s. 0d.'
> Walsh Cat. 24a: 'Warlike Musick, 68 Marches and Trumpet Tunes (for a German Flute, Violin, or Harpsicord). 2s. 0d. Warlike Musick 2d Book D⁰ 1s. 6d.'
> No copy of a 2d Book has been traced.

MUZIO SCEVOLA

1125. The favourite Songs in the Opera call'd Muzio Scævola.

London Printed for & sold by I: Walsh . . . & In⁰ and Ioseph Hare, &c.

Post-Boy, July 31–August 2, 1722. (Now engraving.); August 23–25, 1722. (Musick publish'd this Vacation.)

> Fol. Passe-partout title-page as used earlier for some other work and afterwards for 'Acis and Galatea'. ff. 21. Printed on one side only.
> BM. G. 158. NLS. BH. 68. Rowe. Flower. Coke. Smith.
> Contains overture and four songs from Act III (Giovanni Bononcini); one song from Act I (Filippo Amadei, probably) and three songs from Act III (Handel).
> Same contents as R. Meares edition, in slightly different order. (Bm. G. 192. (2.))

1126. Favourite Songs in Muzio Scævola. 2s. 6d. N⁰ 249.

> [*c.* 1730.]

> Fol.

Walsh Cat. 18. (Two entries.)

As No. 1125, with Walsh only in the imprint and 'N.º 249' added to the title-page.

An issue may have been made by Walsh (including 'Deh serbate' from Handel's 'Teseo') with additional paginations from 'Apollo's Feast', Vols. I and II: 129–30, 228–30, 132–4, 151–2, 229–230 (or 75–76), but no copy is available for examination, and the details are open to correction.

NARCISSUS

The Opera of Narcissus.

See No. 1332. Scarlatti (Domenico)

NARDINI (Pietro)

1127. Six Solos for a Violin with a Bass for the Harpsicord or Violoncello Compos'd by Sig.ʳ Pietro Nardini.

London. Printed for I. Walsh, &c.

Public Advertiser, March 26, 1761.

Fol. pp. 26.
CUL. Pendlebury. Rowe.

NARDINI (Pietro) and FERRARI (Domenico)

1128. Six Sonatas or Duets for Two Violins Compos'd by Sig.ʳ Nardini and Ferari Opera Seconda.

London. Printed for I. Walsh, &c.

Public Advertiser, Aug. 4, 1762.

Fol. 2 parts.
BM. g. 218. d. (5.) RAM.

NARES (James)

See No. 1233. Psalms

NERONE

1129. The Favourite Songs in the Opera Call'd Nerone.

London. Printed for I. Walsh, &c.

Public Advertiser, Dec. 8, 1753.

Fol. Passe-partout title-page. pp. 2–23.
BM. H. 348. e. (3.) RCM. DAM.
Pasticcio. Composers named are Pescetti, Cocchi, Galuppi, Hasse, Abos, and Rinaldo da Capua.
Republished in 'Le Delizie dell' Opere', Vol. VI, pp. 22–47 and Vol. IX, pp. 160–3.

THE NEW COUNTRY DANCING-MASTER.

See No. 515. Country Dancing Master

NEW FLUTE MASTER

1130. The New Flute Master for the Year 1729 Containing The most compleat Rules & Directions for Learners on yᵉ Flute Together with a curious collection of the newest & choicest Aires, Jiggs, and Minuets, with great variety of things of Humour; also the newest French Dances perform'd at Masquerades and publick Enter-tainments, with Preludes Flourishes in all the Keys. The whole done by the best Masters. Price 1ˢ 6ᵈ Note. all the choicest pieces for 2 Flutes, for 2 Flutes and a Bass, and Solos may be had where these are sold.

London. Printed for and sold by I: Walsh . . . and Ioseph Hare, &c.

[1728.]

Obl. 12°. ff. 7 (text 1, 2, 4, 5 foliated). ff. 27 (music). Printed on one side only.
Coke.

1131. The New Flute Master for the Year 1733 Containing The most compleat Rules & Directions for Learners on yᵉ Flute Together with a curious collection of the newest & choicest Aires, Jiggs and Minuets, with great variety of things of Humour; also the newest French Dances perform'd at Masquerades and publick Entertainments, with Preludes or Flourishes in all Keys. The whole done by the best Masters. Price 1ˢ 6ᵈ Note all the choicest pieces for 2 Flutes and a Bass, and Solos may be had where these are sold.

[1732.]

Obl. 12°. ff. 7 (text), ff. 29 (music). Printed on one side only.
GUL.
'33' in the date is in MS. There is no imprint in this work, but it was presumably published by Walsh.

NEW HARPSICORD BOOK

1132. The new Harpsicᵈ Book wᵗʰ Rules for a Thro' Bass. 1s. 6d. Nº 516.

[*c.* 1734.]

Walsh Cat. 18.
Not identified.

NICOLA

See Matteis (Nicola)

NICOLA, *Mr. Jun.*

See Matteis (Nicholas)

NOVELL (MATTHEW)

1133. Novels 12 Sonatas (2 Violins and a Bass). 7s. 6d.

[*c.* 1730.]

Walsh Cat. 18.

This presumably refers to 'Sonate da Camera or Chamber Musick. Being a Sett of Twelve Sonata's consisting of Preludes Allemands Sarabands Jiggs Ayres & Gavotts with many other Musical Intervals composed for Two Violins and Bass with a Thorough-bass for the Theorbo-lute Spinett or Harpsicord by Matthew Novell. London Printed for the Author and are sold by him at Mr Crouches . . . Excud: et Sculp: Cross Junr.' (BM. f. 93. Fol. Parts. 1704.)

Copies were acquired by Walsh and sold by him.

NUMITOR

Opera of Numitor.

See No. 1227. Porta (Giovanni)

NUSSEN (FREDERICK)

1134. Musica di Camera or Some Old Tunes new Sett, and some New ones Compos'd for the Harpsichord, Opera 3za For the Practise and Amusement of the Rt Honble the Lady Frances Greville, To whom these are Dedicated by her Ladyship's Most Dutifull & Obedient Humble Servant Fred: Nussen.

London Printed for I. Walsh, &c.

Public Advertiser, Jan. 4, 1762.

> Obl. fol. pp. 27.
> BM. e. 5. g. (8.)
> Printed from the same plates as the edition 'Printed for the Author', London [1761], with the title-page modified by the Walsh imprint. (BM. e. 5. (4.)) 'Milton sculp' appears on p. 27.
> Walsh Cat. 27 and Randall Cat.: 'Nussen's Lessons, 5s. od.'

1135. VI Solos for a Violin with a Thorough Bass for the Harpsicord or Violoncello. Dedicated To the Right Honble Francis Earl Brooke. Composed by Frederick Nussen.

London. Printed for I. Walsh, &c.

[*c.* 1750.]

> Fol. pp. 1–5, blank, 7–11, blank, 13–17, blank, 19–23, blank, 25–32.
> BM. g. 221. (2.)

1136. — 2d. Edition.

General Advertiser, Nov. 19, 1750. (Of whom may be had, just published. 2d Edit.)

1137. Six Sonatas for Two Violins Violoncello or Harpsicord. Most humbly dedicated to the Lady Augusta By Her Highness' most devoted and Dutiful Servant Fred: Nussen. Opera 2da.

London Printed for the Author by J. Walsh, &c.

Whitehall Evening-Post, Dec. 29, 1753–Jan. 1, 1754.

Fol. 3 parts.
BM. g. 686. RM. 17. c. 6. (11.) Manchester. Oriel College, Oxford. Rowe.

OLIMPIA (OLIMPIA IN EBUDA)

See No. 1014. Merode. The Favourite Songs in the Opera[s] Call'd Merode and Olimpia, &c.

OLIMPIADE

1138. The Favourite Songs in the Opera call'd L'Olimpiade.
London. Printed for I. Walsh, &c.

[*c.* 1753.]

Fol. pp. 21.
RCM.
'L'Olimpiade' is in MS.
Pasticcio. Composers named are Galuppi, Minuti, and Pergolesi.
Randall Cat.: 'L'Olimpiade. Galuppi.'
Republished in 'Le Delizie dell' Opere', Vol. VI, pp. 1–21 and Vol. IX, pp. 118–38.

OPERA AIRS

1139. 2 Collections of Opera Airs for a single German Flute in quarto.
[London . . . I. Walsh . . . and Ioseph Hare.]

[*c.* 1725.]

Not identified.
Advertised on title-page of 'Solos for a German Flute a Hoboy or Violin with a Through Bass . . . Compos'd by Mʳ Handel . . . Part yᵉ first', &c. [*c.*1730.] (Smith, 'Handel. A Descriptive Catalogue', &c. p. 306, no. 3.)

1140. — With Walsh only in the imprints and 'Nọ 155' and 'Nọ 156' added to the respective title-pages.

[*c.* 1730.]

Walsh Cat. 18: 'Opera Aires 1st Collection (for a single German Flute). 2s. od. Nọ 155.' 'Opera Aires 2d Collection (for a single German Flute). 2s. od. Nọ 156.' 'Nọ 155' is also given in Cat. 18 to 'Opera Aires 3d. Collection (for a single Violin)' and 'Nọ 156' to the 4th Collection (for a single Violin).'

1141. Opera Aires 3d Collection (for a single Violin). 2s. od. Nọ 155.
[London . . . Iohn Walsh.]

[*c.* 1730]

4°.
Not identified.
Walsh Cat. 18.
'Nọ 155' is also given in Cat. 18 to 'Opera Aires 1st Collection (for a single German Flute).' (*See* No. 1140.)

1142. Opera Aires 4th Collection (for a single Violin). 2s. od. N̞ 156. [London . . . Iohn Walsh.]

[*c.* 1730.]

40.

Not identified.
Walsh Cat. 18.
'N̞ 156' is also given in Cat. 18 to 'Opera Aires (for a single German Flute)'. (*See* No. 1140.) Walsh advertised '4 Books of Opera Aires for a single Violin in 4ᵗᵒ' on 'Sonatas or Chamber Aires for a Violin and Bass . . . Compos'd by Mͬ Handel', Vol. II. Part II and Part III. (Smith, 'Handel. A Descriptive Catalogue', &c. p. 314, No. 5, p. 315, No. 10.)

Opera Aires (for 2 Violins).

See No. 134. Banister (John)

Opera Airs with Symphonys (for 2 Flutes).

See No. 1143. Opera Songs

Opera Airs not identified as such may have appeared as Collections of Song Tunes.

See Nos. 136, 137. Banister (John) and Nos. 1398, 1399. Song Tunes.

OPERA DANCES

The Opera Dances for the Year 1762.

See Nos. 794, 795. Hasse (Johann Adolph) [Comic Tunes. Vol. IX.]

OPERA SONGS

1143. Six Setts of Choice Opera Songs or Arietts With their Symphonys fitted for 2 Flutes The Second parts, being Compleat and Airy as the First, not thin and heavy as second Trebles usually are, in both parts there are proper Variations for the Humour of the Flute price 2ˢ

London. Printed for I. Walsh, &c.

[*c.* 1730.]

Obl. 8°. 2 parts.
Smith 545 (BM. a. 209. Flauto Secondo part only) with Walsh only in the imprint and 'N̞ 62' added to the title-page.
Walsh Cat. 18: 'Opera Aires with Symphonys (for 2 Flutes). 2s. od. N̞ 62.'

ORAZIO

1144. The Favourite Songs in the Opera Call'd Orazio.
London. Printed for I. Walsh, &c.

General Advertiser, Dec. 15, 1748.

Fol. pp. 2–20.
RCM. Rowe.
Pasticcio. Composers named are Jomelli, Fini, Macchari, Resta, and Paradies.
Republished in 'Le Delizie dell' Opere', Vol. VI, pp. 154–72.

ORFEO

1145. The Favourite Songs in the Opera Call'd Orpheus.
London. Printed for and sold by I. Walsh, &c.

London Daily Post, and General Advertiser, April 7, 1736.

Fol. Passe-partout title-page. pp. 1–4, blank, 5–7, blank, 8–14, blank, 15, 16.
BM. G. 206. e.; G. 206. h. (3.) RAM. Manchester.
Pasticcio. Composers named are Araja, Vinci, and Porpora.
Walsh Cat. 18: 'Orpheus & Sabrina each 2s. 6d. N° 587.'
Walsh Cat. 25: 'Hasse. Orpheus. 2s. 6d.'
Republished in 'Le Delizie dell' Opere', Vol. II, pp. 104–18.

ORIONE

The Favourite Songs in the Opera Call'd Orione, o sia Diana Vendicata.

See No. 119. Bach (Johann Christian)

ORLANDINI (GIUSEPPE MARIA)

Amore e Maestà.

See No. 376. Ciro

ORMISDA

1146. The Favourite Songs in the Opera call'd Ormisda.
London Printed for and sold by I: Walsh . . . and Joseph Hare, &c.

Daily Journal, April 25, 1730.

Large fol. Passe-partout title-page as used for 'Astyanax' (G. Bononcini, 1727), 'Lotario' and other works by Handel. ff. 2–19, and 4 unnumbered folios. Printed on one side only.
BM. I. 49. (2.) RAM. Coke. Manchester. OUF.
Pasticcio. Text by Apostolo Zeno. Music attributed to Francesco Conti, Bartholomeo Cordans, and Antonio Caldara, but was probably arranged for performance by Handel; what part, if any, he had in the composition of the opera is not known.

1147. — With Walsh only in the imprint and 'N° 264' added to the title-page.
[1730].

Walsh Cat. 18.
A selection was included in 'Le Delizie dell' Opere', Vol. II, pp. 214–18, 228, 231–2.

ORPHEUS

See No. 1145. Orfeo

ORPHEUS AND EURYDICE

1148. The Comic Tunes in the Celebrated Entertainment call'd Orpheus and Euridice. as they are Perform'd at the Theatre in Covent Garden. To which is added the Tambourine Dances, and several other Choice Aires Perform'd at both Theatres. For the Harpsicord, Violin, or German Flute. Price 1ˢ 6ᵈ

London. Printed for I. Walsh, &c.

London Daily Post, and General Advertiser, March 25, 1740.

> Obl. 8°. ff. 30. Printed on one side only.
> BM. a. 154.
> The 'Aires' include Handel's 'Dead March in Saul'.

OVEREND (MARMADUKE)

1149. The Second Six of twelve Sonatas or Trios for two Violins and a Violoncello, the Basses of which are correctly figured for the Harpsichord, composed by Marmaduke Overend, Organist of Isleworth, Opera Primo.

Printed for, and sold by the Author, and by Charles and Samuel Thomson . . . and John Walsh, &c.

Public Advertiser, May 24, 1763.

> The 'XII Sonatas: for two Violins and a Violoncello', &c. were published by the Author, London, 1762. (Fol. Parts. 2 Bk.) Rowe.

OVERTURES

Overtures for Violins, &c. in parts.

> The various collections and editions containing works by Handel and other composers, published by Walsh and John Hare from 1723 onwards are listed in Smith, 'Handel. A Descriptive Catalogue', &c. and are therefore not repeated here.

1150. A Collection of Several Excellent Overtures Symphonys and Aires for a Flute and a Bass Compos'd by the most Eminent Masters to which is added that Incomperable Sonata for a Flute and a Bass Perform'd at Court and often at the Theatre by Mʳ Paisible and Mʳ Gasperini the whole fairly Engraven price 3ˢ

London Printed for I. Walsh . . . Nº 128.

> [*c.* 1730.]

> Fol. ff. 12.
> Smith 198 (BM. h. 17. (5.)) with Walsh only in the imprint and 'Nº 128' added to the title-page.
> Walsh Cat. 18: 'Gasperini's Work's. Overtures and Aires with a curious Sonata of Gasperini for a Violin and a Bass. 3s. od. Nº 128.'

1151. Six Overtures in Seven Parts for Violins, French-Horns, Hoboys &c. with

a Through Bass for the Harpsicord or Violoncello from the Late Operas Compos'd by Sig.ʳ Hasse, Vinci, Galuppi & Porpora. [First Collection.]
London. Printed for I. Walsh, &c.

London Evening-Post, Feb. 25–27, 1748.

Fol. Parts.
RM. 17. d. 4. (11.) RM. 26. b. 2. (9.) BM. g. 270. u. (9.) (Violin II and and Violon-
cello parts only.) RAM. RCM. Bod. Coke.
This collection contains the overtures to Galuppi's 'Enrico', 'Penelope', and 'Scipione in
Cartagine', to Porpora's 'Arianna' and 'Polifemo' and to the pasticcio 'Meraspe'.

1152. — New edition.

General Advertiser, Oct. 25, 1749. (New editions.)

Listed as 'The First Set' on the title-page of 'Six Overtures in 8 Parts . . . Compos'd by
Sig.ʳ Bach Jomelli Galuppi Perez Sixth Collection'. (BM. g. 212. a. 1764.) (No. 1158.)
Walsh Cat. 27: 'Hasse and Vinci's Overt.ˢ 1.ˢᵗ Coll.ⁿ 6s. od.'

1153. Six Overtures by Sig.ʳ St. Martini, Galuppi, Jomelli. [Second Collection.]
London. Printed for I. Walsh, &c.

[*c.* 1760.]

Fol. Parts.
Listed as 'Fifth Set' on the title-page of 'Six Overtures in 8 Parts . . . Compos'd by Sig.ʳ
Bach Jomelli Galuppi Perez Sixth Collection.' (1764. BM. g. 212. a..) (No. 1158.).
Walsh Cat. 27: 'Martini and Galuppis Overtures. 2.ᵈ Coll.ⁿ 10s. 6d..'

1154. Six Favourite Overtures in 8 Parts. from the late Italian Operas Perform'd
at the Haymarket. For Violins, Hoboys & French Horns with a Bass for the Harpsicord and Violoncello. Compos'd by Sig.ʳ Cocchi, Galuppi, Graun and Jomelli. Publish'd by M.ʳ Agus. N.B. These Overtures are Printed in such manner that they may
be Play'd as Trios. [Third Collection.]
London. Printed for I. Walsh, &c.

Public Advertiser, July 27, 1762.

Fol. parts.
RAM.
Listed as 'Second Set' on the title-page of 'Six Overtures in 8 Parts . . . Compos'd by Sig.ʳ
Bach Jomelli Galuppi Perez Sixth Collection'. (1764. BM. g. 212. a.) (No. 1158.)
Walsh Cat. 27: 'Cocchi and Jomellis Overtures 3.ᵈ Coll.ⁿ 10s. 6d.'

1155. Abel Arne and Smith's Six Favourite Overtures for Violins, Hoboys and
French Horns. With a Bass for the Harpsicord and Violoncello. From Love in a
Village Thomas & Sally Judith Eliza Enchanter Fairies. [Fourth Collection.]
London. Printed for I. Walsh, &c.

Public Advertiser, Nov. 11, 1763.

> Fol. Parts.
> BM. g. 30. c. (Violino Primo and Corno Primo e Secondo parts only.) Coke.
> Listed as 'Third Set' on the title-page of 'Six Overtures in 8 Parts . . . Compos'd by Sig^r Bach Jomelli Galuppi Perez Sixth Collection'. (1764. BM. g. 212. a.) (No. 1158.)
> > Walsh Cat. 27: 'Abel, Smith and Arne's Overtures. 4th Collⁿ 10s. 6d.'
> > Includes also 'The Tempest'. (*See* No. 1156.)

1156. Abel Arne and Smith's Six Favourite Overtures for Violins, Hoboys and French Horns. With a Bass for the Harpsicord and Violoncello. From Love in a Village Thomas & Sally Judith Eliza Enchanter Fairies. To which is added the Tempest.

London. Printed for I. Walsh, &c.

[*c.* 1765.]

> Fol. Parts.
> BM. g. 30. c. (Violino Secondo, Viola, Basso, Hautboy Primo, Hautboy Secondo, Corno Primo e Secondo parts only.) RM. 6. h. 17. (1.) (Hautboy Primo, Hautboy Secondo, Corno Primo e Secondo parts only.) RAM. RCM. Bod.
> > A reissue of No. 1155, with additions to the title-page.

1157. Abel Arne and Smith's Favourite Overtures From the Latest English Operas Set for the Harpsicord or Organ.

London. Printed for I. Walsh, &c.

Public Advertiser, Jan. 7, 1764. (Also for the Harpsichord.)

> Obl. fol. pp. 2–35.
> Rowe.
> > Walsh Cat. 27: 'Abel, Smith and Arne's Overtures (for the Harpsicord), 5s. od.'

Six Favourite Overtures in 8 Parts . . . Compos'd by Sig^r Bach. [Fifth Collection.]

See No. 126. Bach (Johann Christian)

1158. Six Overtures in 8 Parts for Violins, Hoboys, French Horns, with a Bass for the Harpsicord and Violoncello Compos'd by Sig^r Bach Jomelli Galuppi Perez Sixth Collection.

London. Printed for I. Walsh, &c.

Public Advertiser, Nov. 21, 1764.

> Fol. Parts.
> BM. g. 212. a. Bod.
> No. 1 is by Galuppi, No. 2 by Bach 'Zanaida', No. 3 by Perez, No. 4 by Ciampi, Nos. 5 and 6 by Jomelli.
> > Previously issued separately as Nos. 7–12 of favourite Opera Overtures. Nos. 675, 128, 1192, 369, 873, and 874.
> > Walsh Cat. 27: 'Perez, Jomelli, and Ciampi's 6 Overtures in 8 Parts 6th Collⁿ 12s. od.'

1159. Eleven favourite Opera Overtures for Violins, French Horns, in 8 Parts By Sig. Bach, Jomelli, Perez, Ciampi and Galuppi. Each 2s.
Printed for J. Walsh, &c.

Public Advertiser, June 5, 1764.

Fol. Parts

Separate numbers from the various collections of 'Six Favourite Overtures', &c, Nos. 1154–1158.

1160. Six Medley or Comic Overtures in Seven Parts. for Violins and Hoboys with a Bass for the Harpsicord and Violoncello Compos'd by Dr Arne, Lampe, Charke, &c.
London. Printed for I. Walsh, &c.

Public Advertiser, Nov. 11, 1763.

Fol. 7 parts.
BM. g. 100. c. RM. 26. b. 2. (17.) RAM.
Also contains Howard's Overture to 'The Amorous Goddess' and two Overtures by Prelleur.
Earlier issues under the separate composers' names. (Nos. 83, 352, 843, 902, and 1229.)

OXON AIRS

1161. Oxon Aires (for 2 Flutes and a Bass). 3s. od. N? 99.

[*c.* 1730.]

Smith 614 with Walsh only in the imprint and 'N? 99' added to the title-page.
Walsh Cat. 18.

PAGANELLI (GIUSEPPE ANTONIO)

See No. 858. Ingratitudine Punita

PAISIBLE (JAMES)

1162. Six Setts of Aires for two Flutes & a Bass Consisting of Preludes Allmands Corants Sarabands Marches Minuets Gavotts and Jiggs. Compos'd by Mr Paisible Never before Publish'd.
London: Printed for & sold by I. Walsh... N? 101.

[*c.* 1730.]

Fol. Parts.
Smith 597 (BM. h. 23.) of which this is presumably a reissue with Walsh only in the imprint and 'N? 101' added to the title-page.
Walsh Cat. 18: 'Paisible's Aires (for 2 Flutes and a Bass). 4s. od. N? 101.'
Walsh Cat. 11a: 'Paisibles Sonatas for two Flutes and a Bass. Opera seconda.'

1163. Six Sonatas of two Parts For Two Flute's Composed by Mʳ Paisible Opera Prima.
London. Printed for I. Walsh . . . Nº 70.

[*c.* 1730.]

Obl. fol. Parts.
Smith 142*b* (BM. c. 105. a.) with Walsh only in the imprint and 'Nº 70' added to the title-page.
Walsh Cat. 18: 'Paisible's Sonatas (for 2 Flutes). 3s. od. Nº 70.'
Walsh Cat. 11*a*: 'Paisibles Sonatas for two Flutes. Opera Prima.'

1164. Paisible's Sonatas for Flutes being his Posthumous.
Sold by John Walsh . . . and John and Joseph Hare, &c.

Daily Courant, April 4, 1722.

Not identified.

See also No. 1150. Overtures. A Collection of Several Excellent Overtures . . . Perform'd . . . by Mʳ Paisible, &c.

PALMA (Fɪʟɪppo)

See No. 1076. Minuets. Minuets For His Majesty's Birthday . . . 1753.

PARADIES (Pɪᴇᴛʀo Doᴍᴇɴɪᴄo)

1165. The Favourite Songs in the Opera call'd La Forza d'Amore.
London. Printed for I. Walsh, &c.

General Advertiser, Feb. 26, 1751. (In score, by Sig. Paradice.)

Fol. Passe-partout title-page. pp. 2–21.
RCM.
Pasticcio, music chiefly by Paradies, whose name appears at the top of the arias.
Randall Cat.: 'La Forza d'Amore. Paradies. 2s. 6d.'

1166. The Favourite Songs in the Opera Call'd Phaeton.
London. Printed for I. Walsh, &c.

General Advertiser, Feb. 10, 1747.

Fol. Passe-partout title-page. pp. 2–21.
BM. G. 194. (4.) RAM. RCM. Rowe.
Words by Francesco Vanneschi.
The composer's name appears at the top of the arias.
A selection was included in 'Le Delizie dell' Opere', Vol. V, pp. 185–95, 199–204.

See also No. 37. Annibale in Capua; No. 969. Love in a Village . . . Music by . . . Paradies, &c.; No. 1144. Orazio.

PASQUALI (Nicolò)

1167. XII. English Songs in Score, Collected From several Masques and other Entertainments, Composed by Nicolo Pasquali. And Printed for the Author, With His Majesty's Royal Licence and Privilege. London MDCCL.

Sold by the Author, also by John Walsh . . . and at all the other Musick Shops in Town and Country. Price 7s. 6d.

> Obl. fol. Privilege (dated 14 June 1750). pp. 1–18, blank, 20–36, blank, 38–44.
> BM. E. 527. RCM. Rowe.
> Not published by Walsh.

1168. Twelve Overtures for Violins, &c. in Parts, Price 15s.
Sold by J. Walsh, &c.

Public Advertiser, April 5, 1753.

> Not published by Walsh. An edition was printed in Edinburgh for Robert Bremner, and was presumably the work sold by Walsh.

1169. Six Solos for the Violin and Harpsichord, Price 5s.
Sold by J. Walsh, &c.

Public Advertiser, April 5, 1753.

> Not identified, may refer to a later edition of No. 1170. (This Day are published.)

1170. Sonate a Violino e Basso. Composte da Nicolò Pasquali e Dedicate All' Illustrissimo Signor Giacomo Nelthorpe. Opera Prima.
London. Printed for I. Walsh, &c.

Daily Advertiser, March 16, 1744.

> Fol. pp. 22.
> BM. g. 431. b. CUL. Tenbury.
> Randall Cat. 'Pasquali's Solos 5s. od.'

See also Nos. 789, 790. Hasse (Johann Adolph) The Comic Tunes . . . Compos'd by . . . Pasquali, &c.; No. 858. Ingratitudine Punita; Nos. 1066, 1085. Minuets. Select Minuets Second Book (Vol. IV).

PASQUALINI DE MARZI (   )

1171. Six Solos for two Violoncellos compos'd by Sig.r Pasqualino de Marzis.
London. Printed for I. Walsh, &c.

London Evening-Post, Jan. 14–16, 1748. (Six Solos, for two Violoncellos, with a Thorough Bass for the Harpsichord . . . by Sig. Pasqualino.)

> BM. g. 102. Rowe.
> Opus 1.

PASQUALINO, *Signor*
  See Pasqualini de Marzi (   )

PASQUINI (Bernardo)
  See No. 1528. Voluntaries. A Second Collection of Toccates Vollentarys and Fugues . . . Compos'd by Pasquini, &c.

PELLEGRINI (Ferdinando)
1172. Six Concertos for the Harpsicord or Organ with Accompanyments for Two Violins Tenor & Violoncello. Compos'd by Sig.ʳ Ferdinando Pellegrino of Naples. Op: Sexta.
  London. Printed for I. Walsh, &c.
  Public Advertiser, Jan. 13, 1766.

> Fol. 5 parts.
> BM. g. 640. (2.)

1173. Sei Sonate per Cembalo composte dal Sig.ʳ Ferdinando Pellegrino. Opera Seconda.
  N.B. These Sonatas or Lessons are Printed from the Author's Original Copy, Compos'd in an Easy Familiar Taste for the Improvement of Ladies and Gentlemen on the Harpsichord.
  London. Printed for I. Walsh, &c.
  Public Advertiser, July 3, 1765.

> Fol. pp. 1–4, blank, 6–12, blank, 14–17, blank, 19–26.
> BM. e. 12. (1.) RM. 16. a. 13. (2.) Rowe.

PEPUSCH (Johann Christoph)
1174. The Additional Songs in the Opera's of Thomyris & Camilla as they are Perform'd at the New Theatre Compos'd by D.ʳ Pepusch, &c.
  London Printed & Sold by I: Walsh . . . N.º 331.
  [*c.* 1730.]

> Fol. pp. 20.
> Walsh Cat. 18: 'The Additional Songs in Thomyris. 2s. 6d. N.º 331.'
> Smith 565 (BM. H. 2815. j. (1.)) with Walsh only in the imprint and 'N.º 331' added to title-page.
> Includes only one song in 'Camilla' ('Save me with Joy posess me') headed 'An additional Song set by D.ʳ Pepusch Sung by M.ʳˢ Pulman in the Opera of Camilla.'

  See also No. 1443. Thomyris; No. 184. Bononcini (Antonio Maria) Camilla

1175. Aires for 2 Flutes. 3s. od. N.º 65.

> [*c.* 1730.]
>> Walsh Cat. 18.
>> Smith 327 with Walsh only in the imprint and 'N.º 65' added to the title-page.

1176. M.ʳ Pepusch's Aires for two Violins Made on Purpose for the Improvement of Practitioners in Consort The whole Fairly Engraven and Carefully Corected. London Printed for J. Walsh . . . N.º 429.

> [*c.* 1730.]
>> Fol. pp. 24.
>> RCM. Oriel College, Oxford.
>> Smith 307 and 460 (BM. h. 59.) with Walsh only in the imprint and 'N.º 429' added to the title-page.
>> Walsh Cat. 18.

1177. Six English Cantatas Humbly Inscrib'd To the most Noble the Marchioness of Kent. Compos'd by M.ʳ I. C. Pepusch. London Printed for J. Walsh, &c.

> [*c.* 1730.]
>> Fol. Illustrated title-page. 'To the Lovers of Musick', 2 pp. pp. 31.
>> BM. G. 222. (1.) Fitz. Euing.
>> Smith 353 and 582 with Walsh only in the imprint.

1178. — With 'N.º 290' added to the title-page.

> [*c.* 1731.]
>> Walsh Cat. 18: '12 Cantatas for Voices and Instruments in two Books. 10s. od. N.º 290.'

1179. Six English Cantatas for one Voice Four for a Flute and two with a Trumpet and other Instruments. Compos'd by I: C: Pepusch. Book yᵉ Second. London Printed for J: Walsh, &c.

> [*c.* 1730.]
>> Fol. Illustrated passe-partout title-page. Dedication. pp. 46.
>> BM. G. 222. (2.) Fitz. Euing. (With 'Second Book' in MS.)
>> Smith 581 with Walsh only in the imprint.

1180. — With 'N.º 290' added to the title-page.

> [*c.* 1731.]
>> Walsh Cat. 18: '12 Cantatas for Voices and Instruments in two Books. 10s. od. N.º 290.'

1181. An Entertainment Call'd The Union of the Three Sister Arts as it is perform'd at the Theatre in Lincoln's Inn Fields for S.ᵗ Cecilia's Day 1723 Compos'd by D.ʳ Pepusch Publish'd for December price 2ˢ 6ᵈ.

London Printed for I. Walsh . . . & I^no & Ioseph Hare, &c.

[1723.]

Fol. pp. 28.

BM. G. 222. (3.) Hirsch II. 708. RAM. RCM. Bod. Manchester.

1182. — With Walsh only in the imprint and 'N° 294' added to the title-page.

[*c.* 1730.]

Euing.

Walsh Cat. 18: 'The Union, or the three Sister Arts a Mask made for St. Cæcelia's Day. 2s. 6d. N° 294.'

1183. The Excellent Choice. Being A Collection of the most favourite Old Song Tunes Set for 3 Voices in the manner of Catches. Or for two German Flutes and a Bass. By Dr Pepusch and the most Eminent English Masters.
London. Printed for I. Walsh, &c.

[*c.* 1750.]

Obl. fol. pp. 31.

Rowe.

'The Beggar's Opera' is not mentioned on the title-page as it is in No. 1184.

1184. The Excellent Choice. Being A Collection of the most favourite Old Song Tunes in the Beggars Opera Set for 3 Voices in the manner of Catches. Or for two German Flutes and a Bass. By Dr Pepusch and the most Eminent English Masters.
London. Printed for I. Walsh, &c.

Whitehall Evening-Post, June 24–26, 1755.

Obl. fol. pp. 31.

BM. D. 270. (1.) RM. 8. e. 11. (7.) RAM. Bod. CUL. Dublin. Mitchell. Rowe.

Public Advertiser, Jan. 11, 1760. (The Beggars Opera Songs for Voices or two German Flutes and a Bass. Price 5^s. J. Walsh. Of whom may be had.)

Randall Cat.: 'Beggar's Opera for two Voices, called The Excellent Choice.'

Perseus and Andromeda

See Nos. 1197–1200. Perseus and Andromeda

Rules for a Thorough Bass with a Dictionary of Italian Words us'd in Musick.

Walsh Cat. 18.: Under Dr Pepuseh's Works.

See No. 1299. Rules

1185. 12 Solos for a Flute and a Bass in two Books. 8s. od. N° 110.

[*c.* 1730.]

Walsh Cat. 18.

The notice refers to the two works Smith 232 and 335, with probably Walsh only in the imprints and 'N⁰ 110' added to the title-pages. The title of the first is 'Six Sonatas or Solos for the Flute with a Through Bass for the Harpsicord.' (Rowe. Fol. 2 parts.) The second is 'A Second Set of Solos for the Flute. with A Thorough Bass for the Bassoon, Bass-Flute or Harpsicord.' (BM. h. 250 c. (2.) Large fol. 2 parts.)

1186. XXIV Solos for a Violin with a Through Bass for the Harpsicord or Bass Violin Compos'd by Signʳ Pepusch.
London Printed for I. Walsh... N⁰ 458.

[*c.* 1730.]

Obl. fol. pp. 35.
Smith 264*a* (BM. e. 15. b. With an inner title-page 'Solos for a Violin with a Through Bass for the Harpsicord or Bass Violin Compos'd by Signʳ Pepusch.) with Walsh only in the imprint and 'N⁰ 458' added to the title-page.
Walsh Cat. 18: '24 Solos for a Violin and a Bass. 10s. od. N⁰ 458.'

1187. The Songs and Symphony's in the Masque of Venus & Adonis as they are Perform'd at the Theatre Royal Compos'd by Dʳ Pepusch. Fairly Engraven and Carefully Corected by the Author.
London Printed for J. Walsh, ... N⁰ 320.

[*c.* 1730.]

Fol. 'A Table of the Songs', &c. ff. 41.
Smith 492 (BM. G. 222. (4.) with Walsh only in the imprint and 'N⁰ 320' added to the title-page.
Walsh Cat. 18: 'A Mask of Venus and Adonis. 5s. od. N⁰ 320.'

See also No. 326. Castrucci (Pietro) Concerti Grossi . . . Opera Terza. (Revis'd and Recommended by Dr. Pepusch.); No. 402. Corelli (Arcangelo) The Score of the Four Operas . . . Revis'd . . . by Dr. Pepusch. Vol. I. The Score of the Twelve Concertos . . . Revis'd . . . by Dr. Pepusch. Vol. II; No. 753. Harmonia Mundi . . . Mʳ Pepusch . . . the first Collection, &c.; No. 893. The Lady's Banquet Fifth Book; No. 1392. Six Solos by several Authors; No. 1443. Thomyris; No. 1465. Treatise. A Treatise on Harmony, &c.

PEREZ (Davidde)

1188. The Favourite Songs in the Opera Call'd La Didone Abbandonata By Sigʳ Perez.
London. Printed for I. Walsh, &c.

Public Advertiser, April 18, 1761.

Fol. Passe-partout title-page. pp. 20.
BM. H. 325. RM. 13. c. 20. (10.) London University. DAM. Rowe.
Contains some songs by B. Galuppi.
Republished in 'Le Delizie dell' Opere', Vol. XI, pp. 171–90.

1189. The Favourite Songs in the Opera Call'd Ezio By Sig^r Perez.
London. Printed for I. Walsh, &c.

London Evening-Post, May 15–17, 1755.

> Fol. Passe-partout title-page. pp. 20.
> BM. H. 325. a.

1190. The Favourite Songs in the Opera Call'd Ezio By Sig^r Perez. 2^d [With 'Arie nel Penelope by Hasse.']
London. Printed for I. Walsh, &c.

Public Advertiser, May 27, 1755. (A Second Set of Songs in the Opera of Ezio, by Sig. Perez. With Two favourite Songs of Signora Mingotti in Penelope. Not printed before.)

> Fol. Passe-partout title-page. pp. 20. (Arie nel Penelope by Hasse, pp. 14–20.)
> RM. 13. c. 21. (4, 5.) RAM.
> '2^d' is in MS.
> Both sets republished in 'Le Delizie dell' Opere', Vol. VII, pp. 1–40.

1191. Ezio by Perez 2^d Colln.

[*c.* 1755.]

> Fol. pp. 13.
> BM. H. 325. a.
> The title is in MS. and without an imprint.

1192. No. IX, a favourite Overture for Violins, and French Horns: By Sig. Perez. Price 2s.
Printed for J. Walsh, &c.

Public Advertiser, March 1, 1764.

> Fol. Parts.
> Subsequently issued in a collection as No. 3 of 'Six Overtures in 8 Parts . . . Compos'd by Sig^r Bach Jomelli Galuppi Perez Sixth Collection.' (BM. g. 212. a. 1764.) (*See* No. 1158.)
> Other numbers in this series are under J. C. Bach, B. Galuppi, L. V. Ciampi, and N. Jomelli.

See also No. 60. Arminio; No. 105. Attalo; Nos. 565, 566. Delizie dell' Opere.
Vols. X, XI; No. 1158. 'Six Overtures in 8 Parts . . . Sixth Collection'; No. 1388.
Solimano; No. 1526. Vologeso.

PEREZ (Davidde) and **COCCHI** (Gioacchino)
1193. The Favourite Songs in the Opera Call'd Farnace.
London. Printed for I. Walsh, &c.

Public Advertiser, May 19, 1759.

Fol. Passe-partout title-page. pp. 23.
BM. G. 204. RM. 13. c. 21. (7.) RCM. DAM. Rowe.
The composers' names appear inside the work.
Republished in 'Le Delizie dell' Opere', Vol. IX, pp. 25–47.

PERGOLESI (GIOVANNI BATTISTA)

1194. The Celebrated Salve Regina. Compos'd by Sig^r Pergolesi.
London Printed for & sould by I: Walsh, &c.

Public Advertiser, May 2, 1765.

Fol. Illustrated passe-partout title-page, Collins frame. pp. 13.
BM. H. 1102. i. RCM. Bod. CUL. Liverpool University. OUF.
May have been published before 1765.

1195. Stabat Mater. Compos'd by Sig^r Pergolesi.
London Printed for & sould by I: Walsh, &c.

General Advertiser, May 8, 1749. (Just published.)

Fol. Illustrated passe-partout title-page, Collins frame, pp. 2–26.
Hirsch M. 1445. RAM. Cardiff. Euing. Rowe, and others BUC.
First published in 'Le Delizie dell' Opere', Vol. V, pp. 2–26. (Nov. 22, 1748.)
Later published with 'The Songs in Messiah'. (*See* Smith, 'Handel, A Descriptive Catalogue', &c. p. 120. No. 5, p. 121. No. 11.)

1196. An Ode of Mr. Pope's Adapted to the Principal Airs of the Hymn Stabat Mater. Compos'd by Signor Pergolesi.
London. Printed for I. Walsh, &c.

Public Advertiser, Dec. 24, 1761. (Pope's Ode intitled The Dying Christian to his Soul, &c.)

Fol. pp. 2–26.
BM. G. 285. a. (1.) Manchester. Rowe (2).
Full score of 'Vital spark of heav'nly flame'.

See also Nos. 556, 559–66. Delizie dell' Opere. Vols. I, IV–XI; No. 813. Hasse (Johann Adolph) Number VIII. A Favourite Collection of Canzonets or Duets, &c.; No. 833. Hasse (Johann Adolph) No. III. Venetian Ballads; No. 858. Ingratitudine Punita; No. 1009. Meraspe; No. 1138. Olimpiade.

PERSEUS AND ANDROMEDA

1197. The Tunes, Aires and Dances in the Entertainment, call'd Perseus and Andromeda. As they are perform'd at the Theatre Royal in Lincoln's Inn-Fields. The Tunes Proper for the Violin or German Flute, and several of them within the Compass of the Common Flute. Price 6d.
Printed for and sold by John Walsh . . . and Jos. Hare, &c.

Daily Post, April 18, 1730.

1198. — With Walsh only in the imprint and 'N̪ 139' added to the title-page. [*c.* 1730.]

> Walsh Cat. 18: 'Perseus and Andromeda as Perform'd at the New House (for a single Violin). 6d. N̪ 139.'
> Presumably the work for which J. C. Pepusch arranged the music in 1717, with the title of 'The Shipwreck; or Perseus and Andromeda', and which was revived for Lewis Theobald's production in 1730.

1199. Perseus and Andromeda (for a Single Flute). 6d. N̪ 48. [*c.* 1730.]

> Walsh Cat. 18.
> Not identified. May refer to a flute edition of No. 1198.

1200. The Comic Tunes in the Entertainments of Perseus & Andromeda and the Rape of Proserpine as Perform'd at the Theatre Royal in Covent-Garden. For the Harpsicord, German Flute, Violin, or Guitar. Price 1ˢ 6ᵈ

London. Printed for J. Walsh, &c. [*c.* 1740.]

> 8°. pp. 16.
> Mitchell.
> 'Perseus and Andromeda' is by J. C. Pepusch and 'The Rape of Proserpine' by J. E. Galliard.

The Tunes, Airs and Dances in the New Entertainment call'd Perseus and Andromeda. *See* No. 1282. Roger (   )

PESCATRICI

1201. The Favourite Songs in the Opera Call'd Le Pescatrici.
London. Printed for I. Walsh, &c.

Public Advertiser, May 19, 1761.

> Fol. Passe-partout title-page. pp. 5–19, 2–4.
> BM. G. 808. c. (25.) DAM. Mitchell. Pendlebury. Rowe.
> Pasticcio. Burney. BUC and Grove attribute to F. G. Bertoni.
> Republished in 'Le Delizie dell' Opere', Vol. X, pp. 33–50.

PESCETTI (GIOVANNI BATTISTA)

1202. The Favourite Songs in the Opera call'd Angelica & Medoro. Compos'd by Sigʳ. Pescetti.
London Printed for and sold by I. Walsh, &c.

London Daily Post, and General Advertiser, April 4, 1739.

> Fol. Passe-partout title-page. pp. 2–17.
> BM. G. 216.

La Conquista del Vello d' Oro. [Two Songs from 'Vello d' Oro'. 'Nacqui agli affanni'.—'Spera fors anche'.]

> *See* No. 557. Delizie dell'Opere. Vol. II, pp. 72–73, 86–87.

1203. The Favourite Songs in the Opera Call'd Demetrius. Compos'd by Sig.ʳ Pescetti.

London. Printed for and Sold by I. Walsh, &c.

Country Journal: or, The Craftsman, April 23, 1737. (Just publish'd.)

> Fol. Passe-partout title-page. pp. 2–20.
> BM. G. 193. (2.) RCM. Manchester.
> Republished in 'Le Delizie dell' Opere', Vol. II, pp. 49–70.

1204. The Favourite Songs in Diana and Endymion, by Sig. Pescetti. Price 2s. 6d. Printed for John Walsh, &c.

London Daily Post, and General Advertiser, Jan. 15, 1740. (Just publish'd.)

> Fol. pp. 2–10.
> Republished in 'Le Delizie dell' Opere', Vol. II, pp. 15–23.

1205. Ten Suits of Lessons, &c. for the Harpsichord compos'd by Sig. Gio. Battista Pescetti.

Printed for the Author: And sold by J. Walsh, &c.

Daily Advertiser, Nov. 28, 1743.

> This probably refers to 'Sonate per Gravicembalo . . . Londra nel MDCCXXXIX'. (BM. e. 493. Fol. pp. 59.) This work was printed for the Author, and sold by Walsh, who may have issued an edition with title as above. 'Pescetti's Lessons. 10.ˢ 6.ᵈ' advertised in catalogues of Walsh (Nos. 24a, 25) and in Randall's catalogue.

> *See also* No. 11 . Airs. Select Aires or Duets for two German Flutes . . . By . . . Pescetti . . . 2d Book; No. 32. Alessandro in Persia; Nos. 556, 559–66 Delizie dell' Opere. Vols. I, IV–XI; Nos. 772–85. Hasse (Johann Adolph) [Chamber Airs.]; No. 1014. Merode. The Favourite Songs in the Opera[s] call'd Merode & Olimpia; No. 1061. Minuets. Select Minuets, &c.; No. 1129. Nerone.

PEZ (JOHANN CHRISTOPH)

1206. Sonate da Camera or Chamber Musick Consisting of Several Sutes of Overtures and Aires for two Flutes and a Bass Compos'd by Sig.ʳ Christopher Pez Parté Prima.

London Printed for I. Walsh . . . N.º 88.

[*c.* 1730.]

> Obl. fol. 3 parts.
> Smith 231 (BM. d. 150. (4).) with Walsh only in the imprint and 'N.º 88' added to the title-page, and issued with the second collection.
> Walsh Cat. 18: '12 Sonatas for 2 Flutes and a Bass. 6s. od. N.º 88.'

1207. A Second Collection of Sonatas for two Flutes and a Bass, by Sig.ʳ Christopher Pez, to which is added Some Excellent Solo's out of the First Part of Corelli's

Fifth Opera; Artfully transpos'd and fitted to a Flute and a Bass, yet Continu'd in the same Key they were Compos'd in; the whole fairly Engraven.
London. Printed for I. Walsh . . . N⁰ 88.

[*c.* 1730.]

> Obl. fol. 3 parts.
> Smith 242 (BM. c. 105. i. (2.) Rowe.) with Walsh only in the imprint and 'N⁰ 88' added to the title-page, and reissued with the first collection.
> Walsh Cat. 18: '12 Sonatas for 2 Flutes and a Bass. 6s. od. N⁰ 88.'

1208. XII Sonatas of three Parts for two Violins & a Bass with a Thrō Bass for yᵉ Organ Harpsicord or Archlute Compos'd by Joanne Christopher Pez Opera Prima Duplex Genius, &c.
London Printed for J. Walsh . . . N⁰ 459.

[*c.* 1730.]

> Fol. 3 parts.
> Smith 420 with Walsh only in the imprint and 'N⁰ 459' added to the title-page.
> Walsh Cat. 18: '12 Sonatas for 2 Violins and a Bass Op: Prima. 8s. od. N⁰ 459.'
> Twelve Sonatas for Violins in four parts, Walsh Cat. 11*a*, presumably refers to the same work.

See also No. 753. Harmonia Mundi . . . Signʳ Pez . . . the first Collection

PHAETON

The Favourite Songs in the Opera Call'd Phaeton.

See No. 1166. Paradies (Pietro Domenico)

PHARNACES

The favourite Songs in the Opera call'd Pharnaces.

See No. 209. Bononcini (Giovanni) [Farnace.]

PICCINI (NICOLO)

See No. 1419. Summer's Tale.

PIETRO

See CASTRUCCI (PIETRO)

PIRRO E DEMETRIO

1209. Songs In The New Opera, Call'd Pyrrhus and Demetrius, &c. [Words translated from the Italian of Adriano Morselli by Owen Mac Swiney. Music by Alessandro Scarlatti and N. F. Haym.]

Sold by I: Walsh ... No 219.

[*c.* 1730.]

Fol. ff. 57. Printed on one side only.

Smith 293 (BM. H. 109.) with Walsh only in the imprint and No 219 added to the title-page.

1210. The Symphonys or Instrumental Parts in the Opera Call'd Pyrrhus and Demetrius, &c.

London Printed for I. Walsh, &c.

[*c.* 1730.]

Fol. Parts. 2 ff. not foliated. Printed on one side only.

Walsh Cat. 18: 'The Opera of Pyrrhus. 9s. od. No 219. (With Symphonys for 2 Viol^s & Bass.)'

Smith 293, 294, and 345 (BM. H. 109, BM. h. 17. a. (2.) and Rowe), with Walsh only in the imprint and 'No 219' added to the title-page. (*See* No. 1209.)

1211. The Most Celebrated Aires & Duets In the Opera of Pyrrhus: Curiously Fitted and Contriv'd for two Flutes: With their Symphonys introduc'd in a Compleat man.^{r} The whole fairly Engraven. Note, most of these being here Printed in the same Keys they were Perform'd in at the Theatre, renders them as well proper for two Violins, being very spritely & agreeable to the Instruments.

Printed for J. Walsh ... No 66.

[*c.* 1730.]

Fol. Passe-partout title-page, with 'In the Opera of Pyrrhus' from a supplementary plate. ff. 12. Printed on one side only.

Smith 325 (Rowe) with Walsh only in the imprint and 'No 66' added to the title-page.

Walsh Cat. 18: 'Pyrrhus Airs (for 2 Flutes). 3s. od. No 66.'

Music by Alessandro Scarlatti, with additions by Nicolò Francesco Haym.

1212. Phyrrus and Clotilda Aires (for a Single Flute). 2s. od.

[*c.* 1730.]

Walsh Cat. 18.

Smith 338 and 339 and assumed to refer to separate issues of each work, which probably consisted of the First Flute parts of the editions for Two Flutes, with new tite-pages, with Walsh only in the imprints. (*See* Nos. 1211 and 385.)

1213. Overtures in Pyrrhus, &c. for two Flutes. 2^s o^d

[*c.* 1721.]

Walsh Cat. 9*b*.

1214. Overtures in Pyrrhus (for 2 Flutes). 2s. od. No 77.

[*c.* 1730.]

Walsh Cat. 18.

Nos. 1213 and 1214 may be later issues of Smith 295 with Walsn only in the imprint and 'No 77' added to the title-page: 'Choice Italian and English Musick for Two Flutes', &c. (B.M. a. 209. a. (9.))

PIXELL (JOHN)

1215. A Collection of Songs, with their Recitatives and Symphonies, for the German Flute, Violins, *etc.* with a Thorough Bass for the Harpsichord. Set to Musick by Mr Pixell. To which is added a Chorus for Voices and Instruments.

Birmingham. Printed for the Author, and sold by *Mess.* Walsh and Johnson. London. (Engrav'd and Printed by M. Broome in Birmingham 1759.)

> Fol. 'Subscribers Names', 3pp. pp. 41.
> BM. G. 298. RCM. Birmingham Public Library. BUL. CUL. Rowe. Tenbury.

PLAYFORD (HENRY)

> *See* No. 757. Harmonica Sacra

POGLIETTI (ALESSANDRO)

> *See* No. 1528. Voluntaries. A Second Collection of Toccates Vollentarys and Fugues . . . Compos'd by Polietti, &c.

POLAROLI (CARLO FRANCESCO)

> *See* No. 1527. Voluntaries. Voluntarys & Fugues . . . by . . . Pollaroli, &c.

POLIETTI ( )

> *See* Poglietti (Alessandro)

POLLAROLI

> *See* Polaroli (Carlo Francesco)

POLLY

1216. The Tunes to the Songs in Polly an Opera Being the Second Part of the Beggar's Opera Transpos'd for the Flute Done from the original Songs; which Songs may be had where these are Sold.

London Printed and sold at the Musick-shops Price 1s

Country Journal: or, The Craftsman, July 5, 1729. (Music for the Flute in Polly's Opera. Printed for and sold by John Walsh . . . and Joseph Hare.)

> 8°. pp. 36.
> BM. a. 19. b.; A. 869. a. (5.) (Wanting title-page.)

1217. — With Walsh in the imprint and 'No 50' added to the title-page.

> [*c.* 1730.]

> Walsh Cat. 18: 'Polly's Opera. 1s. 0d. No 50.'

PORPORA (Nicolò Antonio)

Aeneas.

See infra [Enea nel Lazio.]

1218. The Favourite Songs in the Opera call'd Ariadne by Sig.ʳ Porpora. N.º II. 509.
Note. where these are Sold may be had all M.ʳ Handel's Operas and Instrumental
Musick.
London Printed for & Sold by I: Walsh . . . N.º 285.

London Evening-Post, Feb. 21–23, 1734.

> Fol. Passe-partout title-page with 'Ariadne by Sig.ʳ Porpora. N.º II. 509' from a supple-
> mentary plate. pp. 22–37.
> BM. G. 193. (4.) ('N.º II.' has been deleted in ink on this copy.) RCM. Coke. Hall. NLS.
> The pagination continues from Porpora's 'Arbaces' 2–19. (No. 44.)
> Words by Paolo Antonio Rolli.
> Republished in 'Le Delizie dell' Opere', Vol. II, pp. 192–208.

1219. Twelve Cantatas for a Voice, a Violin, and Harpsichord. Compos'd by
Nicolo Porpora. Price 1£. 1s. Dedicated to his Royal Highness the Prince of Wales.
Printed for the Author: And sold by J. Walsh, &c.

General Advertiser, Jan. 7, 1745. (This Day are publish'd.)

> This appears to be a reissue of 'All' Altezza Reale di Frederico Principe Reale di Vallia . . .
> Queste nuovamenti Composte Opre di Musica vocale . . . dedica . . . Nicolò Porpora.
> Londra nel MDCCXXXV.' (BM. D. 359. pp. 82. Obl. fol. Others in BUC.)

[Enea nel Lazio. Two Songs from 'Aeneas'. 'Grazie a te'.—'Consolata par ch'io'.]

See No. 557. Delizie dell' Opere. Vol. II, pp. 119, 171–3.

1220. The Favourite Songs in the Opera call'd Polypheme by Sig.ʳ Porpora. Note.
where these are Sold may be had all M.ʳ Handel's Operas and Instrumental Musick.
London. Printed for and Sold by I: Walsh . . . N.º 285.

London Evening-Post, March 13 to 15, 1735.

> Fol. Passe-partout title-page. pp. 20.
> RCM. XXXII. B. 9 (4.)
> Walsh Cat. 18: 'Songs in Polpheme by Sig.ʳ Porpora. 2s. 6d. N.º 538.'
> Words by Paolo Antonio Rolli.

1221. The Favourite Songs in the Opera call'd Polypheme by Sig.ʳ Porpora.
London Printed for and sold by I. Walsh, &c.

[*c.* 1740.]

> Fol. Passe-partout title-page. pp. 20 (bottom pagination).
> BM. G. 193. (3.)
> With additional top pagination 164–70, 184–6, 174–83 from 'Le Delizie dell' Opere'
> Vol. II.

1222. Six Sonatas for two Violins with a Thorough Bass for the Harpsicord or Violoncello Compos'd by Sig.ʳ Nicolo Porpora Opera 2.ᵈᵃ
London. Printed for I. Walsh, &c.

Public Advertiser, Sept. 13, 1753.

> Fol. 3 parts.
> BM. g. 1037. RAM. RCM.
> This work was originally issued as 'Sinfonie da Camera a Tre Istromenti Opra II. Sculp. da B. Fortier. Londra. MDCCXXXVI'. (BM. i. 76.)

1223. Six Sonatas for two Violoncellos or Violins, by Sig. Porpora.
Printed for J. Walsh, &c.

General Evening Post (London), April 6–9, 1745.

> Not identified. May refer to the work by N. A. Porpora and G. B. Costanza. No. 1226.

1224. — Another edition or re-advertisement.

General Advertiser, Nov. 28, 1747. (Just publish'd. Porpora's Sonatas, for two Violoncellos.)

1225. The Favourite Songs in the Opera Call'd Temistocle. By Sig.ʳ Porpora.
London Printed for I. Walsh, &c.

Daily Advertiser; London Daily Post, and General Advertiser, March 12, 1743.

> Fol. Passe-partout title-page. pp. 2–20, 17 and 18 printed on one side only.
> BM. G. 190. (5.) Pembroke (Cambridge). Rowe.
> Words by Apostolo Zeno.
> A selection was included in 'Le Delizie dell' Opere', Vol. IV, pp. 165–80.

> *See also* No. 44. Arbaces; Nos. 555, 557, 559–66. Delizie dell' Opere. Vols. I, II, IV–XI; Nos. 598, 599. Elisa; Nos. 771, 772. Hasse (Johann Adolph) [Chamber Airs.]; No. 1145. Orfeo; No. 1151. Overtures. Six Overtures in Seven Parts ... Compos'd by ... Porpora.

PORPORA (Nicolò Antonio) and COSTANZA (Giovanni Battista)

1226. Six Sonatas for two Violoncellos and two Violins with a Thorough Bass for the Harpsicord Compos'd By Sig.ʳ Nicolo Porpora and Sig.ʳ Gio. Batta Costanza.
London. Printed for I. Walsh, &c.

Daily Advertiser, Jan. 24, 1745.

> Fol. Parts.
> BM. g. 222. b. (3.) (Wanting the 2nd Violin and 2nd Violoncello parts.) RAM (2).
> *See also* No. 1223.

PORTA (Giovanni)

1227. Songs in the New Opera call'd Numitor as they are Perform'd at the Kings Theatre For the Royal Accademy Compos'd by Sig.ʳ Porta.
London: Printed for & sold by I. Walsh ... N.º 233.

[*c.* 1730.]

Fol. pp. 65.
Smith 588 (BM. H. 297.) with Walsh only in the imprint and 'N.º 233' added to the title-page.
Walsh Cat. 18: 'Opera of Numitor. 9s. od. N.º 233.'

1228. The Aires and Song Tunes With their Symphonys in the Opera of Numitor for a single Flute. Price 1.ˢ 6.ᵈ, &c.
London: Printed for & sold by I: Walsh ... N.º 25.

[*c.* 1730.]
Obl. 8°. ff. 26.
Smith 591 (BM. a. 209. a. (5.)) with Walsh only in the imprint and 'N.º 25' added to the title-page.
Walsh Cat. 18: 'Opera of Numitor for the Flute. 1s. 6d. N.º 25.'

POTENZA (Pasquale)

See No. 105. Attalo; No. 522. Creso; No. 1419. Summer's Tale.

PRELLEUR (Pierre)

1229. Medley Overture in 4 Parts.
Printed for and sold by John Walsh, &c.

Country Journal: or, The Craftsman, Dec. 25, 1736. (Medley Overtures by Arne, Lampe, Charke and Prelure, in Four Parts—Just published.)

Fol. Parts.
Subsequently issued in a collection, 'Six Medley or Comic Overtures', 1763. (BM. g. 100. c.) (*See* No. 1160. Overtures, which includes two by Prelleur.)

PRELUDES

1230. Select Preludes and Vollentarys for the Flute being made & Contriv'd for yᵉ Improvement of yᵉ Hand with Variety of Compositions by all the Eminent Masters in Europe.
London Printed for I. Walsh ... N.º 16.

[*c.* 1730.]
Large fol. ff. 16
Smith 283 (BM. h. 250. g.) with Walsh only in the imprint and 'N.º 16' added to the title-page.
Walsh Cat. 18: 'Preludes and Cibells by the Greatest Masters (Single Flute). 2s. 6d. N.º 16.'

1231. Select Preludes & Vollentarys for the Violin being Made and Contrived for the Improvement of the Hand with Variety of Compositions by all the Greatest Masters in Europe for that Instrument.
> Printed for I. Walsh ... Nº 149.

[*c.* 1730.]

>> Obl. 4º. With an outer illustrated title-page, Smith Ill. 14. 'A Table of the Preludes', &c.
>> ff. 35.
>> Smith 166 (NLS. Glen 102.) with Walsh only in the imprint and 'Nº 149' added to the title-page.
>> Walsh Cat. 18: 'Select Preludes by all Masters (for a single Violin). 2s. 6d. Nº 149.'

PROTEUS

1232. The Comic Tunes and Songs in the Entertainment Call'd Proteus, or Harlequin in China as they are Perform'd at the Theatre Royal in Drury Lane. For the Harpsicord, Violin &c.
> London. Printed for I. Walsh, &c.

Public Advertiser, Feb. 6, 1755.

>> Obl. fol. pp. 2–13, and 3 songs on 2 folio sheets without pagination.
>> BM. D. 282. (3.)
>> Words by H. Woodward.
>> Randall Cat.: 'Proteus or Harlequin in China (For a German Flute, Violin or Harpsichord). 2s. od.'

PSALMS

1233. A Collection of Melodies for the Psalms of David, According to the version of Christopher Smart, A. M. By the most Eminent Composers of Church Music.
> London. Printed for I. Walsh, &c.

Public Advertiser, Oct. 23, 1765; Oct. 29, 1765. (By Dr Boyce and the most eminent Composers of Church Musick.)

>> 4º. 'A Table of all the different Measures'. pp. 1–12, blank, 14–30.
>> BM. E. 485. RM. 8. k. 9. Bod. Liverpool University. NLS.
>> The composers named in this collection are W. Boyce, S. Howard, J. Stanley, J. Baildon, S. Long, B. Cooke, J. Nares, Dr. Randall, E. Ayrton, T. Wood, J. Bennett, and G. Berg.
>> Randall Cat.: 'Smart's Psalms. 3s. od.'

PULLI (Pietro)

> *See* No. 394. Commedia in Commedia. (Includes a song by Pietro Pulli in Orazio.)

PURCELL (Daniel)

1234. The Iudgment of Paris. A Pastoral Composed for the Music Prize by Mr D: Purcell.

London Printed for I. Walsh . . . Nº 328.

[*c.* 1730.]

Large fol. Dedication. pp. 82.
Smith 89 (BM. I. 325.) with Walsh only in the imprint and 'Nº 328' added to the title-page.
Walsh Cat. 18: 'The Judgement of Paris. 7s. od. Nº 328.'
Nº 328 was also used for J. Eccles's 'Judgment of Paris'.

1235. The Psalms Set full for the Organ or Harpsicord as they are Plaid in Churches and Chappels in the mañer given out; as also with their Interludes of great Variety by Mr Danl Purcell. late Organist of St Andrew's Holbourn. 1s 6d Note there are New Editions of severall Curious Pieces for the Organ, Harpsicord and Spinnet which may be had where these are Sold.

London Printed for I: Walsh . . . Nº 178.

[*c.* 1730.]

Obl. fol. pp. 15 (with verso of p. 9 blank).
BM. c. 20. RCM. Euing. Mitchell. Rowe.
The work has a frontispiece of a figure playing the organ, with an imprint 'Musick for the Organ and Harpsicord, Printed for I: Walsh and I: Hare.' (Smith Ill. 25.)
Smith 539, with Walsh only in the imprint and 'Nº 178' added to the title-page.
Walsh Cat. 18: 'Psalms with their Interludes for the Organ. 1s. 6d. Nº 178.'

1236. Solos for a Flute and a Bass. 3s. od. Nº 125.

[*c.* 1730.]

Walsh Cats. 18 and 15*b*.
Not identified.

1237. Purcels Solos for a Violin and a Bass.

[*c.* 1725.]

Walsh Cat. 11*a*.

See No. 1238.

1238. Six Solos for a Violin and a Bass. 4s. od. Nº 399.

[*c.* 1730.]

Walsh Cat. 18.
Presumably No. 1237 with 'Nº 399' added to the title-page.)

1239. Six Sonatas three For two Flutes & a Bass, and three Solos for a Flute and a Bass, Compos'd by Mr Dan: Purcell. The whole Fairly Engraven & Carefully Corected by ye Author.

London, Printed for J: Walsh . . . Nº 72.

[*c.* 1730.]

Large fol. 3 parts.
Smith 377 (BM. h. 250. c. (3.) with Walsh only in the imprint and 'N? 72' added to the title-page.
Walsh Cat. 18: 'Six Sonatas 3 for 2 Flutes and 3 for a Flute and a Bass. 3s. od. N? 72.' (Without any composer's name.)

1240. Purcells Sonatas (for 2 Flutes & a Bass). 4s. od.

[*c.* 1721 or earlier.]

> Walsh Cats. 9*b* and 11*a*.
> *See* No. 1241.

1241. Sonatas for 2 Flutes and a Bass. 4s. od. N? 79.

[*c.* 1730.]

> Walsh Cat. 18.
> Presumably No. 1240 with 'N? 79' added to the title-page.

1242. Seven Sets of Tunes for 2 Violins and a Bass made for several Plays. 10s. 6d.

[*c.* 1730.]

> Walsh Cat. 18.
> Presumably a collection of tunes previously issued separately for various plays. (*See* Smith, Nos. 47, 81, 97, &c.)

See also No. 625. Finger (Gottfried) and Purcell (Daniel) Six Sonatas or Solos for the Flute with a Through Bass for the Harpsichord, &c.; No. 626. Finger's and Purcels Solos (for a Violin & a Bass); No. 749. Harmonia Anglicana. Book II.

PURCELL (Henry)

1243. Four Sets of Aires for 2 Violins & a Bass. 8s. od. N? 464.

[*c.* 1730.]

> Fol. Parts.
> Walsh Cat. 18.
> Presumably refers to copies of 'Sonnata's of III. Parts' published by: 'I Playford and I. Carr for the Author . . . 1683' (BM. K. 4. g. 10.) which Walsh advertised and sold as early as 1707. (*See* Smith, No. 248.)
> No Walsh edition traced
> Walsh Cats. 9*b* and 11*a*.

1243a. Two Books of Celebrated Catches. 5s. od. N? 298. (Hen? Purcell's Works.)

> Walsh Cat. 18, p. 12; p. 27: '2 Books of Catches. 5s. od. N? 297.'
> *See also* Nos. 339, 340. Catch Club.

1244. Opera of Dioclesian. 10s. 0d. № 246.

> [*c.* 1730.]
>
>> Fol. pp. 173.
>> Walsh Cat. 18.
>> Presumably refers to copies of 'The Vocal and Instrumental Musick of the Prophetess' (BM. K. 4, i. 21) previously issued by J. Heptinstall for the Author (1691) and afterwards taken over by Walsh and advertised by him from 1707 onwards. (*See* Smith, No. 248.)
>> No Walsh edition traced.
>> Walsh Cats. 9*b* and 11*a*.

1245. Harmonia Sacra or Select Anthems in Score for one, two and three Voices. Compos'd by the late M̲r̲ Henry Purcell.

> London. Printed for I. Walsh, &c.
>
> [*c.* 1730.]
>
>> Fol. pp. 34.
>> BM. H. 101. a. Add. MSS. 17 818. Gresham. RCM. Fitz. OUF. Others in BUC not examined.

1246. — Reissue or re-advertisement.

> *Public Advertiser*, Dec. 24, 1761.

1247. Lessons for the Harpsicord. 3s. 0d. № 180.

> [*c.* 1730.]
>
>> Obl. 4°. pp. 61.
>> Smith 499 with Walsh only in the imprint and 'N⁰ 180' added to the title-page.
>> Walsh Cat. 18.
>> May refer to copies of 'A Choice Collection of Lessons for the Harpsichord', &c. published by Frances Purcell, 1696, &c. (BM. K. 1. c. 5.)
>> Walsh Cats. 9*b* and 11*a*.

1248. M̲r̲ Hen̲r̲ Purcell's Favourite Songs out of his most celebrated Orpheus Brittanicus and the rest of his Works the whole fairly Engraven and carefully corrected.

> London Printed for & sold by In⁰ Walsh . . . and In⁰ & Ioseph Hare, &c.
>
> [*c.* 1724.]
>
>> Fol. 'A Catalogue [Index] of M̲r̲ Henry Purcells Songs.' pp. 2–62. Some printed on one side only.
>> BM. G. 102. a. (1.) RAM. Manchester. Oriel College, Oxford.
>> Walsh Cat. 11*a*.: 'A Choice Collection of his Celebrated Songs.'

1249. — With Walsh only in the imprint and 'N⁰ 295' added to the title-page.

> [*c.* 1730.]
>
>> Walsh Cat. 18: 'A Choice Collection of Favourite Songs Collected from Orpheus Brittanicus. 6s. 0d. N⁰ 295.'
>> Walsh Cat. 17*a*.: 'Purcell's Songs. Just Publish'd.'

1250. Orpheus Brittanicus, being a Collection of all his Songs. £2. 2s. od.

    [*c.* 1730.]

> Fol.
> Walsh Cat. 18.
> Presumably refers to copies of 'Orpheus Britannicus' issued by J. Heptinstall for H. Playford and others. (BM. G. 100, G. 101, G. 110. a.) which Walsh advertised and sold. (*See* Smith, No. 248 and No. 258.)

1251. Orpheus Britannicus. A Collection of Choice Songs for One, Two, and Three Voices with a Through Bass for the Harpsicord Compos'd By Mr Henry Purcell.

    London. Printed for I. Walsh, &c.

Daily Advertiser, Jan. 31, 1745. (Just publish'd ... Henry Purcell's Songs, Duets, and Diallogues, call'd Orpheus Britannicus. Price bound 10s. 6d.)

> Fol.
> BM. G. 102. RCM. CUL. Mitchell. OUF. Others in BUC not examined.
> This work is merely a collection of single sheet songs engraved at different periods about the beginning of the 18th century.

1252. — Third edition.

    [*c.* 1747.]

> Walsh Cat. 24*a*.: 'Purcell's Orpheus Brittannicus. 3d Edition. 10s. od.

1253. Ten Sonatas for 2 Violins and a Bass. 6s. od. Nº 465.

    [*c.* 1730.]

> Fol. Parts.
> Walsh Cat. 18.
> Presumably refers to copies of 'Ten Sonatas in Four Parts' published by Frances Purcell, 1697 (BM. K. 4. i. 10. (2.)) which Walsh advertised and sold as early as 1707. (*See* Smith, No. 248.)
> Walsh Cats. 9*a* and 11*a*.

1254. The Te Deum and Jubilate, for Voices and Instruments, to be perform'd To-morrow, the 13th instant, before the Gentlemen, Sons of the Clergy, at the Cathedral Church of St. Paul; composed by the late Mr. Henry Purcell.

    Sold by John Walsh ... and John and Joseph Hare, &c.

Daily Courant, Dec. 12, 1722.

> Fol. pp. 48.
> Presumably refers to Smith No. 595.

1255. The Te Deum et Jubilate, for Voices and Instruments. Perform'd before the Sons of the Clergy at the Cathedral-Church of St. Paul. Compos'd by the late Mr. Henry Purcel. Note. Where these are Sold may be had great variety of Church-Musick.

London. Printed for and Sold by Iohn Walsh, &c.

[*c.* 1730.]

> Fol. pp. 48.
> RCM. Manchester.

1256. — With Walsh only in the imprint and 'N.° 216' added to the title-page.

Country Journal: or, The Craftsman, July 17, 1731.

> Walsh Cat. 18: 'The Te Deum and Jubilate. 5s. od. N.° 216.'
> In later catalogues, 1747, &c. at 2s. 6d.

1257. — Another edition.

Public Advertiser, Dec. 24, 1761.

> Fol. Dedication to the Lord Bishop of Durham on one side of preliminary leaf. pp. 48.
> Liverpool University. Manchester. (A hybrid copy, Heptinstall type.)

See also Nos. 341, 342. The Catch Club or Merry Companions . . . Catches . . . Compos'd by . . . Mr. Henry Purcell, &c.; No. 749, Harmonia Anglicana . . . by Hen: Purcell &c.; No. 753. Harmonia Mundi . . . H. Purcell . . . the first Collection, &c.; No. 757. Harmonia Sacra.

QUANTZ (JOHANN JOACHIM)

1258. Solos for a German Flute a Hoboy or Violin with a Thorough Bass for the Harpsicord or Bass Violin Compos'd by Sig.ʳ Quants. Musician in Ordinary to the King of Poland. [Op. 1.]

London. Printed for and sold by I: Walsh . . . and Ios: Hare, &c.

Daily Post, Feb. 14, 1730.

> Fol. pp. 1–4, blank, 6–17, blank, 19–25.
> BM. g. 281. Rowe.
> Op. 1.

1259. — With Walsh only in the imprint and 'N.° 431' added to the title-page.

[*c.* 1732.]

> RM. 17. f. 20. (3.)
> Walsh Cat. 18: 'Quant's Solos. 3s. od. N.° 431.'

1260. Solos for a German Flute a Hoboy or Violin with a Thorough Bass for the Harpsicord or Bass Violin Compos'd by Sig.ʳ Quants. Musician in Ordinary to the King of Poland. Opera Seconda.

London. Printed for and Sold by I: Walsh . . . N.° 432.

Country Journal: or, The Craftsman; Universal Spectator and Weekly Journal, Jan. 15, 1732.

> Fol. pp. 27.
> RM. 17. f. 20. (4.) NLS.
> Walsh Cat. 18: 'Quant's 2d Solos. 3s. od. N? 432.

1261. — Reissue without 'N? 432' on the title-page.

London Daily Post, and General Advertiser, Sept. 6, 1739. (New Musick and Editions of Musick.)

> Fol. pp. 27.
> BM. g. 1090. (1.)

1262. Six Sonatas for two German Flutes or two Violins with a Thorough Bass for the Harpsicord. Compos'd by Signor Quantz. Opera Terza.
London Printed for and Sold by I: Walsh . . . N? 433.

Daily Post, Jan. 10, 1733.

> Fol. 3 parts.
> BM. g. 241. (7.) RM. 17. d. 2. (8.) Manchester. Tenbury.
> Walsh Cat. 18: 'Quants Sonatas. Op. 3ᶻᵃ for 2 German Flutes. 5s. od. N? 433.'

1263. Solos for a German Flute or Violin With a Through Bass for the Harpsicord or Violoncello Compos'd by Sigʳ Quantz Musician in Ordinary to the King of Poland Opera Quarta.
London. Printed for I. Walsh, &c.

Daily Advertiser, Feb. 4, 1744.

> Fol. pp. 24.
> RM. 17. f. 20. (5.) RCM. Tenbury.

1264. Six Sonatas or Duets for two German Flutes or Violins Compos'd by Sigʳ Quantz. Opera Quinta.
London. Printed for I. Walsh, &c.

General Advertiser, Nov. 8, 1750.

> Fol. pp. 22.
> BM. g. 280. b. (9.)
> *See also* No. 11. Airs. Select Aires or Duets for two German Flutes . . . By . . . Quantz . . . 2d Book.

QUARTERLY COLLECTION OF VOCAL MUSIC

1265. The Quarterly Collection of Vocal Musick, Containing The Choicest Songs for the last Three Months, namely January, February & March, being the 'Additional Songs' in Otho. [By G. F. Handel.]

London Printed for and sold by In.º Walsh . . . and Ios: Hare, &c.

[*c.* 1726.]

Fol. ff. 12. Printed on one side only.

B.M.G. 316. r. NLS.

Contains five songs introduced into the libretto of the February and March performances of 'Otho' in 1726. (Smith, 'Handel. A Descriptive Catalogue', &c. p. 44, No. 7.)

1266. The Quarterly Collection of Vocal Music. Containing the Choicest Songs for the last Three Months October November & December being the Additional Songs in Elpidia [by Leonardo Vinci] Compos'd by several of the most eminent Authors.

London Printed for and sold by In.º Walsh . . . and Ios: Hare, &c.

[*c.* 1726.]

Fol. ff. 14 'Elpidia'; 4 unnumbered folios 'Alexander'. Printed on one side only.

NLS.

Includes two songs from Handel's opera 'Alexander'. (Smith, 'Handel. A Descriptive Catalogue', &c. p. 15, No. 15.)

See also No. 1509. Vinci (Leonardo) Additional Songs in Elpidia. 1s.

RAMEAU (JEAN PHILIPPE)

1267. Five Concertos for the Harpsicord Compos'd by M.ʳ Rameau. Accompanied with a Violin or German Flute or two Violins or Viola, with some Select Pieces for the Harpsicord alone.

London. Printed for I. Walsh, &c.

General Advertiser, April 11, 1750.

Fol. 3 parts. (Score pp. 48, Violino Primo, Violino Secondo.)

RM. 17. e. 1. (5.) BM. g. 82. (Score, and Violino Secondo part.) RCM. Fitz. Rowe and others in BUC not examined.

Originally issued as 'Pièces de Clavecin en Concerts . . . Chez l'Auteur, Paris. 1741'. (BM. g. 82. a.)

1268. A Collection of Lessons for the Harpsicord Compos'd by M.ʳ Rameau. Opera Seconda.

London. Printed for I. Walsh, &c.

Public Advertiser, Dec. 5, 1760.

Obl. fol. pp. 2–29.

BM. d. 36. RM. 16. a. 14. (4.) RCM. Fitz. Rowe.

Originally issued as 'Nouvelles Suites de Pièces de Clavecin . . . Chez l'Auteur, Paris'. *c.* 1735. (BM. e. 1300. (1.); another edition, BM. e. 1300. b.)

1269. A 2.ᵈ Collection of Lessons for the Harpsicord composed by M.ʳ Rameau. Opera 3.ᶻᵃ

London Printed for I. Walsh, &c.

Public Advertiser, May 2, 1764.

Obl. fol. pp. 1–7, blank, 19–27.
BM. e. 101. a. (6.) RCM. Fitz.
'2ᵈ' and '3ᶻᵃ' are in MS.
Originally issued as 'Pièces de Clavessin, avec une méthode pour la mechanique de doigts', Paris, 1724. (BM. e. 1300. a.)

1270. A Treatise of Musick containing the Principles of Composition. Wherein the several Parts thereof are fully explained, and made useful both to the Professors and Students of that Science. By Mr. Rameau, Principal Composer to his most Christian Majesty, and to the Opera at Paris. Translated into English from the Original in the French language. Entered at Stationer's-Hall, and Published according to the Act of Parliament.

London. Printed by Robert Brown, For the Proprietor, And sold by John Walsh . . ., and all the other Musick Shops in Town. MDCCLII.

4°. 'A Table of the Contents . Sigs. A–Z, A2, in fours.
BM. 557*. e. 5.
Originally published as Liv. III of 'Traité de l'Harmonie' by J. B. C. Ballard, Paris, 1732.

RAMONDON (Lewis)

1271. A New Book of Songs the Words & Musick by Mr Ramondon never before Publish'd.
London Printed for & Sould by I: Walsh . . . Nº 315.

[*c.* 1730.]

Fol. Passe-partout title-page. ff. or pp. 9.
Walsh Cat. 18: 'Ramondon's Songs. 2s. 6d. Nº 315.'
Smith 585 (Euing Library, Glasgow) with Walsh only in the imprint and 'Nº 315' added to the title-page.

See also No. 185. Bononcini (Antonio Maria) A Collection of the Song Tunes in the Opera of Camilla; Nos. 896, 897. Ladys Entertainment.

RANDALL (John)

See Nos. 265, 267, 268. British Orpheus. Books I, III, IV; No. 1233. Psalms.

RANISH (John Frederick)

1272. XII Solos For the German Flute with the Through Bass for the Harpsicord Composed by Iohn Frederick Ranish Opera Secunda.
London Printed for & Sold by Inº Walsh, &c.

Daily Advertiser, Dec. 8, 1744. (Of whom may be had.)

Fol. Illustrated passe-partout title-page. pp. 49.
BM. g. 73. Cardiff. Rowe.
Walsh Cat. 18: 'Ranish's Solos. 10.s. 6d.'

RAPE OF PROSERPINE

1273. Tunes, Aires and Dances in the Entertainment call'd the Rape of Proserpine, for the Flute, as they were performed at the Theatre in Lincoln's-Inn-Fields. Price 6d. [By J. E. Galliard.]

Printed for and sold by John Walsh . . . Joseph Hare, &c.

Country Journal: or, The Craftsman, March 9, 1728.

Words by L. Theobald.

1274. — With Walsh only in the imprint and 'N° 52' added to the title-page.

[*c.* 1730.]

Walsh Cat. 18: 'Rape of Prosperpine (for a Single Flute). 6d. N° 52.'

See also No. 1200. Perseus and Andromeda. The Comic Tunes in the Entertainments of Perseus & Andromeda and the Rape of Proserpine, &c.

RAVENSCROFT (JOHN)

1275. Sonatas or Chamber Aires for two Violins and a Through Bass. Composed by the late Mr. Ravenscroft Opera Seconda. Engraven in a better Caracter and more corect then the former Edition.

Presented for J. Walsh, &c.

[*c.* 1730.]

Fol. Parts.

Smith 277 with Walsh only in the imprint and 'N° 462' added to the title-page.

Walsh Cat. 18: 'Ravenscrofts Sonatas (2 Violins and a Bass). 5s. od. N° 462.'

RAVENSCROFT (THOMAS)

See No. 354. Church (John) An Introduction To Psalmody . . . containing some . . . Anthems and Hymns by Mr Tho: Ravenscroft, &c.

READING (JOHN)

1276. Reading's Anthems. £1. 1s. od.

[*c.* 1730.]

Walsh Cat. 18.

This probably refers to 'A Book of new Anthems Containing a Hundred Plates fairly Engraven with a Thorough Bass figur'd for the Organ or Harpsicord with proper Retornels By John Reading', London, *c.* 1715. (BM. E. 473. 4°. Advertisement. Dedication. pp. 105.)

RESTA (NATALE)

See No. 1144. Orazio

RICCIOTTI (Carlo Bacciccia)

1277. VI. Concerti Armonici a Quattro Violini obligati, Alto Viola, Violoncello obligato e Basso continuo. Composti da Carlo Bacciccia Ricciotti.
London Printed for I Walsh, &c.

London Evening-Post, Sept. 30–Oct. 2, 1755.

Fol. Parts.
BM. h. 53. RM. 17. a. 3. (12.) RM. 17. f. 2. (4.) RCM. Others in BUC not examined.

RICHTER (Franz Xaver)

1278. Six Solos for a German Flute or Violin, with a Thorough Bass for the Harpsicord or Violoncello Compos'd by Sig͏ͬ Francesco Xave͏ͬ Richter &c.
London. Printed for I. Walsh, &c.

Public Advertiser, March 6, 1764.

Fol. pp. 1–25, blank, 26–29.
BM. g. 71. f. (3.) RM. 17. f. 20. (6.) Leeds.
The only composers named in this work are F. X. Richter (Solo No. 1) and Giuseppe San Martini (No. 2).

1279. Six Sonatas for the Harpsicord with Accompanyments for a Violin or German Flute and Violoncello. Composed by Sig͏ͬ Francesco Xave͏ͬ Richter.
London. Printed for I. Walsh, &c.

London Evening-Post, Feb. 22–24, 1759.

Fol. 3 parts.
BM. g. 673. Hirsch M. 1651. RM. 17. e. 1. (3.) Oriel College, Oxford. Rowe.

1280. Six Sonatas or Duets for two German Flutes or Violins, composed by Signor Richter, Op. 4.
Printed for J. Walsh, &c.

Public Advertiser, Oct. 3, 1764.

Not identified.
Randall Cat.

1281. Six Symphonys in Eight Parts for Violins, Hoboys and French Horns with a Bass for the Harpsicord and Violoncello. Compos'd by Sig͏ͬ Franc͏ͦ Xavier Richter. Opera Seconda.
London. Printed for I. Walsh, &c.

Public Advertiser, June 27, 1760.

Fol. Parts.
BM. g. 673. b. (Wanting Horn parts.) RM. 17. d. 4. (9.) RM. 26. b. 2. (13.) RAM.
See also Nos. 1419, 1420. The Summer's Tale . . . Music by . . . Richter, &c.

RINALDO, *Sig.* (RINALDO DA CAPUA)
    See Capua (Rinaldo da)

ROGER ( )
1282. The Tunes, Airs, and Dances in the New Entertainment call'd Perseus and Andromeda, for the Violin and Hoboy, as they are perform'd at the Theatre in Drury Lane. Compos'd by Mons. Roger. Price 1s.
    Printed for John Walsh . . . and Joseph Hare, &c.
    Daily Post, Dec. 7, 1728.

1283. — With Walsh only in the imprint and 'N⁰ 153' added to the title-page.
    [*c.* 1730.]
        Walsh Cat. 18: 'Tunes in Perseus and Andromeda (for a single Violin). 1s. 0d. N⁰ 153.'

ROMANO ( )
1284. Ten Sonatas for two Flutes & a Bass. Opera Seconda.
    [*c.* 1726.]
        Walsh Cat. 11*a*.
        Presumably reissue of Smith 279.

1285. — With Walsh only in the imprint and 'N⁰ 82' added to the title-page.
    [*c.* 1730.]
        Walsh Cat. 18: 'Romano's Aires (for 2 Flutes and a Bass). 3s. 0d. N⁰ 82.'
        Probably Walsh edition of 'XII Sonate à due Flauti & Basso continuo' Amsterdam [*c.* 1725] by J. H. Roman (or Romano, BUC). Rowe.

ROSAMOND
The Opera of Rosamond.
    See No. 380. Clayton (Thomas)

ROSEINGRAVE (THOMAS)
1286. Six Double Fugues For the Organ or Harpsicord Compos'd by Mʳ Roseingrave. To which is added, Sigʳ Dominico Scarlatti's Celebrated Lesson for the Harpsicord, with several Additions by Mr. Roseingrave.
    London. Printed for I. Walsh, &c.
    General Advertiser, March 17, 1750.
        Fol. pp. 2–25.
        BM. e. 174. m. (17.) RCM. Bod. Fitz. Manchester. Rowe. Tenbury.

1287. Eight Suits of Lessons for the Harpsicord or Spinnet in most of the Keys; with Variety of Passages & Variations Throughout the Work. Humbly Inscrib'd to the Right Honble the Earl of Essex &c. By his Lordships most devoted and humble Servant Tho: Roseingrave,

London. Printed for and sold by I: Walsh . . . and Ioseph Hare, &c.

Country Journal: or, The Craftsman, Dec. 7, 1728.

Fol. pp. 39. blanks between 8–9, 25–26, 36–37.
BM. h. 145. (1.) BUL. Rowe.

1288. — With Walsh only in the imprint and 'N? 192' added to the title-page.

[*c.* 1730.]

St. John's College, Cambridge. Tenbury.
Walsh Cat. 18: 'Roseingrave's Lessons. 5s. od. N? 192.'

1289. Voluntarys and Fugues made on purpose for the Organ or Harpsicord By Mr Thomas Roseingrave Organist of St George's Han^r Square, &c.

London. Printed for and sold by I: Walsh . . . and Ioseph Hare, &c.

Country Journal: or, The Craftsman, Dec. 7, 1728.

Fol. pp. 2–29.
BM. h. 145. (2.) RCM. Durham. Manchester. Rowe. Tenbury.

1290. — With Walsh only in the imprint and 'N? 193' added to the title-page.

[*c.* 1730.]

Fitz. Manchester. Pendlebury. St. John's College, Cambridge.
Walsh Cat. 18: 'Roseingrave's Volentarys 4th Book (Organ). 4s. od. N? 193.'

See also No. 1322. Scarlatti (Domenico) Songs in the New Opera call'd Narcissus . . . With the Additional Songs Compos'd by Mr Roseingrave.

ROYAL CHACE

1291. Tunes in the Royal Chace, or Merlin's Cave. [By J. E. Galliard.]

London Daily Post, and General Advertiser, April 23, 1736. (The Tunes Aires and Dances in Harlequin Restor'd, the Royal Chase, and all the late Entertainments, set for the Violin German Flute and Harpsichord.)

Obl. fol. ff. 12. Printed on one side only.
BM. e. 5. k. (3.) (Without title-page. Wanting fol. 2, 4, and 6.)

RUDIMENTS

1292. The Rudiments or Instructions for the German Flute. 2s. od. N? 137.

[*c.* 1730.]

Walsh Cat. 18.
Not identified.

RUGE (FILIPPO)

1293. Six Concertos in Six Parts For a German Flute, Two Violins, a Tenor, with a Bass for the Harpsicord and Violoncello. Compos'd by Sig.^r Filippo Ruge. Opera Terza.
London. Printed for I. Walsh, &c.

Public Advertiser, April 13, 1753.

Fol. 6 parts.
RAM.

1294. Six Solos for a German Flute or Violin with a Thorough Bass for the Harpsicord or Violoncello. Compos'd By Sig.^r Filippo Ruge of Rome.
London. Printed for I. Walsh, &c.

London Evening-Post, Dec. 7–10, 1751.

Fol. pp. 2–16, blank, 18–29.
BM. g. 79. d. (2.) Rowe.

1295. Six Sonatas in 3 Parts. Four for 2 German Flutes or Violins and a Bass. And Two for 3 German Flutes without a Bass. Compos'd by Sig.^r Filippo Ruge &c. Opera 2da
London. Printed for I. Walsh, &c.

General Advertiser, Oct. 21, 1752.

Fol. 3 parts.
BM. h. 2851. e. (3.) RAM.

1296. A Set of Six Sonatas or Duets for two German Flutes or Violins. Compos'd by Sig.^r Filippo Ruge. Opera Quarta.
London. Printed for I. Walsh, &c.

Public Advertiser, Oct. 3, 1754. (Twelve Sonatas . . . in two books.)

Fol. pp. 2–21.
Rowe.

1297. A 2^d Set of Six Sonatas or Duets for two German Flutes or Violins. Compos'd by Sig.^r Filippo Ruge. Opera Quarta.
London. Printed for I. Walsh, &c.

Public Advertiser, Oct. 3, 1754. (Twelve Sonatas . . . in two books.)

Fol. pp. 22–39.
Rowe.
'2^d'. in MS

U

RULES

1298. Rules for Playing a Bass on a Violin. 1s. 6d. N.° 434.

> [*c.* 1730.]
>> Walsh Cat. 18.
>> Smith 615 with Walsh only in the imprint and 'N.° 434' added to the title-page.

1299. Rules; Or a Short and Compleat Method For attaining to Play a Thorough Bass upon the Harpsicord or Organ. By an Eminent Master. Also an Explanation of Figur'd Time, with the Several Moods & Characters made use of in Musick. To which is added, a Dictionary, or Explanation of such Italian Words, or Terms, as are made use of in Vocal, or Instrumental Musick.

London. Printed for & sold by I:Walsh...N.° 189.

> [*c.* 1730.]
>> 8°. pp. 42.
>> BM. d. 39.
>> Walsh Cat. 18: 'Pepusch. Rules for a Thorough Bass with a Dictionary of Italian Words us'd in Musick. 1s. 6d. N.° 189.'

RUSSEL (DAVIDSON)

> *See* Nos. 265, 267, 268. British Orpheus. Books I, III, IV; No. 1419. The Summer's Tale . . . Music by . . . Russel, &c.

SABRINA

1300. The Favourite Songs in the Opera, call'd Sabrina.
London. Printed for and sold by I. Walsh, &c.

Country Journal: or, The Craftsman, July 16, 1737. (Where may be had, just publish'd.)

>> Fol. pp. 2–14.
>> University of California, Los Angeles.
>> Pasticcio. Founded on John Milton's 'Comus', by Paolo Antonio Rolli.
>> Walsh Cat. 18: 'Orpheus & Sabrina each 2s. 6d. N.° 587.'
>> Orpheus is catalogued separately.
>> Republished in 'Le Delizie dell' Opere', Vol. II, pp. 71, 74–85.

SAGGIONE (GIOSEPPE FEDELLI)

> *See* Fedelli (Giuseppe) called *Saggione*.

SAINT GERMAIN (DE) *Count*

1301. Musique Raisonnée Selon le bon Sens Aux Dames Angloises qui aiment le vrai goût en cet arte. Par [a sign] de S.t. Germain.
London Printed: and sold by I. Walsh, &c.

General Advertiser, Feb. 10, 1750.

> Obl. fol. Privilege (dated 27 November 1749). pp. 135.
> BM. E. 161.
> Walsh Cat. 25: 'Count S! Germains Songs. £1. 1s. od.'

1302. Solos (for a Violin and Harpsicord).

> Walsh Cat. 25: 'Count S! . . . Solos.'
> Walsh Cat. 27: 'C— S! Germain's Solos.'
> Not identified.

1303. Six Sonatas for Two Violins with a Bass for the Harpsicord or Violoncello Compos'd by [a sign] de S! Germain.
> London. Printed: & Sold by I. Walsh, &c.

General Advertiser, April 26, 1750.

> Fol. 3 parts.
> BM. g. 286. RAM (2). London University. Tenbury.
> Walsh Cat. 25: 'Count S! Germain's Sonatas. 10s. 6d.'

See also Nos. 556, 559–66. Delizie dell' Opere. Vols. I, IV–XI; No. 857. Inconstanza Delusa; No. 1419. The Summer's Tale . . . Music by . . . C. S! Germain, &c.

SAN MARTINI (GIOVANNI BATTISTA)

1304. Concerti Grossi Con due Violini Viola e Violoncello obligati con due altri Violini e Basso di Ripieno. Opera Sesta di Gio: Batta S! Martini Questi Concerti sono composti da diversi Notturni del S! Martini da Francesco Barsanti.
> London. Printed for I. Walsh, &c.

Public Advertiser, Oct. 7, 1757. (Six Concertos for Violins, in seven parts, compos'd by St. Martini of Milan. Op. 6. 10s. 6d.)

> Fol. 7 parts.
> BM. h. 57. e. RCM.

1305. Six Solos for a German Flute or Violin with a Thorough Bass for the Harpsicord or Violoncello Compos'd by Sig! Gio. Batista S! Martini of Milan. Opera VIII.
> London. Printed for I. Walsh, &c.

Whitehall Evening-Post, July 12–14, 1759.

> Fol. pp. 2–25, blank, 27–29.
> BM. h. 57. f. Rowe.

1306. Six Sonatas or Duets for Two German Flutes or Violins Compos'd by Sig! Gio. Batista S! Martini of Milan. Opera Quarta.

Bibliography of Musical Works

London. Printed for I. Walsh, &c.

London Evening-Post, March 8–10, 1748.

> Fol. pp. 2–12, blank, 14–26.
> BM. g. 421. n. (3.); g. 421. h. (1.) Cardiff. CUL. Manchester.

1307. — Another issue.
Six Sonatas or Duets for Two German Flutes or Violins. Compos'd by Sig.ʳ Gio.
Batista S.ᵗ Martini of Milan. Opera IV.
London. Printed for I. Walsh, &c.

[*c.* 1748.]

> Fol. pp. 2–12, blank, 14–26.
> BM. g. 70. c. (5.) RCM. Bod.
> 'IV' altered from 'V' in MS.

1308. Six Sonatas for two Violins with a Thorough Bass for the Harpsicord or
Violoncello compos'd by Sig.ʳ Gio. Batista S.ᵗ Martini of Milan Opera Quinta.
London. Printed for I. Walsh, &c.

Whitehall Evening-Post, Dec. 2–4, 1756.

> Fol. 3 parts.
> BM. h. 57. d. RM. 17. c. 5. (7.) CUL. Oriel College, Oxford.
> Assumed to be Set 4 of 'Lampugnani and Martini of Milan's Sonatas', &c. (*See* No. 921.)
> Walsh Cat. 27.

1309. A Second Set of Six Sonatas or Duets for Two German Flutes or Violins.
Compos'd by Sig.ʳ Gio. Batista S.ᵗ Martini of Milan. Opera VII.
London. Printed for I. Walsh, &c.

Public Advertiser, Oct. 20, 1757.

> Fol. pp. 2–25.
> BM. g. 280. b. (11.) Cardiff.
> Sonatas 1–3 are the same as in the following issue of Op. 7, but 4–6 are different.

1310. Six Sonatas or Duets for Two German Flutes or Violins. Compos'd by Sig.ʳ
Gio. Batista S.ᵗ Martini of Milan. Opera VII.
London. Printed for I. Walsh, &c.

[*c.* 1760.]

> Fol. pp. 2–23.
> BM. g. 70. c. (6.) Reid.
> 'VII' altered from 'V' in MS.
> Sonatas 1–3 are the same as in the preceding issue, but 4–6 are different.

1311. Six Sonatas called Notturni's, in 4 Parts, for a German Flute and two Violins,
with a Bass for the Violoncello and Harpsichord, composed by Sig. St. Martini of
Milan. Op. 9.

Printed for J. Walsh, &c.

Public Advertiser, Jan. 13, 1762.

> Randall Cat.: 'St. Martini's Notturnies. 6s. od., (Under Sonatas or Trios for two German
> Flutes and a Bass.)

1312. A Third Set of Sonatas or Duets for two German Flutes, or Violins. Compos'd by Sig.r Gio. Batista S.t Martini of Milan. Opera X.
London   Printed for I. Walsh, &c.

Public Advertiser, Sept. 16, 1763.

> Fol. pp. 2–19, blank, 21–26.
> BM. g. 280. b. (12.) Oriel College, Oxford.

1313. Six Sonatas For two Violins with a Thorough Bass for the Harpsicord or Violoncello Compos'd by Sig.r Gio. Battista S.t Martini of Milan. Sig.r Brioschi & other Masters. 3.d Set.
London. Printed for I. Walsh, &c.

General Advertiser, Nov. 8, 1746.

> Fol. 3 parts.
> BM. h. 57. a. RM. 17. d. 3. (4.) RAM. RCM. CUL. Rowe. Others in BUC not examined.
> Walsh Cat. 24a: 'Brioschi and S.t Martini's Sonatas. (For 2 Violins and a Bass.) 3d Set.
> 5s. od.'
> Walsh Cat. 25: 'Brioschi's Sonatas. 5s. od. (For 2 Violins and a Bass.)'
> For Set I & II *See* Lampugnani (G.B.) and San Martini (G.B.) (Nos. 918, 920.)
> For Set IV *See* San Martini (G.B.) Opera Quinta. (No. 1308.)

> *See also* No. 879. Jozzi (Giuseppe) A Collection of Lessons . . . compos'd by
> . . . S.t Martini of Milan, &c.; Nos. 918–920. Lampugnani (Giovanni Battista)
> and San Martini (Giovanni Battista) Six Sonatas for Two Violins . . . Opera
> Prima (Seconda); No. 1153. Overtures.

SAN MARTINI (GIOVANNI BATTISTA) OR (GIUSEPPE)

> *See* No. 11. Airs. Select Airs or Duets for two German Flutes . . . By . . . S.t
> Martini . . . 2d Book, &c.; Nos. 1061, 1066, 1070, 1085, 1095. Minuets; No.
> 1535. Warlike Music . . . By . . . S.t Martini, &c.

SAN MARTINI (GIOVANNI BATTISTA) AND HASSE (JOHANN ADOLPH)

1314. Six Concertos in 8 parts, for Violins, French Horns, Hoboys, &c. with a Bass for the Violoncello and Harpsicord. Compos'd by Sig.r Gio: Bat: S.t Martini of Milan and Sig.r Hasse.
London. Printed for I. Walsh, &c.

London Evening-Post, Nov. 23–26, 1751.

> Fol. 10 parts.
> RM. 17. d. 4. (5.) RM. 26. b. 2. (5.)
> Nos. 2 and 3 are by Hasse.

SAN MARTINI (GIUSEPPE)

1315. Concerti Grossi a due Violini, Viole e Violoncello obligati con due altri Violini, e Basso di Ripieno. Composta da Giuseppe San Martini. Opera Quinta. Questi Concerti sono composti dalle Sonate a due Violino, e Basso dell' Opera III.
London. Printed for I. Walsh, &c.

General Advertiser, Nov. 10, 1747.

> Fol. 7 parts.
> BM. g. 86. c. RM. 17. a. 3. (9.) RM. 17. d. 4. (4.) RM. 26. a. 6. (2.) RM. 26. b. 2. (3.)
> RCM. Rowe.

1316. — Another edition.

General Advertiser, Oct. 25, 1749. (New editions, &c.)

1317. Giuseppe S.t Martini's Concertos For the Harpsicord or Organ with the Instrumental Parts for Violins Opera Nona.
London. Printed for I. Walsh, &c.

London Evening-Post, Jan. 17–19, 1754.

> Fol. 4 parts.
> BM. g. 86. RM. 17. e. 1. (4.) RCM. Oriel College, Oxford.

1318. Eight Overtures in Eight Parts For Violins, Hoboys, French Horns, &c. with a Through Bass for the Harpsicord or Violoncello. And Six Grand Concertos for Violins &c. Compos'd by Sig.r Giuseppe S.t Martini.
London. Printed for I. Walsh, &c.

London Evening-Post, Nov. 16–18, 1752.

> Fol. 8 parts in each work
> BM. g. 86. e. RM. 17. a. 3. (10.) RM. 17. d. 4. (1.) RM. 26. b. 2. (1.) RCM. Fitz. Manchester. Rowe. (*See* Addenda).
> The overtures are Op. 7 and the Concertos Op. 8. The Concertos have separate title-page and pagination, 'Six Grand Concertos For Violins &c. in Eight Parts Compos'd by Sig.r Giuseppe S.t Martini. Opera 8.va'.
> BUC lists another issue of the 'Six Grand Concertos . . . Opera 8.av', c. 1760. Copies not examined.

1319. Six Solos For a German Flute or Violin with a Thorough Bass for the Harpsichord or Violoncello Compos'd by Sig.r Giuseppe S.t Martini. Opera Seconda.

London. Printed for I. Walsh, &c.

Daily Advertiser, August 15, 1745.

> Fol. pp. 1–13, blank, 15–25, blank, 27–31.
> Tenbury.

1320. — Another issue. With 'Seconda' re-engraved as '2.ᵈ'

[*c.* 1745.]

> BM. g. 422. b. (6.) Inglefield.

1321. Six Solos for a German Flute or Violin with a Thorough Bass for the Harpsi-cord or Violoncello Compos'd by Sig.ʳ Giuseppe S.ᵗ Martini Opera Quarta.
London. Printed for I. Walsh, &c.

[*c.* 1747.]

> Fol. pp. 2–11, blank, 13–28.
> BM. g. 422. b. (7.) Bod. Inglefield. (Leighton Buzzard.)
> Walsh Cat. 24 *c.*

1322. Six Solo's [for a German Flute or Violin and a Bass?].
Printed for and sold by John Walsh, &c.

London Daily Post, and General Advertiser, Nov. 11, 1736.

> Not identified.

1323. Six Solos for a German Flute or Violin with a Through Bass for the Harpsi-cord or Violoncello Compos'd by Giuseppe S.ᵗ Martini of London. Opera XII.
London. Printed for I. Walsh, &c.

Public Advertiser, October 13, 1757.

> Fol. pp. 1–5, blank, 7–11, blank, 13–17, blank, 19–31.
> BM. g. 86. g. Rowe.

1324. XII Sonatas For two German Flutes or Violins with a Thorough Bass.
Compos'd by Giuseppe S.ᵗ Martino.
London Printed for and sold by I: Walsh . . . and Joseph Hare, &c.

Mist's Weekly Journal, Sept. 30, 1727.

> Fol. 3 parts.

1325. — With Walsh only in the imprint and 'N.º 95' added to the title-page.

[*c.* 1730.]

> Fol. 3 parts.
> BM. g. 241. (9.) RM. 17. d. 2. (10.) RAM.
> Walsh Cat. 18: 'St Martino's 12 Sonatas. 5s. od. N.º 95.'

1326. Six Celebrated Sonatas, in three Parts, for two German Flutes, and a Bass, compos'd by Giuseppe S. Martini. Dedicated to his Royal Highness the Prince of Wales.

   Printed for and sold by John Walsh, &c.

London Daily Post, and General Advertiser, Nov. 11, 1736.

   Not identified.

1327. Six Sonatas For two German Flutes or two Violins with a Thorough Bass for the Harpsicord or Violoncello Compos'd by Sigᵣ Giuseppe Sᵗ Martini. Opera Sexta.

   London. Printed for I. Walsh, &c.

   [*c.* 1750.]

   Fol. 3 parts.
   BM. g. 242. (5.) RM. 17. d. 6. (5.) RM. 17. d. 2. (11.) RAM. RCM. CUL. GUL.

1328. XII Sonate a due Violini, e Violoncello, e Cembalo, Se piace, Opera Terza, Dedicata All' Altezza Reale di Augusta Principessa di Vallia da Giuseppe San Martini Milanese MDCCXLIII Londra.

Daily Advertiser, Dec. 8, 1743. (Twelve Sonatas for two Violins, and a Violoncello, with a thorough Bass for the Harpsichord. Printed for the Author, and sold by him . . . and J. Walsh, &c.)

   Fol. 3 parts.
   RM. 16. e. 28. RAM.

1329. — Another issue.

Daily Advertiser, Dec. 15, 1743. (A few copies are printed on Imperial paper, for the curious.)

1330. — Another edition.

   XII Sonate a due Violini, e Violoncello, e Cembalo, Se piace, Opera Terza, Dedicata All' Altezza Reale di Augusta Principessa di Vallia da Giuseppe San Martini.

   London Printed for and Sold by I. Walsh, &c.

General Advertiser, Jan. 28, 1747. (Just published.)

   Fol. 3 parts. pp. 4 and 5 of 'Violino Primo' re-engraved.
   BM. h. 39. a. BM. g. 86. a. (2.) RM. 17. d. 6. (4.) RM. 17. d. 3. (1.) RM. 17. a. 4. (8.) RAM. RCM. Fitz. Rowe. Others in BUC not examined.

See also No. 1278. Richter (Franz Xaver) Six Solos for a German Flute or Violin, &c.; *See also supra*, San Martini (Giovanni Battista) or (Giuseppe)

SANTIS (GIOVANNI DE)

1331. Twelve Solo's by Giovanni de Santis, Opera prima, for a Violin and Bass. Printed for and sold by John Walsh, &c.

London Daily Post, and General Advertiser, Sept. 20, 1738. (Where may be had.)

Presumably the work 'VI Sonate da Camera a Violino e Violone o Cimbalo . . . Opera Prima' issued by G. F. Witvogel, *c*. 1738. (BM. g. 223. d. (I.) Fol. pp. 26.)
Walsh Cat. 18: 'De Santi's Solos (for a Violin and a Bass). 5s 0d.'

SAVAGE (WILLIAM)

See No. 268. British Orpheus. Book IV.

SCARLATTI (ALESSANDRO)

See No. 45. Arianna e Teseo; No. 57. Arminio; No. 891. Lady's Banquet 3ᵈ Book; No. 1009. Meraspe; Nos. 1209–11. Pirro e Demetrio; Nos. 1443–5. Thomyris.

SCARLATTI (DOMENICO)

1332. Songs in the New Opera call'd Narcissus as they are perform'd at the Kings Theatre For the Royal Academy Compos'd by Sigᵣ Domᶜᵒ Scarlatti With the Additional Songs Compos'd by Mᵣ Roseingrave.

London, Printed for & sold by I: Walsh . . . Nᵒ 234.

[*c*. 1730.]

Fol. 'A Table of the Songs', &c. pp. 69.
Smith 590 (BM. H. 315) with Walsh only in the imprint and 'Nᵒ 234' added to the title-page.
Walsh Cat. 18: 'The Opera of Narcissus. 9s. 0d. Nᵒ 234.'

See also No. 32. Alessandro in Persia; No. 1286. Roseingrave (Thomas) Six Double Fugues . . . To which is added, Sigᵣ Domenico Scarlatti's Celebrated Lesson for the Harpsicord, &c.

SCHENCK (JEAN)

1333. Select Lessons for the Bass-Viol, of two Parts, Collected by our Best Viol-lists out of the Works of that Great Master Giovanni Schenk being the Choicest Preludes Allemands Sarabands Corrants Minuets and Jiggs Fairly Engraven. price 3s the First Collection.

London. Printed for I. Walsh . . . Nᵒ 200.

[*c*. 1730.]

Obl. fol. 2 parts.
H. Reeves Cat. No. 107. 1933. p. 23.
Smith 136 (Fitz, imperfect) with Walsh only in the imprint and 'Nᵒ 200' added to the title-page.
Walsh Cat. 18: 'Lessons for the Bass Viol. Nᵒ 200.'

SCHICKHARD (JOHANN CHRISTIAN)

1334. Six Concertos for 4 Flutes, with a thorough Bass for the Harpsichord or Bass Violin, compos'd by Mr. Christian Schickhard.
Printed for John Walsh ... Nº 93.

[*c.* 1730.]

> Fol. Parts.
> Smith 567 with Walsh only in the imprint and 'Nº 93' added to the title-page.
> Walsh Cat. 18: 'Six Concertos for four Flutes. 19th Opera. 6s. od. Nº 93.'

1335. Solos for a German Flute a Hoboy or Violin with a Thorough Bass for the Harpsicord or Bass Violin Compos'd by Mr Christian Schickhardt 20 Overage, &c.
London Printed for I: Walsh ... Nº 438.

[*c.* 1730.]

> Fol. pp. 2–19.
> Smith 542 (BM. h. 3055. (2) with Walsh only in the imprint and 'Nº 438' added to the title-page.
> Walsh Cat. 18: 'Six Solos for a German Flute and a Bass. 20th Op. 4s. od. Nº 438.'

1336. Six Sonatas for one Flute & two Hoboys or two Violins with a Viol Bass and a Thorough Bass for the Harpsicord & Arch Lute Compos'd by Mr Christian Schickhard.
London Printed for I. Walsh ... and I. Hare, &c.

[*c.* 1722.]

> Fol. Parts.
> BM. h. 250. c. (4.)
> A later issue of Smith 467. (BM. h. 250. c. (4.))

1337. — With Walsh only in the imprint and 'Nº 436' added to the title-page.

[*c.* 1730.]

> Walsh Cat. 18: 'Six Sonatas for variety of Instruments. Opera 5ta 6s. od. Nº 436.'

1338. Six Sonatas for two Hoboys, two Violins or German Flutes; with a Thorough Bass for the Harpsicord, or Bass Violin. Composed by Mr. Christian Schickhard. Pr. 2s.
Printed for and sold by John Walsh ... Nº 437.

[*c.* 1730.]

> Smith 571 with Walsh only in the imprint and 'Nº 437' added to the title-page.
> Walsh Cat. 18: 'Six Sonatas for 2 German Flutes or Violins and a Bass, 10th Opera. 2s. 6d. Nº 437.'

1339. XII Sonatas or Solos for a Flute with a Through Bass for the Harpsicord or Bass Violin Compos'd by Mr Christian Schickhard Opera 17 Note all ye Choisest Works of this Author may be had where these are sold.

London Printed for I: Walsh . . . N? 104.

[*c.* 1730.]

Fol. pp. 2–48.
Smith 616 (BM. h. 250. c. (5.)) with Walsh only in the imprint and 'N? 104' added to the title-page.
Walsh Cat. 18: '12 Solos for a Flute and a Bass, 17th Opera. 6s. od. N? 104.'

See also No. 410. Corelli (Arcangelo) Corelli's 6 Concertos Transpos'd by Schickard.

SCOLARI (GIUSEPPE)

See No. 124. Bach (Johann Christian) A Fifth favourite Opera Overture, &c.

SCOTCH AIRS

1340. Original Scotch Aires &c. Set in a Familiar Taste for a German Flute Violin or Harpsicord Price 1? 6?
London. Printed for I. Walsh, &c.

Daily Advertiser, March 18, 1745. (Just published. Forty-eight Original Scotch Airs, &c.)

8°. pp. 1–24.
Mitchell. (Wanting title-page.)

1341. A Second Set of Original Scotch Aires &c. Set in a Familiar Taste for a German Flute Violin or Harpsicord Price 1? 6?
London. Printed for I. Walsh, &c.

Daily Advertiser, June 6, 1745. (Just publish'd.)

8°. pp. 25–48.
Mitchell.
Book 3 is 'A Select Collection of Italian Aires', &c. No. 861.
Walsh Cat. 24a: 'Select Scotch and Italian Airs (for a German Flute, Violin or Harpsicord) in 4 Books, each 1s. 6d.' No copy of Book 4 has been traced.

Scotch Aires (for a Single Flute).

See No. 1349. Scotch Tunes

SCOTCH SONGS

1342. A Collection of Original Scotch Songs, with a Thorough Bass to each Song, for the Harpsicord.
London Printed for and sold by I: Walsh . . . and Ioseph Hare, &c.

Mist's Weekly Journal, August 26, 1727. (A Second Collection of Scotch Songs, &c. Lately published.); *Daily Journal*, April 13, 1728. (Where may be . . . had Two Collections of pleasant Scotch Songs.)

Fol. Printed on one side only.
BM. H. 1374. a. (2.)
A made-up set without pagination. Some sheets bear the numbers used in original works. An earlier collection was issued, *c.* 1715 (Smith 464. BM. G. 316. b.) with the title 'Collection of new Songs With a Through Bass to each Song for the Harpsicord Compos'd by Several Masters.'

1343. — With Walsh only in the imprint and 'N⁙ 321' added to the title-page.
[*c.* 1730.]
Walsh Cat. 18: 'Scotch Songs. 2 Books. 5s. od. N⁙ 321'.

1344. A Collection of Original Scotch Songs, with a Thorough Bass to each Song, for the Harpsicord.
London Printed for and sold by I: Walsh . . . N⁙ 306.
[*c.* 1732.]
Fol. Printed on one side only.
BM. H. 1374. a. (1.)

1345. — A 2ᵈ Collection, &c.
[*c.* 1732.]
Fol. Printed on one side only.
BM. H. 1374. a. (3.)
Title-page same as first collection, with '2ᵈ' in MS.

1346. — A 3ᵈ Collection, &c.
[*c.* 1732.]
Fol. Printed on one side only.
BM. H. 1374. a. (4.)
Title-page same as first collection, with '3ᵈ' in MS.

1347. — A 4ᵗʰ Collection, &c.
[*c.* 1732.]
Fol. Printed on one side only.
BM. H. 1374. a. (5.)
Title-page same as first collection, with '4ᵗʰ' in MS.
Nos. 1344–7 are made-up sets without pagination. Some sheets bear the numbers used in earlier collection, *c.* 1715. (Smith 464. BM. G. 316. b.)
Walsh Cat. 15a: 'A Book of Scotch Songs. 2s. 6d.' 'Scotch Songs 2ᵈ Collection. 2s. 6d.'
Walsh Cat. 17a: 'Scotch Songs. 2 Books. (Just Publish'd.)'
Randall Cat.: 'Scotch Songs. 4 Books. 2s. 6d. each.'
The details of the works under Nos. 1342–7 'Scotch Songs' are open to question and there may have been other sets differently made up. BUC copies not examined.

1348. Thirty Scots Songs for a Voice & Harpsichord. The Music taken from the Most genuine Sets extant; The Words from Allan Ramsay. Price 2sh.-6d.
　　Edinburgh, Printed for, & Sold by R. Bremner, &c.

Public Advertiser, Sept. 6, 1757. (Just published in Scotland. Thirty Scots Songs for a Voice and Harpsichord, the Words from Ramsay. London, sold by J. Walsh, &c.)

　　Fol. pp. 2–31, and 1 leaf without pagination 'For the Flute'.
　　BM. G. 802. b.
　　Others in BUC under Bremner (Robert) who adapted the music.

SCOTCH TUNES

1349. A Collection of Original Scotch Tunes for the Flute. pr. 1s.
　　Printed and Sold by J. Walsh . . . № 14.

　　[*c.* 1730.]
　　　Smith 65 with Walsh only in the imprint and '№ 14' added to the title-page.
　　　Walsh Cat. 18: 'Scotch Aires (for a Single Flute). 1s. 0d. № 14.'

1350. A Collection of Original Scotch tunes for the Violin all pleasant and comical, and full of the Highland humours.
　　Printed for J. Walsh . . . № 144.

　　[*c.* 1730.]
　　　Smith 214 with Walsh only in the imprint and '№ 144' added to the title-page.
　　　Walsh Cat. 18: 'Scotch Tunes for the Violin. 1s. 6d. № 144.'

1351. A Collection of the most celebrated Scotch Tunes for the Violin; with Variety of Whims and Fancies of different Humour; the whole pleasant and comical. Book the 2d. Price 1s. 6d.
　　Printed for J. Walsh . . . and J. Hare, &c.

　　Post Boy, July 6–8, 1721.

　　　The first collection is presumably Smith 214 (No. 1350).

1352. — With Walsh only in the imprint and '№ 145' added to the title-page.

　　[*c.* 1730.]
　　　Walsh Cat. 18: 'Scotch Tunes 2d Book (for the Violin). 1s. 6d. № 145.'
　　　Walsh Cat. 24*a*: 'Scotch Tunes (for a Single Violin). 2 Books, each 1s. 6d.'

1353. A Third Collection of the most Celebrated Scotch Tunes, Curiously fitted for the German Flute or Violin, The whole Pleasant and Diverting, being full of the Highland Humour. Price 1s 6d
　　London. Printed for and sold by Iohn Walsh . . . № 492.

Country Journal: or, The Craftsman, Sept. 29, 1733.

> Obl. 12°. ff. 29. Printed on one side only.
> Perth.
> Walsh Cat. 18: 'Scotch Tunes 3d Collection (German Flute). 1s. 6d. N⁰ 492.'

1354. Three Collections of choice Scots Tunes, for a German Flute, or Violin, &c.
Printed for J. Walsh, &c.

Daily Advertiser, Oct. 4, 1743.

> Presumably refers to Walsh issues Nos. 1350–3.

1355. Scotch Tunes (for 2 German Flutes or Violins). 3 Sets. 4s. od.
[*c.* 1743.]

> Walsh Cat. 21.
> Not identified.

SCOTS SONGS

> *See* Scotch Songs.

SCOTS TUNES

> *See* Scotch Tunes.

SEA SONGS

1356. A Collection of Sea Songs on Several Occasions—Price 1ˢ 6ᵈ—.
London Printed for & Sould by I: Walsh . . . N⁰ 326.

[*c.* 1730.]

> Large fol. 'A Table of the Songs', &c. ff. or pp. 15.
> Smith 594 (BM. H. 35.) with Walsh only in the imprint and 'N⁰ 326' added to the title-page.
> > Walsh 18: 'Sea Songs. 1s. 6d. N⁰ 326.'
> > Walsh Cat. 17a: 'Sea Songs. (Just Publish'd.)'

SELECT HARMONY

1357. Select Harmony; being XII Concertos in Six Parts, for Violins and other Instruments; Collected from the Works of Antonio Vivaldi, viz His 6ᵗʰ 7ᵗʰ 8ᵗʰ and 9ᵗʰ Operas: being a well-chosen Collection of his most Celebrated Concertos. The whole carefully corected, &c.
London Printed for and sold by I: Walsh . . . and Joseph Hare, &c.

Daily Post; Country Journal: or, The Craftsman, Jan. 10, 1730.

> Fol. 6 parts.
> Fitz. (Imperfect.)

1358. — With Walsh only in the imprint and 'N⁰ 454' added to the title-page.

Country Journal: or, The Craftsman, May 13, 1732. (Where may be had.)

> RAM.
> Walsh Cat. 18: 'Select Harmony being 12 Concertos . . . N⁰ 454. 15s. od.'
> 'A 2d Edition' was advertised on the title-page of the Fourth Collection, No. 1364.

1359. — Another issue.

General Evening Post (London), Jan. 17–19, 1745. (New editions.)

1360. Select Harmony, 2d Collection; being 12 Concerto's collected from the latest opera of Albinoni in 7 Parts.
Printed for and sold by John Walsh, &c.

Country Journal: or, The Craftsman, May 13, 1732. (Where may be had.)

> Fol. Parts.
> Walsh Cat. 18: 'Albinoni. Select Harmony 2d Collection being 12 Concertos Collected from his 5th and 7th Operas. 15s. od. N⁰ 343.'
> 'A 2d Edition' was advertised on the title-page of the Fourth Collection, No. 1364.

1361. — Another edition.

General Evening Post (London), Jan. 17–19, 1745. (New editions.)

1362. Select Harmony Third Collection. Six Concertos in Seven Parts for Violins, and other Instruments Compos'd by Sig\.r Geminiani, and other Eminent Italian Authors. Engraven in a fair Character and Carefully Corrected. N.B. The First and Second Collections of Select Harmony contains the most Celebrated Concertos Collected from the Works of Albinoni and Vivaldi.

[1734.] *London Evening-Post*, May 31–June 3, 1735. (Just publish'd.)

London. Printed for and sold by I. Walsh . . . N⁰ 506.

> Fol. 7 parts.
> BM. g. 26. RAM. RCM. (Imperfect.) Rowe.
> At the bottom of the parts of Concerto II is printed 'Geminiani N⁰ 4. 504.'; and on Concerto III, 'Geminiani N⁰ 2. 502.'; Concerto IV, 'Geminiani N⁰ 3. 503' and Concerto VI, 'Facco N⁰ 501'. The work is a collection of the series of Concertos issued monthly by Walsh in 1734. Concerto I was anonymous. Concerto V had appeared as No. 4 in Handel's 'Concerti Grossi', Op. 3, first edition, but was omitted from subsequent editions and transferred with additions to 'Select Harmony Third Collection' as Concerto V, anonymous. (See Nos. 395, 611, 701–3.)
> Walsh Cat. 18: 'Select Harmony 3\.d Collection, being 6 Concertos by Geminiani, &c. 9s. od. N⁰ 506.'

1363. — Another edition.

General Evening Post (London), Jan. 17–19, 1745. (New editions.)

1364. Select Harmony Fourth Collection. Six Concertos in Seven Parts For Violins and other Instruments Compos'd by Mʳ Handel Tartini and Veracini Just Published'd a 2d Edition of Select Harmony 1ˢᵗ Set being 12 favourite Concertos Collected from all Vivaldi's Works. Select Harmony 2ᵈ Set being 12 favourite Concertos Collected from all Albinoni's Works. Select Harmony 3ᵈ Set being 6 Concertos by Geminiani and other Italian Authors.

London. Printed for I. Walsh . . . № 682.

London Daily Post, and General Advertiser, Dec. 11, 1740. (In this is the celebrated Concerto in Alexander's Feast, never before printed.)

> Fol. 9 parts.
> BM. g. 26 a. (Wanting Hautboy Primo and Secondo.) RM. 6. h. 12. (1*) (Hautboy Primo and Secondo of Concerto I only, without title-pages). RCM. (Wanting two Ripieno parts and all title-pages.) Smith. (Wanting Basso and Hautboy Secondo.)
> Concertos I–III are by Handel (H. G. XXI, pp. 63–97), IV by Veracini, V and VI by Tartini, although the composer of VI is not named.

1365. Select Harmony Fourth Collection, &c.
London. Printed for I. Walsh . . . № 682.

London Daily Post, and General Advertiser, Nov. 11, 1741. (This advertisement may not refer to this edition which was issued 1741 or later.)

> Fol. 9 parts.
> NLS. BH. 193. Bod. (11 parts, two duplicated.) Schoelcher.
> Similar in all respects to No. 1364 except that it is printed on Whatman paper, and has pp. 19–20 of the Violino Secondo Continuo part on one folio sheet, pulling out to the width of two leaves, stitched in the spine at the left side of p. 19. In No. 1364 (Smith) p. 18 is followed by a blank, verso of p. 19, then p. 19, then p. 20, verso blank.
> Randall Cat.: 'Handel's Select Harmony, 4th Collection. 9s. od.,

1366. — Other editions or issues.

General Evening Post (London), Jan. 17–19, 1745. (New editions of the following Works . . . 'Select Harmony; being thirty-six favourite Concertos', &c.) *General Advertiser,* Jan. 6, 1750. (Thirty-six Concertos called Select Harmony', &c.) *Whitehall Evening-Post,* Nov. 15–17, 1759; *Public Advertiser,* Nov. 19, 1759. ('The Concerto in Alexander's Feast.') *Public Advertiser,* Dec. 6, 1759. ('The Celebrated Concertos in Alexander's Feast.')

SEMIRAMIDE RICONOSCIUTA

See No. 819. Hasse (Joahnn Adolph) The Favourite Songs in the Opera Called La Semiramide Riconosciuta.

SHEELES (JOHN)

1367. Sheeles's Collection of Songs.

> Walsh Cat. 11a. [*c.* 1727.]

1368. — Sheeles's Songs. 1s. 6d. N°. 308.

[*c.* 1730.]

> Walsh Cat. 18.
> Not otherwise known. Probably a collection of single songs, some of which are in the British Museum and elsewhere. (BUC.)

SHUTTLEWORTH (OBADIAH)

1369. Two Concerto's for ten Instruments, viz. two Hautbois, two Violins, one Tenor, one Bassoon, two Violins ripienos, one Violoncello, and a Thorow Base: The 1st composed for a private Concert, the 2d in Honour of St. Cecilia's Day. By Mr. Obadiah Shuttleworth.

> Printed for, and sold by Joseph Hare . . . John Walsh . . . and John Young, &c.

> *Daily Post*, October 3, 1729.

> *See also* No. 441. Corelli (Arcangelo) Two Concerto's. being the first & eleventh Solos of yᵉ late Arcangello Corelli. as they are made into Concerto's by Mͬ Obadiah Shuttleworth, &c.

SIMONS (HENRY)

1370. Six Sets of Airs for two Flutes, by Mr. Hen. Simons.
Printed for J. Walsh . . . N°. 63.

[*c.* 1730.]

> Walsh Cat. 18: 'Simmon's Aires (for 2 Flutes). 2s. od. N°. 63.'
> Smith 418 with Walsh only in the imprint and 'N°. 63' added to the title-page.

> *See also* No. 1549. Weldon (John) and Simons (Henry) A Collection of Aires, &c.

SIMPSON (CHRISTOPHER)

1371. Simpson's Compendium. 2s. od.

[*c.* 1730.]

> Walsh Cat. 18.
> Presumably refers to 'A Compendium: or Introduction to practical Musick', &c., first published by Henry Brome in 1665 as 'The Principles of Practical Musick', &c. and later as 'A Compendium of Practical Musick', &c. (BM. K. 8. c. 22; 7897. aa. 14, &c. 8°) and sold by Walsh.

1372. Sympson's Division Violist. (Musick for the Harpsicord, Spinnet or Organ.) £1. 1s. 0d.

[*c.* 1730.]

Walsh Cat. 18.
Presumably refers to the work first published by William Godbid in 1659 (BM. K. 1. i. 11. (1.)) and later by others, and sold by Walsh.

SMITH (JOHN CHRISTOPHER)

1373. The Enchanter A Musical Entertainment as it is Perform'd at the Theatre Royal in Drury Lane. Compos'd by Mr Smith.
London. Printed for I. Walsh, &c.

Public Advertiser, Jan. 8, 1761.

Fol. pp. 44.
BM. G. 240. c. RAM. RCM. Euing.
Words by David Garrick.

1374. The Fairies An Opera. The Words taken from Shakespear &c. Set to Music by Mr Smith.

Vide Prologue   GARRICK.

    Struck with the Wonders of his Master's Art
    Whose SACRED DRAMAS shape and melt the Heart
    Whose Heaven-born Strains the coldest Breast inspire,
    Whose CHORUS-THUNDER sets the Soul on Fire!
    Inflam'd, astonish'd! at those magic Airs,
    When SAMSON groans, and frantic SAUL despairs,
    The Pupil wrote—

    -
    -

    If through the Clouds appear some glimm'ring Rays,
    They're Sparks he caught from his great Master's Blaze!
London. Printed for I. Walsh, &c.

London Evening-Post, March 6–8, 1755. (Songs in the New English Opera, call'd The Fairies.); *Whitehall Evening-Post*, March 29–April 1, 1755. (A Second Sett of Songs in . . . To which is prefixed the Overture.); *Public Advertiser*, April 17, 1755. (3rd Set of Songs.); *Whitehall Evening Post*, April 15–17, 1755. (The Fairies. An English Opera.)

Fol. 'A Table of Songs', &c., pp. 2–61, blank, 63–92.
BM. G. 240. a. Gresham. RAM. RCM. Bod. Euing. Fitz.
Adapted from 'A Midsummer Night's Dream' by David Garrick.
Copy of the 1st Set at Tenbury and 2nd Set, Mummery Cat. 24, No. 876. (See Nos. 1375, 1376.)

1375. Songs in the New English Opera call'd the Fairies. as it is Perform'd at the Theatre-Royal in Drury Lane. Compos'd by Mr Smith. N.B. A 2ᵈ Collection will be Publish'd in a few Days.
London. Printed for I. Walsh, &c.

London Evening-Post, March 6–8, 1755.

 Fol. pp. 7–36.
 Tenbury.

1376. A 2nd Set of Songs in the New English Opera call'd the Fairies, &c.
London. Printed for I. Walsh, &c.

Whitehall Evening-Post, March 29–April 1, 1755.

 Fol. pp. 2–6 (Overture), 37–61.
 Mummery Cat. 24, No. 876.

Lessons.

 The details of dates of publication and identification of the different sets are uncertain owing to the use of the same plate for title-pages of different collections and the manuscript alterations on various copies. Randall Cat. gives Smith Lessons Op. 1. 6s. od. Op. 2. 6s. od. Op. 3. 6s. od. Op. 4. 6s. od. Op. 5. 10s. 6d., as identified and indicated on the following entries.

1377. Six Suits of Lessons for the Harpsicord Compos'd by Mr Smith Author of the Opera call'd The Fairies. Opera Terza.
London. Printed for I. Walsh, &c.

London Evening-Post, Nov. 4–6, 1755. (Six Sets of Lessons for the Harpsichord . . . Op. 3.)

 Obl. fol. pp. 41.
 BM. e. 5. (8.) RAM. Coke. Hall. Pendlebury. Rowe. Tenbury.
 Issued with a different title-page as Opera I. (No. 1378.)
 Randall Cat.: 'Smith's Lessons. Op. 1. 6s. od.'

1378. A Collection of Lessons for the Harpsicord Compos'd by Mr Smith Author of the Opera call'd The Fairies. Opera I.
London. Printed for I. Walsh, &c.

[*c.* 1757.]

 Obl. fol. pp. 41.
 Fitz. Rowe.
 Identical with 'Six Suits of Lessons . . . Opera Terza', (No. 1377) except for title-page. Fitz. copy has 'Opera I' altered to 'III' in MS.

1379. A Collection of Lessons for the Harpsicord Compos'd by Mr Smith Author of the Opera call'd The Fairies. Opera IV.
London. Printed for I. Walsh, &c.

Public Advertiser, Feb. 7, 1757.

> Obl. fol. Numbered VII–XII, pp. 42–73, blank, 75–81.
> BM. d. 37.a. RCM. Coke. Fitz. Rowe.
> The 'V' in 'Opera IV' is in MS.
> The Lessons are numbered and paginated in continuation of 'Six Suits of Lessons . . .
> Opera Terza'. (No. 1377.)
> Randall Cat.: 'Smith's Lessons. Op. 2. 6s. od.'

1380. A Collection of Lessons for the Harpsicord Compos'd by Mr Smith Author of the Opera call'd The Fairies. Opera III.
London. Printed for I. Walsh, &c.

> [*c.* 1760.]
>> Obl. fol. pp. 34.
>> Rowe.
>> 'Opera I' altered to 'III' in MS. Consists of Suites 1–3 from Volume II of his 'Suites de Pieces.' (No. 1385.)
>> Randall Cat.: 'Smith's Lessons. Op. 3. 6s. od.'

1381. A Collection of Lessons for the Harpsicord Compos'd by Mr Smith Author of the Opera call'd The Fairies. Opera II.
London. Printed for I. Walsh, &c.

> [*c.* 1755.]
>> Obl. fol. pp. 35–82.
>> BM. d. 37. b. ('Opera I' altered to 'II' in MS.) Rowe. ('Opera I' altered to 'IV' in MS.)
>> A different work from the preceding. Consists of Suites 4–6 from Volume II of his 'Suites de Pieces'. (No. 1385.)
>> Randall Cat.: 'Smith's Lessons. Op. 4. 6s. od.'

1382. Paradise Lost. An Oratorio. Set to Musick by Mr Smith.
London. Printed for I. Walsh, &c.

Public Advertiser, March 8, 1760.

> Fol. 'A Table of the Songs', &c., pp. 90.
> BM. g. 232. (2.) Gresham. RCM. CUL. Euing. Pendlebury. Tenbury.

1383. Rebecca. An Oratorio. Set to Musick by Mr Smith.
London. Printed for I. Walsh, &c.

Public Advertiser, March 12, 1761. (Songs in the New Oratorio of Rebecca.); April 14, 1761. (A Second Set of Songs . . . with the Overture.)

> Fol. Passe-partout title-page. 'A Table of the Songs', &c., pp. 2–80.
> Gresham. RCM. Euing. Rowe.

1384. XII Sonatas for the Harpsichord. Opera Quinta. Most humbly inscrib'd To Her Royal Highness The Princess Dowager of Wales by Her Royal Highnesses most Obedient and most Devoted Servant Iohn Christopher Smith.

London. Printed for I. Walsh, &c.

Public Advertiser, March 7, 1765.

> Obl. fol. pp. 1–7, blank, 9–38, blank, 40–61, blank, 63–75.
> RM. 16. a. 2. Fitz. Pendlebury.
> Randall Cat.: 'Smith's Lessons. Op. 5. 10s. 6d.'

1385. Suites de Pieces Pour le Clavecin. Composées par I. C. Smith. Second Volume.

London Printed & Sold by Iohn Walsh ... N.º 490.

Country Journal: or, The Craftsman, May 14, 1737. (Where may be had just publish'd Six Sets of Lessons for the Harpsichord. Vol. II.)

> Obl. fol. Passe-partout title-page from the plate used by Walsh for Handel's 'Suites de Pieces'. 'A List of Subscribers', 1 p. pp. 82.
> BM. d. 37. RAM. Fitz.
> Vol. 1 was 'Printed for and Sold by the Author ... and by Thos. Cobb.' (*London Evening-Post*, May 2, 1732.) (BM. d. 37. Obl. fol. Subscribers, 2 pp. Dedication, 1 p. pp. 59.)
> Walsh Cat. 18: 'Smith's Lessons. 12s. 6d.' (This refers to copies of the Author's edition of Vol. I, which were being sold by Walsh.)
> Walsh Cat. 21: 'Smith's Lessons. 10s. 6d.' [Vol. II.]

1386. The Tempest. An Opera. The Words taken from Shakespear &c. Set to Music by M.ʳ Smith.

London. Printed for I. Walsh, &c.

London Evening-Post, March 4–6, 1756. (Songs in The Tempest.); *Public Advertiser*, March 23, 1756. (A Second Set of Songs, &c.); *Public Advertiser*, April 3, 1756. (A Third Set of Songs in ... which compleats the Opera.)

> Fol. 'A Table of the Songs', &c., pp. 2–79, blank, 81–110.
> BM. G. 240. Gresham. RAM. RCM. Birmingham. Fitz.
> Text adapted by David Garrick.
> Copy of 1st set only at Tenbury. (No. 1387.)

1387. Songs in the New English Opera call'd the Tempest. as it is Perform'd at the Theatre Royal in Drury Lane. Compos'd by M.ʳ Smith. N.B. A 2.ᵈ Collection will be Publish'd in a few Days.

London. Printed for I. Walsh, &c.

London Evening-Post, March 4–6, 1756.

> Fol. pp. 7–46.
> Tenbury.

See also Nos. 1155, 1156, 1157. Overtures. Abel Arne and Smith's Six Favourite Overtures, &c.

SOLIMANO

1388. The Favourite Songs in the Opera Call'd Solimano.
London. Printed for I. Walsh, &c.

Public Advertiser, Feb. 25, 1758.

Fol. Passe-partout title-page. pp. 21.
BM. G. 201. (4.) RCM. Bod. Coke. Rowe.
Pasticcio. Composers named are Perez, Bertoni, and Handel.
Republished in 'Le Delizie dell' Opere', Vol. IX, pp. 186–201.

SOLNITZ (ANTON WILLEM)

1389. Six Sonatas For Two Violins with a Thorough Bass for the Harpsicord or
Violoncello Compos'd by Antonio Guglielmo Solniz. [Op. 1.]
London. Printed for I. Walsh, &c.

General Advertiser, Nov. 24, 1750. (Just published.)

Fol. 3 parts.
BM. g. 274. (6.) RAM. Manchester. Rowe.
Walsh Cat. 25: 'Solniz Sonatas. 5s. od.'
Randall Cat.: 'Solnitz Sonatas, Op. 1. 5s. od.'

1390. Six Sonatas for two German Flutes or Violins with a Bass for the Violoncello or Harpsicord Compos'd by Sigr Antonio Guglielmo Solniz. Opera Seconda.
London Printed for I. Walsh, &c.

General Advertiser, March 29, 1751.

Fol. 3 parts.
BM. g. 421. v. (4.) (With 2 copies of the Basso part.) RAM. Rowe.
Walsh Cat. 25: 'Solniz Sonatas, Op. 2d 5s. od.'
Randall Cat.: 'Solnitz Sonatas, Op. 2. 5s. od.'

SOLOS

1391. A Collection of New Solo's for a German Flute and a Bass, and for a Violin
and a Bass. Compos'd by several eminent Masters.
Printed for, and sold by J. Walsh . . . and J. Hare, &c.

London Journal, Sept. 2, 1727. (New Musick just published.)

Not identified.

1392. Six Solos by several Authors (for a Violin and a Bass). 4s. od. No 435.
Printed for J. Walsh, &c.

[*c.* 1730.]

Walsh Cat. 18.
Reissue of Smith 224 (an advertisement of 'Six Select Solos for a Violin and a thorough
Bass, Collected out of the Choicest Works of Six Eminent Masters, viz Signior Martino
Betty [i.e. Bitti], Mr. Nicola [Matteis], Jun. Signior Corelli, Signior Torelli, Signior Carlo
Ambrogio, and Mr. Pepusch; the first Collection Engraven and carefully Corrected, price
3s.') with Walsh only in the imprint and 'No 435' added to the title-page.

1393. Six Solos Four for a German Flute and a Bass and two for a Violin with a Thorough Bass for the Harpsicord or Bass Violin Compos'd by Mʳ Handel Sigʳ Geminiani Sigʳ Somis Sigʳ Brivio.

London. Printed for and sold by I: Walsh . . . and Ioseph Hare, &c.

Daily Post, July 22, 1730. (Solo's for a German Flute . . . by four celebrated Masters.)

> Fol. pp. 1-11, blank, 12-19, blank, 20.
> BM. h. 2140. d. (3.) Bod. Coke. CUL. NLS.BH. 233.
> 'Sonata I. Traversa Solo by Mʳ Handel'; 'Sonata II. Traversa Solo by Mʳ Handel'; 'Sonata III. Traversa Solo by Mʳ Handel'; 'Sonata IV. Traversa Solo del Sigʳ Brivio'; 'Violino Solo V. del Sigʳ Geminiani'; 'Violino Solo VI. del Sigʳ Batista Somis'.
> Smith, 'Handel. A Descriptive Catalogue' &c. pp. 241-2.

1394. Six Solos Four for a German Flute and a Bass . . . by Mʳ Handel, &c.
London. Printed for and sold by I: Walsh . . . Nº 398.

[*c.* 1731.]

> Fol. pp. 20.
> Walsh Cat. 18: '6 Solos by Geminiani, Brivio and other Authors. 3s. od. Nº 398.' A later issue, with Walsh only in the imprint and 'Nº 398' added to the title-page.

1395. 3 Solos for a German Flute. 3ˢ oᵈ

[*c.* 1730-2.]

> Listed on the title-page of Walsh's first and second editions of 'Solos for a German Flute', &c. (Op. I. c. 1732, 1733.) Presumably a separate issue of the three Handel Sonatas of the previous item probably with a title in MS. The advertisement may, however, refer to the complete work including the items by Geminiani, Somis, and Brivio as the price is the same.

1396. Six Solos for a German Flute or Violin with a Thorough Bass for the Harpsichord or Violoncello Compos'd by Several Eminent Authors. Not Printed before.
London Printed for I. Walsh, &c.

Public Advertiser, Oct. 28, 1761.

> Fol. Passe-partout title-page. pp. 1-11, blank, 13-23, blank, 25-31.
> RM. 17. f. 20. (8.)
> Contains Sonatas by Frederick II, King of Prussia, A. Besozzi, and G. Fritz.
> Randall Cat.: 'K—g of P—'s Solos. 4s. od.'

SOMIS (GIOVANNI BATTISTA)

See No. 1393. Solos. Six Solos Four for a German Flute .. Compos'd by Mʳ Handel . . . Sigʳ Somis, &c.

SONATAS

1397. Twelve Sonata's in three parts, for two Violins or German Flutes and a Bass. By an eminent English Author.

Printed for and sold by John Walsh, &c.

Country Journal: or, The Craftsman, Feb. 21, 1736.

Not identified.

Sonatas or Chamber Airs.

See No. 772. Hasse (Johann Adolph) [Chamber Airs.]

Six Sonatas 3 for 2 Flutes and 3 for a Flute and a Bass.

See No. 1239. Purcell (Daniel)

SONG TUNES

1398. A Collection of the most Celebrated Song Tunes with their Symphonys out of the late Opera's Neatly fitted to the German Flute for the Improvement of Practicioners on that Instrument by an Eminent Master price 2s. Note the following Pieces may be had, &c.

London Printed and Sold by I: Walsh . . . and Ino. & Ioseph Hare, &c.

[*c.* 1723.]

Obl. 4°. ff. 24. Printed on one side only.
Mitchell.
Contains twenty-three items, all but three by Handel.
See Smith, 'Handel. A Descriptive Catalogue', &c., pp. 277–8.

1399. A 4th Collection of the most Celebrated Song Tunes with their Symphonys out of the late Opera's and Fitted to the Violin or Hoboy for the Improvement of Practicioners on that Instrument by an Eminent Master price 2s. Note the following pieces may be had where these are Sold Mr. Banisters 1st & 2d Collection, &c.

London. Printed & Sold by I: Walsh . . . and Ino. & Ioseph Hare, &c.

[*c.* 1726.]

Obl. 4°. f. 24. Printed on one side only.
Rowe.
Title-page of 3rd Collection, with '4th' in MS. pasted over '3rd'.
No copies of second and third collections, advertised as 'Opera Airs', traced.
Contain twenty-one items, nineteen by Handel.
Smith, 'Handel. A Descriptive Catalogue', &c., p. 278.

SONGS (arranged chronologically)

1400. Four New and Diverting Songs, performed at the Theatres and Publick Entertainments, with great Applause, particularly the Cobbler's-End. Price 6d.

Printed for and sold by John Walsh . . . and Joseph Hare, &c.

Daily Journal, April 13, 1728.

> Not identified. Richard Leveridge composed a song 'The Cobbler's End'. (BUC.)

1401. The Choicest Songs out of yᵉ latest Operas for the Harpsicord by the greatest Masters.

> [*c.* 1729.]

> Walsh Cat. 11*b*.
> Not identified. May be a general reference to separate collections or to the collections of sheet songs issued by Walsh *c.* 1703 and *c.* 1715. (Smith 142 c. and 463.)

1402. Comical Songs. 2 Books. 5s. 0d. Nº 330.

> [*c.* 1730.]

> Walsh Cat. 18.
> Book I is presumably Smith 319 ('A Collection of Comicall Songs'. Walsh Cat. 9*a* 'A Book of Comical Songs. 2s. 6d.'), with Walsh only in the imprint and 'Nº 330' added to the title-page.
> Book II not otherwise known.

Songs and Aires for the Viol.

> *See* No 5. Airs. Aires & Symphonys for yᵉ Bass Viol, &c.

1403. Marybon Songs. each 1s. 6d.

> [*c.* 1755.]

> Walsh Cat. 25.
> Not identified. Refers presumably to various collections of Songs sung at Marylebone Gardens, recorded elsewhere under various composers.

1404. Miss Brents Songs sung at Vauxhall. 5s. 0d.

> [*c.* 1765.]

> Walsh Cat. 27.
> Not identified. May refer to volumes of Arne's 'Vocal Melody'. (No. 91, &c.)

1405. A Second Set of the new Songs and Ballads sung at Vauxhall Gardens, for the Harpsichord, Voice, German Flute, or Guitar.

Printed for J. Walsh, &c.

Public Advertiser, July 16, 1765.

> Not identified.

1406. A Collection of new Songs, sung by Mr. Vernon and Mrs. Weichsell at Vauxhall Gardens. Price 2s.

Printed and sold at, the late Mr. Walsh's, &c.

Public Advertiser, July 24, 1766.

> Not identified.

SPRING

The Pastoral called The Spring.

> *See* Nos. 253, 258 British Miscellany.

STAMITZ (JOHANN WENZEL ANTON)

1407. VI Sinfonies or Overtures in Eight Parts. For Violins, French Horns &c. with a Bass for the Harpsicord or Violoncello. Compos'd by Sʳ Stamitz.

London. Printed for I. Walsh, &c.

[*c.* 1765.]

> Fol. 8 parts.
> RM. 26. b. 2. (12.) RCM. Bod.
> Walsh Cat. 27: 'Stamitz Symphonys. 10s. 6d.'

STANESBY (THOMAS) *Junior*

1408. A new System of the Flute, abec, or common English Flute, wherein is propos'd to render that Instrument universally useful in Concert, without the trouble of transposing the Musick for it. By Tho. Stanesby, Jun.

Printed for John Walsh, &c.

Country Journal: or, The Craftsman, Jan. 18, 1735.

> Not in Dayton Miller catalogue or traced elsewhere.

STANLEY (JOHN)

1409. Six Cantata's, For a Voice and Instruments: Set to Musick by John Stanley, MB Organist of the Temple and St. Andrew's in London.

London Evening-Post, April 1–3, 1760. (Three Books of English Cantatas. Printed for J. Walsh, &c.)

> Presumably a reissue of the original edition with the above title, printed for John Stanley, 1742. (BM. H. 1217. (1.) Fol. Privilege. pp. 3–49.)

1410. Six Cantata's For a Voice and Instruments, Set to Music by John Stanley MB, &c. [Second Set.]

London Evening-Post, April 1–3, 1760. (Three Books of English Cantatas. Printed for J. Walsh, &c.)

> Presumably a reissue of the original edition with the above title, printed for John Stanley, 1748. (BM. H. 1217. (2.) Fol. pp. 3–45.)

1411. Three **Cantatas** and three Songs for a Voice and Instruments Set to Music by John Stanley MB.

London Evening-Post, April 1–3, 1760. (Three Books of English Cantatas. Printed for J. Walsh, &c.)

> Presumably a reissue of the original edition with the above title, printed for the author, 1751. (BM. H. 2818. d. (10.) Fol. pp. 3–27.)

1412. Six Concertos in Seven Parts for Four Violins, a Tenor Violin, a Violoncello, with Thorough Bass for the Harpsicord. Compos'd by John Stanley Batchelor of Musick, Organist of S.t Andrews, and the Temple.

London. Printed for I. Walsh, &c.

Daily Advertiser, Jan. 14, 1745.

> Fol. 7 parts.
> BM. h. 2985. a. RM. 6. h. 17. (10.) (Violin I and Secondo Ripieno parts only.)
> RCM. Cardiff. Fitz. Manchester. Pendlebury. Rowe. Tenbury.
> The music is printed from the same plates as the original work 'Six Concerto's in seven Parts . . . Opera Seconda. London Printed for, and Sold by the Author', &c. (BM. h. 2985.) (*London Evening-Post*, March 30–April 1, 1742.)

1413. Six Concertos for Violins, &c. in seven Parts. . . The 2d Edit.

Printed for J. Walsh, &c.

Daily Advertiser, April 8, 1745.

1414. — Another edition.

General Advertiser, Feb. 3, 1747. (New edn. of Stanley's Concertos for Violins.)

> RAM. RCM. Oriel College, Oxford. (BUC. not examined.)

1415. Six Concertos Set for the Harpsicord or Organ Compos'd by M.r John Stanley Organist of the Temple, and S.t Andrews. N.B. The 1.st & 2.d Ripienos, Tenor, & Basso Ripieno of His Violin Concertos, are the Instrumental Parts to the above.

London. Printed for I. Walsh, &c.

[*c.* 1745.]

> Fol. pp. 1–7, blank, 9–11, blank, 13–17, blank, 19–28, blank, 30–32.
> BM. f. 25. a. RM. 16. f. 1. (2.) Hirsch IV. 1660. a. Fitz. Manchester. Rowe. Tenbury. Welsh Cat. 24a.

1416. — Another edition.

General Advertiser, Oct. 25, 1749. (New editions, &c.)

1417. Six Solos for a German Flute Violin or Harpsicord Taken from the Six Concertos for Violins &c. Compos'd by M.ʳ John Stanley.

London. Printed for I. Walsh, &c.

[*c.* 1745.]

> Fol. pp. 1–7, blank, 9–11, blank, 13–17, blank, 19–22, blank, 24–28, blank, 30–32.
> BM. f. 25. Tenbury.
> Walsh Cat. 24*a*.

1418. Zimri. An Oratorio. Set to Musick by M.ʳ Stanley.

London. Printed for I. Walsh, &c.

Public Advertiser, March 29, 1760.

> Fol. 'A Table of the Songs', &c., pp. 2–69.
> BM. G. 232. (1.) Gresham. RCM. Cardiff. Euing.
> Full score. Words by John Hawkesworth.

See also No. 12 Airs. Select Aires or Duets for two German Flutes . . . 3.ᵈ Book; No. 267. The British Orpheus. No. III; No 1233. Psalms; Nos. 1419, 1420. The Summer's Tale . . . Music by . . . Stanley, &c.

STEFFANI (Agostino)

See No. 1443. Thomyris

SUMMER'S TALE

1419. The Summer's Tale. A Musical Comedy. As it is Perform'd at the Theatre Royal in Covent Garden. The Music by Abel Arne Arnold Boyce Bach Cocchi Ciampi C. S.ᵗ Germain Giardini Hasse Howard Lampe Lampugnani Richter Russel Stanley For the Harpsichord, Voice, German Flute, or Violin.

London Printed for I. Walsh, &c.

Public Advertiser, Dec. 19, 1765 (Book I.); Jan. 6, 1766 (The Second Act. Book II.); Jan. 29, 1766. (The Third Act. Book III.); Feb. 1, 1766. (Price 10s. 6d.)

> Obl. fol. 'A Table of the Songs', &c., pp. 2–37, blank, 39–55, 2 blank, 56–79.
> BM. D. 273. (1.) RCM. CUL. Cardiff. Fitz.
> Besides those named on the title-page, this pasticcio contains compositions by Baildon, Bertoni, Dunn, Galuppi, Granom, Piccini, Potenza and Vernon.
> Words by Richard Cumberland.

1420. The Summer's Tale Set for the German Flute, Hoboy, or Violin The Music by Abel Arne Arnold Boyce Bach Cocchi Giardini Howard Hasse Lampugnani Richter Stanley. Price 1.ˢ 6.ᵈ

London. Printed for I. Walsh, &c.

Public Advertiser, Jan. 13, 1766. (Just publish'd The Airs in the Summer's Tale.)

> 8°. One page without pagination and pp. 32.
> BM. e. 340. h. (3.) Mitchell.

1421. The Airs in the Summer's Tale A Musical Comedy Set for the Guitar. Price 1s. 6d.

London. Printed for I. Walsh, &c.

Public Advertiser, Jan. 13, 1766. (Just publish'd.)

8°. pp. 20.
Pendlebury.

1422. The Overture in the Summer's Tale For Two Violins, 2 Hoboys, 2 French Horns, a Tenor, with a Bass for the Harpsicord, & Violoncello. Compos'd by C. F. Abel. Price 2ˢ.

London. Printed & Sold at the late Mʳ I. Walsh's, &c.

Public Advertiser, March 15, 1766.

Fol. 8 parts.
BM. g. 30. (2.)

1423. The Overture in the Summer's Tale . . . Compos'd by C. F. Abel . . . set for the Harpsicord, Price 6d.

Printed and sold at the late Mr. J. Walsh's, &c.

Public Advertiser, March 15, 1766.

SYMPSON (Christopher)

See Simpson

TAGLIETTI (Giulio)

1424. Taglietti's Concertos (Violins). £1. 1s. 0d.

[*c.* 1735.]

Walsh Cat. 18.
Presumably 'Concerti é Sinfonie a Tre Du (*sic*) Violini Violene (*sic*), o Cembalo da Giulio Taglietti mastro nel Collegio di Nobili di Brescia Opera Seconda. London Printed and sold by Daniel Wright', *c.* 1735. (BM. g. 679. Fol. 3 parts.)
Presumably Walsh sold copies of this work. Not in his later catalogues.

TARTINI (Giuseppe)

1425. XII Solos for a Violin with a Thorough Bass for the Harpsicord or Violoncello Compos'd by Giuseppe Tartini.

London. Printed for and Sold by I. Walsh, &c.

Daily Advertiser, Sept. 18, 1742. (Of whom may be had.)

Fol. pp. 57.
BM. g. 296. (2.)
This work is the same as 'Sonate a Violino e Violoncello o Cimbalo . . . Opera Prima. Amsterdam Spesa di Michele Carlo Le Cene.' [1734.] (BM. g. 296. c.)
Walsh Cat. 18: Tartini's Solos.

1426. — *General Evening Post*, Oct. 12–15, 1745. (Tartini's Solos. Just publish'd.)

1427. —Re-advertisement.

General Advertiser, April 2, 1746. (Of whom may be had.)

1428. Six Solos For a Violin with a Thorough Bass for the Harpsicord or Violoncello Compos'd by Giuseppe Tartini. Opera Seconda.
London. Printed for I. Walsh, &c.

General Advertiser, June 21, 1746. (Just published. Price 4s.)

> Fol. pp. 1–5, blank, 7–11, blank, 13–17, blank, 19–23, blank, 25–29, blank, 31–35.
> BM. g. 296. (1.)
> This is not the same work as 'Sonate a Violino e Basso . . . Opera Seconda', published at Rome. (BM. e. 787.)

1429. Twelve Sonatas in Three Parts, for a German Flute and Violin, or two Violins, with a Bass for the Violoncello or Harpsicord. Composed by Sig.r Giuseppe Tartini. Opera Terza.
London. Printed for I. Walsh, &c.

Public Advertiser, April 12, 1756.

> Large fol. Parts.
> CUL. Rowe.
> With 'N.º XXIV' printed at the top of the title-page.
> This is not the same work as 'XII Sonatas for Two Violins and a Bass', &c. (BM. g. 296. e.)

> *See also* No. 1364. Select Harmony. Select Harmony Fourth Collection. Six Concertos . . . Compos'd by M.r Handel Tartini &c.

TELEMANN (Georg Philipp)

1430. XII Solos for a Violin with a Thorough Bass for the Harpsicord or Bass Violin Compos'd by G: P: Telemann. Opera Prima.
London. Printed for & Sold by I. Walsh . . . N.º 417.

[*c.* 1735.]

> Fol. pp. 28. 25.
> BM. g. 422. i. (2.) RAM.
> These solos were first published by Walsh and Hare under Telemann's pseudonym, Georgio Melande, the first six as Opera Prima and the remainder as Opera Seconda. In Walsh Cat. 18 they appear under Melande with the Walsh numbers 416 and 417. (Nos. 1004–1007.)

1431. Six Sonatas or Duets for two German Flutes or Violins Compos'd by Sig.r G. P. Telemann. Opera Seconda.

London. Printed for I. Walsh, &c.

General Advertiser, June 30, 1746.

Fol. pp. 1–5, blank, 7–15, blank, 17–20, blank, 22–23, blank, 25–28, blank, 30–35.
BM. g. 401. a. (2.)

TEMPLE MUSIC
The Temple Musick: or, an Essay Concerning the Method of Singing.

See No. 147. Bedford (Arthur)

TEMPLE OF LOVE
The Opera of Temple of Love.

See No. 612. Fedelli (Giuseppe) called *Saggione*

TERRADELLAS (DOMINGO MIGUEL BARNABAS)
1432. Dudici Arie e Due Duetti All' Eccellenza Di Melusina Baronessa di Schulem-
burg Contessa di Walsingham, Contessa di Chesterfield Queste Composizioni di
Musica Delle alme Grandi Nobile Sollievo Qual Tributo di Rispetto e d'Ammira-
zione Dedica e Consacra L'Umilissimo e Devotissimo Servo Dominico Terradellas.

London. Printed for I. Walsh, &c.

General Advertiser, April 23, 1748. (Twelve favourite Italian Songs and two
Duets.)

Fol. pp. 2–55.
BM. G. 113.

1433. — Another edition.

[*c.* 1750.]

Fol. pp. 15–55, 2–14 (top corner).
RM. 13. c. 22. (6.)
With additional top centre pagination 27–67 on pp. 15–55 and 68–80 on 2–14 respectively
from 'Le Delizie dell' Opere', Vol. V.

1434. The Favourite Songs in the Opera Call'd Bellerofonte By Sig^r Terradellas.
London. Printed for I. Walsh, &c.

General Advertiser, April 4, 1747.

Fol. Passe-partout title-page. pp. 2–20.
BM. G. 194. (5.) RCM. Rowe.
Republished in 'Le Delizie dell' Opere', Vol. V, pp. 169–84.

1435. The Favourite Songs in the Opera Call'd Mitridate By Sig^r Terradellas.
N^o I.
London. Printed for I. Walsh, &c.

— N.° II.

General Advertiser, Dec. 20, 1746. (The favourite Songs.) Jan. 23, 1747. (A Second Set of the favourite Songs.)

> Fol. Passe-partout title-pages. No. I. pp. 2–17. No. II. pp. 18–33, blank, 34–37.
> BM. G. 194. (3.) RCM. Rowe. Gresham. (No. II.)
> No. I republished in 'Le Delizie dell' Opere', Vol. V, pp. 133–48, No. II republished in 'Le Delizie dell' Opere', Vol. V, pp. 149–68.

1436. — Another issue of No. I.

> [*c.* 1750.]

> Fol. pp. 5–17, 2–4 (bottom centre).
> BM. H. 348. e. (5.)
> Wanting title-page. With additional top centre pagination 133–48 from 'Le Delizie dell' Opere', Vol. V.

See also No. 37. Annibale in Capua (Name given as Terradeglias); Nos. 556, 559–66. Delizie dell' Opere. Vols. I, IV–XI; Nos. 780, 782. Hasse (Johann Adolph) [Chamber Airs.]

TESSARINI (Carlo)

1437. Concerti a Cinque Con 3 Violini, Violetta, Violoncello ò Basso Continuo Da Carlo Tessarini di Rimini Virtuoso di Violino Presentemente in Venetia Opera Prima.

> London Printed for and sold by I: Walsh . . . and Ioseph Hare, &c.

London Journal, Feb. 18, 1727. (Walsh only. New Musick.); *Country Journal: or, The Craftsman*, April 7, 1728. (Lately published.)

> Fol. 6 parts.
> Hirsch III. 540. BM. g. 688. b. (Organo e Violoncello part only.) RCM.

1438. — With Walsh only in the imprint and 'N.° 441' added to the title-page.

> [*c.* 1730.]

> BM. g. 688. a.; g. 688. c.

1439. — Another edition.

General Evening Post, Jan. 17–19, 1745; *General Advertiser*, Oct. 25, 1749. (New editions.)

1440. XII Solos for a German Flute a Hoboy or Violin with a Thorough Bass for the Harpsicord or Bass Violin Compos'd by Carlo Tessarini di Rimini. Opera Seconda.

London. Printed for and Sold by I: Walsh . . . N<u>o</u> 580.

Country Journal: or, The Craftsman, Feb. 7, 1736.

Fol. pp. 1–17, blank, 19–27, blank, 29–33, blank, 35–55.
BM. g. 688. CUL.

1441. Twelve Solos for a German Flute or Harpsichord, by Carlo Tessarini.
Printed for J. Walsh, &c.

Daily Advertiser, July 11, 1744.

May refer to an issue of No. 1440 otherwise not identified.

1442. Six Sonatas for two German Flutes or Violins with a Thorough Bass for the
Harpsicord. Compos'd by Carlo Tessarini di Rimini. Opera Terza.
London. Printed for I. Walsh, &c.

London Evening-Post, Jan. 28–30, 1752.

Fol. Parts.
BM. g. 409. k. (3.) Euing. Manchester.

See also Nos. 753, 755. Harmonia Mundi. The first Collection. (The 2<u>d</u>. Collection.)

THOMYRIS

1443. The Opera of Thomyris, with the additional Songs, as it is now performed
at the Theatre in Lincoln's-Inn-Fields.
Printed for, and sold by John Walsh . . . and Joseph Hare, &c.

Country Journal: or, The Craftsman, Jan. 20, 1728.

Fol.
Pasticcio. Music consists of airs by A. Scarlatti, G. Bononcini, Steffani, Gasparini, and
Albinoni. Adapted and arranged by J. C. Pepusch, first produced in 1707.
The newspaper notice covers issues of Smith 254 ('Songs in the New Opera', &c. BM. H.
113.) and Smith 565 ('The Additional Songs', &c. BM. H. 2815. j. (1.)).
For earlier editions of this opera *see* Smith, 246, 251, and 253.

1444. — With Walsh only in the imprint and 'N<u>o</u> 222' added to the title-page.
[*c.* 1730.]

Walsh Cat. 18: 'The Opera of Thomyris. 9s. od. N<u>o</u> 222.'

1445. The Symphonys or Instrumental Parts in the Opera Call'd Thomyris as they
are Perform'd at the Theatre Royal.
London Printed for I. Walsh . . . N<u>o</u> 478.
[*c.* 1730.]

Fol. Parts.
Walsh Cat. 18: 'Thomyris Concertos (Violins). 6s. od. N<u>o</u> 478.'
Smith 337 and 617 with Walsh only in the imprint and 'N<u>o</u> 478' added to the title-page.
The work was an arrangement for instrumental parts of the opera Thomyris, music by A. Scarlatti, G. Bononcini, &c.
Walsh Cat. 16*a*: 'Thomyris Symp: or Concertos. 6s. od.'

Thomyris. Overture.

> *See* No. 220. Bononcini (Giovanni) and (Antonio Maria) and others. Bononcini's Six Overtures for Violins ... in the Operas of Astartus ... Thomyris, &c.

> *See also* No. 1174. Pepusch (Johann Christoph) The Additional Songs in the Opera's of Thomyris & Camilla, &c.

THORNOWETS (   )

1446. Sonate da Camera Per il Flauto Col Basso Del Seg<u>r</u> Thornowets Trez Exactement Corrigee.

> In Londra A Spese di Giovanni Walsh ... e Giovanni Hare, &c.

> *Daily Courant*, April 4, 1722.

>> Fol. pp. 24.

1447. — With 'N<u>o</u> 105' added to the title-page.

> [*c*. 1730.]

>> BM. g. 280. b. (15.)
>> 'N<u>o</u> 105' has been added in MS. and altered to 'N<u>o</u> 405'.
>> Walsh Cat. 18: 'Thornowet's Solos (for a Flute and a Bass). 3s. od. N<u>o</u> 105.'

TIBALDI (Giovanni Battista)

1448. Tibaldi's Sonata's or Chamber Aires in three Parts for two Violins and a Through Bass Compos'd by Gio. Battista Tibaldi Opera Prima.

> London Printed for I. Walsh ... N<u>o</u> 439.

> [*c*. 1730.]

>> Large fol. Parts.
>> Smith 265 (BM. h. 22.) with Walsh only in the imprint and 'N<u>o</u> 439' added to the title-page.
>> Walsh Cat. 18: 'Six Sonatas for 2 Violins and a Bass. Op. Prima. 6s. od. N<u>o</u> 439.'

1449. Tibaldi's Sonatas in Three parts for two Violins and a Through Bass Compos'd by Gio Battista Tibaldi Opera 2<u>d</u>

> London Printed for I: Walsh ... N<u>o</u> 440.

> [*c*. 1730.]

Large fol. Parts.
Smith 483 (BM. i. 85.) with Walsh only in the imprint and 'N̠o 440' added to the title-page.
Walsh Cat. 18: '12 Sonatas for 2 Violins and a Bass Op: 2da. 6s. od. N̠o 440.'

TITO MANLIO

1450. The Favourite Songs in the Opera Call'd Tito Manlio.
London. Printed for I. Walsh, &c.

Public Advertiser, May 8, 1756.

Fol. Passe-partout title-page. pp. 2–18.
BM. G. 206. g. (5.) RM. 13. c. 22. (7.) RCM. Rowe.
Composers named are Abbos and Lampugnani.
Republished in 'Le Delizie dell' Opere', Vol. VIII, pp. 144–60.
Randall Cat.: 'Tito Manlio, Abbos. 2s. 6d.'

TO

1451. To take in good part, the squeeze of the hand. *A Cock and a Bull*, as Sung by M̠r Beard at Ranelagh.
Printed with the Consent of the Author by I: Walsh.

[*c.* 1756.]

S.sh. fol.
BM. G. 312. (76.)
London Magazine, July 1756, p. 348.
Universal Magazine, March 1757, p. 132.

TOLOMEO

1452. N̠o 1. The Favourite Songs in the Opera Call'd Tolomeo. Price 4ˢ
London. Printed for I. Walsh, &c.

Public Advertiser, Jan. 20, 1762; April 14, 1762. (2 Collections.)

Fol. Passe-partout title-page. pp. 1–13, blank, 15–27 (bottom centre). With additional top-corner pagination 57–59 on pp. 25–27 and top-centre pagination 7–8 on pp. 26–27.
BM. H. 300. a. RM. 13. c. 22. (8.) (With Price 2ˢ First Collection only. pp. 1–13.)
'4ˢ' is in MS.
Pasticcio. Composers named are Cocchi, Galuppi, and Ciampi.
Republished in 'Le Delizie dell' Opere', Vol. X, pp. 193–5 and Vol. XI, pp. 117–40.

TOPHAM (WILLIAM)

1453. Six Sonata's or Solos, for the Flute. With a Through Bass for the Harpsicord Compos'd by William Topham. A.M.
London Printed & Sold by I: Walsh . . . N̠o 126.

[*c.* 1730.]

Obl. fol. 2 parts.
Smith 60 (BM. d. 150. (5.)) with Walsh only in the imprint and 'N.º 126' added to the title-page.
Walsh Cat. 18: 'Topham's 1st Solos (for a Flute and a Bass). 3s. od. N.º 126.'

1454. Six Sonatas or Solos for the Flute with a Through Bass for the Harpsicord Compos'd by W.ᵐ Topham. A. M. Opera Secunda.
London Printed for I. Walsh . . . N.º 127.

[*c.* 1730.]

Obl. fol. 2 parts.
Smith 227 (BM. c. 105. a. (6.)) with Walsh only in the imprint and 'N.º 127' added to the title-page.
Walsh Cat. 18: 'Topham's 2d Solos (for a Flute and a Bass). 3s. od. N.º 127.'

1455. Topham's Sonatas (for 2 Violins and a Bass). 3s. od. N.º 463.

[*c.* 1730.]

Walsh Cat. 18.
May refer to Smith 334 ('Six Sonata's Five in Four & a Sixth in 7 Parts Compos'd In Imitation of Archangelo Corelli By W.ᵐ Topham. M:A Opera Terza.' BM. g. 171. Fol. Organ part only.)

TORELLI (Giuseppe)

1456. Torelli's Solos (for a Violin or (and) Harpsicord). 4s. od.

[*c.* 1747.]

Walsh Cat. 24*a.*
Walsh Cat. 25.
Randall Cat.
Not identified. Presumably published earlier by Walsh.

1457. Torelli's Sonatas (for 2 Violins and a Bass). 5s. od.

[*c.* 1747.]

Walsh Cat. 24a.
Walsh Cat. 25.
Not identified. Presumably published earlier by Walsh.

See also No. 753. Harmonia Mundi . . . Torelli . . . The first Collection, &c.; No. 1392. Six Solos by several Authors.

TORELLI (Giuseppe) AND VIVALDI (Antonio)

1458. Torelli and Vivaldi's Concertos (Violins). £1. 1s. od.

[*c.* 1730.]

Walsh Cat. 18.
Probably refers to copies of Roger's Amsterdam edition of 'Concerts à, 5, 6 & 7 Instrumens . . . Composez par Messieurs Bitti, Vivaldi & Torelli', &c. (BM. h. 917. Fol. Parts.) Smith 550, which Walsh was selling.

TORTORITI (Gabriele)

1459. Twelve Duets for a German Flute and a Violin. Compos'd by Sig. Tortoriti. Corrected by the Author.

N.B. These Duets are entirely new, and of a different Manner and Taste from any thing hitherto publish'd of that kind, properly adapted for the Use of young Practitioners on each Instrument, and likewise are as agreeable for Gentlemen of longer Practice.

Printed for John Simpson . . . and sold by Mr. Walsh . . . and Mr. Walmsley, &c.

London Daily Post, and General Advertiser, Feb. 29, 1744.

This work was issued as 'Twelve Duets for a German Flute & a Violin' by John Simpson. (Rowe, Fol. Parts.)

1460. Twelve Solos, compos'd on Purpose for a German Flute, with a Thorough Bass for the Harpsichord, or Bass Violin. Compos'd by Sig. Tortoriti.

Printed for John Simpson . . . and sold by J. Walsh . . . Mr. Walmsley, &c.

General Advertiser, April 20, 1744.

1461. Six Sonatas for two German Flutes or Violins and a Bass Compos'd by Sig.ʳ Tortoriti.

London. Printed for I. Walsh, &c.

Daily Advertiser, March 24, 1744. (Just publish'd.)

Fol. 3 parts.
BM. g. 241. (8.); g. 70. c. (7.) RAM.

TRAVERS (John)

1462. Proposals for Printing by Subscription. Eighteen Canzonets, or Songs, for two and three Voices. The words chiefly by Matthew Prior, Esq: Set to Musick by Mr. John Travers, Organist to his Majesty's Chapel Royal, and of St. Paul, Covent Garden.

Subscriptions are taken in by Mr. Walsh . . . and by the Engraver and Printer, John Simpson, &c.

General Evening Post. (London.) Nov. 23–26, 1745.

The work was published with the imprint 'London Printed for the Author by John Simpson'. (BM. G. 805. e. (1.) Fol. pp. 64.) Others in BUC not examined.

See also No. 266. British Orpheus. No. II.

TRE CICISBEI RIDICOLI

1463. The Favourite Songs in the Opera Call'd Le Tre Cicisbei Ridicoli.
London. Printed for I. Walsh, &c.

General Advertiser, April 13, 1749.

1464. — Another edition.

[*c.* 1755.]

> Fol. Passe-partout title-page. pp. 2–10 (top corner).
> RCM. XXXII. A. 30 (3).
> With additional top-centre pagination 145–153 from 'Le Delizie dell' Opere', Vol. VI.
> Bound up with this work are two arias from 'Don Calascione' by Latilla, pp. 11–17 (top corner) with additional pagination 138–44 (top centre) from 'Le Delizie dell' Opere', Vol. VI.

TREATISE

1465. A Treatise on Harmony, containing the chief Rules for Composing in two, three, and four Parts.

Printed for and sold by John Walsh, &c.

Daily Journal, Nov. 25, 1730.

> Walsh Cat. 18: 'Pepusch. A Treatise on Harmony. 1s. 6d.'
> This work, 'A Short Treatise on Harmony', &c., was issued anonymously by J. Watts in 1730 (BM. 785. a. 8. Obl. 8º pp. 84. 4 pl.) and a second edition in 1731, printed by W. Pearson. (BM. 785. a.10. Obl. 8º pp. 228.)

TRELDI ( )

1466. Concertos.

London. Printed and sold by J. Walsh, &c.

General Advertiser, Oct. 25, 1749. (Also new editions, &c.)

> Composer and work not identified.

TRIONFO DI CAMILLA

The Favourite Songs in the Opera Call'd Trionfo di Camilla.

See No. 375. Ciampi (Legrenzio Vincenzo)

TRUMPET TUNES

1467. Six Sets of Trumpet Tunes. 6s. od. Nº 479.

[*c.* 1730.]

> Walsh Cat. 18.
> Smith 525 reissued with Walsh only in the imprint and 'Nº 479' added to the title-page.

TUNES

1468. Familiar Tunes for the Violin. 1s. 6d. Nº 148.

[*c.* 1730.]

> Walsh Cat. 18.
> Smith 369 ('A Book of familiar Tunes for the Violin') with Walsh only in the imprint and 'Nº 148' added to the title-page.
> Presumably same work as 'A Book of Familiar Aires, or Song Tunes for a Violin' advertised on 'Caledonian Country Dances'. (Nos. 278, 279.)

1469. Select Tunes (for a Single Violin). 2 Books. each 1s. 6d.

[*c.* 1730.]

> Walsh Cat. 24*a*.
> Not identified.

1470. 24 Sets of Tunes by the Greatest Masters made for several Plays for 2 Violins and a Bass. £1. 4s. 0d.

[*c.* 1730.]

> Walsh Cat. 18.
> A general entry covering many works in Smith, 32, 40, &c.

TURNER (WILLIAM)

1471. A Philosophical Essay on Musick. Wherein is Explained The Nature of Sound both in its Essence and Regulation &c. Contrived for the Use of the Voice in Singing, as well as for those who play on Instruments. Together with a Thorough Explanation of all the different Moods used in Musick for regulating Time in the different Divisions of Measures used therein. All rendered plain and easy to the meanest Capacities by familiar Similies. The Third Edition. By William Turner.
    Printed for J. Walsh, &c.

General Advertiser, Jan. 23, 1749.

> 8°. 'To the Philoharmonical Society', &c. 2 pp. 'Preface' 2 pp. pp. 80.
> BM. 7897. b. 56.
> First published by William Pearson as 'Sound Anatomiz'd,' &c. 1724. (BM. 557.*c. 20. (3.))

TUTOR

1472. The 6th Book of the Compleat Tutor to the Violin or the Practical Musician Containing the whole Art of Playing on the Violin Improv'd by short and easey Rules for Learners, together with a Collection of the Newest Song Tunes, Aires & Marches, with great Variety of Minuets, Rigadoons & French Dances, Compos'd by the best Masters, ye whole fairly Engraven and carefully corrected. Price 1s 6d
1723.
    London Printed for I: Walsh . . . & I: Hare, &c.

> Obl. 8°. ff. 10. 28. Printed on one side only.
> BM. a. 30.
> The First and Third Books are Smith 515 and 562; another book is probably that listed under No. 228. Book, as 'A new Book for Learners on the Violin', &c. The whole series is probably covered by the entry in Walsh Cat. 18: 'Books for Learners. 1s. 6d. Nº 131.'

1473. The 13th Book of the compleat Tutor to the Violin or the Practical Musician Containing the whole Art of Playing on the Violin Improv'd by short and easey

Rules for Learners, together with a Collection of the Newest Song Tunes, Aires & Marches, with great Variety of Minuets Rigadoons and French Dances, Compos'd by the best Masters. the whole fairly Engraven and carefully corrected. price 1ˢ. 6ᵈ. 1730, &c.

London. Printed for and sold by I: Walsh . . . and Ioseph Hare, &c.

> Obl. 8°. ff. 10. 27. With a folding plate of violin bridge. Printed on one side only.
> Newberry Library, Chicago.

TUTORE E LA PUPILLA

1474. N° I. The Favourite Songs in the Opera Call'd Il Tutore e la Pupilla.
London. Printed for I. Walsh, &c.
— N° II.

Public Advertiser, Nov. 29, 1762; Dec. 13, 1762. (A Second Set.)

> Fol. Passe-partout title-page. pp. 2–13, 15–27.
> BM. G. 179. RCM.
> 'Il' has been altered from 'I' in MS..
> Pasticcio. By Cocchi and anonymous composers.
> Republished in 'Le Delizie dell' Opere', Vol. X, pp. 2–27.

VALENTINE (ROBERT)

1475. Six Setts of Aires and a Chacoon for two Flutes & a Bass Compos'd by Mͬ Valentine at Rome, &c.
London Printed for I: Walsh . . . N° 90.

[*c.* 1730.]

> Large fol. 3 parts.
> Smith 552 (BM. h. 250. c. (6.)) with Walsh only in the imprint and 'N° 90' added to the title-page.
> Walsh Cat. 18: 'Six Sonatas for 2 Flutes and a Bass. 8th Op: 3s. od. N° 90.'

1476. Seven Setts of Aires for two Flutes & a Bass Consisting of Preludes Allmands Corants Sarabands Marches Minuets Gavotts and Jiggs Being familliar & easey for Young Practitioners in Concert Compos'd by Mͬ Robͭ Valentine at Rome Opera Nona.

London, Printed for & sold by I: Walsh . . . & I: Hare, &c.

Post-Boy, Oct. 14–17, 1721.

> Fol. 3 parts. Printed on one side only.
> BM. g. 297. (2.)
> 'Nona' is in MS.
> Title-page used also for Op. 10. (No. 1478.)

1477. — With Walsh only in the imprint and 'N⁰ 94' added to the title-page.

[*c.* 1730.]

Walsh Cat. 18: 'Sonatas or Aircs for 2 Flutes and a Bass. 9th Op: 3s. od. N⁰ 94.'
Advertised on Op. XIII (No. 1494) as: 'Sonatas for 2 Flutes and a Bass, Op. 9.'

1478. Seven Setts of Aires for two Flutes & a Bass Consisting of Preludes All-mands Corants Sarabands Marches Minuets Gavotts and Jiggs Being familliar & easey for young Practitioners in Concert Compos'd by Mʳ Robᵗ Valentine at Rome Opera Decima.

London, Printed for & sold by I: Walsh . . . & I: Hare, &c.

Post-Boy, Dec. 7–9, 1721. (Lately publish'd.)

Fol. 3 parts. Printed on one side only.
BM. h. 11. b.
'Decima' is in MS..
Title-page used also for Op. 9. (No. 1476.)

1479.— With Walsh only in the imprint and 'N⁰ 91' added to the title-page.

[*c.* 1730.]

Walsh Cat. 18: 'Sonatas or Aires for 2 Flutes and a Bass. 10th Op: 3s. od. N⁰ 91.'
Advertised on Op. XIII (No. 1494) as: 'Sonatas for 2 Flutes and a Bass. Op: 10th.'

1480 XII. Sonatas of three Parts for two Violins & a Bass with a through Bass for yᵉ Organ Harpsicord or arch Lute Compos'd by Mʳ Valentine at Rome. Opera Prima.

London, Printed for J. Walsh . . . N⁰ 444.

[*c.* 1730.]

Fol. 4 parts.

Smith 419 (BM. h. 11. c. (1.)) with Walsh only in the imprint and 'N⁰ 444' added to the title-page.
Walsh Cat. 18: '12 Sonatas for 2 Violins and a Bass. 1st Opera. 6s. od. N⁰ 444.'
This catalogue lists all Valentine's works under 'Robert Valentine of Rome'.
Daniel Wright published a number of spurious editions of Valentine's works.

1481. Solos for a Flute With a Thorough Bass for the Harpsicord or Bass Violin Compos'd by Mʳ Valentine at Rome Opera 2ᵈᵃ

London Printed for I: Walsh . . . & I: Hare . . . N⁰ 120.

[*c.* 1730.]

Large fol. pp. 34.
BM. h. 11. a. (1.)
Smith 474 with 'N⁰ 120' added in MS. to the title-page.
Walsh Cat. 18: '12 Solos for a Flute and a Bass. 2d Opera. 6s. od. N⁰ 120.

1482. XII Sonatas or Solos for a Flute With a Through-bass for the Harpsicord or Bass Violin. Compos'd by Mͬ Valentine at Rome Opera Terza.
    London, Printed for J. Walsh . . . Nͦ 121.

    [*c.* 1730.]

      Large fol. pp. 37.
      Smith 458 (BM. h. 11. a. (2.)) with Walsh only in the imprint and 'Nͦ 121' added to the title-page.
      Walsh Cat. 18: '12 Solos for a Flute and a Bass. 3d Opera. 6s. od. Nͦ 121.'

1483. Six Sonata's of two Parts made on purpose for two Flutes Compos'd by Mͬ Valentine at Rome Opera Quarta.
    London Printed for I: Walsh . . . Nͦ 58.

    [*c.* 1730.]

      Fol. 2 parts.
      BM. h. 11. c. (2.)
      Smith 468 (BM. h. 11. (9.)) with Walsh only in the imprint and 'Nͦ 58' added to the title-page.
      Walsh Cat. 18: 'Six Sonatas for 2 Flutes, 4th Opera. 3s. od. Nͦ 58.'

1484. Six Sonata's of two Parts for Two Violins Compos'd by Mͬ Valentine at Rome Opera Quarta.
    London Printed for I: Walsh . . . Nͦ 442.

    [*c.* 1730.]

      Fol. 2 parts.
      BM. h. 11. i. (Violino Secondo part only.)
      Smith 480 (BM. h. 11. e.) with Walsh only in the imprint and 'Nͦ 442' added to the title-page.
      Walsh Cat. 15*a*: 'Valentines 4th Opera (2 Violins). 3s. od.'
      Walsh Cat. 18: 'The 4th and 7th Operas of this Author is Transpos'd for 2 Violins. 6s. **od.** Nͦ 443' [i.e. 442 and 443].

1485. XII Sonatas or Solos for a Flute with a Through Bass for the Harpsicord or Bass Violin Compos'd by Mͬ Valentine at Rome Opera Quinta.
    London Printed for I: Walsh . . . Nͦ 122.

    [*c.* 1730.]

      Large fol. pp. 34.
      Smith 554 (BM. h. 11. a. (3.)) with Walsh only in the imprint and 'Nͦ 122' added to the title-page.
      Walsh Cat. 18: '12 Solos for a Flute and a Bass. 5th Opera. 6s. od. Nͦ 122.'

1486. Six Sonatas of two Parts for two Flutes Compos'd by Mͬ Valentine at Rome Opera 6ᵗᵃ
    London Printed for I: Walsh . . . Nͦ 61.

    [*c.* 1730.]

Fol. 2 parts.
BM. g. 71. f. (7.)
'6ᵗᵃ' is in MS. on blocked-out portion of plate.
The plate was used earlier for Op. 7 (No. 1487), which also has 'Nꞌ 61'.
Walsh Cat. 18: 18: 'Six Sonatas for 2 Flutes. 6th Opera. 3s. od. Nꞌ 60.'
Smith 572 with Walsh only in the imprint and 'Nꞌ 61' added to the title-page.

1487. Six Sonatas of two Parts for two Flutes Compos'd by Mꞌ Valentine at Rome Opera 7ᵐᵃ

London Printed for I: Walsh . . . Nꞌ 61.

[*c.* 1730.]

Large fol. 2 parts.
Smith 575 (BM. h. 11. j.) with Walsh only in the imprint and 'Nꞌ 61' added to the title-page.
Walsh Cat. 18: 'Six Sonatas for 2 Flutes, 7th Opera. 3s. od. Nꞌ 61.'

1488. Six Sonatas of Two Parts for Two Violins Compos'd by Mr. Valentine at Rome. Opera 7ᵐᵃ

London. Printed for I. Walsh . . . and I. Hare, &c.

Post-Boy, July 6–8, 1721.

Fol. 2 parts.
Peter Murray Hill, Ltd. Cat. 14. No. 294.

1489. — With Walsh only in the imprint and 'Nꞌ 443' added to the title-page.

[*c.* 1730.]

Walsh Cat. 18: 'The 4th and 7th Operas of this Author is Transpos'd for 2 Violins. 6s. od. Nꞌ 443' [i.e. 442 and 443].

1490. Sonatas or Solos for a Flute With a Thorough Bass for the Harpsicord or Bass Violin Compos'd by Mꞌ Valentine at Rome. Opera XI.

London. Printed for & sold by I: Walsh . . . and Ioseph Hare, &c.

London Journal, Sept. 16, 1727.

Fol. pp. 22.
Rowe (2 copies).

1491. — With 'Nꞌ 123' added to the title-page in MS.

[*c.* 1730.]

BM. h. 11. a. (4.)
Walsh Cat. 18: 'Six Solos for a Flute and a Bass. 11th Opera. 4s. od. Nꞌ 123.'

1492. XII Solos for a Violin with a Thorough Bass for the Harpsicord or Bass Violin Compos'd by Mꞌ Valentine at Rome Opera XIIᵗʰ

London. Printed for and sold by I: Walsh . . . and Ioseph Hare, &c.

Country Journal: or, The Craftsman, March 30, 1728. (Lately published.)
Daily Journal, Jan. 29, 1730. (New Musick, and Editions of Musick, Just published.)

> Fol. pp. 50.
> CUL.

1493. — With Walsh only in the imprint and 'N.º 448' added to the title-page.
[*c.* 1730.]

> Walsh Cat. 18: '12 Solos for a Violin and a Bass. 12th Opera 6s. od. N.º 448.'

1494. Sonatas or Solos For a German Flute with a Thorough Bass for the Harpsicord or Bass Violin Compos'd by M.ʳ Valentine at Rome. Opera XIII.
London. Printed for & Sold by John Walsh . . . N.º 541.

London Evening-Post, April 26–29, 1735.

> Fol. pp. 2–26.
> BM. h. 11. a. (5.)
> The title-page contains a list of Valentine's works published by Walsh, Op. 1–12.
> Walsh Cat. 18: 'Six Solos for a Flute and a Bass. 13th Op: 4s. od. N.º 541.'

VALENTINI (GIUSEPPE)

1495. Bizzarrie Per Camera à Tre Cio a Due Violini e Violone ò Cembalo Di Giuseppe Valentini Fiorentino Opera Seconda. Note: there are other Curious Pieces (for Violins) by this Author which may be had where these are sold.
London Printed for I: Walsh . . . & I: Hare, &c.

Post Boy, Oct. 3–5, 1721.

> Fol. Parts.
> BM. g. 392. b.

1496. — With Walsh only in the imprint and 'N.º 445' added to the title-page.
[*c.* 1730.]

> RCM. LXI. E. 11. (8.)
> Walsh Cat. 18: 'Bizzarias or Chamber Aires for 2 Violins and a Bass. Opera Seconda. 4s. od. N.º 445'.

1497. XII Solos for the Violin or Violoncello With a Thorough Bass for the Harpsicord Compos'd by Giuseppe Valentini Opera Octava.
London Printed for I: Walsh . . . N.º 446.

[*c.* 1730.]

Fol. pp. 52.

> Smith 577 (BM. g. 392. a.) with Walsh only in the imprint and 'N.º 446'. added to the title-page.
> Walsh Cat. 18: '12 Grand Solos for a Violin and a Bass. Op: 8.ᵛ.ª 6s. od. N.º 446.'

VANBRUGHE (George)

1498. Mirth and Harmony. Consisting of Vocal and Instrumental Musick; as Songs and Ariets, for one and two Voices; and a Cantata: Several of the Songs on Diverting Subjects. All fitted for the German Flute, Common Flute, Violin, Hoboy, Harpsichord, or Organ, To accompany the Voice, or to be Play'd alone. The whole Compos'd by Mr Vanbrughe. Price 5 Shillings.

London. Printed for & sold by Iohn Walsh . . . and by the Author next Door to Mr Roome near the Sun Tavern in Fleet-street.

Daily Journal, May 14, 1730.

Fol. 'A Table of Songs', &c. pp. 2–34.
BM. H. 1605. a.; H. 1605. (2.) Gresham. RCM. Birmingham. Euing.
Walsh Cat. 18: 'Mirth and Harmony; or a 2d Book of Songs by Mr. Vanbrughe. 5s. od. Nº 296.' This refers to copies of No. 1498 with 'Nº 296' added to the title-page.
The first book of Vanbrughe's Songs was 'Modern Harmony'. (No. 1499.)
A Second Book of 'Mirth and Harmony' was printed for the author by T. Cobb, 1732. (BM. K. 7. i. 22.)

1499. Modern Harmony or a desire to Please Consisting of Vocal and Instrumental Musick as Songs and Arietts for one and two Voices and a Cantata together with a Solo for a Flute & a Bass and a Solo for a Violin & a Bass as also a Set of Lessons for the Harpsicord The whole Compos'd by Mr Vanbrughe.

London Printed for J: Walsh . . . Nº 325.

[*c.* 1730.]

Fol. pp. 2–23, blank, 24–31.
Smith 583 (BM. H. 1605. (1.)) with Walsh only in the imprint and 'Nº 325' added to the title-page.
Walsh Cat. 18: 'Vanbrughe's Songs. 5s. od. Nº 325.'

See also No. 759. Harpsicord Master. VIIIth Book; Nos. 891, 893. The Lady's Banquet 3d Book (Fifth Book).

VENCESLAUS

1500. The Favourite Songs in the Opera call'd Venceslaus.
London Printed for and sold by I: Walsh, &c.

Daily Journal, Jan. 27, 1731.

Fol. Passe-partout title-page. ff. 16 without foliation Printed on one side only.
BM. G. 206. c. (4.) (Without 'Nº 265' on the title-page.)
Walsh Cat. 18: 'Favourite Songs in Venceslaus. 2s. 6d. Nº 265.'
Words by Apostolo Zeno, English by Samuel Humphreys.
Two numbers included in 'Le Delizie dell' Opere', Vol. II, pp. 225–7.

VERACINI (Francesco Maria)

1501. The Favourite Songs in the Opera Call'd Adriano By Sigr Francesco Maria Veracini.

London. Printed for and sold by I. Walsh, &c.

London Evening-Post, Jan. 3–6, 1736.

> Fol. Passe-partout title-page. pp. 26.
> BM. G. 206. c. (5.) Manchester.
> Walsh Cat. 18: 'Adriano by Veracini. 2s. 6d. N°. 582.'
> Words by Metastasio.
> Republished in 'Le Delizie dell' Opere', Vol. II, pp. 120–45.

1502. The Favourite Songs in the Opera call'd Partenio. Compos'd by Sign. Francesco Maria Veracini.

Printed for John Walsh, &c.

London Daily Post, and General Advertiser, April 21, 1738. (In a few Days will be published.)

> Fol. pp. 2–26.
> Walsh Cat. 18: 'Partenio by Veracini. 2s. 6d.'
> Republished in 'Le Delizie dell' Opere', Vol. II. pp. 24–48.

1503. The Favourite Songs in the Opera Call'd Rosalinda By Sig.ʳ Veracini. London. Printed for I. Walsh, &c.

Daily Advertiser, Feb. 11, 1744.

> Fol. Passe-partout title-page. pp. 2–23.
> Rowe.
> Republished in 'Le Delizie dell' Opere', Vol. IV, pp. 95–116.

1504. XII Solos for a Violin with a Thorough Bass for the Harpsicord or Bass Violin. Compos'd by Francesco Maria Veracini Fiorentino. Opera Prima, &c. London. Printed for and sold by I: Walsh . . . N°. 456.

Country Journal: or, The Craftsman, April 14, 1733.

> Large fol. pp. 2–29, blank, 31–37, blank, 39–45, blank, 47–53, blank, 55–61, blank, 63–69, blank, 71–81.
> BM. h. 1745. RAM. Pendlebury. Rowe. Tenbury.
> Walsh Cat. 18: 'Veracini's Solos (for a Violin and a Bass). 8s. od. N°. 456.'

See also Nos. 556, 557, 559–66. Delizie dell' Opere. Vols. I, II, IV–XI; Nos. 771–85. Hasse (Johann Adolph) [Chamber Airs.]; No. 1364. Select Harmony Fourth Collection. Six Concertos . . . Compos'd by M.ʳ Handel . . . and Veracini, &c.

VERNON (JOSEPH)
See No. 1419. Summer's Tale

VESPASIAN
Vespasian for a Flute.
See Nos. 55, 56. Ariosti (Attilio)

VILLAGE OPERA

1505. The Music for the Flute in . . . the Village Opera.
Printed for and sold by John Walsh . . . and Joseph Hare, &c.

Daily Post, June 28, 1729. (Also may be had.)

1506. — With Walsh only in the imprint and 'N⁰ 56' added to the title-page.
[*c.* 1730.]

    Walsh Cat. 18: 'Village Opera (for a Single Flute). 6d. N⁰ 56.'

VINCENT (Thomas)

    See No. 266. British Orpheus. No. II; No. 925. Latour (   ) A Collection of
Minuets . . . Compos'd by Mʳ Latour, &c.; No. 1068. Minuets.

VINCI (Leonardo)

1507. Arie 6. Composte dal Sigʳ Leonardo Vinci.
London. Printed for I. Walsh, &c.

[*c.* 1757.]

    Fol. Passe-partout title-page. pp. 2–19.
    BM. H. 1653. b. (2.)
    This work is probably the same as that advertised as 'Six favourite Italian Songs'. (No.
1512.)
    Republished in 'Le Delizie dell'Opere', Vol. VIII, pp. 106–23.

1508. [The Favourite Songs in the Opera call'd Elpidia.
London. J. Walsh and J. Hare.]

[1725.]

    Fol. ff. 21. Printed on one side only.
    BM. H. 230. f. (7.) (Wanting title-page.)
    The opera was by Vinci and others.

1509. — Additional Songs in Elpidia. 1s.
[*c.* 1725.]

    Fol. ff. 14?
    Walsh Cat. 15*a.*

    See also: No. 1266. The Quarterly Collection of Vocal Music.

1510. — Favourite Songs in Elpidia with the Addiˡ Songs. 4s. od. N⁰ 255.
[*c.* 1730.]

Walsh Cat. 18. A reissue of the Walsh and Hare editions with Walsh only in the imprint and 'N.° 255' added to the title-page.
Words by Apostolo Zeno.
Republished in 'Le Delizie dell' Opere', Vol. I, pp. 13–18, 21–22, 41–42, 49–50, 57–59, 129–32, 198–9, 220–1, 224–6.
Benjamin Cooke advertised an edition of 'The favourite Songs', &c. *Daily Post*, May 20, 1727.

1511. Overture in Elpidia.
[London. J. Walsh?]

[*c.* 1730.]

Fol. 8 single sheet orchestral parts. Printed on one side only.
BM. h. 3211. (8.) (Bassoon part in MS. Same as Violoncello or Bassoon part in No. 220.)

Elpidia. Overture.

See also No. 220. Bononcini (Giovanni) and (Antonio Maria) and others. Bononcini's Six Overtures for Violins . . . in the Operas of . . . Elpidia, &c.

1512. Six favourite Italian Songs, composed by Sig. Leonardi Vinci.
Printed for J. Walsh, &c.

Public Advertiser, Jan. 29, 1757.

Randall Cat.: 'Vinci's Songs. 2s. 6d.'
See No. 1507: Arie 6.

1513. Twelve Solos For a German Flute or Violin with Thorough Bass for the Harpsicord or Violoncello Compos'd by Sig.ʳ Leonardo Vinci and other Italian Authors.
London. Printed for I. Walsh, &c.

General Advertiser, Nov. 22, 1746.

Fol. pp. 1–10, blank, 12–32.
BM. g. 280. b. (17.) Bod. Manchester. Reid. Rowe.

See also No. 2. Agrell (Johann Joachim) Six Sonatas or Duets for two German Flutes . . . Compos'd by Giovanni Aggrell . . . Leonardi Vinci Opera Seconda; No. 3. Agrell (Johann Joachim) Six Sonatas for two German Flutes . . . Opera Terza; No. 44. Arbaces; Nos. 555–7, 559–66. Delizie dell' Opere. Vols. I, II, IV–XI; Nos. 771–85. Hasse (Johann Adolph) [Chamber Airs.]; No. 1009. Meraspe; No. 1014. Merode; No. 1145. Orfeo; No. 1151. Overtures. Six Overtures in Seven Parts . . . by . . . Vinci, &c.

VINER (WILLIAM)

1514. Solos for a Violin with a Thorough Bass for the Harpsicord or Bass Violin Compos'd by the late Mʳ Viner of Dublin, &c.

Printed for I: Walsh . . . Nº 447.

[*c.* 1730.]

Fol. pp. 2–28.
Smith 532 (BM. g. 1084.) with Walsh only in the imprint and 'Nº 447' added to the title-page.
Walsh Cat. 18: 'Viners Solos (for a Violin and a Bass). 4s. od. Nº 447.'

VIOLIN BOOKS

1515. New Violin and Flute Books; with Instructions for Learners for the Year 1728.

Printed for, and sold by John Walsh . . . and Joseph Hare, &c.

Country Journal: or, The Craftsman, Jan. 20, 1728.

Presumably a general reference to works recorded elsewhere, which cannot be identified.

VISCONTI (GASPARO) *Commonly called Gasparini or Gasperini*

1516. A Collection of Airs purposely made and contriv'd for 2 Flutes, being entirely new. Composed by Signior Gasparini, price 2s.

Printed for and sold by J. Walsh . . . Nº 71.

[*c.* 1730.]

Walsh Cat. 18: 'Gasperini's Works. Aires for 2 Flutes. 2s. od. Nº 71.'
Smith 127 with Walsh only in the imprint and 'Nº 71' added to the title-page.

1517. Gasperini's Solos for a Violin with a through Bass for the Harpsicord or Bass Violin Containing Preludes Allemands Sarabands &c. Composed by Seignʳ Gasparo Visconti Opera Prima.

Printed for I. Walsh . . . Nº 380.

[*c.* 1730.]

Obl. fol. Dedication. pp. 3–31.
Smith 125 (BM. e. 790.) with Walsh only in the imprint and 'Nº 380' added to the title-page.
Walsh Cat. 18: 'Gasperini's Works. Six Solos for a Violin and a Bass. 4s. od. Nº 380.'

See also No. 7. Airs. Aires by 8 Masters (for 2 Flutes); No. 1150. Overtures. A Collection of Several Excellent Overtures . . . to which is added that Incomparable Sonata for a Flute and a Bass Perform'd . . . by Mʳ Paisible and Mʳ Gasperini, &c.

VIVALDI (Antonio)

1518. Two Celebrated Concertos the one Commonly call'd the Cuckow and the other Extravaganza Compos'd by Sig.ʳ Antonio Vivaldi Note, the rest of this Authors Works may be had where these are sold.

London. Printed for and Sold by I: Walsh . . . Nº 453.

[c. 1730.]

> Fol. Parts. 2 Violins, Viola, and Violoncello (Organo e Violoncello).
> RAM.
> Smith 579. (BM. h. 43. a.) With Hare deleted from the imprint and 'Nº 453' added to the title-page.
> Walsh Cat. 18: 'The Cuckow and Extravaganza Concerto. 3s. od. Nº 453.'
> Walsh Cat. 25: 'Vivaldi's Cuckow Concertos. 3s. od.'

1519. Vivaldi's twelve Concertos, call'd The Extravaganza, with other great Pieces of Musick just come from Abroad.

Sold by John Walsh . . . and John and Joseph Hare, &c.

Daily Post, March 28, 1722.

> This refers to foreign editions which Walsh was selling, probably publications of Estienne Roger, Amsterdam.
> *See also* No. 1524. La Stravagangza Concerti, &c.

1520. Vivaldi's most Celebrated Concertos in all their parts for Violins and other Instruments with a Thorough Bass for the Harpsicord Compos'd by Antonio Vivaldi Opera Terza.

London Printed for I: Walsh . . . and I: Hare . . . Nº 451.

Country Journal: or, The Craftsman, July 1, 1732.

> Fol. Parts.
> RCM. Oriel College, Oxford. Tenbury.
> Concertos I–XII of 'L' Estro Armonico', published by Estienne Roger, Amsterdam, *c.* 1710 (Bm. g. 33.)
> Walsh Cat. 18: '12 Concertos for Violins in 8 Parts. Op: Terza. 15s. od. Nº 451.'
> Reissues of Smith 469, 509 and 522, in one volume with one title-page.

1521. Concertos Opera 7ᵐª

> Fol. Parts.
> Walsh Cat. 11*b*.
> Probably refers to edition issued by Jeanne Roger, Amsterdam, *c.* 1725: 'Concerti à Cinque Stromenti . . . Opera Settima.' (BM. g. 33. d. (2.))

1522. XII Solos for a Violin with a Thorough Bass for the Harpsicord or Bass Violin Compos'd by Antonio Vivaldi. Opera 2ᵈª

London. Printed for & sold by I: Walsh . . . & I: Hare, &c.

Post Boy, Feb. 23–25, 1721.

> Fol. pp. 2–47.
> BM. g. 33. h.; g. 420. a. (2.) (Wanting title-page.) Bod.

1523. — With Walsh only in the imprint and 'N⁰ 450' added to the title-page.
[*c.* 1730.]
> CUL.
> Walsh Cat. 18: '12 Solos for a Violin and a Bass. Op. 2da. 6s. od. N⁰ 450.'

1524. La Stravaganza Concerti da D. Antonio Vivaldi. Opera Quarta. Vivaldi's Extravaganzas in Six Parts for Violins and other Instruments Being the choicest of that Authors work Opera 4ᵗᵃ N:B: The rest of the Works of this Author may be had where these are sold.
> London. Printed for I: Walsh . . . and Joseph Hare, &c.

> *Daily Post; Country Journal: or, The Craftsman,* May 11, 1728.

>> Fol. 6 parts.
>> BM. g. 33. a. RCM. Fitz. (Imperfect.)
>> *See also* No. 1519.

1525. — With Walsh only in the imprint and 'N⁰ 452' added to the title-page.
> [*c.* 1732.]
>> RCM.
>> Walsh Cat. 18: 'Vivaldi. His Extravaganza Concertos. Opera 4ta. 8s. od. N⁰ 452.'

> *See also* No. 4. Agrell (Johann Joachim) Sei Sonate, &c. (Book II. Vivaldi's Cele-
> brated 5th Concerto); No. 755. Harmonia Mundi. The 2ᵈ Collection . . .
> Vivaldi, &c.; No. 1357. Select Harmony . . . from the Works of Antonio
> Vivaldi, &c.; No. 1458. Torelli (Giuseppe) and Vivaldi (Antonio) Torelli
> and Vivaldi's Concertos (Violins).

VOCAL MASK

1525a. The Vocal Mask. A Collection of Favourite English Songs.
> Printed for I. Walsh, &c.

> [c. 1740.]

>> Fol. Passe-partout title-page (Smith, pl. 17). 67 single and 10 fol. sheets.
>> W. N. H. Harding, Chicago.

VOCAL MUSICAL MASK

1525b. The Vocal Musical Mask. A Collection of English Songs.
> [J. Walsh.]

> [*c.* 1742.]

>> Fol. Passe-partout title-page (Smith, pl. 17, no imprint). 92 sheets, 3 being folios.
>> W. N. H. Harding, Chicago.

> *See also* Nos. 907–12 Lampe (Johann Friedrich) and Howard (Samuel)

VOLOGESO

1526. The Favourite Songs in the Opera Call'd Vologeso.
London. Printed for I. Walsh, &c.

Public Advertiser, Dec. 15, 1759. (The favourite Songs in the New Opera of Vologeso, by Sig. Perez &c.)

> Fol. Passe-partout title-page. pp. 22.
> BM. G. 206. a. (5.) RM. 13. c. 22. (10.) RCM.
> Pasticcio. Composers named are Perez, Cocchi, and Jomelli.
> Republished in 'Le Delizie dell' Opere', Vol. IX, pp. 2–23.

VOLUNTARIES

1527. Voluntarys & Fugues Made on purpose for the Organ or Harpsichord by Ziani Pollaroli, Bassani and other Famous Authors, Engraven in a fair Character.
London, Printed for J. Walsh . . . Nº 179.

[*c.* 1730.]

> Fol. pp. 28.
> Smith 360 (BM. g. 57. a.) with Walsh only in the imprint and 'Nº 179' added to the title-page.
> Walsh Cat. 18: 'Volentarys for the Organ 1st Book. 4s. od. Nº 179.'

1528. A Second Collection of Toccates Vollentarys and Fugues made on Purpose for the Organ & Harpsicord Compos'd by Pasquini, Polietti and others. The most Eminent Foreign Authors Engraven & Carefully Corrected.
London. Printed for I. Walsh . . . Nº 181.

[*c.* 1730.]

> Fol. pp. 35.
> Manchester.
> Smith 564 (BM. g. 56.) with Walsh only in the imprint and 'Nº 181' added to the title-page.
> Walsh Cat. 18: 'Pasquini's Volentarys for the Organ 2d Book. 5s. od. Nº 181.'

A Third Collection of Toccates Vollentarys and Fugues for the Organ or Harpsichord, &c.

See No. 1562. Zipoli (Domenico)

WAGENSEIL (GEORG CHRISTOPH)

1529. Six Concertos for the Harpsicord or Organ with Accompanyments for Two Violins and a Bass Compos'd by Mr Wagenseil.

London. Printed for I. Walsh, &c.

Public Advertiser, Sept. 26, 1761.

Fol. 4 parts.
BM. g. 481. RM. 17. e. 1. (1.)

1530. Wagenseil's Sonatas (for two Violins and a Bass). Op. 3. 5s. 0d.

[*c.* 1765.]
Walsh Cat. 27.
Randall Cat.

1531. Six Symphonys in four parts for two Violins, French Horns, a Tenor, with a Bass for the Harpsicord or Violoncello. Compos'd by Mʳ Wagenseil. Opera Seconda.

N.B. These Symphonys may be Play'd with or without French Horns.
London. Printed for I. Walsh, &c.

Public Advertiser, April 27, 1762.

Fol. 5 parts.
RM. 26. b. 2. (14.)
Randall Cat.: 'Wagenseil's Symphonies, Op. 2. 10s. 6d.'

WAGNER AND ABERICOCK

1532. Wagner and Abericock (for the Harpsicord, Spinnet or Organ). 2s. 0d. Nọ 191.

[*c.* 1730.]
Walsh Cat. 18.
Presumably the same as 'The Miser, or, Wagner and Abericock,' produced at Drury Lane, 1727.

1533. The Tunes in Wagner and Abericock (for a single Violin). 6d.

[*c.* 1730.]
Walsh Cat. 18.

WARLIKE MUSIC

1534. Warlike Musick. Second Book. Being a Collection of Celebrated Marches Collected from the Operas. Compos'd by Mʳ Handel, and other Authors. for the Harpsicord, Violin, German and Common Flute.
London. Printed for I. Walsh, &c.

[*c.* 1758.]
8°. pp. 20.
NLS. BH. 269.
Presumably Books I, III, and IV were issued with separate title-pages, and the four books were issued together later as No. 1535.

1535. Warlike Musick. Book I Being a Choice Collection of Marches & Trumpet Tunes for a German Flute, Violin or Harpsicord. By M.̲ Handel, S.̲ Martini and the most eminent Masters.

London. Printed for I. Walsh, &c.

— Book II, &c.

— Book III, &c.

— Book IV, &c.

Public Advertiser, Sept. 15, 1758. (In Four Books. Each 1s. 6d.)

8°. Book I. pp. 20. Book II. pp. 21–40. Book III. pp. 41–60. Book IV. pp. 61–80.

BM. e. 438. d. RCM. (4 books in one, with the title-page of Book I only.) NLS. BH. 268. (4 books in one, with extra unpaginated items at end: 'Belleisle March'.) Others in BUC not examined.

The title-pages are all from the plate of Book I with alteration made for Books II and III in MS. and for Book IV by alteration on the plate.

A different work from 'Musica Bellicosa. Or, Warlike Music. Being a Choice Collection of Sixty-eight Marches and Trumpet-tunes', &c. published by Walsh in 1730 and a Second Book later on, and which were not advertised as containing any Handel items. (*See* No. 1124. Musica Bellicosa.)

Randall Cat.: 'Select Marches, in 4 Books, each 1.̲ 6.̲ For a German Flute, Violin or Harpsichord, presumably stock copies of the Walsh edition of 1758.

'German Flute Music. Handel's 4 Books Marches each 1. 6', advertised in 'A Catalogue of Vocal & Instrumental Music Engraved, Printed and Sold . . . by John Welcker N.̲ 9 Hay Market . . . London.' (*c.* 1776.) This is assumed to refer to Walsh Randall copies as sold by Welcker.

WEAVER (JOHN)

See No. 617. Feuillet (Raoul Auger) Orchesography; or, The Art of Dancing by Characters, and Demonstrative Figures . . . Translation from the French of Monsieur Feuillet. By John Weaver, &c.

WEIDEMAN (CHARLES FREDERICK)

1536. Six Concertos in Seven Parts for One and Two German Flutes Two Violins, a Tenor, with a Thorough Bass for the Violoncello and Harpsichord, Compos'd by M.̲ Weideman. Opera Seconda. Publish'd by the Author.

London. Printed for and Sold by Iohn Walsh, &c.

General Advertiser, Feb. 15, 1746. (Just published.)

Fol. 7 parts.

BM. g. 674. a. RM. 26. b. 2. (10.) RAM. Oriel College, Oxford. Rowe.

1537. — Another edition.

General Advertiser, Oct. 25, 1749. (New editions.)

1538. A Second Set Six Concertos in 8 Parts for Two German Flutes, Two Violins, Two French Horns, a Tenor, with a Bass for the Violoncello and Thro' Bass for the Harpsicord. Opera Settima. Most humbly Inscrib'd To His Royal Highness The Duke of York, By His Royal Highnesses most obedient and most devoted humble Servant Charles Weideman.

N.B. These Concertos may be Perform'd without French Horns.

London. Printed for I. Walsh, &c.

Public Advertiser, Feb. 15, 1766. (Printed and sold at the late Mr. J. Walsh's.)

Fol. 9 parts.
BM. g. 674. d. RM. 26. b. 2. (11.)

1539. Six Duets for Two German Flutes Compos'd by Mr Weideman. Opera Sexta.

London. Printed for I. Walsh, &c.

Public Advertiser, Jan. 22, 1765.

Fol. pp. 28.
BM. g. 674. c. (3.); g. 280. b. (18.)

1540. Minuets for Her Majesty's Birth-Day, as they were performed at the Ball at Court, for the Harpsicord, German Flute, or Violin. Compos'd by Mr. Weideman, for 1764.

Printed for J. Walsh, &c.

Public Advertiser, Jan. 24, 1764.

1541. XII Sonatas or Solos For A German Flute with a Thorough Bass for the Harpsicord or Violoncello. Compos'd by Mr Weideman.

London Printed for & sold by Ino. Walsh, &c.

Country Journal: or, The Craftsman, April 23, 1737.

Fol. Illustrated title-page. pp. 46.
BM. g. 674. RM. 17. f. 20. (7.) RM. 26. a. 3. (11.) Manchester. Rowe.

1542. — Another edition.

General Evening Post, Oct. 12–15, 1745. (Just published.)

1543. A 2d Set Twelve Solos for a German Flute and Harpsicord Compos'd by Mr Weideman. Opera Quinta.

London. Printed for I. Walsh, &c.

Public Advertiser, Feb. 23, 1760.

Fol. pp. 2–61.
BM. g. 674. c. (2.)

See also Nos. 11, 12. Airs. Select Aires or Duets for two German Flutes . . By . . . Weideman . . . 2d Book. (3ᵈ Book); Nos. 907. Lampe (Johann Friedrich) and Howard (Samuel) The Vocal Musical Mask, &c.; Nos. 1061, 1068, 1085, 1095. Minuets.

WELDON (John)

1544. Divine Harmony Six Select Anthems For a Voice a lone With a Thorow Bass for the Organ, Harpsicord or Arch-Lute Compos'd on several Occasions by Mͬ Inͦ Weldon Organist of his Majestys Chappell Royal and there Performed by the late Famous Mͬ Richard Elford Very proper not only in private Devotion, but also for Choirs, where they may be Sung either by a Treble or Tenor.
London Printed for I: Walsh . . . Nͦ 206.

Country Journal: or, The Craftsman, July 17, 1731. (Lately printed.)

> Fol. Frontispiece. 'To all Lovers of Divine Musick'. pp. 2–29.
> RCM (2). Manchester (3). Pendlebury.
> Smith 491 (BM. H.820.) with Walsh only in the imprint and 'Nͦ 206' added to the title-page
> Walsh Cat. 18: 'Weldon's Anthems. 4s. od. Nͦ 206.'

1545. Divine Harmony The 2ᵈ Collection being Select Anthems for a Voice a lone as also some for 3 and 4 Voices with a Thorough Bass for yᵉ Organ, Harpsicord, or Arch Lute. Compos'd by Several Eminent Authors and perform'd at yᵉ Chappel Royal being very proper not only in private Devotion but also for Choir's. The whole fairly Engraven. Note Mͬ Weldons Anthems for yᵉ Chappel Royal may be had where these are sold.
London Printed for I. Walsh. . .Nͦ 207.

Country Journal: or, The Craftsman, July 17, 1731. (Lately printed.)

> Fol. pp. 2–32.
> BM. H. 820. a.
> Weldon's name does not appear anywhere on this work as the composer.
> Smith 531 (RCM.) with Walsh only in the imprint and 'Nͦ 207' added to the title-page.
> Walsh Cat. 18: 'Anthems by several Authors. 4s. od. Nͦ 207.'

1546. Mͬ Weldons Songs. 10s. od.

[*c.* 1721.]

> Fol.
> Walsh Cat. 9a.

1547. Weldon's Songs. 10s. od. Nͦ 314.

[*c.* 1730.]

> Fol.
> Walsh Cat. 18.

1548. Weldon's Songs.

[*c.* 1737.]

>Fol. 3 Books.
>Walsh Cat. 17a. (Just Publish'd.)
>Nos. 1546–8 refer to editions of Weldon's three books of Songs: Smith 94, [First Book of Songs.] Smith 95, 'A Collection of new Songs', &c. (BM. G. 301. (2.) ff. 6 not foliated, ff. 1–6.) Smith 123, 'Mr Weldon's Third Book of Songs', &c. (BM. G. 301.a. ff. 19.) Smith 124, 'A Collection of New Songs', &c. Another issue of Smith 123. (BM. G. 301. (1.) ff. 19.)

See also No. 7. Airs. Aires by 8 Masters (for 2 Flutes); No. 749. Harmonia Anglicana . . . by . . . Weldon, &c.

WELDON (JOHN) AND SIMONS (HENRY)

1549. A Collection of Aires For two Flutes and a Bass Compos'd by Mr J: Weldon Mr Henr Simons and others Fairly Engraven price 3s

London Printed for I. Walsh . . . Nº 96.

[*c.* 1730.]

>Obl. fol. 3 parts.
>Smith 134 (BM. d. 150. (6.) with Walsh only in the imprint and 'Nº 96' added to the title-page.
>Walsh Cat. 18: 'Weldon and Simmon's Aires (for 2 Flutes and a Bass). 3s. od. Nº 96.'

WILLIAMS (WILLIAM)

1550. Six Sonata's in Three Parts. Three for Two Violins and Three for Two Flutes. With a Part for the Base-Viol, and a Figur'd-Base for the Organ Harpsicord or Archlute. Composed by William Williams, Servant to his Majesty. Cross sculp.

London . . . John Walsh, &c.

[*c.* 1730.]

>Fol. 4 parts. 1st Treble. pp. 12. 2nd Treble. pp. 12. Bassus. pp. 12. Violone. pp. 12.
>Smith 126 (Fitz. Printed for . . . John Hare . . . and John Walsh), presumably reissued with Walsh only in the imprint.
>Walsh Cat. 18: 'William's Sonatas (for 2 Flutes and a Bass). 4s. od.'

WISEMAN (CARLO)

1551. Six Solos for a German Flute or Violin with a Thorough Bass for the Harpsicord or Violoncello Compos'd by Sigr Carlo Wiseman.

London. Printed for I. Walsh, &c.

Public Advertiser, Nov. 26, 1753.

>Fol. pp. 31.
>RCM. Rowe

WOOD (Thomas)
See No. 1233. Psalms

WOODCOCK (Robert)
1552. XII Concertos in Eight Parts The first three for Violins and one Small Flute the Second three for Violins and two Small Flutes The third three for Violins & one German Flute and the three last for Violins & one Hoboy The proper Flute being nam'd to each Concerto Compos'd by Robert Woodcock.
London Printed for and sold by I: Walsh . . . and Ioseph Hare, &c.

London Journal, Feb. 18, 1727.

> Large fol. 8 parts.
> BM. i. 120. Cardiff.

1553. — With Walsh only in the imprint and N°. 455' added to the title-page.
[*c.* 1730.]
> Walsh Cat. 18.

WORGAN (James) *the Elder*
Three New English Cantatas, set to Musick for a Voice, Violins and Violincello; with a Thorough Bass of the Harpsicord.
See No. 313. Cantatas

1554. Sappho's Hymn to Venus Set to Musick by Mr. James Worgan.
London Evening-Post, Jan. 3–5, 1749. (To be had of Mr. Walsh, &c.)
> Fol. pp. 2–11.
> BM. G. 577. Gresham. Dublin. Manchester. Rowe.

WORGAN (John)
1555. The Agreeable Choice. A Collection of Songs Sung by Miss Burchell, Miss Stevenson, and Mr Lowe at Vaux-Hall Gardens. Set By Mr Worgan.
London Printed for I. Walsh, &c.

London Evening-Post; Whitehall Evening Post, July 18–20, 1751.
> Fol. pp. 2–20.
> BM. G. 378. a. (12.) RAM. CUL. Manchester. Mitchell. NLS.

1556. An English Cantata (Sung at Vaux-Hall by Mr Lowe) and Three English Songs Set to Musick by Mr Worgan.
London Sold by J. Walsh . . . J. Simpson . . . Price 1ˢ 6ᵈ

Daily Advertiser, June 22, 1745.

    Fol. pp. 2–7.
    BM. H. 2815. j. (2.) Manchester.

See also No. 315. Canzoniere

YOUNG (ANTHONY)

1557. Suits of Lessons for the Harpsicord or Spinnet in most of the Keyes with Variety of Passages and Variations Throughout the Work Compos'd by Mᵣ Anthony Young Organist of Sᵗ Clements Danes.
    London Printed for and Sold by I: Walsh . . . Nº 187.

    [*c.* 1730.]

        Fol. pp. 30.
        Smith 569 (BM. g. 443. b. (31.)) with Walsh only in the imprint and 'Nº 187' added to the title-page.
        Walsh Cat. 18: 'Young's Lessons (for the Harpsicord, Spinnet or Organ). 5s. od. Nº 187.'

ZANNETTI (FRANCESCO)

1558. Six Sonatas for two Violins with a Thorough Bass for the Harpsicord or Violoncello Compos'd by Sigᵣ Zanetti.
    London. Printed for I. Walsh, &c.

    [*c.* 1760.]

        Fol. 3 parts. Passe-partout title-page.
        BM. g. 434. c. Rowe.
        Walsh Cat. 27: 'Zanetti's Sonatas. 5s. od.'

ZENOBIA

    The Favourite Songs in the Opera Call'd Zenobia.

    See No. 393. Cocchi (Gioacchino)

ZIANI (PIETRO ANDREA)

1559. Ziani's Aires, or Sonatas in 3 parts for two Violins, and a thorow Bass for the Harpsicord or Bass Violin. Containing the most refin'd Italian Airs; Engraven from the Manuscript, which was never before Printed: the whole carefully Corrected Opera Prima, price 4s.
    Printed for and sold by J. Walsh, &c.

    [*c.* 1730.]

        Obl. fol. 3 parts.
        Smith 133 with Walsh only in the imprint and 'Nº 461' added to the title-page.
        Walsh Cat. 18: 'Ziani's Sonatas (2 Violins and a Bass). 4s. od. Nº 461.'

See also No. 1527. Voluntaries. Voluntarys & Fugues . . . by Ziani, &c.

ZIPOLI (DOMENICO)

1560. Six Suits of Italian Lessons, for the Harpsicord or Spinnet. with great Variety of Passages and Variations. Compos'd by Sig^r Domenico Zipoli: an Eminent Organist & Composer at Rome. Opera Prima.
    London Printed for and sold by I: Walsh . . . and Ioseph Hare, &c.

Daily Post, Dec. 22, 1725.

    Large fol. pp. 27.
    BM. h. 21. a.

1561. — With Walsh only in the imprint and 'N° 183' added to the title-page.
    [*c.* 1730.]
        Walsh Cat. 18: 'Zipoli's Lessons (for the Harpsicord Spinnet or Organ). 4s. od. N° 183.

1562. A Third Collection of Toccates Vollentarys and Fugues for the Organ or Harpsicord with particular Great Pieces for the Church Made upon Several Occasions Compos'd by Domenico Zipoli Principal Organist of Rome.
    London. Printed for I: Walsh . . . [and I: Hare], &c.

    [*c.* 1722.]
        Walsh Cat. 11*a*.: 'Zipoli's . . .Volentarys for the Organ.'

1563. — With Walsh only in the imprint and 'N° 182' added to the title-page.
    [*c.* 1730.]
        Fol. pp. 31.
        BM. h. 21.
        The first and second collections are entered under Voluntaries. (Nos. 1527, 1528.)

ZUCKERT (JOHANN FRIEDRICH)

1564. Six Sonatas for Two German Flutes or two Violins & Thorough Bass; Composed by Iohn Frederick Zuckert. Opera Prima.
    London. Printed for I. Walsh, &c.

Public Advertiser, Oct. 5, 1758.

    Fol. 3 parts.
    BM. g. 222. b. (4.)

ADDENDA AND ERRATA

p. 27. *Add after* ATTILIO:

ATTILIO REGOLO
See No. 872. Jomelli (Nicolò) The Favourite Songs in the Opera Call'd Attilio
Regolo.

p. 53. No. 225. *After* '603' *add* '(Rowe)' *in l.* 4.

p. 88. Cock. *For* 'To take a good part' *read* 'To take in good part'.

p. 93. No. 411. *For* 'Opera' *in l.* 4 *read* 'Operas'.

p. 168, para. 1. *Add* 'Nos. 1398, 1399. Song Tunes'.

p. 172. *Add after* No. 765:
 765a. The Harpsichord Master XIVth Book . . . Price 2s. 1730, &c.
 London. Printed for I Walsh . . . & I Hare, &c.

 Obl. fol. f. 1 ('A scale of the Gamut'). f. 2. ('Rules for Graces'. ff. 4–17 (wanting f. 3).
 Printed on one side only,

 BM. d. 38. d.
 Composers named: Bitti, Pepusch, but also contains items from Handel's operas without
his name.

 Note. Books VIII, X, XII, and XIII of 'The Harpsichord Master' also contain: 'A Scale
of the Gamut', 'Rules for Graces', 'Table of the Lessons, Aires & Song Tunes', omitted from
details of Nos. 759, 761, 763 and 764.

p. 183. No. 811. Hasse (Johann Adolph)
 Substitute:
 No. VI Duets or Canzonets for two Voices or Two German Flutes and a Bass
compos'd by Sig^r Jomelli, Hasse, and the most eminent Italian Masters. London.
Printed for I. Walsh, &c.
 Public Advertiser, April 18, 1759. (A fifth and Sixth Book of Duets, &c.)

 Obl. fol. pp. 12.
 BM. E. 270. y. (4.).
 This is another copy of No. 810, with No. V altered to VI in MS.

Addenda and Errata

p. 183. No. 812. Hasse (Johann Adolph)

Substitute:

No. VII. Canzonets for a voice. German Flute or Guitar. Being a Collection of the most favourite French Songs. Book III. Price 2s, &c.

London: Printed for I. Walsh, &c.

Public Advertiser, July 3, 1760. (Number VII. Twenty French and Italian Canzonets, &c.)

Obl. fol. pp. 12.
BM. E. 270. y. (3.)
Title page of No. 314 (Canzonets Book II.) adapted by erasure and in MS.
For Book I *see* No. 382. Cloes (Nicolas).

p. 194. Italian Canzonets. *Add:*

861a. Twelve Italian Canzonets.

London, Printed for I. Walsh, &c.

[*c.* 1755.]

Obl. fol. pp. 14.
BM. E. 270. y. (6.)
A new edition of the Canzonets only of No. 746. H., A.

p. 222. No. 980. Mancini (Francesco) *For* 'Fitz' *read* 'Rowe' *in l.* 9.

p. 248. First para, l. 4. *For* 'No. 1525 c.' *read* 'No. 1525 a.'

p. 278. *Add after* No. 1241:

Purcell (Daniel)

1241a. Six Sonata's or Solos, three for a Violin, And three for the Flute, with a Through Bass for the Harpsichord, Compos'd by Mr D. Purcell.

London Printed for & Sould by I: Walsh, &c.

[*c.* 1730.]

Fol. Passe partout title-page. Unpaginated.
BM. g. 1039. (Some pages cropped.)
May be a reissue of an earlier edition with Hare in the imprint. Not traced in Walsh catalogues.

p. 294. No. 1318. San Martini (Giuseppe) *Delete* 'RM. 17. a. 3. (10.)' *from l.* 7.

Addenda and Errata

p. 294. *Add after* No. 1318:

San Martini (Giuseppe)
Eight Overtures . . . And Six Grand Concertos, &c.
London, Printed for I. Walsh, &c.

[*c.* 1760.]

RM. 17. a. 3. [10.]
Fol. 8 parts.
A different edition from BM. g. 86. e. (No. 1318) with two title-pages, the first for 'Eight Overtures', &c. as BM. g. 86. e.; the second for 'Six Grand Concertos', &c. has similar wording to that of BM. g. 86. e, but is differently engraved in cursive script. BUC copies (*c.* 1760) not examined may be of this edition.

PRINTED IN GREAT BRITAIN
AT THE UNIVERSITY PRESS, OXFORD
BY VIVIAN RIDLER
PRINTER TO THE UNIVERSITY